UNDER
their
THUMB

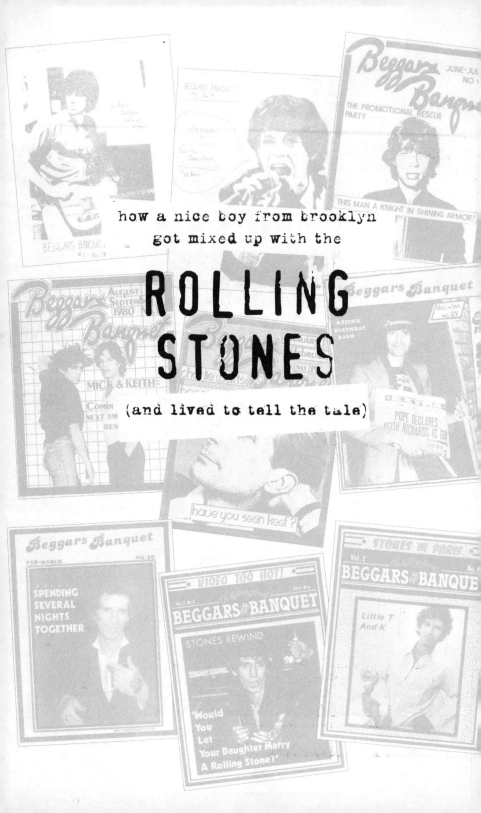

how a nice boy from brooklyn
got mixed up with the

ROLLING STONES

(and lived to tell the tale)

UNDER their THUMB

Bill German

Aurum

First published in Great Britain
2009 by Aurum Press Ltd
7 Greenland Street, London NW1 0ND
www.aurumpress.co.uk

First published in the United States
2009 by Villard Books, an imprint of The Random House
Publishing Group, a division of Random House, Inc., New York

A catalogue record for this book is available from the British
Library.

ISBN 978 1 84513 475 4

1 3 5 7 9 10 8 6 4 2
2009 2011 2013 2012 2010

Printed by MPG Books, Bodmin, Cornwall

Dedicated to my parents, Sylvia and Bernie,
for giving me enough rope;

to my sister, Rhonda,
for selling me her Stones albums;

and to Dessie,
for being my soulmate

Also, to the memories of
Alan Heifetz (aka Alan Andrews),
Bruce Bechtold,
and Sweet Virginia Lohle

contents

introduction

You'll probably want to kill me when I say my only job in life was with the Rolling Stones. Even as a teenager, I wasn't mowing lawns, washing cars, or asking if you want fries with that. I was traipsing after my favorite rock band and writing about it in *Beggars Banquet,* the newsletter I launched on my 16th birthday. When I published the first issue, I had no idea where it would lead or how it would dictate the course of my life.

I shouldn't have been with the Stones in the first place. To be welcomed into their orbit, you have to bring something to their table: drugs, sex, fame, or the ability to carry their luggage better than anyone else. But all I had was my stupid little newsletter.

This is the story of how I made it into the Stones' inner sanctum and how I crawled out. It's also about the overachievers and underachievers—the groupies, pushers, and flunkies—I met along the way. People who dedicated their entire lives to remaining in that sanctum. Some of them are still there, and some of them got carried off in handcuffs or caskets. But all of us lived our dream of hanging with the Rolling Stones.

Be careful what you wish for.

UNDER their THUMB

The first two covers of *Beggars Banquet,* compliments of
my high school's mimeo room.

1

a 'zine grows
in brooklyn

"I'd like to welcome President Clinton," Mick Jagger tells the VIP crowd. "And I see she's brought her husband."

The Rolling Stones are at New York's Beacon Theatre, and Martin Scorsese's shooting it for a documentary. It's October 29, 2006, and, after decades of drug busts, paternity suits, funerals, divorces, rehabs, and chemotherapy, the Stones can still put out. I mean, damn, these guys are *good*. But as my eyes and ears fixate on them at the Beacon, my mind wanders to another time and place.

My eyes see Mick onstage, but my mind sees him in his house, blotting the orange juice I spilled on his rug. My ears hear Keith Richards plucking "I'm Free," but my mind hears him offering me bourbon on his terrace. And Ronnie Wood? I'm peeling potatoes with him in his kitchen.

I used to pal around with these guys. And if this were ten or twenty years ago, I'd have begun my night backstage. I'd tell Keith and Ronnie to break a leg, and then I'd visit them after the show.

But that's not happening tonight. I finagled my way into the crowd, and the Stones don't know I'm here.

For me, there's never been a world without the Stones. They came into existence two months before *I* did. But I didn't hear them until I turned ten. To that point, if you didn't have a Saturday morning TV show, I didn't know you. The Monkees, Beatles, and Jackson 5 were the only bands I could name.

Life changed in 1972, when an announcement came from my sister's bedroom: *Everything seems to be ready . . . Are you ready? . . . Sorry for the delay. . . . Is everybody ready?*

What followed were the strangest words and most violent sounds I'd ever heard: *I was born in a crossfire hurricane! And I howled at my ma in the driving rain!* Followed by: *I think I bust a button on my trousers. . . . You don't want my trousers to fall down, now do ya?* I had no idea what it meant, but it was impossible to ignore.

My sister said it was the Rolling Stones. She showed me their album cover, and they looked pretty tough. Like they could definitely beat up the Monkees.

Until recently, my sister had listened only to "Build Me Up Buttercup" and "I Think I Love You." But somehow, in the summer of '72, she switched her allegiance from Keith Partridge to Keith Richards. She ditched her 45s and bought some Stones albums. One was shaped like a stop sign. Another had a zipper on it.

She pointed to the blond-haired guy and said he was dead. She said the Stones had been busted for drugs, evicted from hotels, and had played at concerts where people got murdered. I thought my head would explode. The chaotic stories, violent music, and wild album covers overwhelmed me. But I craved more.

I borrowed the albums and studied them. They contained words I wasn't allowed to repeat. If Mom were to hear me say "bitch" or "got to scrape the shit right off my shoes," she'd stick a bar of soap in my mouth. And while I didn't understand a phrase like "I laid a divorcée in New York City," I was certain it sounded cool and that *I* wanted to do it. To me, the Stones were the most rebellious people on earth, so I instantly became obsessed with them.

As luck would have it, my sister grew tired of the Stones and offered me her albums for a buck apiece. I suddenly had a Stones collection. When their next album came out, I got sticker shock. *Goats Head Soup* cost me $3.48 at Alexander's Department Store.

The band came to Madison Square Garden in 1975, but Mom wouldn't let me take the subway from Brooklyn to Manhattan. I was only 12. I followed the tour by listening to WNEW and by scouring the pages of *Rolling Stone* and *Creem*. I envied the DJs and writers who covered the Stones and desperately wanted their job.

At school, I had no one to share my enthusiasm with. The kids in my seventh-grade class were into the Carpenters. My teachers complained about my ratty Stones T-shirts, my dirty long hair (patterned after Mick's), and my semi-obscene belt buckle (bearing the Stones' tongue logo). I was attending yeshiva, the Jewish version of parochial school, so there was a dress code. I broke it every day, but I was a straight-A student, so they didn't expel me.

When the Stones released their *Some Girls* album in June 1978, I was 15 years old, attending public high school. Over the summer, I wore that record out. It was as vital as anything from CBGB's and confirmed the Stones' take-no-prisoners attitude. It dripped with sarcasm and pissed off Jesse Jackson, women's groups, and even Lucille Ball.

I bought every piece of memorabilia that album spawned. From the "Miss You" 12-inch on pink vinyl, to the "Beast of Burden" picture sleeve, to all the bootlegs from the *Some Girls* tour.

I was so into it, I passed up my first lay. The hottest girl in school came to my house, ready to do the deed. My parents were at work. She took her clothes off in my bedroom, threw me on the bed, and unzipped my fly. She climbed on top of me, and her boobs and crucifix were brushing against my lips. I was raring to go when the phone rang. I didn't answer, but the person kept calling. I worried it might be a family emergency, so I finally picked up.

It was my friend on a pay phone, outside our favorite mom-and-pop record store. "They got the new Stones boot! From last week's show in Passaic! There's only one copy left!" I zipped up and ran out the door. Losing my virginity could wait. The Stones could not.

The band's only concert in New York that year was at the Palladium, which held just thirty-three hundred people. To purchase a ticket, you needed to send a postcard to WNEW and pray you got picked. I licked a gazillion stamps, but never heard back.

Again, I relied on *Creem, Rolling Stone,* and 'NEW to keep up on the tour. The Stones were a big story that year, so a lot of outlets jumped on the bandwagon. But most of them—local newspapers, local news shows—screwed up. They'd miss the Stones' sarcasm or, worse, get their facts wrong. I can't tell you how many times I'd read that the Stones opened with "Johnny B. Goode" when it was really "Let It Rock." All I could think was, "*That* guy saw the Stones at the Palladium and I *didn't?*"

The *Album Tracks* episode is what pushed me over the edge. *Album Tracks* was a TV show hosted by two DJs from WNBC named Lee Masters and Bob Pittman. They featured a report on the Stones' ill-fated Altamont concert. They said the Stones were performing "Sympathy for the Devil" when a kid got murdered in the crowd, and that the Stones have been too scared to perform the song since.

First of all, if they had watched *Gimme Shelter,* they'd know the kid got stabbed during "Under My Thumb," not "Sympathy." Second, if they cared the least bit about the Stones, they'd know that "Sympathy" was played plenty of times after Altamont. I've got the bootlegs to prove it.

If these guys don't know the most dramatic scene in *Gimme Shelter,* I thought, then maybe they shouldn't be rock journalists. (Pittman later founded MTV. Masters became president of the E! channel.) I wrote them a courteous letter, but got a dismissive response. They said their facts came from a "rock encyclopedia" and that they were sticking to their story.

I realized I could do a better job than most grownups at covering the Stones. And so, in September 1978, armed with a borrowed typewriter, I pecked away at the first issue of my fanzine. It was the week of my 16th birthday, and the start of my junior year in high school.

Fanzines—or 'zines, for short—have been around a long time. But the modern version sprouted from the do-it-yourself punk-rock zeitgeist of the late Seventies. 'Zines took pride in how crappy they looked, and most were handwritten, not typed. Mine was a combination of both.

I had no idea where to print, much less who would read, my little creation, but I didn't care. My primary goal was to report the facts. In my debut issue, I wrote about Keith's upcoming drug trial and about the band's upcoming appearance on *Saturday Night Live*. I wasn't giving you anything *TV Guide* didn't, but at least I was accurate.

In 1978, there wasn't a Kinko's on every corner and no one had a PC. If you wanted to lay out a page, you had to do it the hard way: scissors and glue. "Cut and paste" literally meant to cut and paste. Typos weren't deleted, they were covered up by Wite-Out or by powdery stuff called Ko-Rec-Type, which didn't always work. A simple page could take you a day. But it meant that 'zine publishers were extremely passionate people, dedicated to our subjects. We were in it for love, not money. I dubbed my 'zine *Beggars Banquet* because I wanted it to be—bear with me on this—"a banquet of Stones information that even a beggar could afford."

Back then, copy shops were primarily found on college campuses. If you didn't live near one, you had to go to a bank or library. That's who had the copy machines. For 10 cents, you put your library book or bank statement on the glass and, about thirty seconds later, a horrible-looking copy oozed out. I tried the machine at the Flatlands Avenue bank, but the results were illegible. That's when I remembered my high school's mimeo room. I knew a student volunteer who had the keys. He snuck me in after hours, and we mimeographed a hundred copies of my three-page issue. All on the Board of Ed's dime.

When I left school that night with my published 'zine, I had no idea what to do next. My hundred copies looked like crap, but at least they smelled great.

Keith exits Danceteria on 37th Street. That's me in the
background, two days after my high school graduation,
handing an issue to Woody.

2

the graduate

In 1978, Brooklyn was in the throes of *Saturday Night Fever* fever. The guys in my high school wanted to be Tony Manero. They wore gold chains, slicked-back hair, and tawt it was a good ting to tawk like *diss*. The girls sported Jordache jeans, Farrah Fawcett wings, and would only date guys who dressed like Tony Manero. One kid got so caught up in it, he jumped off the Verrazano Bridge, just like in the movie. They gave him a tribute page in the yearbook.

Whenever I'd pass these guys in the hallway, they'd tell me to "get a fuckin' haircut" or accuse me of not being from Brooklyn. "You don't *tawk* like yooz from Brooklyn." I had a hard time pushing my 'zine on them, and none of them cared what the "Free Keef" button on my jacket meant.

There were a few rock fans in my school, but they were either Floydies or Styx Chicks. The Floydies (Pink Floyd fans) would quote *Dark Side of the Moon* in their everyday conversations and thought a fun time was staring at the ceiling at Laserium. The Styx Chicks were cute, but they'd make you listen to "Come Sail Away" before making a move on them.

I couldn't understand how the Stones' sexuality, sarcasm, and rebelliousness could be lost on my peers, but such was the case. To me, the Stones' raucous appearance on *Saturday Night Live* (October '78) was *our* generation's Beatles-on-Sullivan, but my classmates didn't see it that way. They showed no interest in the Stones or in my crappy-looking 'zine. I was charging just 25 cents, but made no sales.

South Shore High was in the Canarsie section of Brooklyn, and don't let the school's idyllic name fool you. We were a block away from the projects and our closest body of water was the sewage plant on Flatlands Avenue. I wrote for the school's paper and, as the entertainment reporter, covered the "rock vs. disco" debate and the senior production of *Godspell*. When I wrote that disco was geared to conformity-conscious robots who danced their lives away, I almost got beaten up in gym class.

Eventually, I found kindred spirits at the city's mom-and-pop record shops. Places like Bleecker Bob's in Manhattan and Zig Zag in Brooklyn. If you lived near me and needed the latest Ramones 45 or Elvis Costello import, Zig Zag is where you went. I showed the owner my 'zine, and he offered to sell it on consignment. "We'll split the income."

I then headed to the Graham Theatre, the midnight movie house near Zig Zag. They'd screen *The Rocky Horror Picture Show* on Fridays, and everything else—like *Magical Mystery Tour* and *Jimi Plays Berkeley*—on Saturdays. When *Ladies and Gentlemen, the Rolling Stones* came around, I knew it was my cue. I brought a stack of *Beggars Banquet*s and stood near the box office. I approached two guys smoking pot and said, "How much did you pay for that joint? A buck, right? Well, how would you like a banquet of Stones information for the mere price of 25 cents?" The one in the Deep Purple shirt almost strangled me. I didn't sell a single issue that night.

I returned to Zig Zag to tally up my "newsstand circulation." They handed me 13 cents and said I owed them half a penny. They'd sold a grand total of one. I gathered up my rejected issues and noticed that on one of them, someone had scrawled, "What the fuck is this crap?"

Mind you, I'd clearly stated what *Beggars Banquet* was. In big letters on the cover, I wrote, "Stones Newsletter." By using the word "newsletter," I differentiated it from a fan club. I believed there was a place for gushy fan stuff—poems, drawings—but *Beggars Banquet* wasn't going to be it. I may have been a fan, but I was also a journalist. So *that* would be my angle.

Eventually, I showed *Beggars Banquet* to my parents and teachers. My folks kept quiet, praying it was a phase I'd grow out of, while my teachers were mortified. Mr. Weber, my journalism teacher, said I needed to pursue "more significant subjects." And Mr. Royden, my history teacher, said I was wasting my talent on "nonsense." I was his star pupil, and his dream was that I'd be a speechwriter for the White House. He'd have been happier if I'd emulated Bianca Jagger, the political activist, instead of Mick Jagger, the "drug addict degenerate."

Mr. Royden was ancient—at least fifty—and looked like Theodore Roosevelt. When I told him I intended to live the American dream by mixing my hobby (the Stones) with my profession (journalism), he sat me down for a lecture. "Billy," he said, "the problem with mixing hobby and profession is that, yes, it'll make your work feel like fun, but it'll eventually make your fun feel like work."

The Disco Heads thought I was nuts. "You mean diss ain't got nuttin' to do wit school? Fuggedaboudit!" They couldn't believe I was assigning myself work. On a Friday night, while they were dancing at L'Amour, I was toiling on *Beggars Banquet.*

No one understood that the 'zine was where I derived my identity and independence. The fact it had nothing to do with school was the entire point. *Beggars Banquet* was all mine, and no one could tell me what to do with it. I thrived on the decision making: whether to put Mick or Keith on the cover, and whether *Saturday Night Live* or Keith's trial should be the top story. While most kids found self-esteem in a McJob, I found mine in *Beggars Banquet.* No matter the setbacks, I wasn't quitting.

After a few issues, read by almost no one, *Beggars Banquet* found its legs. Like a real journalist, I developed sources. People I'd meet in record stores, who'd see Mick and Keith at New York's nightclubs. For instance, when Keith unexpectedly turned up at the Bottom Line to jam with Dave Edmunds, I had someone on the scene. And when Mick checked out Peter Tosh's show at that same club, I got a full report. I put it in my 'zine and, in a few short months, came a long way from "What the fuck is this crap?"

In March 1979, I placed a classified ad in *Trouser Press:* "Wanna be the first kid on your block to know what the Stones are up to? Then check out *Beggars Banquet,* the fanzine for bona fide Stones freaks." I charged 35 cents, plus a 15-cent postage stamp. People would send a quarter, dime, and stamp to my bedroom, and I'd mail them the latest issue. By summer, I had a few dozen subscribers—3 bucks for six issues—and felt legit.

But I knew something was missing. As a fan and journalist, I wanted to interact with the Stones directly. And so, in September '79, as I turned 17 and entered my senior year of high school, I began tagging along with my older friends to Manhattan's famous nightclubs. Places like Max's, CBGB's, Trax, and the Mudd Club. I was still under the drinking age, which was 18, but no one carded me. I watched bands you never heard of, like the Speedies and the Rattlers, as well as some you have, like the Ramones and Johnny Thunders. But I kept missing the Stones. In my skinny tie and pointy shoes, I'd ask the bartender if the Stones had been in recently, and I'd hear, "Yeah, Mick saw the Contortions last night" or "Keith was here for Doug Sahm."

In November, I learned that Mick and Keith were producing the next Stones LP at Electric Lady Studio on 8th Street. I staked the place out and stood in the cold for hours at a time. I never spotted them, but my readers were impressed by my use of the word "here." Anytime I wrote, "Mick and Keith are here in New York," it brought my 'zine cachet. To someone in Kalamazoo, it was a big deal. I also listed the album's song titles, like "Summer Romance" and "Where the Boys Go," a half year before its release.

My source for that exclusive info was Video James, who I met, oddly enough, through a teacher of mine. He was dubbed Video James because he owned the world's largest collection of Stones footage. The Stones would call *him* when they wanted to watch tapes of themselves. I corresponded with him only by mail at first, but he became my number one source.

One day, he invited me to his Manhattan apartment for one of his patented "videothons." That's when he'd break out his tapes for as many fans as could fit in his living room. I accepted his invitation, but was nervous. I was an innocent teenager, while Video James and his pals were thirtyish. "What if they make me take drugs?"

When I arrived at his apartment, his friends did seem wild. One guy wore snakeskin boots, like Keith in *Gimme Shelter,* and the girls had names like Anastasia and Seven. When the joints got passed around, I said, "No thanks." Surprisingly, Video James refrained from the pot smoking and seemed a bit bookish. He resembled Clark Kent—short hair, thick glasses, buttoned shirt— but carried himself like Ed Norton from *The Honeymooners.* He'd get very worked up over Stones minutiae.

When someone surmised that *The Ed Sullivan Show* marked the Stones' first appearance on American TV, he cried, "No! They did *Sullivan* on October 25, 1964! Their first appearance on U.S. TV was the Les Crane show on June 2. They did 'Not Fade Away' and 'I Just Wanna Make Love to You.' Then they were on the Clay Cole show on June 20, where they did 'Tell Me' and 'Carol.' " He spewed it in a single breath. He was quirky, maybe a little nerdy, but I felt an affinity toward him. Like me, he was an archivist and historian, obsessed with getting the facts right.

His videothon lasted fourteen hours. We watched *Cocksucker Blues,* all the *Ed Sullivan* appearances, and the complete Dallas '78 concert. But the highlight was the rehearsal from *Saturday Night Live.* In an un-aired skit (from the 7:30 run-through), the Stones appeared as themselves, with John Belushi as a bodyguard, Laraine Newman as a groupie, and Bill Murray as record executive Jerry Aldini.

Video James began his collection in 1965, when he brought an 8mm camera to the Academy of Music. He filmed the Stones' concert that day and traded it with others doing the same. But he took it a step further. He knew that local TV stations rarely saved their footage—they'd record over Elvis with the dancing bears—so he asked if he could rummage through their vaults. The grownups didn't consider it valuable, so they said, "Here's the keys, kid. Knock yourself out." He'd even sift through the garbage.

By the mid-Seventies, Bill Wyman became aware of Video James's collection and began trading with him. Bill might say, "I need the *Shindig!* episode of us with Howlin' Wolf," to which Video James would reply, "Okay, but you have to send me the *Ready Steady Go!* clip." Additionally, when the Stones were in town, a roadie would call and say, "Keith wants to see some Otis Redding," or "Woody wants to watch Sam Cooke."

Video James would hop in a cab, schlepping not just a suitcase of tapes to Keith's room, but the video machine itself. This was long before Betamax or VHS, so TV stations—and aficionados like Video James and Bill Wyman—were the only ones with the hardware.

In the spring of 1980, Video James got an advance copy of the Stones' upcoming album. I rushed to his house for a listen and wrote about it in *Beggars Banquet*. I also obtained advance photos of the album cover from someone I knew at Atlantic Records. I was 17 years old and had a world exclusive. But I was still missing that firsthand connection to the Stones. I desperately needed to meet them.

On June 24, 1980, I walked down the aisle in my purple cap and gown at my high school graduation. Two days later, the Stones released *Emotional Rescue*. To commemorate the occasion, they hosted a party at Danceteria on 37th Street. I didn't think I'd get in, but was determined to show up anyway.

The party was set for 3 PM, which seemed odd. I didn't think Keith got out of bed before then. But this wasn't a *party* party, it was a *press* party. The daytime scheduling was to accommodate the 6 o'clock news programs. I got to the club an hour early, and no one was there. Danceteria was in the middle of the garment district, so the only things I saw were minimum-wage laborers wheeling racks of clothes.

Eventually, the press arrived. I watched forlornly as the schnook from Channel 5 and the ditzy chick from Channel 9 got in. They probably needed to ask, "Which one of you is Ringo?"

By 3:30, the door was closed, and all the guests were inside. I figured that the Stones slipped in via a secret entrance. I was the only one left on the street.

I stuck around and, at 4:45, almost two hours behind the scheduled start of the party, a black limousine pulled up. Out popped Mick, dressed in a lime green suit, red tie, and dark sunglasses. He was heading straight toward me, and I had him all to myself. But he wasn't making eye contact and stepped swiftly toward the club. I reached into my manila envelope to give him a *Beggars Banquet,* but thought better of it. The door opened, the door closed, end of my Mick opportunity.

Twenty minutes later, a second limo pulled up. From this one emerged Keith, Ronnie, and Bill. They seemed approachable, but I again didn't pull out my 'zine. I figured that if I gave it to them *now,* they'd lose it, crush it, or dispose of it in the club.

I clammed up as they passed me, but it wasn't because I was nervous. I simply had nothing to say. I was also taken aback by how small they seemed. As a gawky 6-foot-2 teenager, I was accustomed to looking down at the people I looked up to, but I expected the Stones to be larger than life.

With the band members inside, I was again by myself on 37th Street. The party's motif, I later found out, played up the *Emotional Rescue* theme. The walls were decorated with plasma bottles and X-ray screens, and the bartenders were dressed as surgeons. Plastic straitjackets were handed out as party favors. The Stones fielded questions from the media and sat for a photo op.

It felt like forever for them to come out, but it was actually forty-five minutes. By then, a small crowd had gathered on the sidewalk. Passersby would ask me about the limos, and I'd say, "The Rolling Stones are having a party in there." Around twenty people—nine-to-fivers coming out of work—stuck around for a glimpse.

Mick emerged at 5:30. Girls shrieked "Miiiiick!" and guys asked for autographs, but he didn't stop. He put out a don't-fuck-with-me vibe and got in his limo.

When Keith, Ronnie, and Bill came out, the scene was the opposite. They stopped to shake hands and sign autographs. Keith, clutching a bottle of Jack Daniel's he'd pilfered from the party, drew the biggest crowd. Fans were yelling "Keeeef!" in his ear, but he didn't seem to mind. He'd answer, "Yeah!" and sign whatever was put in front of him.

Keith and Bill literally had their hands full, so I set my sights on Ronnie. "Woody," I said, "I wanna show ya something. My newsletter about you guys." (I wasn't being pretentious by calling him Woody. *Everyone* called him that.) I shoved the issue into his hands like a process server. He laughed, glanced at it for a second, and said, "Thanks, it's great." I knew he was humoring me, but I didn't care. A Rolling Stone had finally acknowledged my 'zine.

Woody clutched the issue and kept walking. But when he saw that Keith wasn't ready to board the limo, he studied it a bit. He noticed the issue's cover—exclusive photos from the Stones' new album—and cracked, "How'd you have that? It's not out 'til *today!*"

The three Stones eventually made it to their limo and were safely tucked inside. For some reason, the limo's windows were open and I was able to peer in from the sidewalk. Keith was looking over Woody's shoulder to see what he was reading and, next thing I knew, Woody was pointing at me. Keith glanced at me and then back down at the issue. They didn't know I was 17 or that I'd graduated from high school forty-eight hours earlier, but they had to know I was barely shaving. They smiled at me as their limo pulled away.

With Ian Stewart at 75 Rock. My first-ever Stones interview.

3

puttin'
on the ritz

Location, location, location. If there's an element of luck to my story, it's that the Stones—Mick, Keith, and Woody—lived in the same place as me. If Picasso had a "blue period" and Orson Welles a "film noir period," then this was the Stones' "New York period."

They wrote songs about the city—their new album gave a shout-out to 8th Street—and became part of its fabric. When Mick sang about walkin' Central Park and about *schmattas* on Seventh Avenue, he was drawing from experience. I mean, how many non–New Yorkers even know what a *schmatta* is? (Yiddish for "rag.")

Unlike their iconic peers, the Stones weren't hiding behind moats. While Led Zeppelin were in medieval castles with their Grim Reaper guy, the Stones were pressing the flesh in New York's nightclubs. Often, they'd hop onstage for an impromptu jam.

The Stones felt comfortable in my city, and I loved the fact that they were walking the same streets and drinking the same tap water as me. I obsessively detailed their nightly exploits in a column called "Where the Boys Go."

Of course, when most people think of New York City, they think of the Manhattan part. The skyscrapers and the hustle and bustle. But I was from the Brooklyn part, where some of the blocks have trees. I lived in a nondescript row house, with no garage or front lawn. We weren't poor, but we were far from rich.

From my bedroom window, I could see parts of the Manhattan skyline— the Empire State Building, the World Trade Center—and knew that's where I wanted to be. Even as a little kid, I knew that's where the cool stuff was happening. It's where Felix and Oscar lived, it's where the Macy's parade took place, and it's where the TV and radio stations were stationed. And now it was where I could find the Stones. Mick, Keith, and Woody each had a Manhattan apartment and maintained a midtown office called Rolling Stones Records.

In September 1980, I began commuting every day from Brooklyn to Manhattan. I was attending New York University, where I majored in journalism. I'd been accepted to several schools with good journalism programs, but picked NYU for one important reason: to be closer to the Stones.

After my first day of class, I ventured to Rolling Stones Records. I didn't have an appointment, but that didn't deter me. It was located at 75 Rockefeller Plaza, near the famed ice-skating rink. I took the elevator to the twelfth floor—no security back then—and found a door with a big red tongue on it. I entered the reception area and said to the girl, "Hi, I wanna give you my newsletter."

She nervously buzzed the intercom and out came Earl McGrath and Art Collins, the president and vice president of the company. They leafed through my issue and pretended to like it. Even the office gopher grabbed a copy.

The five of us made a small commotion in the reception area, so a woman came out of her office to see what was going on. She was a tall, busty brunette with a nasal voice. I only exchanged a few words with her, but I sensed she was a stressed-out Type-A personality. She didn't tell me her title, but her name was Jane Rose.

Mr. Collins gave me an *Emotional Rescue* straitjacket and promised he'd invite me to the next Stones bash. He also promised he'd pass my *Beggars Banquet* issues to the Stones. I assumed he was just humoring me.

A short time later, I discovered that Mick was living at 135 Central Park West, around the corner from John Lennon. I visited the building and handed Mick's doorman a manila envelope with my latest issue. Trying to sound official—he could see I wasn't a mailman or FedEx guy—I said, "Please see that Mr. Jagger receives this." It became my new routine. Whenever I'd publish an issue, I'd leave some at Rolling Stones Records and leave one with Mick's doorman. Whether the Stones were actually getting them, I had no idea.

I heard that Woody was living in an apartment near NYU, so I tried to track him down. Someone said he was on Bedford Street, off Barrow. I patrolled the block, hoping to catch him on a cigarette run. I even checked the buzzers in the vestibules, hoping he'd be listed.

Keith was impossible. I heard he had an apartment on 10th Street but got evicted due to noise. (The inspiration for "Neighbors.") Supposedly, he was now on 28th Street or in a building near Washington Square Park or maybe at the Plaza Hotel.

By late 1980, at the age of 18, I'd stepped up my club hopping, even on school nights. I was still living with my parents, but I'd sneak out and take the train to Manhattan. (I never learned to drive.) By using common sense and some old-fashioned detective work, I tried predicting where Mick, Keith, or Woody might turn up. I knew that Keith was into reggae, so I ventured to Max Romeo, Black Uhuru, and Toots Hibbert shows. But I was the only white person in the audience.

I knew that Keith jammed with Matt "Guitar" Murphy at Trax and that Woody jammed with Inner Circle at the Peppermint Lounge, so I checked those places, too. I also frequented a new club called the Ritz, because it's where Keith saw Jerry Lee Lewis and where Mick caught a new singer named Prince. The Ritz's owner was a friend of Mick and Keith's, so they felt comfortable there.

When Chuck Berry came to the Ritz in 1981, I was rarin' to go. Unfortunately, my car ride fell through last-minute, and it was too late to make it by train. Keith showed up, and, although he didn't get onstage, it was a newsworthy night: After the concert, Keith went backstage to say hi to Chuck. Chuck had his back turned, so Keith grabbed Chuck's shoulder to get his attention. But Chuck don't like being touched, y'see, so he whipped around and clocked Keith in the face.

The story has since become part of Stones lore, but, at the time, *Beggars Banquet* was the only publication to cover it. Video James was an eyewitness and called me first thing in the morning. I immediately typed the story and got it to the copy shop. "Keith Hits the Ritz (and Berry Hits Keith)" was my headline. Keith said that Chuck was the only person in the world who could punch him and live.

Incidentally, the Stones never traveled to these clubs with bodyguards. They'd turn up like regular customers. When I finally spotted them around town, they were easy to approach. I didn't ask for autographs or even a handshake. I merely wanted to give them the latest issue of my newsletter and walk away. But they wouldn't let me leave sometimes. At the Savoy one night, Keith said, "I like readin' 'em on the can!" and at Peter Tosh's Ritz show, Woody said, "I've *got* this one, where's the *next* one?"

It meant the Stones were indeed getting my issues from Rolling Stones Records. And they weren't just chucking them. When I gave an issue to Bobby Keys one night at the Ritz, he said, "I just saw this on Keith's coffee table. He was talkin' 'bout you."

Keith? Talking about *me*? Moments like those put me on cloud nine.

I still wasn't sure if Mick was getting my issues—I tried handing him one at the Ritz, but couldn't get his attention—until a paparazzo photographer confirmed it for me. He was staking out Mick's house and saw Mick clutching an issue as he got into a limo. The paparazzo asked, "You read *Beggars Banquet*?" and Mick replied, "Yeah, this kid knows what we're doing before *we* do!"

In the course of my club hopping, I befriended a handful of paparazzi and concert photographers. They'd scope out the clubs, hoping to catch something special. In 1980 and early '81, the paparazzi weren't as vilified as they are today. Especially the rock guys. A few were annoying, but they weren't interested in "Gotcha!" moments and weren't being blamed for killing princesses. *Entertainment Tonight* didn't even exist.

With the paparazzi's help, I was able to back up my odd or interesting stories. If I told you that Mick, sporting a full beard, was zipping around on roller skates, I'd show you Mick, all bushy, on roller skates. When I exclusively reported that Pete Townshend laid down a track for the Stones' new song "Slave," I had photos of him and Mick, taken right after they left the studio. And when the Stones taped their "Waiting on a Friend" video on a downtown street, I ran the pictures before anyone had MTV.

The paparazzi knew that *Beggars Banquet* was a labor of love, so they donated their photos to me. It worked well for them because now they could say to the Stones, "Hey, I'm shooting this for *Beggars Banquet*," and the Stones would actually pose for them.

Everything was moving in a beautiful cycle. By word of mouth, my circulation grew to almost a thousand. I raised my price to $4 a year, and some subscribers offered to pay *more*. Some would send me a $5 bill, but I'd make change through the mail. My readers loved that I was a fan and that I never copped a holier-than-thou attitude. They'd say, "You make the Stones seem human and like anyone can bump into them in New York."

I felt a great sense of accomplishment, but, for an 18-year-old, I was enormously busy. Between school and *Beggars Banquet,* I had no time to date, no time to play sports, and no time to take driving lessons. And as much as I appreciated the Stones' recognition, I still felt something missing: *Creem* and *Rolling Stone* routinely interviewed the Stones and had covered the band on tour. When would *I* get that chance?

One morning in 1981, Mom said, "An Art Collins is on the phone." I jumped from my bowl of Cap'n Crunch and got on the line. Art was now in charge of Rolling Stones Records—Earl McGrath had retired—and said I could interview Ian Stewart *that afternoon.* I changed out of my pajamas, grabbed my tape recorder, and dashed out the door to 75 Rock. I composed my questions on the subway.

Ian, or "Stu" as he was better known, was a founding member of the Stones. He's forever been known as "the Sixth Stone," but was chronologically the *second* Stone. It was he and Brian Jones who auditioned the others. But the first thing Andrew Oldham did when he became manager in 1963 was axe him. The Stones loved Stu, so he continued to play at their concerts, often hidden in the background.

He was visiting New York to promote an album by Rocket 88, the ad hoc boogie-woogie jazz band he'd formed with Charlie Watts. He lived in a sleepy part of England, where his mates included working blokes and pig farmers. "I still live exactly where I used to before the Stones came around," he said. "There are guys I still see who have nothing to do with music."

I was never nervous around Mick, Keith, or Woody, but was nervous meeting Stu. He was a musical purist and had little patience for bullshit. He hated the current state of music—the synthesizers, the poofy hairdos—and hated when bands, including the Stones, put fame ahead of work. When the Stones annoyed him, he'd refer to them as "my showers of shit," and they'd take it from him. That's why I was nervous. If he thought the Stones were manure, I wouldn't rank as a piece of snot.

But the minute I met him, he put me at ease. He was soft-spoken and wore an unassuming golf shirt and Hush Puppies. He was very friendly and taught me about boogie-woogie jazz players, like Wynonie Harris and Louis Jordan.

He opened up to me about the Stones' early days and how he put food in their mouths: "Mick had a university grant . . . but Keith and Brian had nothing." And he said that being axed from the Stones was a blessing in disguise: "I don't like rock 'n' roll as a way of life. I think it's awful. . . . It's nice to get up there and play . . . and then have some peace and quiet. I used to see Bill Wyman come back to the hotel with half his bloody clothes off!"

Stu may have been a "semi-Stone," but this was quite a "get" for my 'zine. My readers loved it. I was about to put him on my next cover, but switched last-minute. A quote from Keith was the bigger story. "We're going to tour this year," he announced. The moment we'd all been waiting for.

Keith takes time from his birthday party to read
my issue onstage.

4

hampton
comes alive

I walked into the kitchen and told my parents, "I'm leaving school to follow the Stones." They did not take it well. But once we picked Mom up off the floor, I compromised: As soon as the 1981 *Tattoo You* tour was over, I'd return to NYU.

The tour's official launch was September 25 at Philadelphia's JFK Stadium. But the Stones first staged a secret warm-up gig at a bar in Worcester, Massachusetts. Only 350 people got into Sir Morgan's Cove, and I wasn't one of them. By the time I learned of the surprise, I couldn't make the two-hundred-mile trek from Brooklyn. I felt ready to cry and vowed "never again."

A few days later, I got a second chance. Video James called, frantic: "They're doing a secret show in Rhode Island tomorrow! Only thirty-five hundred seats!" He said tickets were going on sale in the morning, so we had to leave pronto. I grabbed my toothbrush and dashed out the door.

Like me, Video James didn't drive. And Amtrak couldn't get us to Providence overnight. So Video James phoned some friends with a car. He said he'd reveal the secret to them if they gave us a lift. They accepted, but, like the shampoo commercial, *they* told two friends, who told two friends, and so on and so on. By the time our ride showed up, it was more like a caravan.

We thought we were the only people in the world who knew about the secret show, but, as we zoomed up I-95, the media in Providence caught wind of it. As odd as it seems today, they broke into prime-time programming: "We interrupt this episode of *Dallas* to bring you a special bulletin. The Rolling Stones will play the Ocean State Arts Center tomorrow night. Tickets go on sale tomorrow morning at 8 AM in front of the theater. So get down there *now*!" I'm paraphrasing, but I'm not embellishing.

By the time we got there, around midnight, thousands of people were in front of the theater. Some folks brought lawn chairs and others brought sleeping bags. Some, like us, sat in their cars with the doors open.

The cops tried to break it up. A sergeant got on a bullhorn and said, "No tickets will be sold here," but no one believed him. "I ain't leaving 'til I get a sign from above," the guy next to me joked. A light rain began to fall.

Video James slipped into a phone booth and called his contact in the Stones organization. He jumped back in the car, yelling, "Let's get outta here! The tickets are somewhere else!" According to his source, the location was a parking lot between Union Station and the State House. We drove to the lot and were the only ones there. The gate was locked, but we pulled up anyway. We assumed that, come daylight, the attendant's booth would transform into a box office.

We waited in our cars for hours and, by dawn, had company. A radio station leaked the new info, so we had forty cars behind us, winding around the block. At 7 o'clock, a potbellied guy in a Red Sox cap came hobbling up the street, chomping on a cigar and carrying a coffee cup. He gazed at all the cars and seemed confused. He unlocked the gate and climbed into his little booth. We rolled up and asked, "What's the ticket limit per person?"

"Come again?"

"For tonight's Stones concert. How many can we get?"

He looked at us like we were freaks. "What the fuck are you talking about?"

We explained the story, and he nearly swallowed his stogie. "You don't got your facts straight. I run a parkin' lot here, not a concert joint."

Within minutes, the cops showed up with their predictable announcement: "There will be no Rolling Stones concert tonight. Repeat. No concert. Turn your cars around and disperse immediately."

The cops were right. The Stones had indeed booked the show, but nixed it last-minute, due to the news leak. Management feared a repeat of Sir Morgan's, where fans who couldn't get in threw bottles and got violent. The Stones were hoping to breeze into Providence quietly, but it was too late. "The press has blown it," a Stones spokesperson said.

A front-page article in *The Providence Journal-Bulletin* quoted a fan who'd camped out all night in the rain. "The Stones," he said, "like to mess with people's heads." On the cover of my next issue, I wrote, "The Insanity Begins."

I spent my first-ever Stones concert with 90,000 of my closest friends at JFK Stadium. I bought a ticket through Ticketron, and my seat was up in the nosebleeds. The Stones looked like sprinkles on an ice cream cone. I found someone to give me a lift from Brooklyn to Philly. He was going to the concert anyway, but to see the opening act, Journey. I begged him to stay for the whole show.

I still wanted to see the Stones in a small venue and heard they were doing the Fox Theatre in Atlanta. At 3,960 seats, it'd be the smallest show of the tour, other than Sir Morgan's. Tickets were put on sale in the middle of the night—following a surprise 2 AM radio announcement—and were scooped up immediately. Video James said not to worry. "*I'll* get us in." He suggested we catch the next flight to Florida, watch the Stones at the Tangerine Bowl, and then drive up with his friends for the October 26 show in Atlanta.

At age 19, it was my first time on an airplane. We flew PEOPLExpress, the new discount airline. You didn't need a ticket, you'd just show up and board. You paid your fare after takeoff, in midair, with no ID required.

We landed in Florida and went straight to the Tangerine Bowl in Orlando. We didn't have tickets, but Video James said we didn't need any. I watched as he walked up to a security guard and said, "We're here with JC." The guard got on his walkie-talkie, and we were waved into the stadium, sans tickets. I didn't know who this JC person was, but the mere mention of his holy initials worked miracles.

During the drive to Atlanta, Video James's friends, all in their thirties, recounted their Stones exploits: "Remember the Myrtle Beach show?" "What about Cobo '72?" I felt like I had nothing to contribute and tried to deflect attention. They asked how old I was, and I blurted out "20" because it sounded more grown up than 19. At one point, Video James regaled us with his famous "Paper Bag James" story.

The incident took place a few days before the Stones' appearance on *Saturday Night Live* in October '78. Video James was at a private rehearsal and had a paper bag in his lap. Jane Rose, that woman from Rolling Stones Records, asked him what was in it, and he said a tuna sandwich. She didn't believe him and demanded he open the bag. He admitted it contained a tape recorder, but said, "I'm not taping anything! I have it with me by coincidence!" (This, as he secretly pressed the Stop button.)

Everyone in Studio 8H, including the Stones, overheard the discourse. Video James claimed that Bill Wyman okayed his tape recorder, but Bill didn't defend him. And Keith and Woody were like, "He's not *Video* James, he's *Paper Bag* James!"

For months, if not years, a cloud of suspicion hung over his head. People accused him of being a bootlegger. He was occasionally allowed to hang out—and had *someone* in the organization helping him—but wasn't afforded the access he once was.

When we pulled up to the Fox, it was a madhouse. Thousands of fans crowded Peachtree Street, looking for tickets. Scalpers were asking $500, and a guy was selling T-shirts that read, "I missed the Stones at the Fox Theatre, 10/26/81." Video James asked us each for $50, told us to wait on the corner, and disappeared.

We stood there for nearly an hour. The show was scheduled for 8, but it was past 8:30 when he came running toward us, saying, "Take *these*." They weren't tickets, they were some kind of passes. We entered through the back-stage door, but didn't get to meet the Stones.

The band took the stage, and it was everything I'd hoped for. Unlike at JFK Stadium, the Stones shared lots of interaction with the audience. Mick accepted bouquets of flowers and, during "Miss You," took a dive into the crowd. My pass allowed me down front, so, as both a fan and a reporter, it was a dream come true.

In early November, the Stones set up camp in New York. Two concerts at Madison Square Garden and three at Brendan Byrne Arena. Tickets for all five shows were distributed by lottery. Each place held 20,000 people, so the de-mand was high and the supply was low. Only 100,000 tickets for the largest market in America.

You had forty-eight hours following a radio announcement to get your re-quest and SASE in the mail. Thousands of fans took off from work to write en-velopes all day, but were faced with a dilemma. The radio announcement gave the address as "New York, NY 10116," but there was no such zip code.

People got frantic. "What should I do? Put the zip code they gave on the radio or the zip code that makes sense?" Back then, New York zips were 100-whatever, no exceptions. "What if I write the wrong one, and it doesn't get there in time?" I knew several people who had nervous breakdowns over this.

Then there was the postage panic. Stamps were about to go up from 18 cents to 20 cents. "I put the current stamp on my self-addressed stamped en-velope, but what if the Stones don't respond to me until *after* the increase? I'll never get my tickets!"

Fans were having heart attacks, but I was relaxed. Video James said he'd get me into all five shows. All I had to do was supply a Sony Walkman for each one. I went to Crazy Eddie's, bought five Sony Walkmans (Walkmen?), and de-livered them to his door. Then, on the night of each concert, I met him outside the arena and got my ticket. The seats were pretty good, and the routine be-came tolerable. The nerve-wracking part was the wait. A couple times, Video James didn't show up with my ticket until the Stones were already onstage.

Outside Madison Square Garden one night, I struck up a conversation with someone else waiting for him. "Isn't the Walkman thing odd?" I asked. "This is nothing," she replied. "This tour, it's electronics. Last tour, it was patio products. I chipped in on a swimming pool for the Palladium show."

I wasn't sure how the operation worked, but she suspected that that guy JC was involved. All I knew was: A Walkman was $30 and a Stones ticket was $15—a pretty low markup for a guaranteed seat. The Stones received 3.5 million requests (which is why they were granted their own zip code), so I felt privileged and kept my mouth shut. And if that JC guy was involved, I never met him. My only contact was with Video James.

By December, I'd sampled a good amount of the tour. I'd been to the largest venue (JFK) and the smallest (the Fox). I saw shows in the North, the South, and in every month since the tour began (September, October, November). But at no point during my travels did I hang with the Stones. That would change in Virginia, the tour's final stop. Two shows at the Hampton Coliseum, December 18 and 19.

Video James booked us into the Hilton Hotel in nearby Williamsburg. A bunch of us crowded into one room. I was the youngest, so I got the floor.

When Video James said he'd reserved us a room in the same hotel as the Stones, I didn't believe him. But minutes after we checked in, I spotted Bill Wyman in the hotel's restaurant. And over the course of the weekend, I spotted Shirley Watts drinking beer for breakfast, Ian Stewart buying a newspaper, and Keith's son, Marlon, pumping quarters into a video game. I deluded myself into thinking I was embedded with the entourage, like Chet Flippo of *Rolling Stone* used to be.

The December 18 concert, which fell on Keith's 38th birthday, was televised on pay-per-view. The band's repertoire offered nothing unique, but they added some stage props. Special ramps and scissor lifts allowed the band to get closer to the audience. Mick walked through the crowd during "Let Me Go," Woody hung from a scissor lift during "You Can't Always Get What You Want," and Keith toasted his own birthday before "Little T & A."

But the oddest sight came during "Satisfaction." As balloons rained from the ceiling, I spotted someone from the corner of my eye, running down a ramp. At first, I thought it was a roadie. But he picked up steam and headed straight to Keith. The birthday boy wasn't happy to see this guy, so he took off his guitar and swung it at his head. Security scooped the kid up—never to be heard from again—and Keith put his guitar back on like nothing happened.

After the show, Video James said JC would get us into Keith's backstage birthday party. We waited in the empty arena, but JC never came. Instead, we called out to Art Collins, who told security to let us in.

Art was a man of his word. He had told me a year earlier that he'd get me into the Stones' next party, and there I was. As we entered a banquet room, Bill Wyman was at the door, greeting guests. Mick was in a corner, wearing a ski cap and a don't-come-near-me pout.

The room was decked out for Christmas, with wooden soldiers and giant candy canes. Keith eventually entered, fashionably late. We launched into "Happy Birthday," as he stood over his cake. He grabbed a huge knife and plunged it into the word "Happy." He served slices to his 9-year-old daughter, Dandelion, and to 12-year-old Marlon.

He then worked the room and greeted well-wishers. When he got to me, I reached into my manila envelope and said, "Do you have the latest issue?" He grabbed *Beggars Banquet,* Number 24, and quipped, "I do *now*." He rolled it up in his left hand and continued on. I didn't think the issue would survive the bash, but it was nice of him to take it.

I next spoke with Woody, and told him I loved the show. He said he was surprised that Keith smashed that kid with his guitar, but that Keith told him, "Oh, yeah? How do you know he didn't have a knife or a gun?" John Lennon had taken a bullet the year before and, in just the past few months, President Reagan, the pope, and Anwar Sadat were used for target practice. It was no longer the Sixties, where girls rushed the stage for a lock of your hair. Now your biggest fan could put a hole in you.

As I chatted with Woody, Keith temporarily left his own party. Unbeknownst to most of the guests, he retreated to the stage area. The house lights were on, and the arena was vacant. Roadies were packing things up. But Keith hopped on the stage, unfurled his *Beggars Banquet,* and sat down to read it. A pure moment, nothing fabricated. I'm aware it took place because someone snapped a photo.

When we left the Coliseum that night, a friend of Video James's unwrapped a napkin and showed me his memento. "I took a slice of Keith's cake," he said, "and I'm gonna keep it in my freezer forever." He asked why I didn't do the same, and I said, "I'm holding out for a bigger piece."

"I didn't know there was going to be a program," said Woody.
"There wasn't," I told him, "I did it on my own."
(Keith offered to staple.)

5

waiting
on a friend

The best Christmas/Chanukah gift I ever got wasn't wrapped in a bow and arrived by accident. It was December 1982, and I'd taken the subway from NYU to Rolling Stones Records. Time to drop off my latest issue.

Rockefeller Plaza was teeming with people, admiring the famous Christmas tree, but the Stones office was empty. Oddly, the door was unlocked. I plopped on the sofa and thumbed through a magazine, figuring someone would eventually show up.

After fifteen minutes, Jane Rose entered. She said that everyone was downstairs at the Atlantic Records Christmas party. I cheerily handed her my *Beggars Banquet*s and said, "Hot off the press."

She told me she had to get back to the party and only came upstairs to make a call. "But don't leave until I get off the phone," she added. "I've got something for *you*, too." She sat at the receptionist's desk and began to dial. I tried not to listen in, but it was unavoidable.

"He wants both guitars," I overheard her say. "Can you get them there today? The name is Hurrah. Richard Hurrah. Room 323. Yes, it's 58th and Fifth." When she got off the phone, she reached into the desk and pulled out a tongue-shaped calendar. "Happy holidays," she said, "from Rolling Stones Records."

And that was it. The best holiday gift I ever got. I don't mean the calendar, of course; I mean the phone conversation. Jane had inadvertently given me Keith's current whereabouts and, more important, his current pseudonym. Something she'd never do on purpose. Fifty-eighth and Fifth meant the Plaza Hotel, and the rest was self-explanatory.

I thanked her for the calendar and dashed out of that building like Jesse

Owens. I ran seven blocks to the Plaza in two minutes. For the first time, I had a fixed address for Keith. Previously, the only way I hand-delivered an issue to him was at a noisy nightclub or party. But now I knew where he was living, at least for the rest of the day.

I approached the front desk and asked for an envelope and stationery. I scribbled, "I hope you like the new issue" and put "Richard Hurrah, Room 323" on the envelope. I left it with the concierge and said, "Please see that Mr. Hurrah gets this."

I was about to exit the hotel when an idea struck. I glared at the house phone in the lobby. Could I? Should I? I picked up the receiver and asked for Mr. Hurrah. My only goal was to let him know that my issue was waiting downstairs. The hotel operator asked who was calling and, in my excitement, I simply said, "Bill." She put me on hold and came back seconds later: "Your *last* name, please?"

"Oh! Yes! Sorry! German. Like the country. Or, actually, like a person *from* that country—which I'm not, by the way." Click. She put me on hold.

The next voice I heard belonged to Richard Hurrah. Better known as Keith Richards. "I'm glad you called," he said. "I've been meaning to get together with you."

I nearly dropped the phone. Is it possible he thinks he's speaking to Bill *Wyman*? Did he mishear the operator?

"I really love your rag," he added. "We gotta get together. Do an interview for it."

"Uh, *okay*," I stammered. "When . . . when do you want to do it?"

"Well, I've got Christmas shopping today, but call me tomorrow, round this time." Click. His sign-off was abrupt, but classic Keith.

The next day, I called him from my bedroom in Brooklyn. "We're gonna do it," he vowed. "But I'm out the door to Patti's parents' house. Let's try it after the holiday."

I called after Christmas, but he kept putting it off. Our dance continued for days, then weeks, and became a ritual: I'd call the Plaza, the operator would screen, Keith would take my call, and he'd tell me he was busy. "Try me tomorrow. I'll know more then what I gotta do."

I knew his excuses were legit. Not only was it holiday season, but the Stones were about to release their concert film, *Let's Spend the Night Together*. So when he said, "I'm gonna see Marlon tonight" or "I gotta do some film stuff," he wasn't just blowing me off. He could've gotten rid of me by telling the operator to not let me through. Instead, he'd accept my call and instruct me not to give up.

As December '82 became January '83, his excuses changed a bit. No more holidays. Now it was "I'm gonna see McEnroe at the Garden tonight" or "I'm gonna see Tina at the Ritz tonight." At the very least, he was giving me good dirt for my "Where the Boys Go" column. He replaced Video James as my number one source and, in a weird way, was becoming a friend. He was speaking with me several times a week and, in addition to telling me what *he* was up to, would ask what I, his 20-year-old fan from Brooklyn, was up to. "Yeah? You had a good weekend?"

Meanwhile, fifteen blocks south of the Plaza, Ron Wood was preparing a lecture. Somehow, he got roped into teaching a course at the Learning Annex.

Today, the Learning Annex has branches all over. But at the time, they were a small operation, limited to New York. They offered courses like "How to Strip for Your Mate" and "The Art of Basket Weaving." They were getting trounced by their competitor, Network for Learning, so they needed a splash. They hoped "An Evening with Ron Wood" would be it. Their catalog said he'd discuss his career and maybe teach some guitar licks.

At first, they were going to set Woody up in one of their regular classrooms, down the hall from "Basket Weaving." Fifty or sixty people. But they realized they had something bigger on their hands and booked him into Town Hall, capacity fifteen hundred. They charged $30 a head, which was the same as "How to Become a Notary Public in Your Spare Time." A year or so earlier, people paid *half* that price to see *five* Rolling Stones, but it didn't matter. Town Hall sold out instantly. Fans believed that Mick or Keith would show up and that it'd turn into a Stones concert.

In reality, no one knew what was going to happen. Not the Learning Annex, not the Stones office, and least of all Woody. The only person with a plan was *me*. I correctly assumed that no one had thought about a program, like the *Playbill* at a Broadway show. I nominated myself for the task. I figured it would be great publicity for *Beggars Banquet,* a nice outlet for my creativity, and a good way to ingratiate myself with the Stones camp. I did it without asking permission. I knew that if I approached the Learning Annex, the Stones office, or even Town Hall, they'd say no for the sake of saying no.

I wrote a bio of Woody's career, added some photos, and brought it to the copy shop. The result was a sixteen-page booklet titled *The Banquet.* I produced 1,500 copies at my own expense. On the day of the show, January 7, 1983, I schlepped them to Town Hall. I got there two hours before showtime and told the security guard, "I'm here with the programs." He waved me right through.

Woody was onstage doing a soundcheck, so I put the box down, pulled one out, and headed toward the stage. "Here," I said, "it's the program for tonight."

He looked befuddled. "I—I didn't know there was going to be a program."

"There wasn't," I told him. "I did it on my own."

He was stunned. "That's brilliant, man! Thanks!" He reached down to shake my hand, and our friendship was forged. Woody was so nervous about this thing, he seemed genuinely inspired by my gesture.

The Learning Annex's head muckamuck saw how well Woody received me and assumed we were pals. He came over, shook my hand, and asked whether I'd received my backstage pass. I told him no. He pulled out a sticker and applied it to my jacket. It had no writing on it, just an image of a butterfly. It looked like something you'd get from a gumball machine. I mean, seriously, I think it *was* from a gumball machine.

When Town Hall's head usher saw me chatting with Woody and Mr. Learning Annex, he jumped to his own conclusions. Next thing I knew, he was making an announcement to his fellow ushers: "Okay, everybody, listen up! The programs are in this box. Grab as many as you can, and hand them out when you bring people to their seats."

I was fully prepared to give these things out on my own. I honestly envisioned myself standing on 43rd Street, barking, "Get yer Ron Wood program here! Get yer Ron Wood program!" but now I didn't have to. A team of ushers was doing it for me.

But there's a better part to the story. The night before Woody's Town Hall extravaganza, I phoned Keith at the Plaza, as part of our daily ritual. The one where I ask for Mr. Hurrah, the operator screens, Keith gets on, and then apologizes for not being available. Except that, on this night, at 11:30 PM, he actually said, "Let's do it."

"Huh?"

"Yeah, Bill, I'm free tonight. Let's do it. How soon can you get here?"

Ironically, I was in the middle of preparing the programs for Woody's lecture. I'd spent so much money on the actual printing that I opted to do the rest—the collating and stapling of fifteen hundred booklets—by hand. I was planning to pull an all-nighter to get it done. So I actually heard myself tell Keith Richards, "Um, well, here's the thing. I know we've been trying to hook this up for weeks, but tonight isn't good for me. I, um, well, first of all, are you going to Woody's lecture tomorrow night?"

"Professor Wood," he muttered. "He's gonna have to go that one alone. Another fine mess he's gotten into."

"You should come," I said. "You might learn something."

"Yeah," he shot back. "Learn how to get ripped off!"

Keith wasn't thrilled with Woody's foray into higher education, so I had to sheepishly explain the programs. "Any other night would be good for me, Keith. But I really gotta finish stapling these books by tomorrow."

And that's when he uttered the words I'll never forget the rest of my life. "Bring 'em *here*," he said. "*I'll* help you staple." I honestly think he meant it. I can easily imagine him, Room 323 of the Plaza, going, "Bill, can ya pass me the Swingline?"

I had two Rolling Stones pulling me in opposite directions. I begged some friends to please please please finish my stapling job, and I told Keith I'd be right over. I grabbed my tape recorder, ran out the door, and caught the next train. I got to the Plaza at 1 AM. As a courtesy, I rang Keith from the house phone to tell him I was there.

"I'm sorry," the operator said. "That line is on 'Do Not Disturb.' "

"What? No, you don't understand. He's expecting me."

"I'm sorry," she asserted, "but I can't put you through."

Fuck. What do I do now? I waited ten minutes and tried again. "Sorry, that line is on 'Do Not Disturb.' "

Motherfucker. I gave it *another* ten minutes and, again, "I'm sorry, we can't connect you."

This had to be a mistake. Maybe he doesn't realize his phone's on "Do Not Disturb." I headed up to Room 323 and listened at the door. I heard voices coming from inside, but I couldn't decipher whose. Should I knock? It's 1:30 in the morning, but this *is* Keith Richards and he *is* expecting me. There was a "Do Not Disturb" sign on the doorknob so, ultimately, I didn't disturb. I figured something suddenly came up for him. I decided to wait downstairs and keep trying.

I called every fifteen minutes, but heard "I'm sorry, I can't put you through" each time. It was now 2:30, and hotel security was finally getting suspicious. Two guys with walkie-talkies approached me: "Can we help you?"

"I don't think so," I said. "I'm trying to get through to a guest in Room 323. He's expecting me, but he's got 'Do Not Disturb' on his door and on his phone line."

"What's the guest's name?"

"Mr. Hurrah," I answered. "Richard Hurrah." I guess they were testing me. "You know who Mr. Hurrah is?"

"Yes," I assured them. "I'm supposed to interview him. Keith Richards. He told me to come, but I don't want to disturb him if it says 'Do Not Disturb.' "

They sensed I wasn't a stalker, so they left me alone. But they kept an eye on me. I gave myself 'til 3 AM. If Keith doesn't answer by then, I told myself, I'll get back on the subway to Brooklyn, tail between my legs.

Sure enough, at the stroke of three, my call was put through. The "Do Not Disturb" was lifted. But Keith wasn't the one who answered the phone. It was Art Collins. "You wanna speak with Keith? He fell asleep hours ago. He didn't mention any interview."

Art Collins had always been nice to me, but that's when it came to giving me tchotchkes and getting me into that party. I had no idea if he was kiboshing my private audience with Keith. I took him at his word, because I was too naïve to know that celebrities don't arrange their own interviews. That's what they have publicists, managers, assistants, and agents for. It's just that, well, Keith made it feel so one-on-one.

The ride back to Brooklyn was brutal. The train took forever and I froze my balls off. I got home at 5 AM. The night's upside, at least, was that Keith offered to help me staple—the sign of a true friend.

For me, the highlight of Woody's lecture was before he came out. It was the sight of fifteen hundred people reading my program. Writers don't get that too often, watching people read their work. I sat in my seat anonymously, taking it in with pride.

Woody was greeted with raucous applause when he hit the stage, but it was downhill from there. Within seconds, he looked like a deer caught in the headlights. He had no idea what to do and spent much of the evening with his hands in his pockets. Fans predictably howled "Keeeeeith!" and Woody lost control of the room. He showed videos on a big screen and performed a bass solo, but everyone wanted more. No one paid attention to him, and someone threw a bottle onto the stage.

Woody called time-out for an intermission. Utilizing my butterfly sticker, I ventured backstage for the halftime pep talk. I thought the organizers would instruct him on how to turn things around, but everyone was as lost as he was. Woody seemed disappointed that Keith wasn't there. He told me he'd reserved seats in the front row for three of his closest friends: "One for Keith, one for Dan Aykroyd, and one for Robin Williams." But none of them showed up. "You know things are bad," he said, "when your own fucking best friend isn't here."

Over the next few weeks, *Beggars Banquet* was the lightning rod for Woody's disgruntled customers. I published some of their letters. "A rip-off," one guy wrote. "I was taken for $30, and Ron Wood's performance, or lack of it, was worth nothing. Why he was able to walk off the stage without being given a beating is amazing! But I'm even more surprised that a figure of his stature would be associated with such cheat. The highlights were the videos shown onstage. Not a live performance. Instead we had Wood onstage acting like an ass, drinking a bottle of whiskey. If the man has a drinking problem, I'm sorry I helped finance it."

My program was one of the few positives that Woody took away from that night, and I think he never forgot it.

The next time I spoke with Keith, on a Monday afternoon, he was apologetic about our non-interview. He added that the next few days didn't look good. "I've got to bury Patti's dad, y'see. He died over the weekend."

"I'm sorry to hear that," I told him. "Please send her my condolences."

He thanked me and said, "The interview can wait a bit, but you and I can talk at the party tomorrow."

Party? What party? "I don't know what you're talking about, Keith. Am I invited?"

"*Yeah,* you're invited." A press function at Tavern on the Green, to promote the new film.

"Do I need to be on the guest list?"

"Nah, you just need the invite. Get here now, and I'll give ya one."

Luckily, I was calling from a pay phone in midtown Manhattan. I got to the Plaza in minutes. This time, I went straight to Room 323 and rang the doorbell. A female voice asked me to identify myself.

"Bill German," I stated. "I'm here to see Keith. To *pick something up* from Keith."

The woman didn't answer. I stood for a minute, not knowing what to expect. Eventually, the door opened a crack. A woman's arm came through and handed me a manila envelope. My eyes traced the arm upward, and I realized it was attached to Jane Rose.

"Here," she said. "From Keith." She had one eye peeking through the crack.

"Thanks!" I gushed. "And tell *Keith* I said thanks."

She closed the door before I could say more. I hopped on the elevator and opened the envelope. There was a note from Keith, scrawled on the torn-off cover of the current *Playgirl.* Alongside the cover boy's face—who happened to be Mick Jagger—Keith wrote, "Dear Bill, see you there. If not, call me."

But to my dismay, the wrong invitation was enclosed. My invite was only for the screening, not the after-party. The Stones were not expected at the movie theater, so when Keith wrote "see you there," he meant Tavern on the Green.

But what was I to do? March back to Room 323 and demand the right invite? Accuse Jane Rose of pulling a switcheroo? I felt it best to keep my mouth shut.

I frantically phoned around, trying to score the right invitation. By sheer coincidence, Video James knew an employee at Zarem Inc., the publicity firm handling the party. The guy said he'd give me an invite, but only if I paid him $30. I explained that I was a legitimate member of the press and that Keith Richards was expecting me to be there, but he told me to save my spiel. "Bring thirty bucks and you're in." The party was about to start in a few hours, so I said okay. I'm not sure if it constituted checkbook journalism, but I ran to Zarem and paid this guy his ransom.

Tavern on the Green was the nicest restaurant I'd ever been to, but it was full of media geeks that night. While waiting in the buffet line for roast duck, I was stuck behind Robin Leach. But I sat with some *Harper's Bazaar* editors who were very nice. I showed them my 'zine, and they seemed amused. They loved how a 20-year-old kid was running his own magazine and how he was invited to a Stones party by Keith Richards. As if on cue, Keith stopped by our table to say hi. He snuck up, grabbed my shoulders, and, upon spotting a *Beggars Banquet* on the table, joked, "You still pushin' that rag?" It made everyone's night.

Eventually, I moseyed to the Stones' table. Bill Wyman couldn't make it, but the rest were all there. I chatted with Woody, and he thanked me again for the programs. I didn't speak with Mick or Charlie—they were deep in conversation with Ahmet Ertegun—but I spent some time with Keith. I thanked him for the invite, to which he replied, "*Of course,* man." I never discussed the mix-up.

He gave me some good quotes for *Beggars Banquet.* He told me he hadn't seen the film in its entirety and was relying on other people's opinions. "Everyone's telling me they like it," he said. "But I don't know if they mean it, or if someone's payin' 'em to say it." I told him, as I told my readers in *Beggars Banquet,* that the film was flawed. A fun film to watch, but riddled with sound problems. Not a good thing for a concert film.

Keith told me to stay on top of him regarding our interview. "I gotta be a pallbearer for Patti's dad tomorrow," he said. "But I want ya to keep tryin' me."

Mick stopped for a moment and this is what I got.

Patti, a fellow New Yorker, said, "You're from Brooklyn, right?"
Keith made me feel so welcome, I quit school the next day.

6

bedbugs uptown

Next time I saw Keith, I found myself in an Abbott and Costello routine. He said he was at the Plaza Hotel again, so I asked what name he was under.

"That's it, mate. You got it."

"Huh?"

"I'm Under."

"You're under?"

"Precisely."

He was under Under. He'd left the Plaza for ten days to work with the Stones in Paris, but returned that afternoon, under a new pseudonym, Mr. Under. I had no idea how he'd come up with these things, but, by giving me his nom de check-in, he was encouraging me to stay in touch.

It was February 10, 1983, and we were at a nightclub on Manhattan's Upper East Side. Another party to celebrate the *Let's Spend the Night Together* film. I got in because I paid $30 to that publicist again.

The night began with a red carpet premiere at Loews New York Theatre on Second Avenue. Limos double-parked. I showed up via the Lexington Avenue subway, but walked the red carpet like everybody else. I tried acting famous, but couldn't pull it off. My paparazzi friends waved me over, and I couldn't pretend I didn't know them.

Inside the theater, three people took seats in front of me: Mick, Keith, and Woody. I tried to gauge their reaction to the film, but could only see the backs of their heads. (Note to self: Never sit behind Ron Wood's hairdo in a movie theater.) Occasionally, they'd elbow each other and snicker, but I couldn't hear what they were saying.

The after-party was at Corso, a Latin discotheque on 86th Street. Billy Joel was chatting with Cheryl Tiegs, the Stray Cats were chatting with Bill Graham, and Andy Warhol was snapping pictures of Ahmet Ertegun. As the house band laid down a salsa beat, Mick took to the floor and did a chicken dance. I couldn't tell if he was serious or fucking around, but it was funny either way.

I sidled up to the bar and ordered a drink. Mick came from behind and said, "Hi, Bill," which surprised me. I hadn't bonded with Mick the way I had with Keith and Woody, but he seemed pretty affable. Christopher Reeve, who Keith and Woody knew through Robin Williams (who they knew through Belushi), eavesdropped on our conversation. I asked Mick why I didn't see him at Woody's lecture, and he simply rolled his eyes. "I guess you were lucky not to be there," I said.

"Luck!" he exclaimed. "Lucky! 'Twasn't luck, my lad. I assure you that!"

The other Stones steered clear of the dance floor. Woody again thanked me for the programs, and Keith introduced me to his fiancée, Patti Hansen. "I *love* the newsletter!" she said. "You're from Brooklyn, right?" She was extremely nice. Keith also introduced me to his dad, Bert, a roly-poly chap with a white mustache and Sherlock Holmes pipe. He and Keith had been estranged for twenty years, but, since reuniting in '82, were inseparable.

I asked Keith about the recording sessions in Paris, and he said, "The album's coming along great." As he and I were chatting, Bob Gruen snapped some candid shots of us. Bob is a friend of mine, and he was one of two photographers allowed into the party. Keith and Woody felt comfortable with Bob and me, so we got them to strike some funny poses. "Keith, pretend like you're strangling Woody!" "Woody, pretend like you're reading *Beggars Banquet*." They were extremely accommodating.

The party thinned out at 1 AM, and I realized I never got Mick to pose. He had a bodyguard with him and was itching to leave, so I said, "Mick, is it okay if we get you holding *Beggars Banquet*?" He didn't say anything and seemed annoyed. But he stopped for a second—literally a second—and flashed a smile, before walking away. Bob got the shot, but Mick made me feel like such a pest, I never asked him for another photo the rest of my life.

At around 1:30, Keith got up to leave. As I watched him move through the room, a tall guy with a scraggly beard approached me. "You're Bill German, right? Keith loves your magazine. He's always talking about how you're *everywhere* and how you know more about the band than *he* does. He wants to help you with it."

"Wow," I said. "He's been really nice *already*."

"Well, my name's Svi and I work for Keith. You wanna meet us at Studio 54? Give this to them at the back door"—it was some kind of pass—"and they'll know you're with Keith. We'll meet you there in twenty minutes."

The after-party for the after-party. I don't know whose idea Studio 54 was, but, by 1983, the place had outlived its relevance. No more Biancas on white horses and no more Truman Capotes. As I was whisked through a back entrance and a maze of tunnels, I could hear the Chambers Brothers' "Time Has Come Today." (No more disco, either.) I wound up in a basement, with just a handful of people. Keith arrived with Patti, Jane Rose, and Svi (pronounced "svee"). "You get *around*!" Keith said to me. "All in a day's work," I replied.

I quickly realized this wasn't a party. It was just an intimate get-together. Keith asked if Woody was coming, but no one seemed to know. At one point, Keith disappeared into a private room, to do whatever one did in a private room at Studio 54. When he emerged, he ducked through another doorway that led upstairs. This time, I followed. I stood next to him on a catwalk above the dance floor. Elvis Costello's "Pump It Up" was blasting, and none of the dancers knew that Keith Richards was watching them from above.

By fate or coincidence, the next song was "Brown Sugar." The crowd went nuts, whooping it up and flailing their arms. Keith stood there stoically, not saying a word. But I think he was digging the fact that so many people were digging it. I watched him from the corner of my eye and kept silent. Eventually, he realized Woody wasn't coming and called it a night. "Ring me at the hotel," he said.

"Under Under?"

"Under Under."

During my train ride home, I had time to think. I resolved to quit NYU for good. Keith and Woody were so cooperative with me and made me feel so welcome, there was no turning back. I knew *Beggars Banquet* was my life.

When my parents woke up, I hit them with the news. "School is interfering with my education," I said. "I'm already doing what I want, so why waste time in class?"

Mom and Dad were ready to sit shiva for me (the Jewish mourning ritual), and asked, "What if the Stones *break up*?" but I told them, "I'll cross that bridge when I come to it. Either way, I'm not going back to school."

I was true to my word. After the party at Corso, I never set foot in NYU again. I'd been to class Thursday afternoon, the party was Thursday night, and it was now Friday morning. I got a couple hours sleep and took the train back to Manhattan to visit Bob Gruen. My plan was to pick up his photos and lay out my issue over the weekend. This wasn't the digital age, so for me to obtain Thursday night's photos on Friday afternoon was a journalistic coup. Unheard of in the 'zine world.

There was another reason for rushing to Bob's place: I wanted to beat the snow. The weatherman was predicting the worst storm in decades. By the time I got to Manhattan, the snow was up to my ankles. I hung out at Bob's, as he printed a stack for me and a stack for Keith. "He and Patti are gonna love these!" I said.

I left Bob's and made it to the Plaza. The snowdrifts were up to my knees and the city was a ghost town. I gave the photos to the concierge and enclosed a note I thought was clever: "Keith and Patti, I hope you're enjoying the white stuff."

I struggled back to the subway station, yearning for home. It felt like my face was being whipped. My train took forever and went out of service somewhere in Brooklyn. It was 2 AM, and I had no idea where I was. I began walking, but it was like *Doctor Zhivago.* The drifts were up to my neck. I never called my parents because I didn't want to alarm them. I walked for an hour, with no signs of humanity. I eventually made it to a friend's and collapsed on his couch.

Of course, I should've realized that Mom would be frantic. When she got up in the morning and found my bed empty, she yelled, "Billy's in a snowdrift somewhere!" She called my friends—except, ironically, the one whose house I was at—and one of them said, "He was headed to the Plaza last night."

Mom called the hotel immediately. "I need to speak with Keith Richards."

"I'm sorry, ma'am, but there's no one here by that name."

She began sobbing and told the guy the story. How her son is either dead in a snowdrift or warm and dry with Mr. Richards. "Look," sighed the operator, "I'm not supposed to do this for nonguests, but I'll make an exception. I'll page your son, and everyone in the lobby will hear it."

Mom stayed on the line and listened in: "Bill German, please pick up the courtesy phone. Bill German, please pick up the courtesy phone." I can imagine Keith and Patti, enjoying a quiet brunch in the café, when they hear that announcement. He spits out his mimosa like Danny Thomas and goes, "Man, that kid is *everywhere!*"

The whole Brooklyn-to-Manhattan thing was wearing me down. All those pain-in-the-ass back-and-forths in the middle of the night. I desperately needed to be in Manhattan on a twenty-four-hour basis, closer to the Stones. I loved my parents, but it was time to fly the coop. If I lived in Manhattan, I'd have had my interview with Keith by now, and I would not have risked my life in that blizzard.

One day, I was on the phone with Svi. He said he was going away for a while and did I know anyone to take over the lease of his Manhattan bachelor pad. "Only $386 a month, rent-controlled."

"Yeah!" I said. "Me!" I rushed to his house that day to pick up the keys. It was a run-down railroad flat on 89th Street and Second Avenue. The size of a prison cell. The walls were chipping, the ceiling looked ready to collapse, and the medicine chest was full of roaches. It had only one closet, and Svi said he once found a rat in there. But I was so desperate to live in Manhattan, I didn't care.

Svi left behind a bed and a black-and-white TV, which had a coat hanger for an antenna. He also left some books and cassettes. One was a homemade tape from Keith called "Somewhere over the Counter," featuring Keith's renditions of Hoagy Carmichael and Merle Haggard songs.

Svi's books included Hebrew texts and pharmaceutical guides. It turned out that Svi was both a licensed pharmacist and Talmudic scholar. He could rattle off the table of elements and quote Rabbi Akivah verbatim. Not what I was expecting from Keith Richards's personal assistant. "Svi," incidentally, was not his real name. It was his Hebrew name, assigned when he lived on a kibbutz.

So how did this pharmacist and Talmudic scholar get involved with the Stones? It began in 1979, when Svi made a trip to Morocco. He slept on the beaches for a month, smoking hash, having sex, and taking life as it came. He didn't like staying in one place too long, so he headed north. He ventured through Spain and made it up to France. He did this, by the way, by driving a decommissioned British taxi. He smuggled a huge stash of hash in the cab's partition (the window separating the driver from the passenger), and the border patrols never found it.

One night in Paris, Svi was at a dinner party. He broke out his Moroccan hash, and everyone loved it. One guy asked, "Are you selling?" and Svi said yes. The guy knew some people who'd be interested. "Here's their address."

Svi went to meet his potential clients at a place called Pathé-Marconi Studio. He was buzzed in and told to wait in the lounge area. Someone with a bushy beard came in, but left without a word. Svi knew he looked familiar, but couldn't place the face. About twenty minutes later, two other guys came in. But they, too, grabbed a drink and left. Eventually, it clicked. The more Svi thought about it, the more he could mentally shave off the first guy's beard. He realized it was Mick Jagger. The other guys were Keith Richards and Ron Wood.

Svi thought the Stones were okay and owned a copy of Hot Rocks, but this was a business deal for him. They kept him waiting so long, he said "Fuck it" and left. He got a call the next day, saying, "Why'd you leave?"

Svi told the roadie he felt jerked around. "Do they want my stuff or not?" The roadie swore things would go better next time. Svi returned with his hash, and Keith fell in love. Over the course of the summer, Svi made a bunch of trips to Pathé-Marconi and netted a tidy profit.

Keith was intrigued by the guy who'd initially walked out on him and who was driving around Paris in a decommissioned taxicab, so they became friends. And when Keith and Woody broke off from the Stones sessions to do a one-off concert in England (as the New Barbarians), they brought Svi to serve as their bodyguard. His job was to stand in front of their trailer and say, "You can't come in." He also had to guard a paper bag full of cash. Svi liked to keep a low profile, but it was difficult with his 6-foot-7 frame. From a distance, he resembled baseball's "Big Unit," Randy Johnson. Lanky and scraggly.

After the summer, the Stones returned to New York, to mix *Emotional Rescue* at Electric Lady. Svi returned to his job at the pharmacy, which benefited Keith and Woody. Obviously, some senile old lady wasn't gonna notice if her prescription was shortchanged one pill. Do it to *several* old biddies, and it's gonna be a fun night.

When the Stones embarked on their '82 tour of Europe, Keith put Svi on the official payroll. "Personal Assistant" is how it reads in the tour program. His job was to tend to Keith's needs. Whether it was guitar strings or shoelaces, if Keith requested it, Svi fetched it. When Patti Hansen needed panty hose in Paris, Svi skipped dinner to scour Avenue Victor Hugo. When 12-year-old Marlon had a midnight craving for Snickers, it was Svi who searched the candy shops of Vienna.

Of course, Svi's "professional experience" was also put to use. He became the tour's pharmacist. If the queen has a food taster, then Svi was the Stones' drug taster. In every city, Svi would chat up the local dealers. He'd summon a few to Keith's suite, and they'd sit in the foyer. Keith would look them over and pick one. "You, in the red bandanna. In the kitchen with Svi." Svi would determine the quality of the guy's wares. If he liked it, he'd walk out of the kitchen and flash Keith a thumbs-up. If he didn't, he'd flash a thumbs-down. Like Siskel and Ebert.

Sometimes, drugs would be purchased in one country and brought to another. Svi ensured that the stash got there safely and that no one got arrested. Often, customs would board the Stones' private plane to conduct a search upon landing. But Svi knew every nook and cranny of the aircraft. He also knew they'd never pull the heads off of Marlon's GI Joe dolls. Pounds of blow safely made the trip between Spain, Italy, and Switzerland, thanks to Svi. He quickly became known as the tour's problem solver.

Svi was paid a meager salary by the Stones organization, so he was expecting a large off-the-books gratuity when the tour was over. But all Keith did was whip out $5,000 in cash. Svi was upset and reminded Keith that he could've made more money by working in the pharmacy that summer.

"Hang on," Keith said sternly. "What the fuck were you doing with the $700 every day?"

Svi, you see, began each day with 700 bucks in cash. It was given to him by the tour's accountant (usually in the local currency) to purchase stuff for Keith. At the end of the day, Svi would go to the accountant and tell him what he bought: guitar strap, $20; panty hose, $8. No matter how much it totaled, the accountant would replenish Svi's cash flow so that he'd start tomorrow with $700 again.

But there were "certain items" Svi purchased for which the seller did not provide a receipt. The accountant would take Svi's word as to how much was spent and would mark it in the ledger as "miscellaneous" or "sundries." Keith was under the impression, and had hoped, that Svi was skimming two hundred bucks off the top each day by lying to the accountant. "Hey," Keith said to him after the tour, "you shoulda been savin' up to buy boots when we were in Milan. Or a watch when we was in Zurich. I thought you knew that."

Svi felt like an ass. He prided himself on his street smarts, but was clueless as to how things worked on a Stones tour. Feeling shortchanged, he came back to New York and jumped at the first chance to have the Stones pay off for him. As luck would have it, he bumped into an old high school pal named Bill Zanker. Zanker owned a company called the Learning Annex, and Svi pitched him the Woody idea. The Learning Annex needed a Rolling Stone, and Svi and Woody needed cash. (They split around 30K.) Svi caught grief from the Stones organization—"What next, you're gonna have him work with puppets?"—but he didn't give a shit.

It wasn't the first time Svi drew the ire of the Stones camp and wouldn't be the last. His main nemesis was Jane Rose. She and Svi were constantly bickering. During the '81 rehearsals in Massachusetts, Svi gave Keith a pill that knocked him out. Keith missed a day of rehearsals, and everyone was pissed. Jane blamed Svi, but Svi said, "Keith's a big boy and doesn't do anything he doesn't want to." They argued for hours until Keith woke up and took Svi's side.

One of Svi's jobs on the '82 tour was to roust Keith out of bed and get him to the concert each day. Or to dinner. When the tour reached France, the Stones were guests of honor at a fancy restaurant in Nice. As Keith was getting his shit together at 6 PM, Jane burst in and told Keith to get a move on. "You should've woken him up an hour ago, Svi! We're late! The rest of the band is on the way!"

Of course, if there's one thing Keith Richards don't like, it's being hounded. He commanded Jane to "shut the fuck up and wait in the car." She followed his instructions and sat in the limo. But Keith and Svi snuck out the back door and took a cab. By the time Jane figured it out and got to the restaurant, everyone was downing dessert. "So nice of you to join us!" Keith proclaimed. "Late as usual!"

I realized these were Svi's one-sided accounts, but, considering the personalities involved, I knew they weren't far off.

I moved into Svi's apartment in June of '83. According to my parents, I was running away to join the circus. First I quit school and now this, all to follow the Stones. I did not want to fall on my face and come crying back to them.

I could not have pulled it off if I didn't take in a roommate and if the rent wasn't so cheap. Our phone and electric bills were next to nothing, and we didn't have cable. After splitting everything, my share was $300 a month. My *Beggars Banquet* income (around $4,000 a year) was enough to sustain me. But I could only afford one meal a day and, because the apartment was so small, I had to sleep in the same bed as my roommate. It's something two heterosexual guys can do if they're desperate to live in Manhattan.

In addition to the TV and bed, Svi let me keep his phone number. I hoped that Keith might call by accident, but it never happened. I did hear from a roadie named Gary, who said he'd left a bag in the closet that I should burn. I also heard from 13-year-old Marlon, who probably wanted a Snickers bar.

Ironically, the best "Stones call" I got wasn't for Svi, it was for me. The guy said, "Mick and Keith told me to call." I thought it was a put-on, but the more I listened, the more he seemed legit. He said Mick gave him my Brooklyn number, and my mom gave him my Manhattan number, so here he was. His name was Gordon Bennett, and he was setting up an official Rolling Stones fan club. Mick and Keith insisted he get me involved.

"*Beggars Banquet* will become the Stones' official newsletter," he said, "and will be sent to thousands of fans throughout the world. Mick and Keith also want to advertise *Beggars Banquet* via an insert in the next Stones album."

When my head stopped spinning, I agreed to meet this guy and have him lay out the details. I can't say this was a dream come true for me because, frankly, it was beyond anything I ever dreamed.

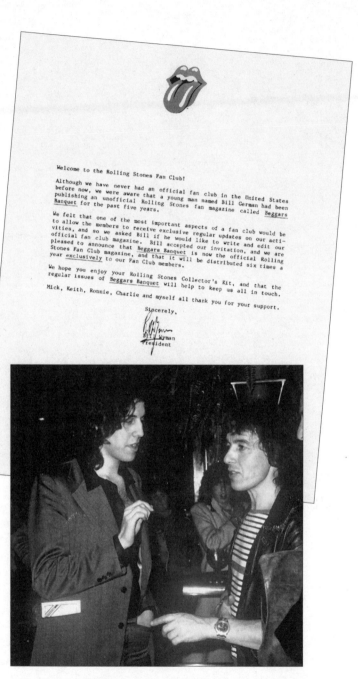

Welcome to the Rolling Stones Fan Club!

Although we have never had an official fan club in the United States before now, we were aware that a young man named Bill German had been publishing an unofficial Rolling Stones fan magazine called Beggars Banquet for the past five years.

We felt that one of the most important aspects of a fan club would be to allow the members to receive exclusive regular updates on our activities, and so we asked Bill if he would like to write and edit our official fan club magazine. Bill accepted our invitation, and we are pleased to announce that Beggars Banquet is now the official Rolling Stones Fan Club magazine, and that it will be distributed six times a year exclusively to our Fan Club members.

We hope you enjoy your Rolling Stones Collector's Kit, and that the regular issues of Beggars Banquet will help to keep us all in touch.

Mick, Keith, Ronnie, Charlie and myself all thank you for your support.

Sincerely,

Bill Wyman
President

Chatting with Bill Wyman at the ARMS after-party about our
new venture. His letter went out to 20,000 fans.
Charlie, meanwhile, had no idea who I was.

7

the merger

Within weeks of that phone call, I was spilling orange juice on Mick's rug, watching Keith pull a knife on my ginger ale, and covering up the Stones' sexual infidelities. I was also the subject of various newspaper and magazine articles.

"Little Stones fanzine becomes official," read the headline in *Circus*. "German has sources . . . that surprise even the members of the band," wrote columnist Lisa Robinson. "As a result, *Beggars Banquet* is now the official Rolling Stones fan club newsletter. . . . German's little fanzine has become a real success story."

Meanwhile, in the *Detroit Free Press,* columnist Gary Graff reported: "The Stones [have] bought out Bill German, a Stones freak who has been independently publishing a fan magazine titled *Beggars Banquet.* The Stones are now bankrolling it, claiming to be giving German free editorial control. We'll see whose side time is on with this one."

It all stemmed from my conversation in early August with Gordon Bennett. He had just signed a deal with Prince Rupert Loewenstein, the Stones' business manager, to become the Stones' licensing agent. It was Bennett's job to take the Stones' tongue logo and market the crap out of it. He revealed his plans to me for Jagger Jeans and Satisfaction perfume, as well as Rolling Stones bubble gum, watches, jigsaw puzzles, air fresheners, and telephones.

Rather than unleashing a crass marketing campaign, the idea of a fan club was hatched. Like slipping your kid's aspirin in the ice cream. Fans would join the club and receive all sorts of merchandise offers. A central part of the fan club would be a newsletter, so Mick and Keith said, "Get Bill German." They wanted someone who thought like, and possessed the unbridled enthusiasm of, a true Stones fan.

I met with Gordon Bennett shortly after he phoned me. His office was in Hollywood, but he was staying at an Upper East Side hotel. "Your newsletter," he said, "will be advertised in the next Stones album. It will be declared the official Stones newsletter, and thousands of fans around the world will receive it. We'll provide you with a new masthead that will incorporate the Stones' tongue logo. We'll pay you a salary per issue, and we'll pay your expenses, including all printing costs and photographers' fees. Plus, you'll receive full co-operation from the band and their employees."

He asked if there was anything I needed for my first official issue, and I wisecracked, "Yeah, how about interviews with Mick and Keith?"

"Consider it done," he said.

I thought he was joking, so I was caught off guard when Jane Rose woke me on September 28, 1983, the day after my 21st birthday. "Be at 304 West 81st Street at noon," she instructed over the phone. "That's where you'll interview Mick. Then you'll come to the office to interview Keith."

I had less than an hour to shower and shave and meet up with Mick. On my way out the door, I realized I had no blank tapes. So I reached into my roommate's bag of cassettes and pulled out *Willie Nelson's Greatest Hits* to tape over.

Mick was directly across town, so it took me five minutes by cab. Jane was so trained to not give out the Stones' personal information, she never let on that "304 West 81st" meant Mick's new home, but I already knew. The five-story townhouse was a tourist attraction. Mick had hoped he could move in quietly, but a deranged groupie graffitied the front wall. "Jerry Hag Hall pant pant filth filth," it said. If the yentas at Zabar's deli counter didn't know who their new neighbor was, they knew it now.

I rang the doorbell at high noon. The "Hag Hall pant pant" stuff had been steamed off, and a guy on the intercom told me to look in the camera and identify myself. He buzzed me in and said, "Mick and Jerry are out shopping, but you can wait in the kitchen."

I sat at the counter and rehearsed my questions. When Mick finally arrived, he shook my hand, apologized for being late, and introduced his long-time girlfriend to me. "Jerry, you know Bill, right? From *Beggars Banquet*?"

"Oh, yes, I enjoy reading that," she replied.

As Mick looked through a stack of mail, she asked if I wanted something to drink. She was reaching for a container of orange juice, so I said, "I'll have *that.*" She was charming, tall, and, contrary to the famous line in Andy Warhol's diary, completely devoid of body odor.

"Alright, then," said Mick. "Let's go up and *do* it!"

I grabbed my notes, my tape recorder, and my glass of OJ, and followed him up the stairs. As we passed each floor, he pointed out the renovations that were being done. "They've been working on this place forever," he said. "Sorry it's such a mess."

We eventually got to Mick's study on the top floor. It was a beautiful autumn day, so the windows were open. We were facing 81st Street and could hear the shrieks of young girls. "Must be recess," he said. "This is the best neighborhood in New York, but it can get pretty noisy sometimes." You'd think there'd be a law against it, but Mick Jagger was living next to an all-girl middle school.

His study was very neat, with a bookcase on one side and a VCR on the other. The VCR was blinking "12:00," and I remember thinking, "Wow, even Mick Jagger can't program his machine." He suggested we rearrange the chairs to face each other for our interview. They were heavy, but Mick said he'd do it himself. He dragged them to the center of the room, but then sat on the floor. I opted for a chair, placing my tape recorder and orange juice at my feet.

Mick grabbed the tape recorder and pressed some buttons. "Two, two. One, two." He knew more about recording than I did, so I let him tinker with it. "Alright," he said, "it's working." I informed him we were erasing Willie Nelson.

Before I posed my first question, he asked if I'd heard the upcoming Stones album. I told him I hadn't. The record wasn't due until November. "Well," he said, "we'll have to remedy that." Within moments, *Undercover* was blasting from his stereo. I realized it was eating into my interview time, but I didn't complain.

I felt I had a personal stake in this album—what with the *Beggars Banquet* ad to appear—so I was eager to hear it. The first song was about brutal Third World regimes.

Because of the volume, Mick and I couldn't talk much while the record was on. He spent most of the time dancing and prancing around the room as I sat in my chair, tapping my toes. I think he was playing it for himself as much as for me. He was wearing gray sweatpants and a maroon T-shirt, which would occasionally hike up and expose his navel as he danced. During the fourth song, "Wanna Hold You," he pounded his fists in the air and proclaimed, "I played drums on the demo for this!"

Eventually, he flipped to Side Two. The first song was about a guy hacking up his girlfriend. "True story!" he shouted over the music. "Guy in France! Cut her up and put her in the freezer!" It sounded like the chorus went, "There's too much blow," but I wasn't sure. It'd make sense—the guy was on so much blow, look what it made him do—so I asked, "Are you singing 'too much *blow*'?"

"Noooo!" he replied. "Too much *blood*! *Bloooood*!" He pinched the veins in his forearm for emphasis.

To prevent further confusion, he dashed across the room to grab some papers. He handed me his handwritten lyrics for each song. The song I connected with most was "All the Way Down." Its opening line—"I was 21, naïve, not cynical, I tried to please"—described *me* that day. The rest of the songs were about S&M, poverty, beatings, and assassinations.

I told Mick it was a bleak album, and he concurred: "Bleak, I'll say, sir. Bleak house. But it's not *all* bleak. It's *tough,* that's all. What comes out, comes out. A lot of it's antitotalitarian."

Within minutes, we got into a flow of conversation, hitting all sorts of topics. He grew evasive, however, when I asked about the Stones' new deal with CBS, set to take effect in 1984. It was reportedly worth $28 million, an astounding amount at the time. "I don't know what the figures are," he claimed. "[But] you know, it has to get shared. I don't get all the money."

"I didn't expect you to! But you did guarantee CBS four albums, right?"

"No, you can't be guaranteed anything. I might get hit by a bus, or the group might break up. . . . I'm not being very positive about that, but I'm being honest."

I asked what it was like to be a rock star at 40. He'd hit that milestone weeks earlier, and the press went berserk with it. "They criticize you for being old," he replied. "Like it's a fault. Like I should've died years ago.

"Living your life in public is not something to be recommended," he added. "Anyone who lives their life in public is affected in some way. . . . Some people can't deal with it. They go round the bend."

I asked how he'd managed to not pull an Elvis, and he quipped, "I've not reached his age yet! I might get there yet, with the help of a Greek pharmaceutical manufacturer and a doctor named Nick!"

We spoke for almost two hours, and I got some good quotes. I also got some insight when the phone rang in the middle of our interview. Mick assumed Jerry would pick it up and grew annoyed when she didn't. After seven or eight rings, he grabbed it himself. "Halloooo," he said. "Who eeez calleeeeng?" He was putting on a fake accent. If I'm not mistaken, he was trying to sound like an old Spanish lady. As soon as he recognized the caller, he reverted to his normal voice: "Oh, yeah, hang on, I think she's downstairs." He left the room, walked to the staircase, and shouted, "Jerry! It's for you! Pick up next time! We can't get any work done if the phone keeps ringing!" The point is, Mick Jagger was pretending to be his own maid to screen his phone calls.

To round out my interview, I asked Mick what kind of music he was listening to. "Huh-ho! *Good one!*" he said. "I haven't been to the record store lately, but let's see. I just listened to Bette Midler's version of 'Beast of Burden' and to the Eurythmics. Also, Herbie Hancock's new one. . . . But let me see."

He sprang up again and disappeared into an alcove in the corner of the room. I heard him flip through a stack of albums. While he was occupied with that, I decided to check out what books he was into. I stood up to look at the shelf and—PLINK!—there went my glass.

My first visit to Mick Jagger's house and I spill Minute Maid orange juice on his sixteenth-century Persian rug. There was no way I could pretend it didn't happen. "Um, hey, Mick? Mick?" I peered into the alcove, but he wasn't there. I stood over the puddle like an idiot, not knowing what to do. But Mick came to the rescue. He'd seen the whole thing and went to fetch a towel. He was now on his hands and knees, blotting up my mess.

"I am so sorry," I told him. "Please don't tell Jerry."

"Nah, s'alright. Besides, this is *my* room."

The image of me, 21 years and a day old, standing over Mick Jagger on his hands and knees, is something I'll carry with me as long as I live. The guy couldn't have been more gracious. And to think my day wasn't over. I still had to meet up with Keith.

I told Mick I needed blank cassettes, and he suggested I try the newsstand at 79th and Broadway. He was right. I then rushed to 75 Rockefeller Plaza, where Keith kept me waiting. I got to Rolling Stones Records around 4 o'clock, but sat in the reception area until 6. Keith was in Art Collins's office, testing Fenders. I suppose there are worse ways to kill two hours than listening to Keith Richards play guitar.

At 6 o'clock, I was ushered into the room. The first thing he said was, "We've *merged.* Welcome to the club." He added that, as far as he was concerned, my newfound status was a formality. I was *already* part of the extended Stones family. "That's why we're together in this room right *now,*" he said into my tape recorder. "Because we [the Stones] always say to each other, 'Have you seen the new *Beggars Banquet?*' It works, and it's always more interesting than anything else that comes out about us."

Keith was seated behind Art Collins's desk. A cigarette was dangling from his lips, and an unplugged Fender was resting on his lap. He plucked it throughout our interview. He wore a scarf around his neck and had a bottle of Jack Daniel's within arm's reach, sitting atop a stereo speaker. A copy of *The Village Voice* was resting on the desk between us. He glanced at it and, upon seeing Jesse Jackson's face on the cover, said, "I wonder what he'll hassle us for *this* time." (In 1978, the reverend picketed that very building to protest the "Black girls just wanna get fucked" line from "Some Girls.")

Jane Rose asked if we needed anything before she left us alone. Keith said he could use more ginger ale, and I said I'd take some, too. She brought us each a can from the office fridge. Keith mixed some into his glass of Jack. He offered me his booze, but I said I take my ginger ale straight. When I tried to open the can, however, I accidentally pulled the ring-thingy off. No luck with beverages that day.

"Not a problem," said Keith. He whipped a huge knife out of his back pocket, flung open the blade, and stabbed the top of the can for me. "*Now* you got it."

Jane closed the door, and I began asking Keith some pretty heavy questions. When I look back on it today, I'm surprised I had the balls to bring up what I did. I don't know if I was brave or naïve. I confronted him about his drug addiction, his estranged father, and the death of John Belushi. He didn't duck a single question.

Belushi died the year before, and I knew he and Keith were friends. They were together weeks before that fateful night at the Chateau Marmont. Did Keith see it coming?

"Yeah, always, [but] not that I ever expected it to happen. You never expect it to happen. It's kind of a retrospective point of view. But there was a very certain Brian Jones–type of vibrations in John Belushi. Even if you recognized it while John was still alive, you didn't want to admit it to yourself or say it to him. There was that certain recklessness [and] insatiable 'overdo it.' You know you can't say anything to him because the more you'd *tell* him he was overdoin' it, the more he'd *overdo* it. I never expected Brian to die, either, it was a terrible shock. . . . You only recognize it when it's too late, when it's all over and done with."

I also knew that Keith did not speak to his father for two decades. What was the reunion like?

"I was so scared to meet him, I took Ronnie . . . 'cause I needed the support. This is the father I'd left because we couldn't stay in the same house together anymore. It was time for me to leave the goddamned nest, and, soon after that, my mother broke up with my father, and one's inclination is to take care of Mum. . . . You're in one camp or the other. You can't put the foot right. Either you're on Mum's side or Dad's side, so you take care of Mum. And then I wasn't anywhere capable or geographically near enough to deal with it, so I got very used to it. 'I haven't seen my dad in two years, I haven't seen my dad in five years, ten years, fifteen years.' It could've gone on forever. . . . But now, all the things we couldn't stand about one another twenty years ago is water under the bridge. . . . He's given me a lot of insight into why I am like I am. He was at every [recording] session and [we found] forty-two bottles of beer stashed under his bed—an emergency supply—when he left."

Before I brought it up, Keith had never discussed his father or Belushi publicly. Journalists were either too scared or too unaware to broach those subjects. But Keith made me feel so comfortable, I didn't think twice. I asked him how his heroin addiction affected the band.

"Hey," he acknowledged, "for ten years, or at least for five years undoubtedly, I was the weak link in the chain. From *my* point of view, no way. But I was, in retrospect, in no condition to judge. That's the horrible, terrible fascination of dope. That when you're on it, everything's cool. And the more you take it, the more cool it is, and the more necessary it is to be cool. It's only in retrospect that you're able to say, 'Ah, this boy, you been led astray.' When all is said and done, I'm either damned lucky or, as I like to kid myself, real smart, that I didn't manage to top myself in that period. After all, the only thing I was topping the charts in then was the one most likely to kick the bucket. And I held that position for several years. It's one of my minor joys that I'm no longer on the list. Sid Vicious beat me to it. Loads of others. That shows how wrong the charts can be."

The one eerie similarity between Mick and Keith that day was how they both contemplated their mortality. I'm not the one who brought it up, *they* did. First there was Mick, saying he couldn't make guarantees: "I might get hit by a bus." And then there was Keith, dodging that same Greyhound. "We're all still here," he said. "You come across problems, and you deal with 'em or you don't. So far we've dealt with 'em, [but] nobody can deal with 'em all. Eventually there's the one you don't deal with, and that's the one that gets ya. That's only in our hands to a certain extent. I mean, you can do things to stay healthy and then get run over by a fuckin' bus. You can be the healthiest man ever run over by a bus."

I told myself, "Wow, this must be the stuff you think about at 40." My conversation with Keith filled two ninety-minute cassettes. He was willing to keep going, but eventually said, "I'm starved, man, and I gotta take a pee." When he returned from the restroom, Jane locked up the office.

It was 9 o'clock, so we had to use the freight elevator. While waiting, Keith saw someone with a mop and said, "Good to see ya." The four of us boarded the elevator, and Keith kept up the conversation. "So how's your daughter?" he asked. "Started school, right?" "Yes, yes," answered the porter in broken English. "She like college very good." They spoke for just a minute, but it gave me as much insight into Keith's character as did my three-hour interview.

Five weeks later, on November 7, *Undercover* was released. The album went to Number 4 on the *Billboard* charts and sold over a million copies. In each one was a flyer that said: "Subscribe to *Beggars Banquet* and get in touch with the Stones." Six bimonthly issues for $6.

The flyer depicted a mock cover of *Beggars Banquet* and touted its features, like "Where the Boys Go" and "Photo Flashback"—things I thought up in my bedroom as a teenager. Of the million people who saw it, I'm sure many said, "What the fuck is this crap?" but others were intrigued. Twenty thousand people sent money to Gordon Bennett in L.A.

Those people then received a letter from Bill Wyman, the fan club's ceremonial president. "Welcome to the Rolling Stones Fan Club," it said. "Although we have never had an official fan club in the United States before now, we were aware that a young man named Bill German had been publishing an unofficial Rolling Stones fan magazine called <u>Beggars Banquet</u> for the past five years. We felt that one of the most important aspects of a fan club would be to allow the members to receive exclusive regular updates on our activities, and so we asked Bill if he would like to write and edit our official fan club magazine. Bill accepted our invitation, and we are pleased to announce that <u>Beggars Banquet</u> is now the official Rolling Stones Fan Club magazine."

I was now part of the Stones' business plan. I hoped it would bring me closer to them on a personal and professional level, but that took some time. In December, weeks after the *Undercover* release, Bill and Charlie were in New York, taking part in the ARMS charity project. Following an all-star concert at Madison Square Garden, there was a get-together at the Berkshire Hotel. I approached Charlie and said, "Hi, I'm Bill German," but he stared at me like I was nuts. "From the *Beggars Banquet* newsletter," I added, but he continued to stare. I don't think he had the slightest clue what I was talking about.

Keith and Patti, meanwhile, were in Cabo San Lucas, about to wed. The nuptials secretly took place on Keith's birthday, December 18. Only a handful of guests were invited, including Jane Rose and the best man, Mick. No other Stones.

When Jane got back to New York, she hooked me up with the wedding photographer and gave me the exclusive play-by-play. "Keith stepped on the wineglass," she said. "The Jewish wedding custom. It was my idea and he liked it."

With Keith's wedding, the ARMS concerts, and my interviews with Mick and Keith, my first official issue was packed. I couldn't wait to lay it out and get it to my printer. Last time I was there, I told the guy I needed 2,000 copies of my eight-page booklet. It was a $200 order. But now I needed 30,000 copies of a twelve-page booklet, and it cost 3 grand. My printer knew me and trusted me, so he didn't require a deposit. I left him my paste-ups, and he got on the job immediately. But Gordon Bennett called me that night, going, "Stop the presses! Mick doesn't like the cover photo! You have to change it!"

And so, here's the part about editorial control: I did agree to submit my issues to the Stones organization prior to publication. They wouldn't tell me what to put *in,* but they'd tell me what to take *out.* I felt it was a worthwhile concession for my Mick and Keith interviews and my newfound access. But I quickly discovered that each Stone had special needs.

The process would begin with a dummy copy of my upcoming issue. Several people on the Stones' totem pole would get their hands on it. In New York, Jane Rose and Art Collins combed through it, as did the band's lawyers and accountants. I also had to send copies to London: One for the Stones' office on Munro Terrace and one for Bill Wyman's separate office on King's Road.

The annoying part about Mick rejecting my cover is that I'd submitted it to him in November 1983 and it was now January 1984. Also, the photo he rejected was the same close-up of him and Keith that was used on the *Undercover* flyer. He already let a million people see it, but *now* he decides he doesn't like it?

I immediately called my printer, but it was too late. Thirty thousand copies of the cover had already been printed, and you'd better believe he was charging for it. In fact, the printer was so upset, he now demanded full payment to continue the job. I talked him down to a $1,000 deposit and called Gordon Bennett.

Bennett was responsible for all the printing costs—as well as for my salary—but I hadn't seen a penny from him yet. Despite the 20,000 checks he'd received from fans, he claimed he was short on cash. He couldn't pay the $1,000 deposit for another two weeks. I told him we couldn't wait that long— "*Beggars Banquet* is time-sensitive"—but he stuck to his guns. I had no choice but to clean out my life savings and give it to the printer. Anything to get the presses rolling again.

In January 1984, the Stones went to Mexico City to shoot some videos. A party was thrown one night at a club called Quetzal. All the Stones were in attendance, except for Mick. Which is exactly how I worded it: "All the Stones were in attendance, except for Mick." But Jane Rose said, "You can't write that. Mick doesn't want you to make him conspicuous. It might reveal certain things he doesn't want revealed."

Mick, you see, had opted for some "taco" that night. There'd have been nothing to hide if he was a single carefree guy, but he wasn't. Jerry Hall was home in New York, seven months pregnant with their first child. My task, then, was to create a diversion. Instead of, "All the Stones were there, except for Mick," I wrote, "Keith, Bill, Charlie, and Woody attended [the] party." Jerry Hall can connect her own dots. I work for Mick.

I was about to print a harmless photo of Bill Wyman and his girlfriend, Kelly. He'd introduced me to her at the ARMS party, and she was very nice. Except that she was *one* of his girlfriends along the ARMS tour. He didn't want Kelly to find out about the ones in California and Texas, and he didn't want the ones in California and Texas to find out about Kelly. So he told me to never print photos of him with *anyone*.

In the span of a few months, I'd gone from wanting to know everything about my favorite rock stars to knowing too much. I wasn't sure if I felt good or bad about that.

The person who requested the most deletions was Jane. They were usually on behalf of Keith and were pretty nitpicky. She once made me remove the word "stumbled." I wrote something like, "Keith stumbled into Tramps to catch Buster Poindexter," and she didn't like it. I told her it was a figure of speech, but she said "stumbled" implies Keith was stoned, and we wouldn't want anyone to think that.

Another time, she made me delete a song title. Keith was covering Cole Porter's "I Get a Kick out of You" in his hotel room (the song made famous by Sinatra), but she didn't want it known. She feared that someone would steal Keith's idea to perform it, the way Blondie nicked "The Tide Is High" from him. (Keith had been playing that song—originally released in Jamaica, circa 1967, by the Paragons—when Debbie Harry was still waitressing. But some Blondie members allegedly heard Keith's private tape of it in 1979.)

I never argued with Jane because, overall, she volunteered twice as much stuff to put in as she made me take out. There were days I'd stop by her office and sit with her for hours, getting items for my "Where the Boys Go" column. She'd recite from her diary—"Keith had dinner with McEnroe at Da Silvano last Sunday"—and lend me her personal photos of the band. Jane had a reputation for being very territorial when it came to the Stones, so people took note of how cooperative she was with me.

"It's part of her job," sniffed Svi. "Keith told her to be nice to you, so she's nice to you. She doesn't wanna piss off Keith."

Either way, I was grateful. It could not have been easy for Jane to climb the corporate ladder in a male-dominated business like rock 'n' roll. Females were either groupies or secretaries. But here was Jane, a very important cog in the Stones' machinery.

She got her start in the early Seventies with Howard Stein, the concert promoter. He owned the Academy of Music on 14th Street, which later became the Palladium. She then worked for another promoter, Peter Rudge, whose clients included Lynyrd Skynyrd and the Stones. She went on tour with Skynyrd and, in 1975, went on tour with the Stones. She had various administrative duties and was in charge of Mick's wardrobe.

She told me she hated being addressed as "Mommy," which the Stones would do from time to time. "When people ask my title, I say, 'I'm Jane Rose' and leave it at that."

She once asked me to omit something for personal reasons, and I obliged. I'd started a column called "Five Years Ago in *Beggars Banquet,*" the title of which is self-explanatory. A story I covered in 1979, which I intended to rehash in 1984, was about the kid who died at Keith's house. Although Keith was separated from his common-law wife, Anita Pallenberg, he still shared a house with her in Westchester County, just outside New York. A 17-year-old "friend" of Anita's, named Scott Cantrell, was spending lots of time there. One night (when Keith was away), he picked up a gun he found in the bedroom and, according to Anita, played a solo game of Russian roulette. He lost.

The story was reported in every newspaper, and it affected me deeply. I was the same age as that kid, and I knew how easily I could have been lured to Keith's house like he was. I've heard all kinds of funky rumors about what might've happened, but the death was ruled an accidental suicide. Anita was charged with possession of an unregistered firearm and was let go after twelve hours of questioning.

"I'm a nice Jewish girl from Long Island," Jane told me. "My father's a doctor. What do I know from guns? It was the worst night of my life. I met Anita at the police station, and she had blood all over her. I don't want to be reminded of it. You are not putting this in *Beggars Banquet.*" The story was a matter of public record, but I'd never heard it from such a personal angle. I obviously couldn't say no to her.

I soon discovered, however, that there was a subject more taboo than murder and sex when it came to the Stones. And that was their finances. I needed to be *very* careful about that. If I wrote that the Stones massacred a Mexican village, it wouldn't be as bad as something that could elevate their tax bracket. Jane began training me early. The night I interviewed Keith, she kept saying, "Keith lives in Jamaica. Don't ever write that he lives in America or England. He lives in Jamaica."

It's true that Keith owned a house in Ocho Rios, Jamaica, but the fact is, he considered himself a New Yorker. He spent more time in Manhattan than

Ocho. He'd purchased a four-story condo on East 4th Street (which he'd yet to move into) and had owned a home in England since the 1960s. But for tax purposes, he was registered as a resident of Jamaica, nowhere else.

To maintain his status, he couldn't spend 180 days of any calendar year in England or America. His attorneys stayed on top of it: "Keith, you need to leave the country. You're getting close to 180 days, so go to Mexico or Antigua for a while."

The whole game got started in the 1970s when the Stones' financial adviser, the aforementioned Rupert Loewenstein, told them to flee England and become tax exiles. (Thus the album title *Exile on Main Street.*) Rupert, an actual prince of Bavarian descent, was an expert in the Franco-American Double Tax Avoidance Treaty. Don't ask me to explain it—when I hear "Franco-American," I only think SpaghettiOs—but it offered tax relief to earners like the Stones. It meant they would only be taxed by the countries they worked in, not the countries they lived in. And when you're talking Stones money, the difference is in the millions.

It affected many of the band's plans. It's why they recorded in France, not America or England, and it's why they taped their videos in Mexico City, not New York or London. As a fan, it depressed me to learn how many decisions— when and where to record, when and where to perform—were determined not by artistic inspiration, but by lawyers and accountants.

It was all pretty complicated, and determined what I could and couldn't write in *Beggars Banquet.* I sometimes couldn't use the word "work" in a sentence, and I couldn't refer to Keith's homes in New York and England as homes, only "houses."

It struck me as improbable that the INS or IRS would try to snare Keith Richards via the pages of *Beggars Banquet,* but the Stones' lawyers weren't taking chances. If the only things certain in life are death and taxes, Keith was determined to beat 'em both.

From a barstool on 78th Street, Keith peruses my first official
issue and offers me legal advice. "Do what's right for *you*."

8

the mouse
that roared

Unfortunately, I was born into the one Jewish family without a lawyer. The deeper I got involved with the Stones' business associates, the more I needed one.

I should've seen the red flags. When I was at Mick's house in September 1983, he didn't give the fan club venture a ringing endorsement. He said some nice things about *my* involvement—"You've been doing [*Beggars Banquet*] a long time . . . we thought it was the kind of thing to have with it"—but he seemed less than enthusiastic about the merchandising campaign. "We're doing it because it was *suggested*," he said. "If it makes people happy, great. Besides, we might as well get paid for all the garbage that's out there, instead of letting the bootleggers get it."

When I asked if he had any advice for me, he barked, "Yeah! Make sure you get paid!" He was speaking on the record, so I assumed he was joking. But when I hooked up with Keith that day, things got cryptic. At the end of our interview, Keith said, "I can tell you more about Gordon Bennett later, when the tape is off," but he never got into it. That's when he took his pee and when he got distracted at the elevator, before taking off in his limo.

When the *Undercover* album came out in November, I still didn't have a written contract from Bennett, only a handshake agreement. He was selling thousands of *Beggars Banquet* subscriptions without my legal permission.

When the contract finally showed up, it did not reflect what we'd discussed in person. "You shall transfer to us the following assets pertaining to the newsletter," it said. "The name and goodwill thereof."

In other words, I would no longer own *Beggars Banquet*. My compensation? Zilch. I would merely be paid a salary of $2,500 per issue, to write and edit the newsletter I used to own. I'd be nothing more than an employee of *Beggars Banquet*. And then, when my contract was up, at the end of six bimonthly issues, they would have the right to fire me. I'd be out on my ass, with no newsletter, no job, and just $15,000 to show for it.

As if that weren't enough, the contract required me to transfer the copyrights to "all back issues of the newsletter." Again, for no compensation. The thirty-two issues I'd produced in my pajamas since age 16 would now be owned by Bennett and the Stones. They could reprint them whenever they wanted, without paying me a cent.

The contract was between me and Musidor, the company the Stones owned with Prince Rupert Loewenstein. Bennett was the company's agent. The Stones and Rupert owned several companies together, each handling a different facet of the band's career, and Musidor was their licensing-and-merchandising arm.

It was Rupert who fell in love with Bennett's "fan club" idea, and it was Rupert who got the Stones to sign off on it. When Mick says, "It was *suggested*," the person doing the suggesting was Rupert. It was then Rupert and Bennett who hired the superpowerful law firm of Mitchell Silberberg & Knupp to draw up that hideous contract for me. They must have figured, "The kid's a fan. He'll give it to us for nothing."

To say this was David vs. Goliath would be an understatement. I was 21 years old, all on my own. Svi said he knew a lawyer, so I phoned immediately. The guy was a real-estate attorney, but I was too naïve to think that mattered. All I knew was, he took my call, so that made him my lawyer. I'd sit in his office, talking about my 'zine, while he was cutting deals for strip malls in Paramus. He made some futile phone calls to Bennett and rewrote the contract a few times, but nothing got resolved. By February 1984, weeks after publishing my first official issue, I still hadn't been paid. So much for Mick's advice. To add insult to injury, the attorney billed me $2,000.

I was completely exasperated and had no idea how the situation would turn out. I desperately needed moral support and legal guidance from someone who could relate to the situation. I searched and searched and found that person on a barstool in my neighborhood. His name was Keith Richards.

Keith had been in Mexico for December '83 and January '84, but flew back to New York for February. He checked into the Carlyle Hotel, but I didn't have his pseudonym. I discovered, however, that he was at JP's Bar on 78th Street, taping a TV interview. I walked over uninvited and tapped on the window. A sound engineer unlocked the door, and I said, "Tell Keith that Bill German is here."

The guy came back a few seconds later and let me in. Keith was seated at the bar, under bright lights and a boom microphone, with a bottle of Jack Daniel's close by. When his interview was over, I presented him with *Beggars Banquet's* first official issue and unburdened myself to him. He already knew the story. "I was just tellin' someone that German's the lunchmeat," he said. "You're sandwiched between our crap and Bennett's crap."

It's possible that Keith felt bad for getting me involved. I know that he and Mick had the best intentions when they recommended me for the job, but things weren't going as planned. I told Keith about the contract, and he advised, "Hey, Bill, you don't have to sign it. Do what's right for *you*. What *you* feel comfortable with. 'Cause you're not doin' the *Stones* a favor by signin' it. We're *already* handcuffed."

Keith didn't like this Bennett fellow and didn't trust him. Keith wanted out of the deal, but it was too late. I mean, seriously, Jagger Jeans? I can imagine Keith waking up in the middle of the night in a cold sweat. He looks over at his night table and discovers the nightmare he'd had was real. A bottle of Satisfaction Pour Homme is staring him in the face. He grabs it, throws it against the wall, and it shatters into tiny bits.

Keith's advice was truly empowering for me. *I don't have to sign the contract. I can stand up for myself, and the Stones won't be upset with me.* I was grappling with Keith's own business associates, but he was on *my* side.

Keith reiterated to me his reasons for bringing me aboard in the first place. I don't remember how he worded it at JP's, so I'll refer to our September '83 interview: "Where does the fan club stop being a fan club and become a mail-order list? It's a commercial enterprise, true, but how much can we merchandise the Stones without ruining our integrity? *Beggars Banquet* is a way of avoiding just pushing it on the market, y'know, tryin' to flog it. 'We've got this bunny rabbit, wind it up, and the tongue pops out.'"

He went on: "I know you're not gonna compromise your integrity, Bill, the stuff you've built up, just to become a mail-order list, y'know, one page editorial and ten pages a catalog. And so, this is the way we can control it, and make it work within the Stones' framework of what's acceptable and what's not. By keeping it with people like you, who know a little bit about us. Because we [the Stones] aren't able to sit around each month and do a quality control." Keith was deputizing me with the role of watchdog, and I took his appointment seriously.

He also let me in on something else. He convinced me that I, not Gordon Bennett or Rupert, was the one holding the cards. Consider the public relations disaster: They'd already put that ad in a million *Undercover* albums.

They'd already mailed 20,000 copies of that letter from Bill Wyman. And the feel-good story had already hit the press about the Stones hiring a fan. So think how bad it'd look if that fan walked away in disgust. Keith was telling me to turn the screws on his own company.

I told Bennett I wasn't signing that piece-of-crap contract and that I wasn't giving up ownership of my newsletter. I said we should operate on our original handshake agreement: He pays me $2,500 salary per issue, he pays my photographers, and he's responsible for all printing and mailing costs, period.

He said okay, but he didn't put his money where his mouth was. When it came time for my second issue in March, I still hadn't been paid for the first one in January. Nor had my photographers. I began production on the next issue anyway, praying that things would be resolved. But when I brought it to the printer, they refused to start the job. Bennett hadn't sent the deposit.

Days ticked off, then weeks. He finally paid the deposit, but, upon completion of the job, didn't pay the balance. Thousands of issues gathered dust. After a few more weeks, he paid the printing bill, but not the postage. As a journalist, I found this excruciating. My latest issue was outdated before anyone read it.

As you might expect, things got contentious. I asked, "Why is it taking so long to pay everybody?" and he blamed *me*. He accused me of padding my printer's and photographers' prices and taking kickbacks. I didn't even understand what "kickbacks" meant. I thought it had to do with Australian football. If anything, my printer and photographers charged Bennett their *lowest* prices, because of my goodwill with them.

Whether Bennett believed his own spiel, he ran to Prince Rupert and Bill Wyman and said I was the root of his problems. "Bill German is ripping us off, and he's not letting us advertise the bubble gum and air fresheners in *Beggars Banquet*." (I'd stipulated from the beginning that *Beggars Banquet* was to remain ad-free.)

He pointed fingers at everyone but himself. He believed that Stones fans would want bubble gum and jigsaw puzzles, but he was wrong. And the higher-ticket items that fans *might've* gone for, like the jeans and perfume, never materialized. He grew uptight as his business crumbled, and he took it out on *me*. He played on my sensibilities as a fan and shouted, "The Stones are all angry with you!"

I didn't bother telling him that Mick and Keith had warned me about him or that I'd become a frequent guest at Ron Wood's house. I simply said, "I'm pretty sure the Stones are on *my* side."

"Oh, yeah?" he retorted. "Rupert and I can take *Beggars Banquet* from you any time we wish! The Rolling Stones own the rights to the name 'Beggars Banquet.' We can just as easily start a newsletter called *Beggars Banquet* and leave you out of it! We don't need you!" I told him he *did* need me and that the Stones *don't* own the name. I would never have answered him that way if Keith hadn't given me the courage.

Unfortunately, the innocent victims were the fans. In November 1983, they paid for six issues of *Beggars Banquet,* but, by mid-1984, had received just one. They flooded my P.O. box with hate mail. "You're a fucking rip-off, Bill German! I'm calling the authorities!"

They had no idea that I'd never touched their money or that I myself had not been paid. (I was still owed $5,000 for two issues' work.) Some of them vaguely recalled that they'd sent their subscription checks to Los Angeles, but that didn't matter to them. It was Bill German in New York, not Gordon Bennett in L.A., who was the personification of *Beggars Banquet,* so I caught all the grief.

I was extremely upset and answered every piece of hate mail. "You might be my reader," I tried explaining, "but you're not my customer. You sent your money to Los Angeles, not to me, so I never knew your name until you justifiably complained." I spent hundreds of dollars to make peace with Bennett's irate customers, but it was worth it to stop the hate mail.

After clearing my name with a thousand or so people, I next set things straight with fan club president Bill Wyman. I wrote him a six-page letter, and it obviously resonated. He forwarded it to the band's lawyers. After enough pressure was applied, Bennett sent the money for postage, photographers, and my salary. Bennett's customers received their second issue in August, five months late.

After producing six bimonthly issues—which took a year and a half—my oral agreement with Bennett, as well as the Stones' written agreement with him, expired. If there was an upside, it's that the Stones felt I "survived" something with them. It was a painful process, but it brought me closer to them.

Woody enjoyed the Cat Club (above, with Billy Idol) and the
Limelight (below, with yours truly). One night, after meeting
baseball great Willie Stargell at the Limelight, Woody turned
to me and said, "Star Gel? That's what I use in my hair!"

9

the usual
suspects

Since moving to Manhattan, I was like a doctor on call. My phone would ring at any hour, and I'd rush to the scene for a Stones sighting. One night in April 1984, a paparazzo called me from the Cat Club on 13th Street. "Ron Wood just walked in."

It was 1 AM and I was watching Letterman, but I raced out the door. A cab got me there in ten minutes. I spotted Woody in the club's VIP section. Somehow, we made eye contact, and I pretended it was a coincidence. I mouthed, "What are *you* doing here?"

He waved me into the VIP area and suggested I sit at his table. He was with his live-in girlfriend, Jo, and their friend Perri. Woody explained who I was— "Bill runs the Stones' fan magazine!"—but Perri was unimpressed. In fact, she seemed annoyed that Woody didn't shut up about me. "Bill's magazine is how I know what the other Stones are up to. And it's been helping me with my artwork."

As Perri zoned out, Woody told me how he used the photos in *Beggars Banquet* as references for his paintings. "I used that one of me at the ARMS concert to do a self-portrait of myself. I also used that one of Keith from your interview page and the one of Mick with Stevie Ray Vaughan. It's really been helping me."

Woody had attended art school as a kid and dreamt about being the next Van Gogh. But he let it slide when he became a rock star. Now, with the lull in Stones activity, he was picking it up again.

He made me feel welcome at his table and offered to help with *Beggars Banquet*. He said Jo had photos to lend me and that I should stop by their house to pick them up. He scribbled his address and phone number on a napkin.

After ten minutes, someone approached our table. It was Perri's boyfriend, returning from the bathroom. I didn't realize I'd been sitting in his seat. I began to rise, but Woody insisted I stay. "Sit where you are," he told me. "He can get a chair from over *there.*" The boyfriend wasn't about to argue with Ron Wood of the Rolling Stones, but he did not seem pleased. In fact, he sneered at me and said, "Yeah, 'cept you're sittin' on m'jacket, mate."

That's when I realized it was Billy Idol. This wasn't as bad as spilling OJ on Mick's rug, but reminded me I was still a dork, no matter how many VIP rooms I found myself in. I apologized to Mr. Idol, lifted my left ass cheek, and handed him his leather jacket.

Before I had the chance to call Woody, Video James did. Somehow, he had the number and invited himself over. By 1984, Video James's collection was losing its luster—*Cocksucker Blues* and *Ed Sullivan* had long made the bootleg rounds—so he had to dig deeper to maintain his status. He told Woody he'd bring some Bo Diddley clips, and Woody said, "Absolutely." I asked if I could tag along, and they both said yes.

Woody and Jo were no longer in Greenwich Village. They now owned a five-story townhouse on 78th Street, between West End and Riverside. Woody gave me a tour of the place, and I was struck by how much it reflected his personality. In other words, it was a mess. And I mean that in the best possible way. You could tell that a creative, free-spirited person lived there. Guitars were leaning against the walls, cassettes were piled on the staircase, and unfinished drawings were strewn behind candleholders on the mantel. And, oops, I almost tripped on a *Black and Blue* gold album slumped against a railing.

We settled into the living room and watched Bo Diddley. Jo gave me some photos to borrow. Overall, a surprisingly quiet night. Woody suggested I stop by more often and said I didn't need an escort.

A week or so later, I called and said, "I need to return the pictures." Woody told me to come right over. This time, the atmosphere was more of what I expected. A dozen people packed the dining room, watching Woody paint. He seemed happy to see me and introduced me around. "Bill, you know Peter, right?"

"I don't *know* Peter," I replied, "but I know *of* Peter." It was Peter Max, the legendary artist. He and Woody were hunched over their respective canvases. Sort of a jam session, but with paint instead of music.

"And you know Matt, right?"

"I don't *know* Matt," I replied, "but I know *of* Matt." It was Matt Dillon, the actor.

The other guests that night weren't famous, but were "interesting." Most of them went by nicknames and had jobs they didn't want to talk about. It took me a while to figure out they were Woody's drug connections. Dope dealers, all of 'em. One of them said, "You run a magazine? Gimme a free prescription." But he refused to give me his address or real name.

There was a genuine sense of electricity in that house. Some people were high on creativity, some were high on dope, and some, like Woody, were high on both. Lots of noise, lots of motion, and nobody knowing when to quit. By 3 or 4 AM, not a single person had gone home. Woody finished his portrait of Dillon, which he placed next to his portrait of Dylan.

Svi took me aside to offer advice. "When you hang around the Stones," he said, "it's better to leave too early than too late." There are plenty of people who burn themselves out around the Stones, even on their first night. They get turned on by the drugs or by the starfucking and don't know their place. Things often get hairy. Someone OD's or property gets destroyed. A human inventory is then taken, and whoever was in the room at the time is suspect. Punishments are meted out, in the form of banishment from all Stones-related activities.

Svi should know. He was once at Woody's house when a TV went missing from the living room. Amidst all the chaos, nobody saw it disappear. But when Woody went to flip on the evening news the next day, there was nothing to flip. He and Jo did a mental head count from the previous night and narrowed the suspects down to Svi. They came right out and accused him. Svi swore he didn't do it, and Woody and Jo eventually believed him. But the mere suspicion proved his point: Leave before the shit goes down.

It was 4 AM when I made my way to the door. When I bid good night to Woody, he said, "Why so early?" and he wasn't joking. All I know is, I didn't burn myself out or overstay my welcome. I was invited back many more times and soon became a fixture at the Woods', where every night was party night.

When the coke got passed around, I'd wear a dumb smile and say, "No thanks." I was 21 and had never done coke in my life. (Still haven't.) I'm sure I passed up some killer blow—if Ron Wood could afford it, it *had* to be good—but I did not want my first experience to be with these people. They were professional coke inhalers, and I knew zilch. What if I turned blue and dropped dead or something? What if I sneezed like that scene in *Annie Hall*?

Besides, I wanted to stay alert so I could remember it all. Hanging out in Ron Wood's house was a dream come true for me as a fan, and I was conducting newsgathering as a reporter. But my abstinence sometimes led to tension. A few guys got paranoid and accused me of being a narc. "Woody, what's the deal with *this* guy?" He'd have to defend me: "Nah, Bill's alright. He's here to interview me and get pictures from Jo, that's all." I was proud that *Beggars Banquet,* not drugs, was my ticket into the Stones' inner sanctum, but it made me feel like an outsider.

I was the only person Woody could talk to about the Stones. His dealer friends knew nothing and were there for the money and starfucking. I discovered that fact when one of them gave me a lift home. As we cut through Central Park, he popped in a cassette and said, "This is rare stuff. Woody made it just for *me.*" Great, except that it was *Goats Head Soup.* I said, "This is a regular Stones album—you can buy it at Sam Goody's," and the guy lost his cool. "You don't know what the fuck you're talkin' about! Woody made this tape for me special!" He wasn't someone you wanted to piss off, so I dropped the argument.

Woody found most of his dealers at the city's nightclubs. His and Jo's favorite spot in 1984 was the Limelight, a deconsecrated church on 20th Street. The VIP room was the church's former library and a lot of shady characters hung out there. On June 1, Woody had his 37th birthday party in that room, and I was invited. (To play up the church theme, Woody's cake had a nun on it, with the phrase "God Bless You Ronnie.")

Woody's dealers might have been Stones illiterates, but they were around him so much, they became good sources of mine. If Woody forgot to tell me something, I'd hear it from them first: "Did Woody tell you he's meeting Keith in Jamaica next week?"

Another good source was Woody's refrigerator. He'd stick his backstage passes on it, so I'd always take a peek. I'd say, "Woody, you didn't tell me you saw the Pretenders at Radio City last week," and he'd either come back with "Yeah! David Letterman was backstage and told me to get some sleep!" or "The Pretenders? I can't recall."

It took me a while to realize that coke can affect your judgment sometimes. There were nights when Woody would grab his guitar and exclaim, "Listen to this great song I wrote!" but it wasn't so great. Or he'd blurt out ideas like "I'll get Peter Max to paint your next cover!" that'd never come to pass. Things said in that house at 3 in the morning were often meaningless by 3 in the afternoon.

In October 1984, Woody did a special appearance at the Hard Rock Cafe. I wanted to tag along and get him to pose with Brian Jones's Vox guitar, which hung on the club's wall. The night before (at 3 AM), he said he'd put me on the guest list. But when I showed up (at 3 PM), the bouncer said I wasn't on it.

The scene outside was like Beatlemania. A ton of fans, who'd learned of the appearance on the radio, lined 57th Street. When Woody's limo pulled up, it was bedlam. People grabbing him and trying to get his autograph. Miraculously, I caught his attention: "Woody! You forgot to put me on the list!" He stretched out his hand and told me to grab on. Hard Rock security pushed Woody through the mob as he pulled me along. He may have been absentminded, but always offered me a helping hand, sometimes literally.

Later that month, the Stones convened in Amsterdam to discuss their future. They picked Holland because that's where their holding companies were, such as Musidor and Promotone, the parent of Rolling Stones Records. It was basically a shareholders' meeting, so Woody, the salaried Stones employee, wasn't invited. I don't even think they sent him the minutes. But he had some juicy gossip for me, as did Svi.

They both heard it from Keith and, although their accounts differed slightly, one thing was clear: There was trouble in Stonesville. At some point in the proceedings, Mick referred to Charlie as "my drummer." Something like, "None of this should matter to you because you're only my drummer." Mick might've been joking, but it didn't sit well with Charlie. According to Svi, Charlie kept it bottled inside until he got back to his hotel room. He then clicked off his TV, put on his shoes, walked down the hall, and knocked on Mick's door. When the lead singer of the Rolling Stones opened it, his drummer clocked him in the jaw. Charlie then turned around and calmly walked away. By happenstance, Keith saw Charlie in the hallway and asked him where he was coming from. The laconic Charlie answered, "I've just punched Mick Jagger in the face," and kept walking.

The version that Woody gave me also ends with Charlie informing Keith, "I've just punched Mick Jagger in the face." But in Woody's version, the "my drummer" part takes place on the phone. Mick calls Charlie in his hotel room and starts asking, "Is my drummer there? Is this my drummer?" Charlie hangs up the phone and the rest of the story synchs up with Svi's—Charlie leaves his room, knocks on Mick's door, and kapow!

I've heard embellishments through the years. One version says Charlie didn't punch Mick, he just grabbed him by the lapels, pushed him into a plate of salmon, and made him cry uncle. Another version has Charlie holding Mick out the window by his ankles. The point is, Mick upset Charlie, and Charlie took it out on him physically.

The story didn't reach the public for years and has since taken on mythical proportions. But for me it was breaking news. I heard about it days after it happened, not years, and was faced with a dilemma: What do I do with it?

In November 1984, I was still in the midst of my Musidor/Bennett deal, and everything I wrote went through Mick, his people, and the lawyers. I knew it wouldn't pass through the sieve, so I didn't even submit it. No one else had the story—not *Rolling Stone,* not MTV—so I consoled myself with "My readers won't miss what they don't know." I instead reported on the positive aspects of the Amsterdam meeting: "The Stones [resolved] to enter a Paris recording studio in January [1985]."

CBS had given the Stones that huge advance and was finally demanding product. But Mick was more interested in his *own* album, *She's the Boss.* For months, he'd been recording in the Bahamas without the Stones. His solo album was written into the Stones' contract with CBS, but only as an option, not a commitment. Keith never imagined that Mick would exercise that option, much less make it a priority.

In baseball, they call it "twenty-four plus one"—when one player gets so self-interested, he alienates himself from the other twenty-four. He won't ride the team bus and gets a limo instead. He won't share a room and gets a private suite instead. For the Rolling Stones, it was "four plus one" and it's what got Mick Jagger punched in the face. And just because Charlie got it out of his system didn't mean the others had.

The Stones' Paris sessions began in January 1985, as planned. This time, I had Woody and Svi, two of my main sources, right on the scene. Svi was there in his capacity as Keith's pharmacist, and Woody was there in his capacity as Rolling Stones employee. With the tension in the air, I didn't even *think* about flying over.

The band worked through February, before breaking in March. They all came back to New York, and I heard the rough tapes. The aggression in the music was surpassed only by the aggression in the lyrics. There were songs called "I Wanna Fight," "Had It with You," "One Hit to the Body," and "Knock Yer Teeth Out." They were written by Keith and Woody and contained lyrics like, "I'm beginning to hate ya," "I'm gonna pulp you to a mass of bruises," and "You dirty fucker . . . singing for your supper . . . I had it, had it, had it with you!"

Mick shot his load for his solo album, so he hardly contributed to the Stones' writing process. Instead, Keith and Woody created these songs in the studio, based on how they were feeling. Then Mick, the reluctant vocalist for the Rolling Stones, would come in and sing them. But what Mick didn't realize is that most of the songs were addressed to *him.* In essence, Keith was telling Mick, "I'm gonna pulp you to a mass of bruises" and "I had it with you."

Historically, Woody was the peacemaker in the Stones. But even he had resentment toward Mick. It bothered him that Mick skipped his wedding. It took place in England on January 2, right before the recording sessions. Charlie and Keith were co–best men. Bill Wyman gladly attended, as did Peter Frampton, Jeff Beck, Ringo Starr, and Rod Stewart. But no Mick.

It seemed like another example of "four plus one" and made the Paris sessions more tense. As Woody later told me, "We were spared long jail sentences by being able to play our music. A few times, Keith and I felt like killing people, but we picked up our guitars and wrote songs instead." Woody's the one who came up with "Knock Yer Teeth Out."

It seems amazing that the Stones didn't break up at this point, but here's something you should know. They *did* break up. From an administrative point of view, all five Stones went to opposite corners of the ring. Rolling Stones Records folded, and the Stones' employees got chosen up like a schoolyard pickup game.

It had long been understood that Jane was Keith's gal Friday and that a guy named Tony King was Mick's gal Friday, but now it was official. Jane got her own office in New York, and so did Tony. (Art Collins quit to manage Iggy Pop.) Jane's office was called Raindrop Services and was located at Broadway and 57th. Tony's office was a block away.

In London, at an office called Munro Sounds, Mick had another guy working for him named Alan Dunn. Charlie had a woman at that same location named Sherry Daly. Bill had his own office on King's Road, called Ripple Productions, and Woody had a manager named Nick Cowan.

For me, it meant a lot more legwork. I could never, for instance, ask Jane to answer a question about Mick or ask Tony King to answer a question about Keith. And if there was something that pertained to the entire group, I'd have to call five separate places to get a consensus. The lines in the sand were more defined than ever.

Mick's solo album came out in March. The opening track was "Lonely at the Top," a Jagger-Richards composition that had gone unreleased by the Stones. I don't know if Mick put it there as a way of appeasing Keith, but, if he did, it backfired. Keith felt that if Mick was gonna make his big break from the Stones, he should at least make it a clean one.

In April, when the Stones returned to Paris for more recording sessions, their lead singer had a foot out the door. *She's the Boss* was getting radio airplay, and MTV had scheduled a "Mick Jagger Weekend." As the Stones were in the studio one evening, Mick and MTV set up in the café across the street for an interview. It made Keith's blood boil. Keith was slaving away on the Stones album while Mick was plugging a solo album within earshot. If Keith didn't need Mick to sing on a few more songs, he probably would've knocked his teeth out right then and there.

It didn't help that, during this period, Mick disparaged the other Stones in the media. He likened them to "a bunch of pensioners" and said they were out of touch with the 1980s music scene. Keith, of course, took the latter statement as a compliment. He hated that Mick was hanging around "untalented jerk-offs" like Duran Duran (Keith's description, not mine) and inviting them to the studio when he wasn't there. Keith had a sneaking suspicion that Mick was getting ready to tour behind *She's the Boss,* so he laid down the gauntlet in the press: "If Mick tours without the Stones, I'll slit his throat."

You'd think that Bill and Charlie, the two "stable" members of the band, could've brokered a cease-fire, but they had their own turmoil to contend with. British authorities were mulling statutory rape charges against Bill—his latest girlfriend was 14—and Charlie was in the midst of a nervous breakdown.

Charlie's wife, Shirley, was going through a much-publicized booze problem and his teenage daughter, Seraphina, got tossed out of school for pot possession. "Stones Girl in Drug Shocker," screamed the front page of London's *Daily Star.* Charlie didn't need this crap, and one of his outlets was his drum kit. His other was heroin. Charlie was always the "clean" Stone, but the stresses in his life became too much to bear. If his favorite jazz musicians could shoot up, why couldn't he?

He also sought solace in Paris from a woman named Sylvie. From what I was told, he merely went to dinner with her a few times, nothing more. He simply needed a calm human being to talk to. But when Jerry Hall visited Paris one day and saw them together, she got right on the phone to Shirley.

Within an hour, Shirley and her brother were on a plane from London to Paris. Shirley burst into the studio and began carrying on. Screaming, punching, kicking, throwing things. Keith and Woody stood there with their guitars strapped on and their mouths hanging open. She refused to calm down and ran out to the studio's terrace. She said she was going to jump. Everyone ran after her and pleaded with her to calm down, but over the railing she went. Luckily, they were only on the second floor, so it wasn't much of a drop. But an ambulance was summoned, and Charlie rode with her to the hospital.

The fact that Mick's girlfriend was the one who started it—Mick, the *real* philanderer of the band—added to Keith's anger. He felt Mick was responsible for another disruption and that Mick should've reined in his own girlfriend.

I can report today that Charlie and Shirley are fine. One of the longest-running marriages in rock 'n' roll. But in 1985, things were bad for them and bad for the band. The Stones had a lead singer who didn't want to be there, a bassist running from the cops, a drummer whose heroin addiction rivaled Billie Holiday's, and a guitarist who wanted to slit his lead singer's throat.

Amazingly, they got through the Paris sessions with no homicides, no arrests, and only one ambulance trip. And the best part was, the "dirty work" wasn't over. The band had plenty of mixing and overdubbing to do, and they were bringing it to New York. My own backyard.

At the Lone Star Cafe two nights before Live Aid. I thought
this would be the last photo they'd ever take together.

Woody and "Brenda" in the control room at RPM.
Keith must've been sleeping—or pretending to be.

10

a nice bunch
of guys

To complete their *Dirty Work* album, the Stones booked themselves into RPM Studio on 12th Street as the "Runny Noses." A pseudonym was necessary to maintain anonymity and prevent theft. If the janitor wanted to steal the Stones' tapes, he'd find no boxes with "Rolling Stones" on them.

On most nights, Keith and Woody would get to RPM after midnight and leave past sunrise. They told me to stop by whenever I felt like it, as long as Brenda wasn't there. "Brenda" was their code name for Mick and it wasn't a term of endearment. It was Keith who came up with it, after stumbling onto a book by an author named Brenda Jagger. In the summer of 1985, Keith was ready to stab Mick in the eyeballs, so referring to his prima donna lead singer as "Brenda" was a healthier way to vent. Only a handful of us were in on it, so I couldn't mention it in *Beggars Banquet*. It would've ruined Keith's fun if Mick found out.

One night, I asked Woody if Mick was really as bad as he and Keith made him out to be. "Well," Woody sighed, "he has his moments, you know. The thing that me and Keith always say is that Mick Jagger is a nice bunch of guys. It all depends which one you get. He changes his accent every time you speak to him, and he can turn you on or turn you off on any given day. You never know which Mick you're going to get."

My routine for visiting the studio worked like this: I'd phone Woody at his house around 6 PM, when he was first waking up. He'd be groggy, but would usually know the agenda. He'd say, "Brenda's not coming tonight" or "He's coming, but he'll probably leave around 1, so check with us after that."

On most nights, Mick would get to the studio at dusk and leave around midnight, as Keith and Woody were reporting for duty. Mick and Keith's time in the studio barely overlapped. Other than a few "pass the salt" remarks regarding the album, they tried to avoid each other all summer. Mick would pop in, work on his parts, and leave. Then Keith and Woody would handle the rest.

The first time I visited RPM, Mick had stayed late and the coast wasn't clear until almost dawn. I got there at 4 AM, and Svi buzzed me in. From the reception area, I could hear a steamy version of Sam Cooke's "Bring It On Home to Me." I walked toward the main studio, where a sign read: "DO NOT ENTER— even if you met Mick or Ronnie at a club and they said call in." I believe it was Keith's handwriting.

I entered the room to find Keith, Woody, and Charlie jamming with R&B legends Bobby Womack and Don Covay. As the music blared, Svi unfolded a metal chair and placed it next to Charlie's drums. "Sit here," he hollered in my ear. "Now you're on your own."

With that, Svi exited for the night. I was the only nonmusician in the room. It was dark, smoky, and noisy, so Keith and Woody had no idea I'd entered. Charlie could see me—I was sitting five feet from him—but was oblivious to all but the music.

I was privy to three-fifths of a Rolling Stones concert. Keith and Womack on guitar, Woody on bass, and Covay singing lead. If you're not familiar with Covay and Womack, it's a shame. Covay wrote Aretha Franklin's "Chain of Fools" and lots of other classics. The Stones covered his "Mercy Mercy" on their *Out of Our Heads* LP, and Mick stole every falsetto he's ever sung from him. When Mick goes high on "Emotional Rescue" or "Melody," it's because Covay's records taught him how.

Womack, back in the day, played with Sam Cooke. And, in 1964, he wrote and recorded "It's All Over Now." Two weeks after he released it, a bunch of white kids named the Rolling Stones stole it from under him by recording their own version. Theirs became a hit, while his languished in obscurity. His version kicks ass on theirs, but hey, more people bought Pat Boone's "Tutti Frutti" than Little Richard's.

Keith was doing a good job singing the "yeah-yeah" response in "Bring It On Home to Me." From there, the five of them launched into another Cooke classic, "Having a Party," before Jimmy Reed's "Baby What You Want Me to Do," Otis Redding's "I've Got Dreams to Remember," Freddie Scott's "Are You Lonely for Me," and the Beatles' "Please Please Me." There was no other place I wanted to be.

Eventually, Keith took off his guitar and sat at the piano. He sang "Your Cheatin' Heart" and "(You Make Me Feel Like) a Natural Woman." I listened to these guys for three hours and kept my mouth shut. Keith noticed me only when he got up to take a pee. When we greeted each other, Woody recognized my voice in the darkness and said, "Who-zat? Bill German?"

I answered, "Yeah," but didn't get out of my seat. I didn't want to interrupt the vibe. Keith returned from his pee and sat back down at the piano, leading them through a mock version of "Satisfaction." Keith, Womack, and Covay sang the song in such a high register, it could've shattered the glass in a Memorex commercial. Then they gave the same treatment to "Time Is on My Side." Keith got such a kick out of it, he lay back on the piano stool and cackled for a full minute. Even Charlie smiled.

In the three hours I sat next to Charlie, we never shared a single word. He kept pounding the drums, looking off into space. There were a few moments when we made eye contact, but all he'd do was nod, nothing more. I still don't think he had a clue who I was, and he never bothered to ask. At the same time, I was too bashful to introduce myself. I knew he was an introverted guy and that he preferred raising sheepdogs in the British countryside to chatting with 22-year-old kids from Brooklyn.

At 7 AM, things wrapped up in the studio, and we retreated to the lounge area. I was hoping Keith and Woody would finally introduce me to Charlie, but they never did. Instead, the three of them spoke nonstop about subjects I couldn't follow, like old jazz records and British comedians. Gerry Mulligan. Spike Milligan. Charlie Parker. I sat there like a fly on the wall. We left the studio around 9 o'clock and were greeted on the street by a throng of autograph hounds. The waiting limos must have tipped them off.

I felt more at ease during my next visit. I was hoping to break the ice with Charlie, but he wasn't there. He'd flown home to England, where he promptly broke his leg. As I reported in *Beggars Banquet,* "He accidentally fell on the cement floor of his wine cellar." Charlie's leg was in a cast, and he was unable to kick a bass drum. He wasn't returning to New York that year, so my scintillating conversation with him would have to wait.

Over the course of the summer, Keith and Woody made me feel like I belonged. "A studio's my home," Keith told me. "So I make it a comforting environment. I've probably been in the studio more time than I've been in bed. Once you're in there, it's Studioland. Doesn't matter if it's in Australia or Hong Kong or Siberia. It's nighttime, the phones don't ring, nobody's around. It's home."

One night, we were pleasantly surprised when the legendary Les Paul walked in. Keith had invited him, but didn't think he'd show. It would've been a treat to see Les jam with Keith and Woody, but the four of us instead hung out in the control room. Keith told Les he was "a fucking genius" and joked, "I wish *I* was the one who came up with the electric guitar!" Woody was so intim-idated, his childhood stutter returned.

There was one night when it was just me and Keith, sitting in the control room. "I'm thinkin' of starting Side Two with 'I Wanna Fight,' " he informed me. "And then into 'Winning Ugly' and 'Deep Love.' Albums can be made or broken based on the order of songs." (This was, of course, before remote-controlled CD players.) He tweaked the lineup several times over the summer, dropping "Deep Love" completely.

After a few weeks, I learned not just how to mix an album, but how to mix drinks. Keith and Woody liked "Jack & Ginger"—Jack Daniel's with ginger ale—but didn't want to unplug their guitars sometimes. So they'd ask if I could go to the studio lounge and be their bartender. I got pretty good at it.

Usually, I'd stick around until they punched out at 8 AM or so. Quite often, there was no limo waiting, and they had to fend for themselves. One time, we crowded into the elevator with producer Steve Lillywhite and roadie Alan Rogan. Keith and Woody traded jokes until we got to the ground floor. Keith: "Ladies undergarments, floor number three." Woody: "Rubber masks, second floor." When we got to the street it became a game of who-can-hail-a-taxi-first. Keith and Lillywhite (destination midtown) vs. me, Woody, and Rogan (up-town).

Woody ran east and thought he found a cab on University Place. But it said "Off Duty." Keith ran toward Fifth Avenue and snagged a Checker. We weren't just competing with *each other,* we were competing with stressed-out nine-to-fivers headed to work. Guys in suits, holding briefcases, fighting with Keith Richards. Suit: "I gotta get to my office!" Keith: "I gotta get to *bed*!"

For much of the summer, the 800-pound gorilla in the room was Live Aid. When the Stones left Paris at the end of June, they agreed they wouldn't go near it. If their recording sessions told them anything, it was that they were not functioning as a unit. Why go in front of the world—a billion TV viewers—and pretend otherwise?

Furthermore, the Stones did not trust the charity itself. Live Aid was the feel-good concert of the decade, and the Stones didn't question the motives of anyone participating. But they did question the realities on the ground. Would the food and money get to the famine victims? Or would it be intercepted by Ethiopian warlords and corrupt government officials? The Stones sincerely debated that point, and their concerns would later prove warranted.

Lastly, the Stones, as a group, were never big on public displays of charity. They did a benefit for Nicaraguan earthquake victims in 1973, but had otherwise steered clear. "I don't trust big charity events" is how Keith put it to me. "An admirable cause, but it's not for rock 'n' roll to take these things up."

Individually, and away from the glare of the public, the Stones were generous with their time and money. Mick contributed to an orphans' fund, Bill did a ton for MS research, Woody taught art classes in hospitals, and Keith did the Babe Ruth bedside thing with terminally ill fans. But in public, charity wasn't their bag.

Enter Bill Graham, the concert promoter behind Live Aid. He began telling the press the Stones were going to be there. Led Zeppelin, Black Sabbath, and CSN&Y were reuniting for it, so why not the Stones?

The media ran with the speculation: "Stones to Perform at Live Aid." Now, if none of them showed up, it'd look like they backed out. The Stones would be the one group that didn't care about the starving Ethiopian kids with flies in their eyes.

Bill Graham used his bully pulpit—and the worldwide media—to emotionally blackmail the Stones. Mick was the first Stone to cave. "Alright," he basically told Graham, "I'll do it, but not with the Stones. And only if you give me the 9 PM slot."

Nine o'clock meant Mick would be the headliner and that his performance would be seen on network television (ABC), instead of cable (MTV). In the process, he could promote his new album, *She's the Boss.*

He enlisted Hall and Oates as his backup band and rehearsed with them at SIR Studio in New York. One of the songs they attempted was "Beast of Burden." And I want you to know, if they'd actually performed it at Live Aid, we would've witnessed a murder on live television. Keith would've lunged from behind the curtain to strangle Mick on the spot.

"Beast of Burden," you see, is one of those Jagger-Richards songs that's more Richards than Jagger. Keith feels very possessive over it. So when he heard that Mick was rehearsing "Beast" without the Stones, he blew a gasket. If you're gonna go solo, why do *any* Stones songs, let alone *that* one?

Keith was annoyed, but he tried to focus on his work at RPM. Woody, however, had other plans. He learned that Bill Graham had asked Bob Dylan to participate and to go on *after* Mick. So how great would it be, thought Woody, if he and Keith could back up Bob?

To make it a reality, Woody pulled a move straight out of a Hayley Mills film. First he went to Keith: "Bob wants us to back him up at that Live Aid show." And then he went to Dylan: "Me and Keith'll do that show with ya if you want."

Problem was, the next time Dylan came to Woody's house, he thought he was strictly paying a social call. He never took Woody's offer seriously. Keith, on the other hand, showed up at Woody's house ready to rehearse with Bob. Here's how Woody described it to me: "Bob arrives and the first thing he says is 'Hey, are you guys gonna go to the gig on Saturday or stay home and watch it on TV?' [And that's when] Keith began to strangle me. 'What did you get me round here for? You bastard! You wasted my time! We got an album to make!' "

Dylan didn't see Keith strangling Woody because he'd gone to take a pee at that point. But as soon as he came out of the loo, Woody corralled him. He assured Dylan that Keith was into it, so long as Dylan asked him directly. "So [Bob] runs downstairs, grabs Keith. Bam! 'Would you play this gig with me?' And Keith goes, 'What the fuck do you think we're here for? Of course I would!' So we started playing." They had a week to rehearse.

Two nights before Live Aid, Keith and Woody told me they were going to sit in with blues legend Lonnie Mack at the Lone Star Cafe. It turned into one of those special nights. Keith and Woody were onstage for half an hour, and you could tell how much they'd been itching to play live. Keith was in such a good mood, he blew kisses to the audience and ran his fingers through Woody's hair.

I watched it from the club's tiny balcony, where I sat next to Patti Hansen and Jo Wood. Mick decided to stop by, and so did Dylan and Paul Simon. When Keith and Woody finished their set, they came upstairs to join us. We all had a good laugh when a fan asked for my autograph. The kid thought I was Donovan.

The Lone Star was conveniently located on 13th Street, around the corner from RPM. Keith told me they were about to stroll over. Dylan would be joining them, and so would Mick, which meant I wasn't invited. But before they exited, I urged a photographer to get a shot of Keith and Woody with Mick. The way things were going, I felt it might be the last photograph they'd ever take together.

On Saturday, July 13, the American portion of the Live Aid concert kicked off before noon at Philadelphia's JFK Stadium. Mick flew down from New York the day before, in a private jet with Hall and Oates. They soundchecked on Friday.

Keith, Woody, and Dylan eschewed a soundcheck and meandered down the day of the show. The concert was in full gear by the time their caravan left Manhattan. They made a pit stop at a Howard Johnson's on the Jersey Turnpike. The cashier had the radio tuned to the concert, so she was a little surprised when Keith Richards and Bob Dylan came in to use the restrooms.

In all likelihood, you were one of the 1.6 billion people who caught the concert on TV, so I'll merely refresh your memory. Mick, in prime time, performed five songs, including two duets with Tina Turner. During "It's Only Rock 'N Roll," he ripped Tina's skirt off, exposing her million-dollar gams. It was a premeditated move, not a "wardrobe malfunction," but it made for great TV and was a hard act to follow.

Next up was Dylan, with his ragtag team of elves. There were no Stones songs in their repertoire and no backup band. Just Dylan, Keith, and Woody on acoustic guitars. They were clearly under-rehearsed and weren't helped when Dylan popped a string or when their onstage monitors went dead. Also, they performed two Dylan numbers that most people had never heard of—"The Ballad of Hollis Brown" and "When the Ship Comes In."

To the viewing public, Mick stole the show. Many fans considered his performance the rock 'n' roll highlight of the decade. But Keith couldn't give a fuck. As far as Keith was concerned, he'd trumped Mick at his own game by going on last and by staying on message. The songs Keith and Woody played with Dylan may not have been chart toppers or toe tappers, but they were relevant. "Hollis Brown" is about a South Dakota farmer whose wife and five kids are starving. The guy can't bear to see them suffer, so he shoots them all before shooting himself. And "Ship Comes In" provides the stirring reminder "that the whole wide world is watching."

It was hard for Keith not to feel morally superior. To his thinking, Mick went up there to promote his solo album and do his cutesy schtick with his poofy-haired backup band. But his own performance, with Dylan and Woody, was selfless and to the point. Additionally, Keith viewed himself as a reluctant warrior, pressed into action because Mick went back on his word.

In the next issue of *Beggars Banquet,* I reported the Live Aid situation like I saw it: "As a group, the Stones had agreed not to do it, but slowly, individually, they caved in to emotional blackmail."

Two weeks after Live Aid, Mick turned 42. He invited all the Stones to his party as a conciliatory gesture. I heard about it through Woody. "I'm sure Mick wants you there," he said. "Ring him up." He thumbed through his little black book and provided me with Mick's latest number.

I immediately got on the horn to the Jagger residence. It rang four times before an old Spanish lady picked up. "Halloooo?"

"Can I speak with Mick, please?"

"Who eez calleeng?"

"Bill German, from *Beggars Banquet.*"

"Oh, hi, Bill," replied a British male.

It was Mick all along. Once again, he was screening his phone calls by pretending to be his own cleaning lady. As soon as he heard it was me, he reverted to his Mick Jaggerness, offering no explanations. "How've you been?" he asked.

"Well," I told him, "I'd love to come to your shaboozle tomorrow night."

"Oh, yeah," he replied. "Putcha down for a plus-one?"

It was the old Jagger charm. He never questioned how I got his number or how I heard about the party. He asked me to hold for a second while he searched for the guest list. "Better do it now before I forget." He called out to someone in the room, "Hey, can you hand me the list for the party? I wanna put one of my friends on."

That was cool, having Mick refer to me as a friend. "I look forward to seeing you," he added. "Make sure you go through the back entrance."

The party was on 14th Street at the Palladium. Same place the Stones did their surprise gig in 1978. It was now a dance club, owned by Studio 54 magnates Ian Schrager and Steve Rubell. It was open to the public on Mick's birthday, but the party was held in the exclusive "Mike Todd Room," accessible via the club's back door.

When my yellow cab pulled up, amidst a sea of black limousines, the paparazzi let out a collective groan. Apparently, I was the only nonfamous person in attendance. Mick prohibited photographers from coming inside, but they had plenty to shoot on the sidewalk: Jack Nicholson, the Stones, and Duran Duran.

Inside, I mingled with Bill Wyman and with one of the backup singers whom Keith had hired. Her name was Patti Scialfa and she'd someday be Mrs. Bruce Springsteen.

Mick was great this night. He approached me and my date, thanked us for coming, and kissed her hand. "I know all the *guys* here," he said, "but I don't know any of the *girls*. And Jerry told me I'd better keep it that way!"

The party thinned out around 2 AM. Keith and Woody were nowhere in sight, and my date was getting tired. I told her I needed to make a quick pit stop. I opened the door to the men's room and discovered that's where the party was. A dozen people, including Keith and Woody, were smoking, drinking, and carrying on. Woody was leaning against the sink and Keith had his boot on a urinal. "William!" exclaimed Keith. "Welcome to our new office!"

Weeks later, I showed up to the studio around 1 AM. Woody assured me that Brenda would be gone by then. But lo and behold, Mick stayed overtime. He was walking out as I was walking in. For whatever reason, he acted like he didn't know me. He didn't offer a handshake, didn't greet me by name, and didn't ask how I was doing. He merely gave off a don't-get-close-to-me vibe.

As soon as I got in the control room, I complained to Woody. "A few weeks ago, he's calling me his friend, inviting me to his party, and kissing my girl-friend's hand. But now he acts like he doesn't know me."

"That's Mick," he replied. "A nice bunch of guys."

Keith was in the control room, too, but was passed out in a chair. Or at least *pretending* to be. He'd occasionally react to things that Woody and I were saying by opening his right eye and staring at us. Then he'd close it again. I asked Woody if Keith was sleeping when Mick was there, and he said yes. So maybe that was Keith's way of enduring his time with Mick. By making him think he was asleep.

Several weeks later, I was at Woody's house when the bell rang unexpect-edly. In walked Mick with his bodyguard. Rowan was a dreadlocked muscle-bound guy, and it amused Woody to no end that Mick would require his services to walk three blocks in a well-to-do neighborhood. Woody lived on West 78th Street and Mick was on West 81st, but Mick would never take that walk alone.

At first, Mick made it seem like a casual visit. We chatted in the kitchen for twenty minutes about nothing in particular. But then Mick said he wanted to check out Woody's new studio in the basement. "I've got this new song," Mick told us. "And I wanna try it out. It's called 'Soul City.' " Rowan and Jo remained in the kitchen while Mick, Woody, and I headed downstairs.

Woody's basement was an artistic playground. He had his recording stu-dio on one side and his painting stuff on the other. If a song idea hit him, he'd grab his guitar and plug in his amp. If a visual idea hit him, he'd grab his paint-brush and run to his easel. I'd sometimes see him do both at the same time, paint with his guitar strapped on. The basement's walls were covered with Woody's artwork and with photos of Jo from her modeling career. I also recall an 8 × 10 of Dick Clark and a photo of naked aborigines with overgrown testi-cles.

This "Soul City" song of Mick's was not for the Stones. It was for Mick's next solo album. As Keith toiled on the Stones' first album for CBS, Mick was plotting his second solo album under that deal—and taking advantage of Woody's good nature and recording equipment to do so. If Keith knew Woody was accommodating Mick's solo aspirations, he would've beaten him sense-less.

Keith often used Woody's studio, but merely to keep his chops together. He'd fuck around with Woody on Jimmy Reed and Buddy Holly covers. He once helped Jo record a rendition of "Will You Still Love Me Tomorrow?" But he'd never come to Woody's house for something as "anti-Stones" as what Mick was doing.

I asked Mick if "Soul City" bore any connection to "Sun City," the anti-apartheid anthem getting airplay at the time.

"Nah," Mick answered. "It's really the antithesis of that song."

"You mean it's *pro*-apartheid?"

"Noooo! Just that that one is so *negative* and this one is so *positive*. 'Soul City' is a place you *wanna* be."

Woody got behind the drums, and Mick sat on an ottoman in the corner. He grabbed one of Woody's guitars and plugged it into a tiny amp. Mick tossed me a tambourine and suggested I play along. Mick didn't teach us the song—we merely had to keep the beat. The tapes were rolling on Woody's Akai 12-track.

I tried the tambourine for a bit, but was really fucking it up. "I think I'll pass," I told Mick, but he encouraged me to stick with it. "You'll get it eventually," he said.

Mick and Woody recorded two takes of the song, *without* me on tambourine. This was a demo for Mick's own reference, so he kept it pretty simple. Guitar, drums, and a scratch vocal track. But he enlisted me and Woody to help thicken the chorus. "You'll be my backup singers," he said. "It goes, 'Soul city, free and easy, soul city, the girls are pretty.' So that's all I need you to do."

I felt I could wing that part. There was only one mic, so the three of us shared it. We stood shoulder to shoulder and began to sing the chorus. I knew this was the perfect time to deliver my dead-on impersonation of Mick, so I gave it a whirl. Seriously, I've had tons of people tell me how good I am at nailing the Jagger swagger and voice. I've done it at bars, barbecues, and bar mitzvahs, and I know everyone was laughing *with* me, not *at* me. But doing Jagger for Jagger? I couldn't handle it. I started singing, but I sounded more like Dwight D. Eisenhower than Mick Jagger. I simply could not get it up for Mick, and he had no clue what I was even attempting.

Nevertheless, we laughed and drank for a couple hours straight. Mick wanted to hear the tape so Woody played it LOUD. (The song, by the way, did turn up on Mick's next album, *Primitive Cool,* under the title "Peace for the Wicked.")

At 3 AM, Jo yelled down to us. Someone was at the front door, and Rowan was going to answer it. Woody ran upstairs to see who it was, leaving Mick and me in the basement alone.

We were standing near the tape machine. I tried to make small talk about the song, but, before I had the chance, Mick got in my face. And when I say "in my face," I mean he got within two or three inches of my nose. And then he ripped into me: "I don't like what you wrote! About Live Aid! It's not true! I don't like it!"

Yikes. I gulped and said, "Um, well, waddaya mean?"

"You know what you wrote! The bit about emotional blackmail! It's not true! That's not why I did it! Was no emotional blackmail!"

I began to stutter. "Um, well, th-that's what I heard, so I—"

"Well, it's not true! Was no emotional blackmail, not at all! How dare you!"

I physically couldn't get away from him. The guy was coming in for the kill. I couldn't believe how quickly the climate in the room had changed. One minute he was friendly, the next minute he was pouncing. Like something you see on National Geographic. The lion's sitting there, yawning, and then rips apart a baby zebra.

Mick was so close to my face, I thought he was going to bite my cheek off. I guess he does that to intimidate people, but I've got to admit it worked. I could only shrug and back away, but he wouldn't let me. We went around in circles, literally and figuratively. Me: "Well, um, that's what I heard." Him: "Well, it's not true! I don't like it!" I was 23 years old and had one of the most famous people in the world ripping into me.

My only hope was that it was "coke rap." He and Woody had been dabbling in the powder all night. In fact, while Mick was up close, I could spot the white rings around his nostrils. It reminded me of that *SNL* skit where Belushi plays Steve Rubell, standing in front of Studio 54. He denies there's drug use at the club, but there's white stuff all over his nose. At the end of the skit, the camera pulls out and you see he's eating a powdered donut.

In Mick's case, there was no donut. Mick had had a lot to toot, so I hoped that's why he was so pumped. (When he was done grilling me about Live Aid, he rambled on about the Jamaican soccer team being racist. I couldn't understand a word.) Either way, he was pissed, and it was not fun being chewed out by one of my favorite rock stars. When Woody came back—the doorbell was the cops, telling us to lower the music—I excused myself and went home. I was a bit shaken by Mick's tirade.

Now to Christmas. I was pleasantly surprised when the florist brought me beautiful poinsettias. The card said they were from Mick. I realize he may have had a hundred people on his list that year, but I was one of them. Mick Jagger, that nice bunch of guys, was my pal again.

I should have quit while I was ahead.

Patti (and Keith) began inviting me to
non-Stones-related parties.

love and hope
and sex and
dreams

Despite the Stones' chaos, Keith kept insisting through the summer of '85 that they'd tour behind *Dirty Work*. It got me excited. He also raised an intriguing proposition at RPM one night.

Woody greeted me in the reception area and said, "Go see Keith. He wants to talk to you." I opened the door to the studio and found Keith alone, behind a black Steinway. He was singing a ballad he wrote, called "Some of Us Are on Our Knees." The room was dark and he wasn't facing the door, so he had no idea I'd entered. I let him finish the song before making my presence known. Atop the piano was an empty whiskey glass, next to a billowing ashtray. To be clever, I put a dollar in the glass and said, "You take requests?"

"Ah, *William*. We were just talkin' about you."

"About *me*?"

"Yeah." He took the cigarette from the ashtray and stuck it in the corner of his mouth. "Listen, man [puff], we gotta get you some money. Y'know, to keep things goin' [puff]." He was referring to *Beggars Banquet*. To the fact that my deal with Musidor—that fan club mess—had recently expired.

I was blown away by his gesture, and I knew he was sincere. But I told him I liked being on my own again. I didn't have to submit my issues for approval, and I didn't have to follow the corporate rules. I was paying my own way— printing, postage, photos—but making my own money. My readers were sending their checks to me directly again, and not to some company in Los Angeles.

I told Keith that his moral support was enough for me, and I meant it. He and Woody showered me with so much hospitality that summer, I began to feel they were the brothers I never had. Their support came at just the right time, as two of my main sources, Svi and Video James, began to dry up.

Svi, to his credit, took his own advice: He left early instead of late. He cleaned up his life and extricated himself from the Stones' inner sanctum. He knew he was popping too many pills and finding himself in too many dodgy situations.

One of the things that scared Svi straight was the band's new song "Dirty Work." It's about getting a "loser," "jerk," and "dumb ass" to do everything for free and to "take the blame when the trouble comes." "Even if it's not about *me*," Svi said, "it *could* be." He knew that, with his kind of intelligence and life experience, he was selling himself short by working for the Stones. He went back to school, got a master's degree in education, and became a high school teacher. His subject? Chemistry.

He's the only person I ever met through the Stones to do a true 180. He knew that if he'd left the Stones too late instead of too early, it would have been in handcuffs or a box. His parting words to me were "I'm gonna walk before they make me run."

As for Video James, his ticket was wearing thin. His videos weren't so rare anymore, and he was committing faux pas after faux pas. It was uncomfortable seeing how much our roles had reversed. He was now asking *me* for info and access. He begged me to sneak him into Mick's birthday party, which I did, and to bring him to RPM, which I also did.

He knew he had to up his video ante, so he brought something to RPM that Keith and Woody had never seen. It was a tape of Woody's first-ever solo concert in 1974, featuring Keith as a special guest. Video James made copies for them and presented it in person. For Video James, it was like a Hail Mary pass in football. His last shot.

The four of us retreated to the studio's lounge. We popped in the tape, and the words "KEITH'S COPY" flashed in bright yellow letters at the bottom of the screen. I assumed it would disappear after a few seconds, but it didn't. A minute or so in, Keith posed a most logical question. "Is that thing gonna be there for two fuckin' hours?"

And that's when Video James uttered the last thing Keith and Woody ever needed to hear from him. In full Ed Norton mode, he exclaimed, "Yeah! That's so you and Woody won't get the tapes mixed up! I wrote 'Keith's copy' on yours and 'Woody's copy' on Woody's! After the first few songs, you'll forget it's there!"

Keith and Woody shot me a look like, "Why the fuck did you invite him here?" They knew that this was Video James's way of "branding" the tapes the way ranchers brand cattle. He was trying to prevent Keith and Woody from circulating it to their friends and having it hit the black market. But in doing so, he pissed them off and shot himself in the foot.

.   .   .

I don't know what Keith and Woody saw in me, but they encouraged me to hang out more often. One night, I was at Woody's house when the phone rang. No one else was around—no Matt Dillons, no drug dealers—so Woody grabbed it himself. "I've got Bill German here," he told Keith on the other end.

Woody listened to what Keith had to say and then made a face like, "Uh-oh, I think we're in trouble." He muffled the phone on his chest and said, "Keith wants to talk to you. I think he's jealous."

Keith's first words to me were, "Hey, man, you and Woody are spending a lot of time together."

"Um, well . . . [gulp]."

"What are you guys, havin' some kind of scene?"

"Having a scene" was Keith's euphemism for a sexual liaison. His sarcasm indicated he was genuinely annoyed that Woody and I had become so close. Of course, if you had told me as a teenage Stones fan that Keith Richards would one day be jealous of the time I was spending with Ron Wood, I would have had you committed.

My hunch is that Keith was feeling lonely and going through a midlife crisis. He had no idea where his life was headed—waiting for answers on the Stones' future—and needed some friends.

I told him I'd see more of him if I had his current phone number. He gave it to me immediately, but I knew it'd be obsolete pretty soon. Keith changed locations as much as he changed underwear. At the moment, he and Patti were in a rented apartment on East 47th Street. I called a couple times, and they also began calling *me*. Or at least Patti did.

Out of the blue, she'd say, "Keith and I love the latest issue. He's right here, finishing it." He wouldn't get on the phone, but Patti would pass along his messages and invite me out. "Keith and I hope you can make it to Area tomorrow night. It's a party for my hairdresser, Maury."

Most of the events had nothing to do with the Stones, but she and Keith wanted me there as a friend. And it's possible that Patti was trying to fix me up with her niece, Marisa, who was roughly my age.

Like her aunt, Marisa was blond, beautiful, and charming, and I did have a crush on her. I enjoyed seeing her at these parties, but never asked her out. It'd be like dating the boss's niece and could lead to all sorts of complications. I mean, let's say we had a spat. Now I can't talk to Uncle Keith anymore? My business would be ruined.

Even after I turned down his financial offer, Keith was still conjuring ways to help me. He suggested I shack up with Jane Rose. She had a spare room in her office, so he said I should run *Beggars Banquet* out of there. I never broached the subject with her, but Keith saw me in that room several times and assumed I'd actually moved in.

Ultimately, I did find a way for Keith to aid me financially. "Hey," I said, "do you remember that interview we did for *Beggars Banquet*? Is it okay if I reprint it somewhere else?" I'd heard that a new magazine called *Spin* was hoping to compete with *Rolling Stone* and needed a big "get." I brought it to Bob Guccione Jr., the magazine's publisher, and he bought it on the spot. He put it on the October 1985 cover—the magazine's fifth issue—and cut me a check for $2,000. An enormous amount of money, I felt, for such a small amount of work.

Compared to my work on *Beggars Banquet,* what I did for *Spin* was nothing. I simply woke up one morning, and my article was on the newsstand. I didn't have to lay out the issue, bring it to the printer, or lick any stamps.

By 1985, my workload with *Beggars Banquet* had become insane. I felt like I was running the New York City Marathon every day. After a long night at the studio, Keith and Woody slept it off, while I kept going. By 9 or 10 AM, I'd be calling Bill Wyman's office in London. Then I'd run to Bob Gruen to pick up photos and to Jane so she could recite from her diary. Then I'd be at the printer discussing color separations, at the bank depositing itsy-bitsy checks, and at the post office buying thousands of stamps.

I'm not telling you my job was more strenuous than being a coal miner or cotton picker, I'm just telling you the work was never-ending. There was never a moment when I could punch the clock and leave it behind. I didn't go to sleep for weeks on end, running on nothing but adrenaline.

What I mean is, I didn't go to sleep *intentionally.* I wouldn't brush my teeth, put on my pajamas, or tuck myself in bed. I'd pass out and grab an unintentional catnap. It didn't matter if it was 4 in the afternoon or 4 in the morning. I'd wake up with my face on my typewriter or my body sprawled out near a file cabinet. I'd be in my street clothes and the lights would be on, so I'd pick up where I left off.

I felt like the guy on *Ed Sullivan* who spun the plates. Something constantly required my attention. In addition to the writing, layouts, and printing, I had to maintain a mailing list of several thousand people without a computer. When an issue was published, I then had to affix the Xeroxed address labels, affix the postage stamps, and stuff the envelopes. And because it was more efficient than using a sponge, I'd *lick* the three thousand stamps and *lick* the three thousand envelopes to get it done as quickly as possible. If George Costanza's fiancée died from a handful of envelopes, I should've been dead long ago. I'd then make several trips to the post office to get it all out. If you thought it was exhausting mailing your Christmas cards, try a few thousand pieces in a day.

Obviously, I wished I could hire someone, but, because I made so little money (charging $7 a year, times three thousand people), I couldn't afford it. I inquired about interns, but colleges don't send kids to bachelors' houses to lick stuff. Some Stones fans volunteered, but they were only interested in the *fun* part of my job, not the crummy part. None of them wanted to schlep boxes, unless it was to Keith's house. So whether I liked it or not, *Beggars Banquet* remained a one-man operation.

My readers had no idea how *Beggars Banquet* affected my private life. My tiny apartment was no longer a home; it was an office, warehouse, and newsroom. My roommate moved out, but *Beggars Banquet* took over. I had to stuff photos under the bed and store back issues in the fridge.

Obviously, none of this was conducive to a healthy dating or sex life. Guys say to me, "You musta got a lotta pussy from knowing the Stones," but I have to be honest. I spent the prime of my virility licking more postage stamps than anything else.

I had no time to be on the prowl, and I rejected all the female subscribers who professed their love for me. I wanted a girl to want me for me, not for my Stones connections. Besides, sex is supposed to *relieve* the stresses of your job, not *remind* you of them. After working 24/7 on *Beggars Banquet,* I did not want to lie in bed and talk about the Stones. I therefore maintained a "non–Stones fan" policy when it came to my dating life. The girl I brought to Mick's birthday party couldn't give a shit about the Stones, and that's why I took her. I knew she wouldn't freak out in front of them. (She freaked out in front of Nicholson, but I didn't mind so much.)

Girls loved my work ethic, but it would ultimately ruin my relationships. They'd ask where I saw myself in five years, and I'd say, "On tour with the Stones, writing a book about it." That was my biggest dream. Not marriage or a white picket fence.

If a girl slept over, she'd have to play hopscotch to get to my bathroom. "Don't step on that picture of Mick! That's my next cover!" Or, instead of serving her a candlelit dinner, I'd ask her to collate and staple. As for the girl I brought to Mick's party, she got annoyed when I leaped out of bed one night to visit RPM. She stopped calling me around Labor Day, but I was too consumed with *Beggars Banquet* to even notice. There were plenty of girls in the sea, but only one Rolling Stones. *That's* the relationship I needed to nurture.

When my Keith interview came out in *Spin,* I brought a copy to Woody. He devoured it and said, "It's brilliant. I want you to do that to *me.* Can you do that to *me*?"

Around that time, there was a house cleaning at Woody's. A lot of the people who stayed "too late" got sent up the river or were running from the law. Included in that group was Brother John, who *was* the law. (I've changed his name to protect my kneecaps.) He was a huge bald black guy who resembled an NFL linebacker. By day he was a police sergeant, and by night he was Woody's main dealer. He knew nothing about the Stones, but was a big damn fan of Bobby Womack.

When Bobby booked a show at the Beacon Theatre for October 18, Brother John asked Woody to get him tickets and passes. A bonus for being Woody's main man that year. On the night of the concert, Brother John showed up at Woody's house with his wife, mother-in-law, sister, and brother-in-law. They were all dressed in their church clothes. Woody said he'd be jamming on "It's All Over Now," so I tagged along. Woody lived four blocks from the Beacon, so we walked. We watched the first few songs from the wings, before taking seats in the audience. Woody, Jo, and I were the only white folk. Nobody knew Woody, but one guy said he recognized the hairdo: "Aren't you Ron Stewart?"

Bobby was scheduled to play two concerts that night. The late show, which Woody promised to play at, was set for midnight. But it didn't start until 2 AM because everyone walked back to Woody's house after the early show. About twenty of us, including Womack's personal masseuse and Brother John's family, packed into the kitchen. At midnight, I reminded everyone that there was a theater full of people waiting for Bobby, but it didn't faze anyone.

It was well past 1:30 when Woody packed a guitar and made it back to the Beacon. This time, we took limos. It was a great show, and Woody's performance of "It's All Over Now" was duly noted in *Beggars Banquet*. We got out of the theater around 4 AM and returned to Woody's, where, at sunrise, we began to shake, rattle, and roll. It was a rare New York City earthquake and was like a sign from God: "Better to leave too early than too late."

We exited Woody's house at 6 AM and, a few weeks later, Brother John exited for good. He was busted for his night job. Internal Affairs confiscated the big black man's little black book, which contained Woody's phone number.

Keith chided Woody for letting Brother John get so close. Keith may have patronized Brother John once or twice that year, but he *never* gave him his phone number and *never* had him to his house. For a few days, Woody was jittery about the potential fallout. He was questioned by an Internal Affairs detective, but never implicated. A huge sigh of relief.

The people who continued to frequent Woody's house were now of a more artistic nature. They were almost exclusively musicians, actors, and painters. In fact, it was around this time, late '85, that Woody landed a book deal for his artwork. He reportedly scored $100,000, which was astronomical back then.

Woody was under the impression it would strictly be an art book. Reproductions of his paintings and drawings, with maybe a few captions. But he soon learned it'd be more text-heavy and would require a ghostwriter. Which is when I remembered his mantra: "Do that to *me*! Can you do that to *me*?"

I was a 23-year-old novice with no résumé, but would not have forgiven myself if I didn't throw my hat in the ring. It so happened that I needed to visit Woody anyway. He'd promised to do some drawings for a *Beggars Banquet* Christmas card. Keith had already contributed something, but Woody was taking forever. It was now two weeks 'til Christmas, so Woody told me to come over and make sure he got it done. As my taxi zigzagged through the 79th Street transverse of Central Park, I practiced my marriage proposal: "Woody, will you take me to be your ghostwriter?" I knew I was the right person for the job, but I was nervous.

We settled in the dining room with his manager, Nick. Woody popped a rough mix of *Dirty Work* in his boom box and drew two different Christmas scenes: one depicting himself as Santa and one depicting Keith and him with a Christmas tree. I knew I had to make my move and began a countdown in my head. I started at T-minus-30 and decided that when I hit zero, I'd blurt, "Woody, I want to be your co-author!" But when I got to T-minus-15, Woody stole my thunder. Out of nowhere, he turned to Nick and said, "Y'know, I think we've got our co-author right *here*!"

All I could say was, "Damn straight you do!"

And that's how I was hired to pen Ron Wood's semi-autobiography/semi–art book, *The Works*. Woody asked *me* to do it, not the other way around. I still had to pass muster with Woody's literary agent and publisher, but this was the biggest thing that ever happened in my writing career. It wasn't the book I longed to do about the Stones on tour, but it was pretty damn close. I was going to be the first person on earth to co-author a book with one of the Stones. I was so excited, I couldn't sleep when I got home. This was *better* than sex. I wanted to call everyone I knew, but had to wait. It was 6 o'clock in the morning.

Around 7, I allowed myself to doze off. My intention was to wake up in a few hours and start spreading the news. Instead, at 8:30, I was the one getting the phone call. A source from overseas was telling me that Ian Stewart, the "Sixth Stone," had died of a heart attack in London that morning. The air was instantly let out of my balloon. What should have been the most joyous day of my *Beggars Banquet* career turned out to be its gloomiest.

Townshend joins the band at the 100 Club. My all-time
favorite Stones concert.

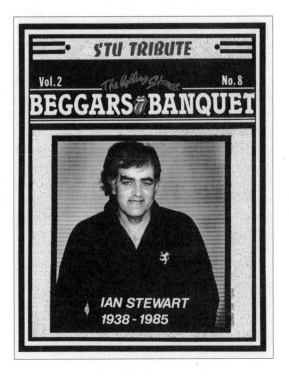

STU TRIBUTE

Vol.2 *The Rolling Stones* No. 8

BEGGARS BANQUET

IAN STEWART
1938 - 1985

12

the last laugh

To the Stones, it was a sick joke. If there was one guy in or around the band who wasn't supposed to go at age 47, it was Ian Stewart. He was the one without the booze, coke, heroin, or cigarettes. It was like God picked Stu to send the rest of them a message.

I decided to memorialize Stu in my next issue. I put him on the cover and reran my 1981 interview with him. In my search for exclusive photos, I found myself at Woody's house, shortly after New Year's 1986.

Jo whipped up her famous shepherd's pie and invited me and Keith. After dinner, she went upstairs to fetch her photo albums, leaving me, Keith, and Woody in the kitchen. I reached into my briefcase to pull out some pictures of Stu, sent to me by a subscriber.

I passed them across the table to Keith and told him not to get his fingerprints on them. Woody was at the sink washing dishes. Keith grinned as he skimmed through the photos. Woody, with a dishtowel in his hands, leaned over Keith's shoulder to have a look. The two of them began impersonating Stu, by squaring their jaws and reciting his favorite expressions: "Good morning, my showers of shit. My three-chord wonders." They even joked about Stu's dandruff problem. I could tell they were really going to miss him.

Woody went back to the sink as Keith kept glancing at the pictures. There was one he stared at for thirty seconds, without saying a word. Then he began talking to it. "Why'd you have to leave us like that, you sod?"

He looked up at me and Woody. "At least he went out on an upswing. He was excited about the new album. . . . But I thought *he'd* be the one holding the shovel, the one to bury all of *us*. What a hole he's left, such an obvious gap. He would always be there to comment on everything, and sometimes you'd think he was crazy. But then you'd go and realize that he was right all along. I mean, no one has a bad word to say about him. You know, I've had other friends pass on, and you'd go, 'Gee, it's a shame,' but Stu was different. I could think of a hundred other fuckers who should have gone instead of him. He wasn't even on my list."

It was a spontaneous and heartfelt eulogy. In fact, I knew it was too good not to print in *Beggars Banquet* verbatim. So I excused myself from the table and ran to Woody's bathroom, to avoid any distractions. There, I pulled a pen and index card out of my pocket and scribbled Keith's thoughts as fast as possible, before I forgot a single word. Then I returned to the kitchen. "Keith," I said, "that was really great what you just said about Stu. Is it okay if I print it?" He said yes, like I knew he would.

Keith left at 3 AM, but I stuck around to work with Woody. The early stages of our book project. "Hang on a minute, though," said Woody. "I'd like to write something about Stu, as well." He grabbed a yellow legal pad and told me to leave him alone in the basement. Jo had already gone to bed, so I occupied myself with a *Mary Tyler Moore* rerun in the guest room. After twenty minutes, I went downstairs to peek in.

He was in a reclining chair, eyes closed, deep in thought. I didn't know how he could concentrate, because a Vivaldi CD was blasting through the speakers. I noticed he hadn't written a single word on the legal pad, but I didn't want to rush him. I gave him fifteen more minutes.

When I returned, I noticed that the pad was still on his chest, with the top page blank. The pen was lodged in his hand, and his eyes were still closed. Memories of Stu rushing through his head. Again, I left him alone.

Next thing I knew, it was 4 o'clock in the morning, and he was in the exact same position. The music was shaking the room, so I told myself, "He's either a very deep sleeper or I've got Ron Wood dead right here." I moved close to his face, but couldn't feel his breath. His chest wasn't moving, either. I called his name and nudged his leg, but he still didn't respond. I figured, "If he's asleep, let him sleep. If he's dead, there's nothing I can do about it."

I tiptoed out of the house, hoping for no witnesses. I expected the next day's *Post* to read, "Stone Cold Dead on Upper West Side," but we know how it turned out.

A few weeks later, I found myself in an enviable yet unnerving situation. I was alone in a room with all five Rolling Stones for the first time in my life. Nobody but me and them. It only lasted a few minutes, but the tension was so great, their presence so powerful, I nearly passed out from lack of oxygen.

We were at a studio on 54th Street for one of the band's obligatory get-togethers. A video shoot for the upcoming single, "Harlem Shuffle." They were wearing zoot suits and lip-synching on a mock Harlem street.

During a break, I greeted Keith and accompanied him to the Stones' dressing room. We passed Mick, who was seated in a makeup chair, with a bib on. I wasn't sure which Mick I was going to get that day. In recent months, he'd both chewed me out and sent me flowers. On this day, February 7, he was cordial. He made some joke about the Stones resembling Cab Calloway.

In the lounge next door, I found Charlie on the floor, massaging his bare feet. I didn't want to interrupt him. Bill Wyman was eating Chinese takeout and suggested I try the snow peas. A couple of CBS execs, who reminded me of Bill Murray's Jerry Aldini, were talking to Jane Rose and Tony King.

Eventually, Mick returned from the makeup chair, and all the periphery people left the room, except for me. I was suddenly alone with all five Rolling Stones. This was different from just hanging out with Keith and Woody. When it comes to the Stones, the whole is so much greater than the sum of its parts, it takes on a life of its own. Like Frankenstein's monster.

The tension among *them* made it even more paralyzing for *me*. My only choice was to clam up and be a fly on the wall. At first, none of them said anything. It was painfully silent. But then, in a hushed tone, Charlie cracked a joke about the video they were shooting. He said it was similar to some British TV show they used to watch when they were teenagers. I had no idea what he was talking about, so I stood there with a dumb smile on my face, pretending I got the reference.

They talked about the upcoming memorial for Stu. It was slated for February 23 in London, and each Stone vowed to be there. Not a religious service, but an intimate get-together at the 100 Club on Oxford Street. Stu's band, Rocket 88, would provide a boogie-woogie tribute. About two hundred of Stu's friends would be invited. And, with all five elements in place, a jam from the Stones—a preview of their '86 tour?—was a slight possibility.

Watching the Stones lip-synch in a studio was one thing, but the specter of seeing them play a tiny nightclub was mind-boggling. When Keith and Woody invited me, I booked my flight immediately, despite not having a passport. I'd never been overseas before.

Our sleeping arrangements in London were as follows: Keith was at the Savoy, Woody was at Simon Kirke's house (former Bad Company drummer), and I was at the YMCA. My room was just 40 bucks a night (24 British pounds), but had a private bath and phone.

I got in the day before the memorial and planned to stay a week. Woody gave me a map of the tube system, which helped me get around. He marked all the important spots with Xs. We were supposed to visit his parents one day, to interview them for our book, but Woody couldn't make it.

A few hours before the Stu event, I visited Jane at the Savoy to pick up my guest pass. It always felt awkward seeing Jane outside her office, like seeing your math teacher at the ice cream shop. She held up two dresses and asked, "Which one do you think I should wear, the black one or the red one?"

I told her the red one looked nice, but that black might be more appropriate for a memorial. Then again, this wasn't a typical memorial. Or at least not the depressing things we Jews put on. This one would feature boogie-woogie music and maybe a set from the Rolling Stones.

The 100 Club was blocks from the YMCA, but I hailed a taxi to avoid getting lost. I had taken well to Britspeak—referring to the elevator as "the lift" and the bathroom as "the loo"—but, for the life of me, I couldn't figure out the cityscape. The streets are laid out in circles, not squares, and everyone drives on the wrong side of the road.

When my taxi pulled up to 100 Oxford Street, I was swarmed by London's paparazzi corps. They had no clue who I was, but their logic was "Shoot first, ask questions later." Professional photographers were not allowed inside. In fact, of the two hundred people invited, I was the only journalist.

Keith spotted me inside and said, "You made it! 'Cross the big pond!" And Woody introduced me to a friend of his. "Jeff, this is me co-author, Bill German. And Bill, this is Jeff. He and I were in a band together. He was so good on guitar, I had to move to bass!" It was Jeff Beck, of course.

Woody next introduced me to Pete Townshend. Pete said he was amazed that anyone would want to read a book about Ronnie Wood, and I'm pretty sure he wasn't joking. Either way, it was nice to have Woody introduce me as his co-author. I liked the sound of that.

No one knew whether the Stones would play this night. Woody told me "something *might* happen," but I never broached the subject with Keith.

I don't know what was discussed or how it came together, but, soon after Rocket 88 left the stage, the Rolling Stones took their place. All of them except for Charlie, who wasn't there yet. "Let's do some songs Stu would want to play," announced Mick. Simon Kirke sat in on drums, as they launched into "Route 66." From there, it was "Down the Road Apiece," one of Stu's all-time favorites. "This is totally improvised," Mick said. "Any requests? Yell 'em up."

Seeing the Stones play an impromptu concert in a tiny nightclub was already a mindblower for me, but it reached surreal proportions when some of their friends joined them onstage. Eric Clapton came up to play "Key to the

Highway," "Confessin' the Blues," and "I'm a Man." And Jeff Beck crammed in for "Bye Bye Johnny."

Clapton then made way for Townshend. "Pete's gonna come up and do the whole *Tommy*," joked Mick. In reality, they did "Harlem Shuffle."

Next came "Little Red Rooster," during which each guitarist—Beck, Townshend, Keith, and Woody—took a lead. Except that Woody's was on slide. He stuck his middle finger in a Heineken bottle and twanged away, as droplets of beer trickled down his knuckles.

Upon the song's conclusion, rumors of a Charlie sighting reached the stage. Townshend stepped up to the mic: "Now that the pubs are closed, Charlie's decided to show up. Charlie, if you don't come up here, Woody's gonna play drums."

Charlie emerged from the darkness wearing a business suit. He got behind the kit without loosening his tie or removing his hat. The Stones' reunion was now complete. Ian Stewart pulled off in death what no concert promoter could pull off in life: a Rolling Stones concert in the mid-1980s.

At that point, Clapton came back onstage to groove on "Meet Me in the Bottom," "Dust My Broom," and the evening's finale, "Little Queenie." When it was all said and done, eleven songs in all, I felt drained. Everyone, including the performers, knew they'd experienced something special. It ranks as my favorite concert of all time.

When I got to the street, it was freezing, pitch-dark, and desolate. I knew my hotel was a few blocks away, but I immediately got lost. I hailed a cab, but the driver refused to take me. "Sorry, mate, I can't mislead ya. It wouldn't be right. You're just a few short blocks." In New York the cabbies are too nasty, and in London they're too nice. I stumbled around for two hours until I found the Y. It was a miracle I didn't freeze to death or get hacked to pieces by Jack the Ripper. I got to bed around dawn.

At 10 AM, my phone rang. British telephones don't "riiiing"—they "ring-ring, ring-ring"—so it took me a few seconds to realize it wasn't my alarm clock. I picked it up, half asleep, and was greeted on the other end by Bill Wyman. Not his secretary, but Bill himself, bright-eyed and bushy-tailed, calling me from his office on King's Road. I'd put in a request to interview him and told him he could reach me at the Y.

When I informed Woody I was going to interview Bill, he said, "Make sure your heads don't explode!" He was referring to my and Bill's shared knowledge of Stones minutiae. But I had no intention of matching trivia with him. I wanted to get inside the man himself, and ask probing questions about his life and career.

Bill greeted me at the door of Ripple Productions and gave me a quick tour. In the main office, I saw photos of him with Prince Charles and Princess Diana. We started our interview by discussing Stu's death.

"I'll never play golf," Bill said sarcastically. "I'll never play golf or eat cheeseburgers. I mean, those were his only vices." (Stu's heart attack was caused by hardening of the arteries.)

I asked Bill to reflect on his own life: Does he wear any scars as the result of his fame?

"So you want me to analyze myself?" he said. "To do a Freud on my-self? . . . I like to think I haven't changed over the last twenty-five years, but of course I *have*. I *liked* the person I was twenty-five years ago. . . . I find it hard now to trust anyone. Managers, photographers, journalists. I wish I was able to trust people.

"And the bigger scar," he added, "is that your personal relationships, your love life, gets all fucked up. Home, family, the way you live, friends, social things. You can't live a normal life, so all your close personal relationships get fucked up. I mean, look at the Stones. There's only one of us who's with the same person he was with in '64, and that's Charlie. Look at Mick with all his re-lationships—Marianne, Bianca, Chrissie Shrimpton, Jerry. Brian Jones with children here and there, being sued by everyone, hated by the girls' parents. I've gone through a marriage, a divorce, and another relationship with some-one I'm no longer with. . . . I mean, this life is incredibly destructive."

"But haven't you overcome all that by now?"

"Yes, but the scars are still there. You still have bad dreams. And you still need a crutch sometimes to get you through. I'm lucky because I don't know what my crutch has been. I suppose it's been women. There are so many fa-mous people who turn to drugs and alcohol, but I suppose I've become totally girl-mad as my crutch. All of us need to compensate somehow. You're not nor-mal anymore. Look at any member of this band. They're not normal people. We're all completely nuts in a certain way, aren't we?"

I let that stand as a rhetorical question. But I did ask him about his new-found reputation as a ladies' man. Supposedly, he was pulling Wilt Chamber-lain numbers.

"Wouldn't *any* man like that reputation?" he said. "We all *aim* for it!"

The press had not yet broken the story of Bill's relationship with teenager Mandy Smith. But a few months after our interview, headlines like "Stone's Lover Aged 13" began appearing in the Fleet Street tabloids (even though she was 15 by then). Once it was made public, I took the liberty of needling Bill in the pages of *Beggars Banquet*. I once ran a photo of him and Mandy, with the caption "Look! Mandy's permanent teeth have grown in!"

And the crazier part of the story is that Bill's twentysomething son, Stephen, had begun dating Mandy's fortysomething mother, Patsy, with talk of a double wedding. In one issue of *Beggars Banquet,* I laid out the ramifications: Bill's mother-in-law would become his daughter-in-law, his son would become his father-in-law, his step-granddaughter would now be his wife, and, if I'm not mistaken, Bill might've become his own third cousin twice removed.

Eventually, our discussion turned to his role in the Stones. "My job is as bass player," he stated. "That's what I do. I don't mix, master, or choose the LP covers."

"Well, what if you wanted to have a larger say in the decision-making process? Couldn't you push for it?"

"If someone pushed themselves in situations like that, this band wouldn't be around any longer. It would have folded up fifteen years ago. You can't have too many egos in the same band. You've got to just swallow your pride. Some people have to swallow their egos, and some have to fly with them. We know who's who in this band."

It was then that Bill revealed to me that Mick, on several occasions, had tried to throw him out of the band. "You're not *serious*," I countered.

"Oh, but I *am* serious," he said. "*Very* serious. You know, Mick does funny things at funny times. But he gets shouted down. Sometimes he gets his way, and sometimes he doesn't.

"The Stones can obviously go on without me," Bill recognized. "I'm sure of it. Mick's not replaceable, and Keith's not replaceable. But you could replace Woody and you could replace *me.* You *might* be able to replace Charlie, although Keith would say no. But yes, I could be replaced. Mick's tried to do it on several occasions, although I didn't know it at the time. Luckily for me, everyone else stopped him."

In February 1986, this revelation was a bombshell. In fact, I'm not sure why Bill was letting me in on it. He was giving me an exclusive. I'm embarrassed to admit that I sat on it. Mick's temper tantrum in Woody's basement had a chilling effect on me, and I didn't want him in my face again.

Besides, it was in my own best interests not to open past wounds. I wanted the Stones to tour that year, and it seemed like they healed some wounds at the 100 Club.

Capping the Stones' busy week in London that cold February was their Grammy Award acceptance at the Roof Garden Club. It was for a noncompetitive award—the Stones were *definitely* receiving it—so the whole thing was prescheduled and coordinated. As usual, the Grammy telecast was emanating live from the Shrine Auditorium in Los Angeles. So, for the Stones to accept their Lifetime Achievement Award during prime time in the States, they'd appear via satellite at 3 AM London time.

After twenty-three years of making records, the Stones had never won a Grammy. Yet here they found themselves, receiving a Lifetime Achievement Award, and they weren't thrilled. Usually, that award is for a 90-year-old composer who has to be wheeled out with an oxygen tank.

The Stones agreed to do it for their record label. CBS brokered a deal whereby, if the Stones accepted on live TV, the producers would air their "Harlem Shuffle" video. Two and a half minutes of free airtime and better exposure than MTV. I mentioned the Grammy-for-video quid pro quo to Keith, and he said, "Why do you think I'm here? I'm no schmuck."

The Roof Garden Club was located on Kensington High Street, a fancy part of London. The Stones didn't get there until 2 AM. Eric Clapton, who was to present the Stones with their plaques, was primping and rehearsing his lines. I heard him apologize to the producers for not donning a tux.

When Kenny Rogers, the Grammy host in Hollywood, threw it live to London, the Stones couldn't keep a straight face. Charlie was sitting on a potted plant, smoking a cigarette, and Keith was pinching him. Clapton flubbed most of his lines, before handing out plaques to each Stone. When Charlie got his, his reaction was, "There's no wheels on it! No wheels!"

As the camera focused on Mick, the other Stones elbowed each other in the ribs and snickered like schoolchildren. "Thank you to all the people who stuck by this band through thick and thin," said Mick. "And to everyone who took the piss [the band's detractors], the joke's on you." The Rolling Stones had finally joined the pantheon of Grammy greats, alongside Christopher Cross and Debby Boone.

As soon as the camera's red light went off, the Stones piled their plaques into the waiting arms of Jane Rose and walked away. Keith breezed past me, muttering, "*That's* done. Where's the *money*?"

He made a beeline toward his mother. I'd never met Doris before, so I asked him to introduce me. "Mum," Keith said, "this is Bill German. If you ever need to find me, call *him* first. He knows where I am at every hour of the day."

Keith suggested that Doris be put on the *Beggars Banquet* mailing list. She scribbled her address on a napkin, and I promised her a complimentary lifetime subscription. She was so kind, it was hard to believe she'd once carried Satan in her womb for nine months.

By 5 AM, the Roof Garden Club cleared out. The caterers were packing up, and the porters were bringing out the mops. Keith, Woody, and I were the last ones left. Keith grabbed me under the arm and started walking with me like we were bride and groom. "William," he said, "you're coming with *me*." He then called across the room to Woody: "Ronaldo! Clapton's movin' out of his flat tomorrow, so let's take the place apart!"

Keith and I exited the building and crawled inside a waiting limo. Woody and Jo hopped in next to us. Jane Rose and Bill Graham were already in the front seat. The ride took about twenty minutes. This wasn't Clapton's estate or anything, just a crash pad he kept in town. He'd already moved most of his stuff, so the place was virtually empty. Just some chairs and a coffee table in the living room. And several cases of booze.

Some of us hung out in the living room, and some of us hung out in the kitchen. Steve Lillywhite, the producer of *Dirty Work*, was there with his wife, singer Kirsty MacColl. So were Chuck Leavell, the Stones' keyboardist, and Stash, a friend of Keith's since the Sixties.

I'm not sure why, but Eric began interrogating me: "What brings *you* here, young man?"

"Um, well, *Keith* brings me here. I guess I'm his date for the night."

"Bill does our fan magazine," interjected Woody.

"Oh, yeah?" said Eric. "How old are you, then?"

"I—I prefer not to divulge that information," I stammered. As much as I hated being stubborn, I liked keeping my exact age a secret around the Stones. I was embarrassed by my youth and feared it could be used against me. Keith, Jane, and Woody had a rough idea, but never knew the exact numbers.

"Well," said Eric, "I'll put you round 23. And when I was that age, I was playing Albert Hall and finishing up with Cream. *Yardbirds* were long gone. I was about ready for Blind Faith, I suppose."

I had no idea where he was going with this. Was he trying to make me feel insignificant or was he trying to make himself feel good? Probably just reminiscing out loud. God doesn't need to pat himself on the back.

"Where are you staying?" he asked. "At the Savoy?"

"Um, no, I'm at the Hotel Y. Oxford Street and Tottenham Court Road."

"Tottenham Court Road. I used to live round there. *Many* years ago."

I don't know why he took such an interest in me, but I was relieved when he began picking on someone else. He next set his sights on Stash: "So you're a prince, are you? Where is your principality?"

Stash was indeed a blueblood from Rolle, Switzerland. I'd send his *Beggars Banquet*s to the castle. His full name was Prince Stanislaus Klossowski de Rola, and he was the son of Balthus, one of the greatest painters of the twentieth century.

Anyway, I don't want you to get the wrong idea about Eric. He was a very gracious host. I think he was just having fun with us. At 7 AM, it was time to leave. Keith to the Savoy, Woody to Simon Kirke's house, and me to the Y. Jane said three limos were waiting downstairs, including one for me alone. "It's on *us*," she said. I thanked her and said it would probably be a first for the driver, going from Eric Clapton's house to the YMCA.

Eric walked us to the door, but said he had a concern. "I've got all these crates of whiskey," he said. "And if *you* don't take them, I'm gonna leave 'em for the landlord."

With that, Keith and Woody dashed back to the living room. They proceeded to stuff bottles of Jack Daniel's into their coat pockets.

"Glad to be of service," said Keith.

Keith Moon lives! This is the photo I messengered
to the publishers.

13

every story tells
a picture

Woody and I spent 1986 on our book project. We began in January and had no set schedule. If he had a free night, I'd get the call: "Big Bill Broonzy! Jo's watching TV and the kids are asleep, so why doncha come over?" I'd hop in a taxi and show up around midnight. I'd unpack my briefcase, and we'd set up in his kitchen. For Woody, my Samsonite was a never-ending source of amusement: "You look like an encyclopedia salesman!"

We'd pop a cassette into Woody's boom box and push Record. We never knew what we'd end up with when the rooster crowed in the morning. I had questions prepared in advance, but, with Woody, things could veer off into a myriad of directions. For the first month, we sifted through his artwork and wasted a lot of time. One night, we made crank phone calls to people who'd placed "Guitarist Wanted" ads in *The Village Voice*.

I dialed the numbers, then passed him the receiver. "Yes, I'm answering your ad in the *Voice*. You're looking for a guitarist?" They hung up on him as soon as he gave his résumé. "Well, I used to play with Rod Stewart and Jeff Beck, and right now I'm in the Stones, but we might not tour this year, so I—" Click. It was a fun way to procrastinate, and we came *this* close to sending pizzas to Mick's house.

It took me most of January to decipher his stories. In the beginning, I'd let him ramble without interrupting. I figured I'd make sense of it at home when I listened to the playback. But that didn't always work. Take, for instance: "I drew this picture of Sandie 'cause of the night me and Mick rode in his ambulance with Linda Ronstadt and Governor Brown behind us and then we had to stop near Sunset to let out Warren Beatty . . . but when we got to Cedars-Sinai, Mick helped me with the cesarean papers."

Then there was someone named El Vee he kept talking about: "El Vee was wearing his feather boa." "Me and El Vee went round the pub." "El Vee stole my girl."

I had no idea who this person was. Some Mexican revolutionary? I finally asked him and he seemed amazed by my ignorance. "LV," he said. "Lead vocalist. Like Rod. Or Mick. LV."

The other mystery was Karen Dash. He kept telling me how she made him a better artist: "Without Karen Dash, I couldn't have done these two portraits." "Karen Dash helped me get the skin tones for this piece." Eventually, I said, "Woody, who is Karen Dash? A teacher of yours from art school? An ex-girlfriend?"

He pulled out a box of colored pencils. "Nah, it's *these*. Caran d'Ache." The brand name of the pencils.

After adapting to his lingo, I had to get used to his idiosyncrasies. He had this amazing ability to stop midsentence and disappear from the room. He'd be saying, "I appreciate Picasso's work, but I couldn't stick with cubism because—" and then interrupt himself. "Hang on a minute. I'm goin' upstairs to get a cig." He'd leave me alone in the kitchen for almost an hour.

I'd be downstairs, wondering: "Is he coming back?" "Did he go to sleep?" "Is he having marital relations with Jo?" I wasn't about to knock on his bedroom door at 3 in the morning to find out.

If he were a ten-year-old, they'd have diagnosed him with attention deficit disorder and put him on Ritalin. He did, at least, grant me refrigerator privileges. "You know, Bill, while I'm gone, you can grab something from the fridge, if you like."

I was hesitant at first, but ultimately took him up on it. I needed the free grub. I never took anything substantial—just cheese, cookies, or bananas—and I'd make up for it by pitching in with chores. There were several nights when Woody and I, with the tapes rolling, peeled potatoes and shucked corn for the family's next dinner.

Regardless, my alleged mooching became a running joke between Keith and Woody, inspiring the eventual blurb on the book jacket: "Bill German lives in New York City, attended NYU, has written for magazines such as *Spin,* and ate the Woods out of house and home while co-writing this book."

After a month of late nights at Woody's, I was asked by the publishers for a sample chapter. I didn't think I had enough material, but I realized he'd spoken a lot about his family. Some priceless stories about his parents and brothers.

Woody's dad played in a twenty-four-piece harmonica band. When he lost his leg to a blood clot, he went around saying, "What has two heads, four arms, and three legs? Mr. and Mrs. Wood!" You could see where Woody got his carefree attitude.

Woody had two older brothers who heckled him as a kid. They'd spit on him and make him do their chores. But he looked up to them and desperately wanted to please them, the way he now did Mick and Keith.

I felt that my "family chapter" was charming and offered insight into how Woody became Woody, but the publishers thought it was boring. They wanted me off the project, and I was devastated.

It was Woody who came to my defense and convinced them to give me another chance. I spiced things up for my next sample. I got him to talk about the celebrities he'd painted. Some of whom he'd met, like Hendrix, Muddy, and Belushi, and some of whom he *wished* he'd met, like Elvis, Otis, and Marilyn Monroe.

I also got him to talk about Keith Moon. As pals in the Seventies, they shared lots of benders and wrecked lots of hotel rooms. Yet for some reason, Woody had never done a portrait of him. I dug up a great photo of Moonie wearing a top hat and gave it to Woody as a reference. He drew his own rendition, and I was blown away by how good it was.

This, by the way, was an exception to the rule. Usually, it was Woody's artwork that generated the stories, not the other way around. In other words, Woody had already done portraits of Hendrix, Muddy, and Belushi, so it was my job to ask him about them. But in the cases of Keith Moon and Groucho Marx, the stories came first.

Woody mentioned to me in passing that he'd once attended Groucho's Passover seder. He wasn't invited, but he tagged along with Ahmet Ertegun and Elliott Gould. It was Hollywood in the mid-Seventies, and Groucho was still Groucho. His opening line to Woody was "Now that's the silliest haircut I've *ever* seen." Later, after the *afikomen,* he pulled Woody aside. "I'd give up every dollar I ever earned," he said, "if I could just get one more erection." I knew it was too good to leave out of the book, so I said, "Woody, you gotta draw Groucho."

The publishers loved the new sample, and I was back in. They also had a suggestion: "When you're writing as Woody, imagine him at a party. A drink in one hand, a cigarette in the other, shooting the bull and looking over his artwork."

So that's what I did. Whenever I finished a chapter, I'd read it back to myself in Woody's voice, with a drink and an unlit Marlboro. It was like method acting. I walked around my apartment for hours, pretending to be Woody. If the phone rang, I wouldn't break character. My mom had no idea why her son had suddenly turned British.

The most liberating part of "being Woody" was that I *intentionally* got Stones facts wrong in the book. Woody had some fuzzy recollections, and it wasn't my place to interfere with them. You want accuracy? Read *Beggars Banquet.* You want Woody's perspective? Read *this.*

The hardest part of being Ron Wood's co-author was that I was also his babysitter. The Woods were moving on July 30—to live in England—so every night we had was precious. I couldn't let Woody waste time.

But with his ADD and with all the distractions of being Ron Wood, it wasn't easy. His doorbell, for instance, could ring at any hour and take us on a journey we hadn't planned. It was like a vaudeville skit or something out of *Pee-wee's Playhouse.* You never knew who was on the other side of the door until you opened it. Ding-dong, it's Mick Jagger. Ding-dong, it's Keith. Could be anybody.

I remember when Mick surprised us. Woody and I were working in the kitchen, so Jo answered the door. The unmistakable voice of Mick Jagger could be heard from the foyer, getting louder as he approached. "Quick," Woody told me, "put everything away. I don't want him to know about the book yet."

I swiftly grabbed my notebook and cassettes and chucked them in my briefcase. Mick was still needling Woody for his Learning Annex debacle—and for any attempt to break his "second banana" mold—so that's what Woody was scared about.

Keith came by a few times, and, although we told him what we were up to, he never showed interest. In general, Keith would monopolize Woody's time and dictate where the proceedings would go. Speaking strictly as Woody's babysitter/co-author, the night was shot to hell the minute Keith walked through the door.

One night, Keith brought over a tape of Billy Connolly, the Scottish comedian. I couldn't understand a single word of his brogue, but Keith and Woody were rolling on the floor laughing. They played the tape over and over, and I got no work done.

Another night, Keith picked up an acoustic guitar and settled into the kitchen. Woody grabbed one, too. As I sat across the table from them, they began fooling around with some Buddy Holly covers. "Peggy Sue," "Learning the Game," and "Rave On." Keith sang most of 'em, but Woody sang "I'm Gonna Love You Too." They also did Beatles numbers, like "Day Tripper."

Part of me was saying, "We've got a book to write here, let's not waste any time," and the other part of me was saying, "Well, this is a cool fucking place to be right now. Two of the Rolling Stones are giving me a private concert at a kitchen table. This is the *good* part of my job, not the *stressful* part."

I must reveal, however, that their jam that night devolved into an earth-shattering fart contest. Some serious Hall of Fame cheese-cutting. In the middle of "Not Fade Away," Keith stopped, lifted his guitar, and went, POOF! Woody answered with one of his own. They alternated flatulence for three or four more songs. "That'll be the day-ay-ay that I—" *Zap!* I told Keith, "You're a real farter figure to me."

One night, the guys from the reggae band Third World stopped by. They were not the type to whom you say, "Hey, me and Woody are trying to do some work here." There were a lot of 'em, and they were big. Seven feet tall, if you count the dreadlocks stuffed in their hats. There was no room left in the kitchen, so I hovered in the corner. One of them accidentally knocked a toy off the shelf and broke it. Then they lit up spliffs the size of farm animals. The house got so smoky I thought we were in a Cheech and Chong movie. They turned out to be nice guys, but Jo was initially scared of them. "We're being invaded by a Third World nation," I heard her mutter.

Other than Keith, my favorite surprise guest was the one who rang the bell one night in June, around 3 AM. Woody and I were working quietly in the kitchen. "Who the fuck can *that* be?" he said.

We walked to the front door and found Stevie Ray Vaughan with his guitar strapped on. No case, no bag, just the guitar. "You mean to tell me," asked Woody, "that you hailed a cab on the street like that, with your guitar strapped on?" And the answer was yes.

He said he got bored at his hotel and needed someone to play with. He and his girlfriend came inside. The girlfriend kibbitzed in the kitchen with Jo, as we three boys retreated to the basement. A searing jam session ensued, with me as the lone spectator.

I'd never met Stevie Ray before. He seemed like a very nice person, but didn't say much. He let his guitar do the talking. He was wearing his trademark hat, a tank top, and an unbuttoned dress shirt. When he removed the dress shirt, I noticed purple suction marks on his back. Woody later told me they were "some kind of treatment."

Stevie Ray told his girlfriend to take my name because he was inviting me to his upcoming gig at Pier 84. Woody and I vowed to attend. But when the day rolled around, Woody was a no-show. I went by myself and, as soon as I gave my name to the backstage bouncer, I was confronted by Stevie Ray's publicist. "We're waiting for Woody," he said. "You've got to convince him to come."

The publicist and I knew each other because he once worked at Rolling Stones Records. He led me inside a trailer and pointed to a phone. "You've got to get him here." I felt awkward about it, but told him I'd try. I dialed Woody's number, but it rang and rang. Not even the machine picked up.

I realized how odd it all was. It was six years to the day since I'd met Woody for the first time, as a dorky 17-year-old outside the *Emotional Rescue* party. But now I stood backstage at a Stevie Ray Vaughan concert, deemed a Rolling Stones confidant—and someone who could dictate Ron Wood's social calendar. "Stevie Ray is far too modest to call there himself," the publicist added. "But I know he's counting on Ronnie coming onstage. Can you try again?"

I did, but there was still no answer. If I recall correctly, that was the week Woody went incommunicado. He was harboring Don Johnson.

Donnie was in the midst of negotiating a new contract with *Miami Vice* and wanted $150,000 an episode. To scare the show's producers, he hid out at Woody's house. They took no incoming calls. But Don left a message on the producers' answering machine: "If you don't gimme what I want, I'm gonna join the New Barbarians!"

The threat apparently worked. Don got his money and, as a token of appreciation, sent Woody a pine box. It was engraved "From one Barbarian to another" and contained a Smith & Wesson.

When Woody's 39th birthday rolled around, Jo threw him a surprise soiree at the house. I got there late, so I was spared the indignity of shouting "Surprise!" But it would've been fun seeing Ahmet Ertegun and Andy Warhol jump out from behind the sofa.

I was late because I was picking out gifts for the birthday boy. I wanted to express my gratitude to him—for the opportunity he gave me and for the faith he showed in my work—so I searched for something special. I knew he had a fascination with the Wild West, so I almost got him a cigar store Indian. I instead spent a hundred bucks at the Rizzoli bookstore, which was a lot of money for me. The other guests showed up empty-handed or with small trinkets. Ahmet gave him novelty sunglasses and an inflatable toy frog—the crap you buy at a candy store.

I brought a book on the Louvre, a book on Van Gogh, and a book on Marilyn Monroe. Woody unwrapped them in front of me and went, "Oh, great, you're finally returning the books I lent you." Sad thing is, he probably wasn't joking. He had no clue what came in or out of that house and had no clue what books he already possessed or didn't possess.

The party was a lot of fun and turned into a jam session by the end of the night. At first, Woody was floating between floors, mingling. In the upstairs living room, you had the literary/art crowd: Warhol, Jerzy Kosinski, and Peter Max. In the downstairs kitchen, you had the music crowd: Paul Shaffer, Don Covay, and Foreigner's Mick Jones. And in the backyard, you had Matt Dillon and Michael J. Fox.

Around midnight, Paul Shaffer began playing the piano in the kitchen. Mick Jones grabbed a guitar. Don Covay was singing Fats Domino covers. Woody rushed to the scene, Telecaster in hand. And that's when Michael J. Fox came in, saw Mick Jones, and cried, "You and Bob Seger are my favorite musicians of all time! I can't believe I'm meeting you!"

Now that the calendar had hit June, it was crunch time. Eight weeks to go before Woody moved out of New York. His schedule was packed with extracurricular activities. During June and July alone, he flew to Detroit to play with Aretha Franklin, Memphis to play with Carl Perkins, New Orleans to play with Fats Domino, and London to play with Rod Stewart. Not to mention jams in New York with Bob Dylan and Chuck Berry.

Compounding the deadline pressure was Woody's missing artwork. The publishers sent a photographer to his house to shoot everything for the book, but it did not match my manuscript. I'd written stories about Otis Redding, Billie Holiday, Jimmy Page, Bob Marley, Dan Aykroyd, and Whoopi Goldberg, but there were no portraits to support them. No Keith Moon, either. Woody told the publishers he never did them.

"Never did 'em?" I exclaimed. "Oh, no, he *did* 'em, alright. The whole reason I *asked* him about those people is because he *showed* me the portraits *first.*"

"Well," said the publishers, "Woody's insisting they don't exist. So that's what we have to go on."

I felt like Mrs. Kravitz on *Bewitched.* She *knows* she saw Samantha wiggle her nose and make the couch fly, but nobody believes her. I ran to the *Beggars Banquet* photo archive (located under my bed) and dug up some proof. It was a shot of Woody in his basement, standing next to his Keith Moon and Bob Marley. I messengered it to the publishers.

"Well," they surmised, "maybe he traded his artwork for drugs."

It was a horrible thought, yet plausible. I mean, the man did have an expensive habit. He rarely had dealers to the house anymore, but was still using. During many of our interviews, he'd have a huge rock in front of him. He'd put it into a grinder thingy and make it come out powdery. Then he'd either snort it or put it into his cigarette. On some of our audiotapes, you can hear him grinding, sniffing, and puffing.

You can also hear the clanking of ice cubes in our glasses. On the Jack & Ginger front, I confess he had a companion in me. I knew it'd make him nervous and less talkative if I sat there like a teetotaler, so, if *he* got drunk, *I* got drunk. There were mornings I reached the point of slurred speech. Like the time I asked him about Hank Greenberg.

"Alrrrrright, Woody, tell me about how D-D-Dylan turrrrned you onto Hank Greenberg."

He looked at me like, "Wha? Who?"

"Hank Greenberrrrrg. You told me Dylan played you, he played for you, some Hank Greeeenberg stuff."

"I don't have a *clue* what you're talking about."

"Hank Greenberg, Woody! You did a f-f-frickin' drawing of him!"

Of course, I meant to ask him about Hank *Williams* and not the Jewish first baseman for the 1938 Detroit Tigers. To think that, even for a night, I was drunker than Ron Wood, is, well, a sobering thought. As a matter of fact, the closer I got to Woody, the more concerned I grew for him. I wished I could help straighten him out somehow, to get him to slow down on the white stuff, but I knew I was out of my league. I was a 23-year-old *putz* from Brooklyn, so who was I to lecture a rich and famous rock star?

Instead, I sent him hints through my writing. In the chapter about his kids, I concocted a quote about how he was going to clean himself up for them. "Kids have been a real stabilizing influence," I wrote. "You have to set a good example for them. . . . When I see little Leah putting things in her lunchbox to bring to school—Twinkie, little tiny sandwich, little tiny apple—it just puts things in perspective. Lets you see what really counts."

I completely fabricated that paragraph, the prerogative of any co-author, but my hope was that he'd read it, *think* he said it, and try to live up to it. To stay clean for his kids.

On the whole, Woody had no qualms with anything I wrote. The only bits he made me take out pertained to Duane Allman and Janis Joplin.

Woody met Duane Allman without knowing it. He was backstage before a Faces concert when someone opened the door. Woody was a big fan of Duane's—still considers him his biggest influence on slide guitar—but had no clue what Duane looked like. So when the guy said, "Hey, you got anything to drink?" Woody thought he was a stalker and yelled, "Fuck off! Find your own!" By the time Woody discovered it was Duane Allman, it was too late to apologize. A few weeks after the incident, Duane was nearly decapitated in a fatal motorcycle accident. (His head got bashed, and his helmet went flying.)

Woody was okay with me recounting the story, but he didn't like my punch line: "I'm real sorry I lost my head with Duane Allman because two weeks later he lost *his* head." It's something Woody *could* have said, but he didn't. I was fairly proud of that line, but Woody insisted I cut it.

As for Janis, Woody had no problem revealing to our readers that he'd re-buffed her advances. "She used to drink Southern Comfort non-stop and had a complexion like a boy in puberty. She was what you call a double-bagger." Woody came up with those lines, not me, but when he saw it in print, he pulled back. "The 'boy in puberty' line can stay, but take out the 'double-bagger' part. That's cruel."

"Hey," I told him, "it's not like *we* voted her the ugliest man on campus!"

In mid-July, after seven months of work, it was time to negotiate my con-tract. In typical Stones fashion, no one had paid me a cent, and I still did not possess a written agreement. A meeting was arranged between me, Woody's manager, Woody's literary agent, and a rep from the publishing house.

The meeting was set for 6 PM in Woody's living room. I showed up early, and Woody answered the door. He'd just rolled out of bed and seemed out of sorts. "I'm worried about Jerry Garcia," he told me.

Jerry Garcia? I had no idea he knew Jerry Garcia.

Turns out, he didn't. But he was maintaining a vigil nonetheless. Jerry had lapsed into a diabetic coma that week, and Bob Dylan was keeping him up-dated.

Woody's other concern that day was his financial standing with the Stones. Since joining the band in 1975, he'd been a salaried employee and not an equal partner. He also wasn't getting proper credit for some of the songs he'd co-written. His manager told him to take a stand and to demand a fair share of all future record sales and concert receipts. Keith endorsed the move and suggested Woody's take be retroactive to the Seventies, a notion that made Mick's veins pop out.

It was a big step for Woody because he was so used to being a second-class citizen. He was nervous about having to assert himself. He showed me his manager's proposal and asked my opinion. It was written in legalese, so all I could say was "Woody, you deserve what you deserve." I had my own damned contract to worry about.

By 6:15, all parties were present and accounted for. Jo sat in on the talks, but Woody disappeared. He had to get a Garcia update from Dylan. The first subject of discussion was my byline. Woody's manager, who was usually nice to me, said he didn't want my name on the cover.

He was probably using it as a bargaining chip, but I made it clear that not having my name on the cover was unacceptable and non-negotiable. In a move that surprises me to this day, I slapped my hands on my knees and said, "Okay, then I guess there's no book."

I'd remembered what Keith taught me two years earlier, during that fan club mess. That after putting in so much work without a contract, it was I who held the cards. I'm the one who came to Woody's house and put up with his ADD. I'm the one who asked the questions, taped the answers, and made sense of it all. Who else could they find to tolerate his overnight hours and his disappearing acts—especially this close to the deadline? All the tapes and transcriptions were in my possession, case closed.

They looked at me in astonishment.

"I'm *serious*," I said. "That credit is very important to me. If my name's not on the front cover of the book, there *is* no book. Does anyone have a problem with that? Woody, do you have a problem with that?"

Woody had not been in the room the entire time, but amazingly, at that very moment, he popped in to get a cigarette. "Wazzat?" he asked.

"I said, Woody, do *you* have a problem with my name being on the book?"

"Of course not," he declared. "It's *got* to be there." And with that, he lit his cigarette, turned back around, and left the room. His timing was impeccable.

"Well, then," I announced. "*That's* settled. What else is on the agenda?"

Next they asked me how I wanted it to read. "Ron Wood *and* Bill German" or "Ron Wood *with* Bill German." Or perhaps even "Ron Wood, *as told to* Bill German." I went with "with."

Then we discussed the book's title. Woody had already nominated *The Works,* but I hated it. My suggestion was *Every Picture Tells a Story.* Not only is that phrase familiar to Woody's fans—he co-wrote the hit song of that name— it completely describes the purpose of the book: Every picture tells a story. But Woody feared the wrath of Rod. He hated making waves and was afraid that Rod, who shares the song's writing credit, might think he was co-opting it. So *The Works* it was.

Eventually, our conversation turned to money. My contract was going to be with Woody, not the publishers, and my money would come from the $100,000 he'd already been paid. His manager handled the negotiations, and I doubt Woody was ever informed. I settled for $18,000 flat, no royalties. I don't possess any copyrights, I'm just the schnook they hired for a one-time fee. But hell, I'd have paid *them* for this gig, and I'm sure Woody's manager knew that.

Whatever the case, it was a relief to square things before Woody's exodus on July 30. I visited him right before he left for the airport. We sat in his back-yard, puffing on cigars that Keith brought over. I'm not a smoker, but Woody said, "Light up for a job well done," so I went for it.

Unfortunately, as Woody flew across the Atlantic, his artwork was still AWOL. Woody's roadie packed the house and didn't recall seeing Whoopi Goldberg, Dan Aykroyd, or Jimmy Page. Ditto, Otis Redding and Keith Moon. The hope was that they'd turn up when the crates got unpacked in England, but it wasn't to be.

Woody got $1.1 million for his house (he was asking $1.9), and when the new family took over, their contractors set up a huge Dumpster out front. A *Village Voice* reporter who lived on the block—78th between West End and Riverside—wrote an article titled "Garbageology Update, Rolling Stones Division." It told how she and her neighbors had been Dumpster diving in front of the Woods' old home. It featured descriptions and photos of her loot: "Good sketch of Johnny Winter, beside the lettering, 'Johnny Winter is a veritable sissy' "; "Likeness of Wood rowing a speedboat called 'Adrift,' about to go over the falls"; "Intricate pen cartoon of a 'trodden upon type of person.' " About a dozen items in all.

A doorman on the block told her she came too late. Her neighbors got the good stuff. When I read it, I didn't know whether to laugh or cry. Could it be that someone dug up the Billie Holiday and Otis Redding? What about Jimmy Page and Keith Moon? Bob Marley, anyone? Lord knows what Woody left behind and what was now being retrieved by the bums, yuppies, and yentas of the Upper West Side.

Maybe someone found *me*. I didn't mention this earlier, but Woody did a real nice sketch of his co-author. We were in the middle of a conversation, and I had no idea what he was working on. But then he turned his pad around and said, "Look what I just did."

"Wow," I told him. "That's great."

"Let me hold on to it," he suggested, "so that when the photographer comes, he'll shoot it, and we can put it on the back of the book."

Fantastic idea, but it was the last time I saw it. I imagine some garbageologist on 78th Street dug it out of the Dumpster, crumpled it up, and went, "Who the fuck was *that* guy?"

Keith poses with the fuzz, outside Panavideo Studio
on 38th Street.

Earlier, Paul Shaffer got Keith to autograph an issue
of *Beggars Banquet*.

14

the sunshine
boys

When the cops got out of their squad car and approached me and Keith on 38th Street, we had no idea what the problem was. I elbowed Keith in the ribs and muttered: "They're finally comin' to get ya." He pretended to strangle me and told the cops, "I'm innocent!"

They said they got a call about the noise. Keith and I were part of a larger group, chatting on the sidewalk, and were apparently too loud for people trying to sleep. It was well past midnight. The two officers told us to quiet down, but, when they realized Keith Richards was one of the noisemakers, they asked for his autograph.

I got the three of them to pose for *Beggars Banquet*. One of those man-bites-dog situations. Nowadays, you wouldn't think twice about the Stones posing with the fuzz. But in June 1986, it signified the changing of the guard. The last time Keith Richards had been photographed with cops, he wasn't smiling. But in the Reagan era, the times they were a-changin'. The rock 'n' roll demographic that made up the counterculture was slowly *becoming* the culture. *We* were now the cops.

"In the old days," Keith observed, "those guys would've been lookin' to bust me. But now they're lookin' to shake my hand and get my autograph. Their fathers on the force probably *did* bust me."

In 1986, things weren't just changing *around* the Stones, but *in* them. Mick distanced himself from the band and left the task of promoting *Dirty Work* to Keith. That's why we were on 38th Street in the first place. Keith had just taped a segment for NBC's *Friday Night Videos*. When the previous Stones album came out in 1983, Mick and Keith *both* appeared on the program, but this time only Keith. He was interviewed by Paul Shaffer and sang the album's closing number, "Sleep Tonight." Keith forgot the lyrics, but my ever-present briefcase came to his rescue. I'd packed a copy of *Dirty Work* because I needed him to autograph it for a contest. The album's innersleeve contains the lyrics, so I lent it to Keith as a cheat sheet.

After the taping, Keith and I headed to the street with Paul, Jane Rose, and some of the show's staffers. That's when the cops showed up. It's also when Keith told me about his upcoming project with Chuck Berry.

Keith's first choice in '86 was to tour with the Stones. When we were in London back in February, he was very optimistic. The five Stones played at Stu's memorial and set aside their animosities. But as soon as we got back to New York, everything fell apart. In March, Mick sent a telegram to the other Stones, saying he wasn't going to work with them.

Keith knew that the band's fans were counting on a *Dirty Work* tour, so he went on network TV in April to explain the situation. "I've only got two hands," he said on NBC's *Today* show. "I need both to play a guitar. So I can't put a gun to his head. You can't force someone to go onstage if they don't want to. I still don't know why [Mick doesn't want to tour with us]. I thought it would be a smart thing to do. It's been five years since we played here. But there you go, folks. It weren't my fault." Anyone watching at home could sense his exasperation.

It was during this time that the Mick-vs.-Keith thing played out in the press. Rather than plugging *Dirty Work,* Mick was saying, "I have other interests than just the Rolling Stones." He chose lame projects like the *Ruthless People* soundtrack over touring with the Stones, which Keith found hard to swallow. A front-page headline in the London *Sun* read, "Mick's Feud with Stone Keith: 'We could finish trading punches.' "

Against this backdrop, the Stones were obligated to reunite for a day on May 1. A video shoot in London for their new single, "One Hit to the Body." I didn't fly over—witnessing the "Harlem Shuffle" shoot was stressful enough for me—but I got a full report from Woody. He told me that Mick and Keith staged a mock brawl during the song's guitar break. He also told me how he himself nearly killed Mick. He was running full steam down a ramp when— KLUNG!—the neck of his guitar went smack into Mick's skull. He swore to me it was an accident and said, "Good thing it was an acoustic guitar. 'Cause if it was a solid body, we'd have had to peel Mick's head off the floor."

Accident or not, the blow to Mick's cranium did nothing to change his mind. He still wasn't touring with the Stones. And Keith was annoyed that Bill and Charlie refused to get involved. Keith believed there was strength in numbers. That if they applied enough pressure to Mick, they could persuade him to go on the road. But Charlie was fighting his own demons, and Bill was giving Mick a pass.

"Physically," Bill said, "the hardest working person [on a Stones tour] is Mick. He has to tune himself up to run for two-and-a-half hours. I know *I* couldn't do that. And he's the one who'd get shit in the press. 'He didn't dance well, he's looking older, a parody.' Eighty percent of every article is about *him*. The other twenty is Keith, maybe Woody. I get mentioned maybe once if I'm lucky—or *unlucky*, depending on what they say. So Mick's got a lot to answer to. I can sympathize with him."

Bill gave me that quote for *Beggars Banquet*. And when I showed it to Keith, he was like, "Screw that. I got no sympathy. If Mick doesn't want to tour with us for physical reasons, no problem. We don't need the ramps and big stage this time. Mick Jagger is the best goddamned front man there is. He can get the job done if he stood on a milk crate."

Losing the Stones hit Keith hard. With no tour to look forward to, he seemed lost for a while. He'd pass the time aimlessly at Woody's house, listening to Billy Connolly tapes, playing Buddy Holly tunes, and farting around.

So when the chance came to work with his idol, Chuck Berry, he jumped. On June 11, as we stood on 38th Street, he was telling me how he'd just spent several days in Chicago with Chuck. They jammed at Checkerboard Lounge and Grant Park, while planning their film project. Keith felt like he'd finally bonded with his idol, and I could tell it lifted his spirits.

The film would document Chuck's career. It'd culminate with a concert in St. Louis on Chuck's 60th birthday in October. It was going to be titled *Hail! Hail! Rock 'n' Roll* and feature Keith as a second guitarist and music director. Keith had always felt he owed a debt to Chuck—"I lifted every lick he ever played"—so this was his way of paying it back.

Between June and October, Keith's task was to assemble Chuck's backup band and to line up guests like Eric Clapton and Julian Lennon. After spending the first half of 1986 in a daze, Keith finally had a purpose. His top priority was to recruit Chuck's original pianist from the Fifties. Johnnie Johnson wasn't on speaking terms with Chuck and wasn't easy to find. He was driving a bus to make ends meet and living in obscurity. Keith tracked him down at a fishing hole and begged him to come on board. Whatever he said, it worked.

Over the summer, Keith visited Chuck's house in Wentzville, a suburb of St. Louis. Chuck drove Keith around in his Winnebego and introduced Keith to his father. "A weird kind of honor" is how Keith described it to me. "Sweet old guy, 91 years old, sittin' there watchin' *The Flintstones* and eatin' his grits. Chuck goes, 'Dad, this is Keith Richards from the Rolling Stones. Been together longer than anybody else ever.' The old boy looks at me and goes, 'You're lookin' pretty good!' And I said, 'Thanks very much, reverend.' "

It didn't take long, however, for Keith to realize that Chuck was as schizo as Mick. "One minute he could be the most charming, amusing, and interesting guy. And [the next minute] he'll just cut you off.... These incredible changes in mood. Everyone would look around the room, asking, 'Did *I* say something? Did *you* say something?' Because the guy would go *poop* . . . disappear physically or, sometimes, he'd be there, but nobody home. An incredible ability to tune you out."

Keith's relationship with Chuck was never a rosy one. In 1972, Chuck threw him off the stage at the Hollywood Palladium. In 1981, Chuck gave him a shiner. And in 1983, Chuck set his clothes on fire.

Keith told me it happened at LAX: "I fly [in] and who do I see sittin' on his suitcase . . . but Chuck Berry, who I haven't seen since he blacked out my eye at the Ritz. . . . We're talkin' while he's waitin' for his car, and he gives me his number. At the same time, he lights a cigarette and drops it down my shirt and almost burns my stomach open. My shirt's on fire! Every time him and me get in contact, whether it's intentional or not, I end up wounded."

Needless to say, I wasn't going to miss this thing in St. Louis. If Chuck ended up killing Keith—or vice versa—I could say I was there. And if they *didn't* kill each other, I'd get to see a fantastic show.

I was a huge fan of Chuck's, thanks to the Stones. I remember being ten years old, holding *Get Yer Ya-Ya's Out* for the first time. I couldn't understand why, next to the songs "Carol" and "Little Queenie," it said "Berry" in parentheses.

By reading interviews with Mick and Keith, I discovered that Chuck was one of their biggest influences. So were the names-in-parentheses on *other* Stones albums, like Ellas McDaniel and McKinley Morganfield—aka Bo Diddley and Muddy Waters. The Stones led me down an investigative path that rewarded me with Chuck, Bo, Muddy, Buddy, Otis, Jerry Lee, and the Wolf. Kids sadly don't have that today. I don't think Britney Spears and Avril Lavigne have ever encouraged their fans to check out Aretha or Janis.

Of course, having Keith and Woody on hand provided me with an additional advantage. I kept my ears open and wasn't scared to ask stupid questions: "Keith, who originally did that song you just jammed on?" "Woody, why do you keep calling me Big Bill Broonzy?"

One day, I visited Keith's new condo on East 4th Street, above the Tower Records store. I bought some Otis Redding and Buddy Holly LPs before heading upstairs to seek his opinion. "The Buddy could do with 'Learnin' the Game,' " he said, "and the Otis needs 'Dreams to Remember.' " I told him he should rent himself out as a guru. He could sit atop Tower Records like the Delphic Oracle, offering advice to potential customers. Or wear a button that says, "I'm Keith. Ask me about Muddy."

I got into St. Louis the day before the concert and headed straight to the rehearsals at the Fox Theatre. As a kid in the 1930s, Chuck tried to see movies at the Fox, but they didn't sell tickets to Negroes. Now, he was there to be feted.

I entered through the backstage door and felt someone grab my shoulder. It was Keith, and he looked frazzled. As a joke, I put my hands on his face and pretended to examine him. "No black eyes yet," I said. "You and Chuck must be getting along swimmingly."

"Oh, yeah?" he snapped. "Just hope I don't give him a *white* eye!"

That was my first clue that things weren't going well. Keith walked out to the stage and tried to get the rehearsal going. He kicked into "Maybellene," but when the cue arrived for Chuck to sing, nothing came out. Chuck was playing the riff on guitar, but he wasn't singing. Keith waved off the band and stopped the song.

He started it again, but again Chuck didn't sing. When Keith was expecting to hear "Maybellene, why can't you be true," he instead got silence. Chuck kept playing his guitar, ignoring the situation, until Keith stopped the song. He stared at Chuck for an eternity, daggers shooting from his eyes. Chuck acknowledged Keith's agitation and slithered to the mic. "I *will not* sing the night before a show. I gotta save my voice for *tomorrow.* Keith, you gotta let me do it *my way.*"

Keith shook his head in disgust and started the song again. This time, Chuck played the lyric line on guitar. Keith rolled with it for twenty seconds or so, before waving it off again. "Chuck, man, you *gotta* sing. Just *once.* Or else, what the fuck are we *here* for?"

Long pause. Keith slowly clasped his hands and began to beg. "*Please,* Chuck. Can you sing for us *just once?*" He kissed Chuck on the cheek. He then launched into "Sweet Little Sixteen" and Chuck sort of capitulated. He still wasn't singing, but he was whispering. Keith knew it was the best he'd get from him, so that's how it went for the next two hours. As Keith told me later, "I swallowed a lot of things I could've said because I knew it wouldn't be productive."

I told Keith that it reminded me of the film *The Sunshine Boys*. Walter Matthau and George Burns play two vaudevillians who are asked to unite for one last show. One codger is more stubborn than the other and it's a contest of who's gonna strangle who first. Miraculously, they pull it together come showtime. I told Keith that I wished the same for him and Chuck.

October 16, 1986. The joint was rockin' and the place was packed. To everyone's relief, Chuck behaved for the cameras. The band opened with "Maybellene" and, this time, Chuck actually sang.

But the concert turned out not to be a concert. The filmmakers kept stopping the show to reset the camera angles. Chuck and Keith would get into a groove, but then they'd get a stop sign—an actual red card, held by the director—and everything would grind to a halt. "I feel like a bull," Chuck said of the card.

Some of the pauses were excruciatingly long. Chuck would recite indecipherable poetry, and Keith would nervously pace the stage and chain-smoke. The capacity crowd, some 4,500 people, grew restless. It was like a Broadway show with twenty intermissions.

At one point, a local DJ got onstage to read telegrams from President Reagan and Mick Jagger. (Mick was big on telegrams that year.) The president called Chuck an American icon, and Mick apologized for not being there. The audience wasn't impressed.

By the end of the so-called concert, everyone walked out disappointed. The whole thing felt like a chore. But the filmmakers gave themselves a second chance by scheduling a separate show for the same night. I had extra tickets for the late show and hoped to give them away. I ventured outside the Fox Theatre, but couldn't find takers. "You couldn't give us those tickets if you *paid* us!" I was told. "We were at the early show, and it sucked!"

The second show ran more like a concert, and it cooked. I feel bad for the people who skipped it. By night's end, Keith felt drained, but knew he'd gone a long way toward squaring his debt to Chuck. "I just paid off a lump sum," he told me. "But then there's always the interest!"

In many ways, Keith viewed the Chuck Berry project as an extension of the Stones, not a departure. But it did prepare him to work with people not named Mick or Woody.

In early December, Keth and I were at the Ritz in New York, watching the Charlie Watts Orchestra. Charlie had gotten his life together and had moved on without the Stones. He was touring with a 33-piece jazz band. Keith spotted me and literally table-hopped through the crowd to get to me. "Excuse me, pardon me, excuse me, pardon me." He climbed over a railing and plopped down in the seat next to me.

With "Caldonia" playing in the background, Keith told me how record companies were courting him that week. Atlantic, Virgin, PolyGram, and Arista all wanted him to sign a solo deal. "They're wining and dining me at the Russian Tea Room tomorrow."

It was never Keith's idea to do a solo album. He entertained the notion only after accepting reality. During the course of 1986, I saw him go through all five stages of grief over losing the Stones: denial, anger, bargaining, depression, *acceptance*. The Rolling Stones were dead, and there was nothing he could do about it.

No one would've blamed me if I'd folded *Beggars Banquet* at this point, but I was already in too deep. I resolved to follow each person's solo career and wait for a reunion. Maybe *I* was the one in denial.

"Leave me alone! I'm stayin' up with Colonel Kentucky!"
Woody's first-ever exhibition in England.

15

over the river
and to the woods

Jane Rose's new strategy was to de-Woodify Keith. She was Keith's de facto manager and felt Keith needed to make a clean break to be taken seriously as a solo commodity. As hard as it was for Keith, he didn't invite Woody to the *Hail! Hail!* concert in St. Louis or to play a single lick on his solo album. In the past, that would've been unthinkable.

I knew something was up when, in July '86, Keith and Woody flew to Detroit to play on Aretha Franklin's cover of "Jumpin' Jack Flash." Jane told me, "You better not print pictures of Woody with Aretha. This was *Keith's* project. Woody tagged along and invited him*self*. He *thinks* he's on the record, but he's not. We mixed him down."

For Woody, it was a blessing in disguise. He moved to Wimbledon, England, honed his painting skills, and became his own man. I visited him there in October 1987. He was hosting an art exhibition in London that was affiliated with the release of our book. I told him I'd stay at the YMCA again, but he wouldn't hear of it. "You're staying with me and Jo! We've got a spare bedroom upstairs."

I got in the day before the exhibition. The Woods' tree-lined street was the picture of serenity. On this crisp autumn morning, the only thing I could hear were birds chirping and the crackle of fallen leaves under my feet. It was the perfect location for Woody. Close enough to central London, but far enough from the 3 AM distractions he'd had in New York. A much healthier atmosphere.

I rang the bell, and Jo quickly swung the door open. She barely said hello and seemed scattered. She scurried through the house, gathering up the kids. "We're off shopping," she said. "We'll be gone two hours. Ronnie won't be home 'til dinner, but you can listen to him on radio in the living room." With that, she and the kids dashed out the door, leaving me alone in a five-story Victorian mansion.

I didn't know where anything was, and I'm not the type to snoop around, so I confined myself to the living room. I planted myself on the sofa, intending to sleep off my jet lag. But dozing wasn't easy with Woody talking about me on the radio. The DJ asked Woody about *The Works,* and my name came up.

When Woody's interview was finished, I turned off the radio. Next to the receiver, I noticed several homemade cassettes, each with an intriguing handwritten label: "Me and Womack," "Me and Johnny Marr," "Me and Keith." If I were a different kind of person, I could have had a field day—attached to Woody's radio was a dual cassette deck—but I suppose that's the point. If I were a different kind of person, I wouldn't have been there in the first place. To me, those tapes were Woody's private stuff, case closed.

I finally nodded off on the sofa before the doorbell rang. Jo hadn't told me to expect anyone, so I didn't answer it. But the dog began barking like a lunatic. I didn't know the Woods *had* a dog until it came running downstairs, growling its head off.

The person kept ringing for several minutes, but I kept ignoring it. I mean, how did I know some criminal wasn't casing the joint, waiting for an unsuspecting houseguest to open the door? If I believed someone's spiel and let them in, I could've been tied to a chair as they loaded up the silverware.

An hour or so later, Jo burst through the door with the kids. Tailing them was Jo's friend Julie. "Why didn't you open the door?" Jo yelled. "Julie's been out there for hours!" Jo claimed she'd told me to expect her, but I swear to you she hadn't.

Julie was the wife of Woody's manager, Nick. She was a beautiful blonde who came from a prestigious family, and I don't think she was accustomed to doors not opening for her. Julie forgave me, but Jo made me feel like shit.

At dusk, Woody walked through the door and gave me a big hug. "Great to see ya, mate!" I was hoping to spend time with him—hadn't seen him in over a year—but he said he had to go back out. "Me and Jo have a charity banquet with Princess Di." He asked if I'd seen the final version of our book, and I told him no. He handed me a copy before he left for the night.

On almost every page, there was something that upset me. Some of my words had been altered, and you needed a magnifying glass to read my name on the cover. But the gut-wrenching part was the missing illustrations. No Otis Redding, no Eric Clapton, no Bob Marley, to name a few. The stories about them appeared anyway and, in the case of Otis, a page was awkwardly left three-quarters blank where the portrait should have been. The Keith Moon never surfaced and, for some inexplicable reason, a drawing of Bobby Keys was in its place.

To prevent such mistakes, I'd put a ton of notes in the margins of my manuscript. I knew Woody's artwork better than anyone, including Woody himself, so I knew where everything was supposed to go. But they listened to me only a handful of times, and, as a result, the *Mustard Painting* appears on page 43, while its description appears on page 38. I took the book to bed and cried myself to sleep with it.

In the morning, Woody knocked on my door and woke me up. "Big Bill Broonzy! Grab your cocks and put on your socks! Breakfast in the dining room!" The whole Wood clan was assembled, including Herman the dog. Jo prepared bubble and squeak, a common British breakfast.

I wasn't sure if I should discuss our book at the breakfast table, but I couldn't resist. "Um, hey, Woody, do you know what happened to the portraits of Otis, Keith Moon, and Jimmy Page?" He simply replied, "Dunno," so I dropped it. But it drove me nuts that it didn't drive him nuts.

Woody's exhibition was sponsored by Christie's Contemporary Art, but took place at the Katharine Hamnett clothing store on Brompton Road. Racks of designer dresses were pushed aside to make room for his work. I hitched a ride with Jo's brothers.

Upon arrival, we were besieged by fans and paparazzi. I had the surprise of my life when some girl broke from the crowd, ran up to me, and kissed me. I was so stunned, I kept walking like nothing happened. I was dressed in my pointy Beatle boots, a black velvet jacket, and a western-style tie I bought at Trash and Vaudeville in New York. As soon as Woody noticed the tie, he teased me relentlessly. "Look! Colonel Kentucky is at my exhibit!" It became my new nickname.

The turnout was great. Our book got lots of publicity, and Woody sold a bunch of his stuff. Guests included Jeff Beck, Dave Edmunds, Bob Geldof, Bill Wyman, and Chris Jagger. Chris's brother, Mick, was in town, but said he couldn't make it. He sent a telegram that read, "Break a leg, Leonardo!"

The next day, things were quiet at the Woods' house. But at night, they held a backyard barbecue to celebrate both Jesse Wood's 11th birthday and Halloween. It was also a bon voyage party, because Woody, Jo, and I were flying to Florida in the morning. Woody threw some hamburgers on the grill, and Jo brought out the potato salad. Woody hopped into the empty swimming pool to light some bottle rockets. The kids, who were dressed as witches and goblins, were thrilled. They were completely enamored of their daddy.

After the party, Jo put the kids to bed, and I helped Woody clean up. He suggested we pull an all-nighter. We had a 9 AM flight, but our car was coming at 7. Jo yelled to Woody from upstairs, insisting he get some sleep, but he snapped, "Leave me alone! I'm stayin' up with Colonel Kentucky!"

"Ronnie," she argued, "you're going to need some sleep!" But he yelled back, "Leave me alone! I'll sleep on the plane!" She slammed the bedroom door.

Woody and I listened to Bo Diddley tapes overnight and even watched a World Series game (tape-delayed by a week). I tried teaching him the rules of baseball, but he kept making jokes. When the announcer said, "Two balls on Ozzie Smith," he replied, "I certainly *hope* so!" When the game was over, he popped in a Pretenders video. "I found out recently," he said, "that I shagged Chrissie Hynde."

I'd never heard the word "shagged" before, but I could figure out what it meant. The part about Chrissie Hynde is what confused me. "She and her friend came to see the Faces," he explained, "and after the show, they came back to the hotel. Her friend went to Rod's room, and *she* came to *my* room. She just told me a few weeks ago." I thought it was cool to have bedded Chrissie Hynde and not remember it.

Before we knew it, the sun was up, and we were on our way to Gatwick Airport. Our Virgin Airlines flight was headed to Miami, to preview Woody's latest venture. A nightclub/restaurant/cabana called Woody's on the Beach. For Woody and Jo, it was the first stop of a six-week tour of art exhibitions, book signings, and concerts with Bo Diddley.

The Bo idea sprung from a concert Woody did a year earlier, when he was still living in New York—a co-bill with Chuck Berry at the Ritz, before Keith monopolized Chuck for *Hail! Hail!* Woody did his own set before backing up Chuck, and he killed. He sang "Ooh La La," "Love in Vain," and "I Can Feel the Fire," and the place went nuts for him. It sounds corny, but I felt my pal had a breakthrough that night. Backstage after the show, I said, "Woody, you can *do* this. You can do shows on your own."

But he still preferred the second-banana role. So in 1987, his management teamed him up with Bo Diddley for a concert tour of U.S. nightclubs. They arranged it so that everything coincided. In some cities, Woody would do a book signing during the day and then an art exhibition or Bo concert at night.

When we got to Gatwick Airport, we headed to the first-class lounge. Woody and Jo had first-class tickets, but I was paying my own way and traveling coach, so I wasn't allowed in. Woody put up a stink, and they made an exception for me. On the plane itself, Woody stuck his head through the first-class curtain and waved me in. I knelt beside his seat for twenty minutes, until a stewardess said I didn't belong there.

At Miami customs, an officer searched Woody's guitar case and jokingly gave him a hard time. "So you're a musician, huh? What band are you in?" He totally knew who Woody was. "Those guys used to tear us apart," Woody told me. "But now they're so nice to me, they sometimes forget to stamp my passport. They're too busy asking me if the Stones are gonna tour."

Woody's on the Beach was located on Ocean Drive and 4th Street in Miami's South Beach district. Today, it's one of the hippest addresses and hottest pieces of real estate in America. But in 1987, the area was depressed. Beset with crime, racial tension, and urban blight. As our limo hit Ocean Drive, we spotted nursing homes and small shanties selling pork sandwiches. When we pulled up to our hotel, at Ocean and 13th, two kids approached: "You got any money? You *look* like you got money."

At our hotel, we were the only guests. No one was staying on the strip back then, and most of the hotels were boarded up after thirty years of neglect. It took forward-thinking investors to revive the area to its Deco-era glory. They were counting on Woody's club to play a major role in that. The city was so optimistic, they resanded the beach and the mayor turned up for a groundbreaking ceremony. He and Woody posed with gold shovels, and he gave Woody the key to the city.

"What does it open?" Woody asked.

"My office!" said Mayor Daoud. "You can use it anytime!"

I featured a photo of Woody on the next cover of *Beggars Banquet,* with the headline "Woody Does It All!" In the span of several weeks, he'd established himself as an artist, an author, and now a nightclub owner. Keith wasn't as proud of Woody as I was. He couldn't understand why a member of the Rolling Stones would get into the "cabana business." But Keith didn't need the ancillary income the way Woody did.

From Florida, it was up to New York. After dropping off my luggage, I rendezvoused with Woody at Top Cat Studio on 28th Street. There, he and Bo rehearsed for their tour. I was honored when Woody introduced us. Bo, who was sporting his trademark black Stetson and thick-rimmed glasses, said, "Pleased to meet you, young man." He then pulled out a card from his pocket and handed it to me. It read: "Kids, don't do it. Stay drug free."

The tour took Bo and Woody to big cities and small towns—from Chicago to Poughkeepsie. They traveled on the cheap, often by car or train, the way Bo'd been doin' it for decades.

Bo was magical. Pushing 60, he was still performing leg kicks onstage and would sometimes switch places with his drummer, midconcert. Woody's role was to back up Bo, but he also shined on his own. He'd lead the band through "Honky Tonk Women" and numbers from his solo albums. Bo would say, "Ladies and gentlemen, Brother Ronnie Woods of the Rolling Stones!" and Woody would answer, "Mr. Bo Diddley of *himself!*"

I flew at my own expense to Woody's signings and exhibitions in California. In Los Angeles, the line at Book Soup curled around Sunset Boulevard. Similar situation at Books, Inc., in San Francisco. At each location, there were twenty or so people who said, "Hey, aren't you Bill German? You gotta autograph my book, too!"

As if that weren't enough, Woody was mentioning me in his interviews. "Bill German's got a nice turn of phrase," he'd say. I heard my name on radio shows like *Larry King* and *Rockline* and saw my name in the *Chicago Tribune, Dallas Morning News, Philadelphia Inquirer, Los Angeles Herald-Examiner, New York Post,* and even *Playboy.* My picture appeared in the *Oakland Tribune,* and excerpts of our book appeared in *Star* magazine. It made me feel great.

Woody's exhibitions were also a treat. At the gallery in San Francisco, known as the Art Exchange, I got to chat with Bill Graham. Woody's portrait of Graham appeared in our book, but, when the impresario saw it in person, he wasn't flattered. A reporter asked him if he liked it, and he replied, "Well, let's just say I like *Ron Wood.*"

I have to admit, Woody's celebrity portraits were hit-or-miss back then. The one of Bowie in our book looks more like Geraldine Ferraro, but the one he did of Belushi is stellar. To me, Woody works best when he doesn't use photo references and instead reaches into that wonderfully warped mind of his to create completely original images. Like the one called *Bird of Death Flying over New York with a Hamburger,* which sadly didn't appear in our book.

But celebrity sells. And that's why, for these '87 exhibitions, Woody did portraits of people like Madonna. At the San Francisco exhibition, the first piece that sold was a portrait of Clapton. It went to a Rabbi Earl Kaplan of Temple Beth Israel in Pomona, who said he "wouldn't hesitate to hang it at the temple."

On November 25, the Wednesday before Thanksgiving, Woody was back in New York to appear on Letterman. We arranged to meet at NBC. He brought a huge entourage. Not just Jo, Nick, and Julie, but a slew of people I'd never met before: two publicists, two secretaries, and a temporary co-manager named Phil. Woody's dressing room was like the stateroom scene in *A Night at the Opera.*

Outside, a pit bull was using the hallway as a bowling alley. Practicing for Stupid Pet Tricks. A producer from the show came to pre-interview Woody, but my co-author couldn't recall a single anecdote from our book. "Tell the one about Groucho," I suggested. "Or how you tried to meet Elvis when he was in the hospital."

Unfortunately, everyone in Woody's entourage frowned at me like I was speaking out of turn. They made me feel like I was a nuisance and in the way. I realize that ghostwriters don't normally go on book tours, but I honestly felt I could help.

Woody sat in with Paul Shaffer's band before an eight-minute interview with Dave. Everyone on Team Woody watched from the green room. Woody seemed stiff in the chair. He told Dave about meeting Groucho, but forgot the punch line about Groucho's erection. It could have gone better.

We then escorted Woody across the hall for WNBC's highly rated news program *Live at Five*. Sue Simmons, the program's popular anchorperson, got Woody to open up. She asked him about his proverbial role as second banana, and he told her, "Bill German made me accept that. My ghostwriter. He put that phrase in, and I didn't object because I think it's true. I feel a bit more comfortable being second banana."

I was hoping that hearing Woody mention my name on live TV would make the members of Team Woody stop treating me like an irrelevant hanger-on, but it didn't. When I asked one of the secretaries if she knew the time, she snapped, "I'm not the town crier!" "You're the ghostwriter," added Jo, "so why aren't you invisible?"

Woody and Al Roker were the only people who were nice to me that day. Al was the *Live at Five* weather guy and, shortly after Woody's appearance, he burst into the green room, proclaiming, "I'm the world's biggest Stones fan!" Woody didn't have a clue who he was, but he shook his hand, and introduced me as his co-author. "Best of luck," said Al. I'm not sure he was the world's biggest Stones fan, but this *was* before the stomach surgery.

Hours later, Woody was onstage with Bo at the Ritz. The audience went berserk when Woody did "Plynth" and when the Temptations guested on the closing number, "Who Do You Love." After the show, I went backstage to see Woody. But when I walked through the door, Jo yelled to the club's security guard, "Don't let him in!" I thought she was joking, but she added, "I'm serious! I don't want him back here!" She'd had enough of my Colonel Kentucky tie, of Woody mentioning me in his interviews, and of my constant tagalongs. So I sloped off and went home.

Except that I really needed to speak with Woody. If I didn't see him before he left town, I'd be out $1,800.

A lot of my subscribers wanted autographed copies of *The Works,* but lived nowhere near Woody's signings. So I ordered two hundred copies from the publisher—at a nonrefundable author's discount of $1,800—and got Woody to promise he'd sign them. But if I never hooked up with him, I'd lose my money and be stuck with two hundred unnecessary books. Woody said he'd do it Thanksgiving Day, but we still needed to pin down the time and place.

I knew he was staying at a friend's house, so I phoned on Thanksgiving and left a message. My parents were expecting me across the East River in Brooklyn, but I told them I'd be late. I waited all day for Woody to call back, but he never did. It was the first time I ever missed Thanksgiving with my folks.

On Friday, Woody was signing books at Shakespeare & Co. on 81st Street. I loaded my two hundred books in the trunk of a friend's car and brought them over. I had no specific game plan, other than to get my books as close to Woody as possible.

Unfortunately, things didn't go smoothly at the bookstore. The event was poorly scheduled (holiday weekend) and underpublicized, so no one showed up. Literally a dozen people. As soon as Woody signed the twelve books, his pissed-off co-manager said, "We're outta here," and physically pulled him out. I never got to speak with Woody, and I had to schlep my 200 pounds of books back home.

I tried Woody's friend all weekend, but kept getting the machine. I knew Woody was leaving town Sunday night, so I had no choice but to stare at the phone and wait. I was a nervous wreck.

After four days of waiting, I finally heard from Woody at 6 PM on Sunday. He was cool, calm, and collected. "Colonel Kentucky, wanna do the books? I'm here on 46th Street. But get here now, 'cause we're leaving in an hour."

Within seconds, I was out the door with the books. I had a friend with a car on stand-by. He was a huge Faces fan and wanted to meet Woody, so he offered to help. We got the job done in thirty minutes, despite Jo's constant badgering: "Aren't you finished already? When are you leaving?"

Jo apologized to me years later. She revealed that she was quite ill at the time. "I was in excruciating abdominal pain," she said. "They told me I had Crohn's disease and put me on steroids, but it made me feel worse. Then I found out I was misdiagnosed. I was living with a perforated appendix. I know I was mean to a lot of people back then, so I'm sorry."

I feigned ignorance and said, "Well, you were never mean to *me.*" Even during her moods, I knew she was a decent lady who had Woody's best interests at heart. He wouldn't be alive if it were not for her vigilance.

. . .

Woody's nightclub lasted a year or so, and he never cashed in on the South Beach boom. It was poorly managed and faced lawsuits from the neighboring old-age homes. But it was great while it lasted. Woody brought in acts like Billy Preston, Mick Taylor, and Jerry Lee Lewis, and gave the residents of Miami a cause for optimism. He was ahead of his time.

Keith wasn't saddened by the club's demise. He never gave Woody the satisfaction of showing interest, but I know he was curious. He'd ask *me* how "Woody's cabana" was doing.

"Extremely well," I once told him. "Last week, a thousand people flew in from France. But Woody had to explain it was Jerry *Lee* Lewis."

Tom Hanks and Keith. Or is it Keith and Tom Hanks?

Partying at Acme in my synagogue clothes.

16

live from
new york

With the help of Tom Hanks, Keith got ready to unleash his first-ever solo album.

Hanks: "I'm Keith Richards."

Keith: "I'm Tom Hanks."

Hanks: "We've switched bodies for this week's *Saturday Night Live*."

Keith: "Man, you look *terrible!*"

This was no ordinary episode of *SNL*. It was the 1988 season opener. Huge exposure and a huge step for Keith. His first TV appearance as a front man.

I attended the 7:30 PM dress rehearsal. Keith performed "Take It So Hard" and "Struggle," two of his new songs. When he finished the former, some guy in the audience yelled, "You don't need Ol' Rubber Lips!" Everyone laughed, but Keith pretended not to hear it.

In between the rehearsal and the 11:30 broadcast, I grabbed a snack near Rockefeller Center. On my way back to NBC's Studio 8H, I bumped into Patti Hansen, who was with John F. Kennedy Jr. We chatted in the hallway, causing us to enter late. No problem for Patti or JFK—they had reserved seats—but I couldn't find a single space to park my rear. A page said it would be okay to crouch in the aisle, so that's what I did.

Except that when I looked to my left, I realized I was crouching next to my all-time idol in journalism, Tom Snyder. I got so nervous, my heart began to pound and my palms began to sweat. For the next ninety minutes, I was paralyzed. I wanted to introduce myself during the commercial breaks, but I couldn't speak.

I know it's weird that I was never nervous around the Stones, yet I was scared of a quirky old dude with a bad hairdo. But here's the thing: As much as I loved the Stones, they were never my role models. I wanted to be *near* them, but I didn't want to *be* them. I wanted to be a journalist. As a teen, I watched Snyder on the *Tomorrow* show every 1 AM, even on school nights. I counted on him to calmly sort out the day's events for me, like the Son of Sam mess. A journalist's job is to make sense out of chaos and, after watching Tom do it, I knew that's what *I* wanted to do. The Stones gave me plenty to work with.

Tom was fuzzy on Keith's identity, but had an inkling. After Keith did "Take It So Hard," I heard him turn to his date and say, "Now he's the *naughty* one, right?"

On September 13, 1988, Keith had a private listening party for his album at Acme Bar & Grill. Guests included Iggy Pop and Paula Abdul. As a fan, journalist, and friend, I wanted to be there, but was faced with a dilemma. The party fell out on the second day of Rosh Hashanah, the Jewish New Year. I was visiting my parents in Brooklyn and observing the traditions, such as attending synagogue and refraining from travel. To make Keith's party—boarding the D train to Manhattan—I'd be breaking the tenets of my religion.

It meant a lot to my folks, so I sought their permission. Dad conceded that although Sandy Koufax didn't play baseball on Yom Kippur—the capo de tutti capi of Jewish holidays—he did play on Rosh Hashanah. So that made it okay. I rushed to Acme in my synagogue clothes and hung with Keith and Iggy.

I reminded Keith of the things he withstood to get the album done. When I visited his sessions one night in 1987, the studio went up in smoke and everyone had to evacuate. Then, when his sessions shifted to Montserrat, his car slid down a ditch during a torrential downpour and he was knee-deep in mud. "I'm exhausted," he told me back then. "I never worked so hard in my life. The Stones was easy compared to this." But he persevered and saw it through.

The *Talk Is Cheap* album was a critical and commercial success. As a result, Keith found himself all over the media. I tried booking an interview through Jane, but she kept me hanging. She instead had *Rolling Stone,* MTV, and the *New York Post* come to her office to speak with him. I felt slighted.

But being me ultimately had its privileges. I wasn't on the formal docket because I was viewed more casually. When Keith had nothing better to do one day, he told Jane to send me to his house. Within an hour, I was on the subway to 4th Street.

Keith's mother-in-law, Beatrice, answered the door and told him I was there. He greeted me barefoot. He grabbed two glasses, a bottle of ginger ale, a bottle of Jack, and told me to follow him. We headed to the top floor of his apartment and out to the terrace. Along the way, we passed an exercise bike. "Do you use it?" I asked.

"*Sometimes,*" he said. "But mostly Patti."

We sat at a wooden table on the terrace, where he poured me a drink. This was more like a friendly hang than an interview. But at some point, it was my job to hit Record on the boom box. I asked him about excluding Woody from the album.

"It's very difficult not to have Woody," he said, "but I thought it was very necessary for me to make a complete break from the Stones on this one. It's Keith Richards. I didn't want that sort of murky gray area."

He seemed pleased with the results. "There's very few records that you make, or at least that I've made, that you wanna hear by the time you finish it. You're just so full with it. It's the last thing you wanna hear. But with this one— I don't know if it's because it's a novelty, my first solo album—but I actually sit around and enjoy listening to it, put it on while I'm taking a shower."

I asked if Mick had given him any feedback.

"I played him the album, but he talked all the way through it. The only time I got any insight from him was when I went to take a pee. I come out of the john, and he's dancing around the room. For a minute I watch him, and he's just enjoying it. So I went back into the john and slammed the door and walked out again, and he's just sitting on the couch. But that's Mick. I know the bloke. I guess I saw him liking it when he didn't know I was looking."

The album featured a song called "You Don't Move Me," which was a poison-pen letter to Mick. Lyrics like "You made the wrong motion," referring to Mick's break from the Stones, and "You already crapped out twice," referring to Mick's two solo albums.

"It's just an expression of what I think went down," Keith told me. "A little diary of events. . . . Because the obvious thing happened. [Mick's solo material] is not as good as the Rolling Stones. It didn't seem to be a competent alternative. . . . What I don't think Mick ever realizes is that without the Stones, half his power is gone. It's like Samson having his hair cut off."

Keith told me that he'd yelled at Mick a couple weeks earlier. "But I was sick at the time, and I did apologize to him. Yelling wasn't necessary. But he still makes me mad, his attitude. The Stones spent a lot of time building up integrity, as much as you can get in the music industry, and I got the very definite impression that the way Mick handled [his solo career] jeopardized all that. . . . I've known him for forty years, and our fights are on many different levels, not just about who runs the Stones, blah, blah, blah. It's more to do with knowing somebody for so long. And you get to a point where you think a mate of yours is screwing up and you try to tell him because that's what friends are for. . . . I still have lots of reservations about Mick, but I think that's something natural we all go through as people. Eventually, we'll work it out."

The nice part about interviewing Keith on his terrace was that we had no one watching over us or telling us when to quit. We ended our interview only because it was getting chilly and because Keith polished off the Jack. The interview appeared in *Beggars Banquet*'s "Tenth Anniversary Issue."

For most of October, I worked tirelessly on that issue and on planning an anniversary party. I wanted to thank everyone who'd ever helped me in the previous ten years. From the Rolling Stones themselves to the anonymous people whose small deeds made a difference: the neighbors in 1978 who lent me their typewriter, the kid who snuck me into the mimeo room, the guy who stocked my first issue at his record store.

Beggars Banquet's actual anniversary was September, but a club called U.S. Blues on Bond Street said they'd give me the room, free of charge, on November 3. I pulled twenty-hour workdays for several weeks to get everything done. Cranking out the anniversary issue, putting together the guest list, printing the invitations, and arranging stuff with the club. I went days without bathing, eating, sleeping, or brushing my teeth. And although Murphy's Law says, "Everything that *can* go wrong *will* go wrong," it seemed like things that could *not* go wrong went wrong.

When my all-important Tenth Anniversary Issue came back from the print shop, I discovered that thousands of them had been collated backwards. Meaning, page 3 was where page 9 should be, and page 7 was where page 5 should be, and so on. None of it made sense. Some insignificant note about Bill Wyman became the issue's top story, and my big Keith interview was on the last page.

Meanwhile, MTV kept calling. They wanted to send a camera crew to my party, but only if I could guarantee a Stones sighting. I kept saying I couldn't. Keith was the one Stone in town that week and, although he lived near the club, it didn't guarantee a thing. In fact, Jane gave me the following proclamation: "Keith is definitely not coming to your party. He has a rehearsal that night." I knew she was right about the rehearsal—Keith's solo tour was set to launch November 24—but I wished she wasn't so adamant.

I mailed an invitation to 4th Street and followed it up with a phone call. Patti said Keith was standing there in a towel, about to take a shower. I heard him speak, but couldn't make it out, so she translated: "He says he's got a rehearsal that night, but he'll try to come. He doesn't know yet." I told her that she and Keith had done so much to help me, it'd mean a lot if they were there.

MTV wasn't the only one who wanted to know if the Stones were coming. So did my readers. My phone rang off the hook, and I did invite a few. But even my dearest friends wanted to know if Mick and Keith had RSVP'd. They didn't want to come out on a work night if there wasn't going to be a "payoff."

In the midst of this tornado, my ceiling caved in. And I'm not being metaphorical. My bathroom ceiling became one with my bathroom floor. Svi had warned me of this eventuality, but the timing could not have been worse. As I was getting dressed for my party and talking to MTV on the phone, I had construction workers chiseling and drilling in the background.

When I finally exited my apartment and headed downtown, I was completely exhausted. I'd had enough of everything associated with *Beggars Banquet,* including the lousy apartment I had to live in because of my income. As my taxi approached Bond Street, I thought about walking into my party and saying, "Thanks for coming. I quit."

"You've got quite a boy there." Keith, Bernie, and Sylvia
go nightclubbing.

17

chip off the
old block

MTV didn't send a camera, but that was for the best. There was enough going on at this party to overwhelm me. The turnout was enormous, and my life flashed before my eyes. Almost every person who'd ever helped me with *Beggars Banquet* was in one room at the same time.

The neighbors who lent me their typewriter in 1978 mixed with Art Collins, the ex-president of Rolling Stones Records. The high school pal who mimeoed my first issue spoke with Lisa Robinson, the journalist who'd profiled me in her column. And the ex-girlfriend who once helped me staple was sitting next to Don Covay, the legendary R&B singer. It was an incredible mix of people.

About an hour into the party, someone got onstage and proposed a toast to me. It was Debby Hastings, the bass player for Bo Diddley. I'd befriended her a year earlier, during the Bo-Woody tour. Everyone raised a glass in my honor and encouraged me to get onstage for a speech. A cake was rolled out to the center of the room. It depicted the *Beggars Banquet* logo and "Tenth Anniversary" masthead. A friend of Woody's paid for it, and it was a total surprise to me. I was such a do-it-yourselfer, I couldn't fathom anyone doing something so nice for me without my knowledge.

I hopped onstage, donning my Colonel Kentucky tie, and the room got quiet. After years of shining the spotlight on the Stones, the light was suddenly on *me*. "You're all here for a reason," I told my guests. "And that's because, in some way, you've each contributed to *Beggars Banquet*. Whether you helped me in 1978 or today, I'll never forget it. So I just wanna say thanks, and I'm glad you all could make it."

I guess this is where I was supposed to deliver my retirement spiel, but I couldn't do it. The warmth I felt at this party made me look forward to *another* ten years. I walked away from the mic, but, as everyone was applauding, I thought of one last thing and ran back. "By the way," I joked, "don't think I don't know that some of you are here because you think the Stones are coming. Well, I hate to tell ya, but the Stones *aren't* coming!"

I leapt off the stage and onto the floor, where I noticed everyone laughing. And that's because the joke was on *me*. Keith Richards of the Rolling Stones was standing right in front of the stage. He was there during my entire speech, but I couldn't see him with the lights in my eyes.

Keith hugged me and said he was playing hooky from his rehearsal. I used lyrics from his new album to express my gratitude. "It means a lot," I told him. "You could've stood me up, but you didn't."

He was sporting a red headband and a T-shirt that said *Obergruppenführer*. German for "leader of the group." He retreated to a booth with Patti, Don Covay, and Sarah Dash, the backup singer from his album. He hung out for almost an hour and was friendly to everyone who greeted him, like my ex-roommate and ex-girlfriend.

At one point, I was approached by the club's manager. He said someone had phoned his office, asking to speak with Keith. He assumed it was a crazy Stones fan, so he hung up. But the person called again, this time asking for Bill German. The caller said his name was Charley Drayton.

I was escorted to the office, where I picked up the phone. It was indeed Drayton, the bassist from Keith's backup band, the X-Pensive Winos. He said they were all waiting for Keith at the rehearsal studio, and could I please relay that fact to the Obergruppenführer. I returned to the booth and thanked Keith for coming.

"Wunna missed it for anything," he said.

As he made his way to the exit, he gave every one of my guests a door prize. Anyone who wanted a handshake, an autograph, or a photo with him, got one. He was phenomenally gracious and patient.

I lost sight of him and was busy mingling when I noticed a commotion near the door. I squinted and thought I saw Keith yukking it up with my parents. I rubbed my eyes and realized it was true: Keith Richards, the Prince of Darkness, was kibbitzing with Bernie and Sylvia, the two kosher deli workers from Brooklyn. I raced to the scene.

"I just met your *parents*," Keith told me.

"That's a sign of the Apocalypse," I replied.

Witnesses later recounted the story for me: Keith was walking toward the door when my dad grabbed him by the shoulder. "Keith," he said, "we're Bill's parents." And Keith responded, "Well, you've got quite a boy there!"

Introducing my folks to Keith had never occurred to me. I didn't think they'd care to meet him. But I was wrong. Bernie and Sylvia weren't Stones fans, but they considered Keith an important person in my life and wanted to thank him for helping me.

The fact is, I almost didn't invite my folks at all. This party was for *young* people, not for people in their midfifties. I got along great with my parents, but didn't think they belonged. Then it occurred to me: My parents are so proud of me, it's scary. Their dining room is like a *Beggars Banquet* shrine. Tons of framed pictures, showing me with the Stones. Not to mention how *verklempt* they got when Woody mentioned me on *Live at Five*. There's no way I couldn't invite them.

I mean, because of me, these *Fiddler on the Roof* lovers took an interest in the Stones. To this day, Mom will sniff out scoops for me. She recently called to report that "Mick's movie, *Freeze Jack,* will be on TV tonight." I had to tell her, "It's *Freejack,* Mom—Freeze Jack is what you put in the car," but I was grateful nonetheless.

The week of my party, she read something in the paper about Keith. "He'll be doing a jig soon," she informed me.

I replied, "No, Mom, it's pronounced '*gig*,' not '*jig*.' He's not wearing a kilt and doing a dance."

But at least she tries. And if this was a party about people who helped me, my parents topped the list. They inspired me by quiet example, and there would not have been a *Beggars Banquet* without them.

In the early Seventies, Mom edited the newsletter for her local chapter of Hadassah. She'd gather tidbits from the neighborhood yentas—"mah jong at Sadie's this Tuesday"; "the Horowitz bar mitzvah on Saturday"—and put it in her 'zine. She'd crank it out on her manual Underwood, paste up some cutesy-tootsy graphics (like that little guy with the megaphone), and bring it to the print shop.

I'd watch her do it and thought the process was cool. I wanted a newsletter just like Mommy. I was nine and not yet into the Stones, so I started a scrapbook of my favorite baseball team, the New York Mets. From 1972 to 1977, I reported on almost every game. Good practice for *Beggars Banquet.*

To complement Mom's creativity, there was my dad, the symbol of stability and self-discipline. The guy can literally stop at one potato chip. He took some tough jobs, like driving the deli's delivery van in winter, just so he could pay the bills. By watching him, I inherited a sense of responsibility, which I needed to run my business. I could've easily gotten swept up in the Stones' bad habits, but I never forgot I had work to do.

And while my parents didn't encourage me to spend my life following the Stones, they didn't *dis*courage me, either. They gave me lots of freedom, and, as a result, I never wanted to disappoint them or abuse their trust. A brilliant experiment in reverse psychology.

When I look back, I can't believe how lucky I was to have the three people I was most grateful to—Bernie, Sylvia, and Keith—in the same room at the same time. My folks got new pictures for their shrine and, this time, they were *in* them. About once a year, a TV repairman will walk past their dining room and stop dead in his tracks. "Hey! That's *you* with Keith Richards! How did *that* happen?"

In one of the photos, it looks like Sylvia and Keith are sharing a private joke. I believe that's when she told him to "have a nice jig."

10TH ANNIVERSARY ISSUE

Vol. 2   *The Rolling Stones*   No. 15

BEGGARS BANQUET

Keith
Gives
Cheap
Talk

18

fun with bill
and jane

Yoko broke up the Beatles. I broke up the Stones. At least according to Jane Rose.

I was feeling pretty good in the days following my party. I visited Jane's office to leave extra copies of my Tenth Anniversary Issue. But when I walked in, the first thing she said to me was, "I'm not talking to you! I can't believe what you did! I can't believe you would do this to us! To me! To Keith! You ruined everything! Wait outside until I'm ready to talk to you!"

I skulked to the reception area like a puppy that had peed on the couch. Jane's secretaries heard the whole thing and suggested I not take it personally. "Oh, you know Jane, she's like that with everybody."

They had no clue why Jane was pissed at me, but, at this point, nothing would surprise them. Jane treated these girls like crap, and I'd often see them flip her the bird when her back was turned. The turnover rate was pretty high in that office. In just a few years, Jane burned through Kathy, Joanne, Debby, Michele, and Linda, like the running gag on *Murphy Brown*.

Jane kept me waiting in the reception area for over an hour. I read the paper, twiddled my thumbs, and wondered what I could have done that was so bad. She finally summoned me to her office and explained my mortal transgression. "You ruined everything! Because of what you put in that issue, the Stones won't get back together! Do you realize that? Mick is going to read it, and there's no way he'll get back together with Keith! You ruined everything! A Stones tour won't happen now because of *you*!"

All I could think was, if I wielded that much power over the Rolling Stones, no one ever told me about it and I certainly wasn't capitalizing on it.

There was a quote in my Tenth Anniversary Issue, said Jane, that was so divisive, so explosive, it'd mark the end of the Rolling Stones. It wasn't something I came up with on my own, it was something I quoted from Keith. "You should've checked with me before you printed it!" she hollered.

Keith said a lot of nasty things about Mick during his *Talk Is Cheap* media blitz, yet *this* was the offending quote: "I'd very much like to use the same cat who engineered [my solo] album, Don Smith, [to engineer the next Stones album]. And Steve Jordan, too, as co-producer. Because we've had such a good thing going, we're on a roll. I'd like to take what I've done in the last two years and bring it to bear on the Rolling Stones. . . . Even if [Don Smith] didn't do [my] record, if I'd heard his work with some other band, I'd want him to do the Stones because I think he's the best guy for the job, for the way the Stones record."

That's the quote she was having a cow about. She believed that Mick would perceive it as Keith trying to take control of the band and that it'd upset him enough to make him walk away. "Why didn't you check with me first?" she yelled. "Just because Keith said it doesn't mean you could print it!"

Well, actually, just because Keith said it *did* mean I could print it. I was under no obligation to submit my drafts to her, the way I was during that fan club thing. Keith's a big boy, and he knew he was speaking on the record. If he realized he'd said something damaging—and really, what could've been worse than his poison-pen song to Mick or his quote about slitting Mick's throat?—he'd have told me to scratch it and I would've obliged. But he didn't.

I stood there, curling my toes, as Jane scolded me like a child. I tried to defuse things—"Hey, my folks enjoyed meeting you at my party the other night"—but she yelled, "Don't try to change the subject! You really screwed up!"

Days after this encounter, several of Keith's friends told me that Jane was dead set against Keith coming to my party. Supposedly, she even called him from the club's pay phone and said, "Do not come down here! Just go to the studio!"

I didn't want to believe it, but I'd understand if it was true. Jane had recently signed a contract to become Keith's official manager. She was *already* overprotective of him, but, with her new title and *his* new album, the stakes got higher. So, even though his tour was three weeks away, she was nervous about rehearsals and concerned about his press. I mean, what sounds better on Page Six of the *New York Post:* Keith dines at Da Silvano with JFK Jr., or Keith attends a fanzine party with Bernie and Sylvia?

Ultimately, Keith's album went gold, and his tour played to wildly enthusiastic audiences. I witnessed four of the junket's fifteen concerts and loved each one. The finale was at Brendan Byrne Arena in New Jersey, the eve of Keith's 45th birthday.

Two nights later, on December 19, a party was held at Keith and Patti's house on East 4th Street. Patti invited me directly. It was a birthday, anniversary (Keith and Patti's fifth), Christmas, and end-of-tour celebration. When Keith and Patti opened the door, I said, "Happy *everything*!"

Keith's dad, Bert, was there, as were Keith's kids, Marlon and Angela (formerly known as Dandelion). I chatted with Keith's X-Pensive Wino band members and flirted with Patti's niece, Marisa. Jane told me to play down the X-Pensive Winos angle in *Beggars Banquet*. "I don't want Mick thinking that Keith has another band."

Keith and I bumped into each other in the kitchen. I was carving lasagna out of a tin, while he was popping a cassette in his boom box. It was a tape of the previous week's concert in Hollywood, which I'd attended.

He sat on the kitchen floor, as I pulled up a chair and rested the plate of lasagna on my lap. Keith was wearing jeans, suede boots, and a sleeveless T-shirt, holding a glass of bourbon. He said he was sad the tour was over. More than just the Winos and the music, he was going to miss the fans. He'd had a unique opportunity to press the flesh, both onstage and off. "In Detroit," he recalled, "this chick, musta been 15 years old, runs up onstage and starts kissin' and kissin' me. I haven't had girls runnin' after me in over twenty years!"

In another town, he gave a fan a lift home. The kid was limping and wearing a neck brace. Keith spotted him on the street after the show. "Hey," Keith said to his driver, "there goes the kid from the third row. We gotta pick him up."

The saddest moment of the tour, Keith said, was when he learned that Roy Orbison had died. He dedicated that night's show in Cleveland to Roy's memory. And the scariest moment was the flight to Oakland. "Turbulence," Keith said. "This way, that way, strugglin' to stay airborne. I told the guys, 'Get ready to meet the Big Bopper.' "

As I listened to Keith tell me these stories, I began to study the lines on his face. They're like rings on a tree, except that, in Keith's case, each line represents not just a year, but a close call. I also fixated on his shoulders. Due to the way he sat on the floor and the way I hunched in my chair, I got a good look. They appeared to be riddled with cellulite. Dimples around the deltoids. It wasn't the first time I'd seen them, but it was the first time I could study them up close. "When Keith first noticed them," Woody once explained to me, "he thought they were bruises that'll go away. But they're still there." I've since learned that they're the result of Keith's heroin use in the Seventies. Instead of injecting into his veins, he'd shoot into his muscles. It deadened the skin and created cottage-cheese-like crevices. Another ring on his tree.

Eventually, our conversation turned to the Stones. Keith told me he was meeting with Mick after New Year's to determine the band's fate. It'd be just the two of them on the island of Barbados. No wives, no kids, no managers. "He still pisses me off," Keith declared, "but we're like Siamese twins. It'd take a lot to separate us for good."

Keith and I noticed that Charley Drayton was sitting on the floor at the other end of the long kitchen. He was listening intently to the Hollywood Palladium tape, while weeping. For twentysomething Charley, working with Keith was the experience of a lifetime. But now it was over.

Almost everyone in that house had grown closer to Keith in the last five or six years. People like me, Bert, and the X-Pensive Winos. But if things worked out between Keith and Mick—if Mick could get past those quotes I printed in *Beggars Banquet*—then we'd have to share Keith with the rest of the world. As much as I yearned for a Stones tour, I sensed that this night was the end of something very intimate and very special.

Mick, Mick, and Keith at the Waldorf. "It was very superficial,"
said Mick T. of his reunion with Mick J.

19

one man's
treasure

It's silly to think you can institutionalize rock 'n' roll. You can't take something that rebellious and try to put a roof over it. When Jerry Lee Lewis first belted "Great Balls of Fire," he did not have the Rock and Roll Hall of Fame and Museum in mind. In fact, the words "rock 'n' roll" and "museum" shouldn't even appear in the same sentence.

And yet, considering the latest crop of fake-titted lip-synchers and sissy-boy pop bands, I've begrudgingly concluded that the Rock and Roll Hall of Fame is a necessary evil. As a culture, it's incumbent upon us to show the next generation that rock stars were once discovered at the Marquee Club and not the Mickey Mouse Club. Personally, I have no need to visit the Rock and Roll Hall of Fame anytime soon. But as an archivist and historian, I'm happy it exists. So long as they never dismantle the Muddy Waters exhibit to make room for the Justin Timberlake exhibit.

Although the Hall of Fame is in Cleveland, the inductions usually take place at the Waldorf-Astoria in New York. The first one was 1986, when folks like Elvis, Bo, and Chuck Berry were enshrined. Keith stepped to the podium to induct Chuck, and then jammed with Woody, Jerry Lee Lewis, and Neil Young.

In 1987, Keith gave the induction speech for Aretha Franklin, before jamming with Springsteen. And in 1988, Mick inducted the Beatles, before singing "I Saw Her Standing There" and "Like a Rolling Stone" with George Harrison and Bob Dylan.

January 18, 1989, was the Stones' turn to be inducted. It was going to be Mick and Keith's first public appearance together in years. If the night went well, it'd herald a reunion tour. If it didn't go well, it'd herald the end of the Rolling Stones.

Back then, the ceremonies weren't televised, as they are today. You'd be lucky to catch a sound bite on MTV or *Good Morning America*. So if you wanted to hear Mick and Keith's speeches, decipher their body language, and witness their potential jam, you had to be there in person. But the Hall of Fame was charging $1,250 a plate, which priced out mere mortals.

I heard the press would be placed in the balcony (no food, no chairs, no cover charge), so I put in a request. The Hall of Fame told me no. I then phoned Jane, hoping to squeeze in with the Stones. I knew they were getting three tables, gratis. She said she'd get back to me, but kept me in limbo. The night before the ceremony, I still didn't know.

Video James had no official way of getting in, so he bootlegged the invitation. He knew someone who had one and brought it to a copy shop. Except that it contained a gold-colored logo and the copy shop didn't have color machines. He applied gold nail polish, and it looked insane. Besides, the invitation by itself was worthless. Your name had to be on the guest list. Video James said, "I've got a plan," but I wanted no part of it.

On January 18, I sat by the phone, waiting for Jane to call. At 6 PM, she finally said, "You're in." I threw my Colonel Kentucky tie on and raced to the Waldorf.

You had to go through an anteroom to check in. You were then given a card with your table assignment—I was Table 9—which was your credential into the ballroom.

I saw Video James in the anteroom, where he posed as someone else. I think he said he was Cousin Brucie. Amazingly, no one was checking IDs, so it worked. He got his table assignment, flashed it to the guard, and entered the ballroom. He had no legitimate place to sit, so he stayed ahead of security by playing busboy. Emptying ashtrays was a small price to pay for a Stones jam.

I, meanwhile, was seated at the Stones' kiddie table. They had two tables up front, where Mick, Keith, and Woody were seated with their wives and Jane Rose. But they had an ancillary table in the corner, for peons like me. I sat next to Jane's new secretary and the guy who took care of Keith's dad. Phil Spector was seated at the very next table, and I had a good vantage point. I looked up Tina Turner's dress as she bent down to kiss Phil, and I was nearly blinded when author Tom Wolfe, decked in bright white, patted Phil on the shoulder. Phil's table was surrounded by five of his own bodyguards, conspicuously packing heat in their cummerbunds, so I was careful not to make fast moves. I didn't even lift my butter knife.

You'd think that for $1,250 a plate, they'd serve something worthy of the Waldorf. The place has hosted presidents and kings. But nope, they fed us microwaved chicken potpies that came straight from the freezer. Honest to goodness, there was a note on everyone's plate that said, "We are serving a meal that guarantees you'll remember the music most of all."

Around midnight, Pete Townshend delivered the honors. "The Stones," he said, "feel to me as though they still have a future. But it won't be easy. And if it wasn't for the vast sums of money they can make, they wouldn't bother at all, really. Or at least Mick wouldn't. So it's lucky for us fans that Mick has such expensive tastes."

At times, the speech bordered on a Friar's Club roast. Townshend alluded to Keith's rumored blood transfusion, to Bill Wyman's lechery, and even to Charlie's heroin addiction. He described Woody, the youngest member of the band, as the only Stone who "still has his own teeth." And he alleged that Mick gave him "a bad case of VD." "Sorry, sorry, that's wrong!" he added. "Mick's CD had a bad case, it says here!"

Pete had the place in stitches. At the end of his speech, the Stones rose from their seats and climbed onstage to accept their Hall of Fame statuettes and say a few words. On this night, honoring a quarter century of recorded Stones history, the band was represented by Mick, Keith, Woody, and Mick Taylor.

All eyes were on Mick and Keith. Up there onstage, the two of them acted like pals. Hugging, laughing, slapping each other on the back. I wasn't buying it, but they put on a good show.

"It's slightly ironic," Mick told the crowd, "that tonight you see us on our best behavior, but we're being rewarded for twenty-five years of bad behavior." He was reading from a prepared statement, which he'd pulled from his pocket. Similar to his acceptance at that Grammy thing, he didn't feign enthusiasm or tell us what an honor it was. He sarcastically referred to the Hall of Fame as "the waxworks of rock" and quoted a line from Jean Cocteau: "Americans are funny people. First you shock them and then they put you in a museum."

"But," he concluded, "we're not quite ready to hang up the number yet."

As soon as he said that, a burst of applause came from the crowd. It was the only indication that the Stones might exist past this night.

Keith came to the mic next. He didn't mention a single word about the Stones' future. Instead, he used the occasion to thank Leo Fender—"for making the goddamned things we gotta play!"—and to remember Ian Stewart. "I still feel like I'm working for *him*. It's *his* band."

Woody said a few words, before pulling Mick Taylor to the podium. In a very soft tone, the ex-Stone described the night as "a great honor" and thanked everyone who made it possible. Of the four men standing on that stage, it was clearly Mick Taylor to whom it meant the most. He said he appreciated it "more than words can say."

The crowd gave him a nice ovation. But before he could savor it, the other Mick gestured with his index finger, as if to say, "We're outta here." Mick J. made his exit and the two and a half Stones had no choice but to follow him out of the spotlight, off the stage.

They all returned to their seats, except for Keith, who detoured to Stevie Wonder. He bent down and whispered a few words to him. Woody and the Micks were seated by the time they realized where Keith was. They didn't come over, but Woody waved to Stevie from across the room.

Stevie was the final inductee of the night, after which the anticipated superjam took place. A who's-who of rock 'n' roll overloaded the stage. Keith, Woody, and Mick Taylor plugged in with Townshend and Springsteen. The Temptations shared a mic with Little Richard and Dion.

Stevie kicked things off with "Uptight," which he medleyed into "Satisfaction." But Mick, who was practically hiding at the back of the stage, acted as if he didn't know the song. He offered a few hand claps and a subtle back vocal, but that was it.

After the ensemble ran through "Lucille," "Respect," and "Be My Baby," the event's music director, Paul Shaffer, walked to the front of the stage and did some cajoling: "I think it's time for some 'Honky Tonk Women.' "

Mick finally stepped up. He did a duet with Tina on "Honky Tonk" that rivaled their set at Live Aid. Mick was on fire, and he changed the entire complexion of the evening. An amazing ability to turn himself on or off at will. Even the suits at the Warner-Elektra table were on their feet.

When "Honky Tonk" was done, Mick launched into "Can't Turn You Loose" and "Bony Maronie" with Little Richard. Again, it was magical. Then, Keith cut through the din like a clap of thunder, by striking the opening chords to "Start Me Up." Mick ripped off his jacket and stripped down to his white undershirt. Keith and Tina shared a mic on the "You make a grown man cry" part. It more than made up for the chicken potpie.

At no point, however, were Mick and Keith within twenty feet of each other. And at no point did they make eye contact. But I'll say this: If it wound up being the last time they ever played together onstage, it was a great way to go out.

Keith spotted me when he came offstage and invited me to a private reception upstairs. "Room 39H." But when I got there, I seemed like the only guest. There were a dozen people, most of whom were married to, or employed by, a Rolling Stone. Curiously absent was Mick Taylor.

Mick Jagger stood in a corner by himself, while Keith was on a sofa. Away from the public, the backslapping and laughter were nonexistent. In fact, the room was eerily quiet. I sat down next to Keith and was about to ask how his healing with Mick was going, but Mick was within lip-reading distance.

Woody popped into the room briefly, easing the tension a bit. He plopped onto the sofa and told us about his exchange with Springsteen during "Start Me Up." "He asked me what key we were in, and I told him, 'You're on your own, Boss!' "

Keith and Woody's Hall of Fame trophies were resting on the coffee table in front of us. Keith noted that the statuette had no genitalia. It was a gold-colored naked person with an important piece missing. Upon closer observation, Keith discovered he could disassemble the thing. Or at least the disc part. The statue, you see, was a faceless, dickless, titless person holding a disc. But if you gave it enough force, you could yank the disc out of the eunuch's hands.

Keith gave it enough force. At first, he used the disc as a coaster. Then, he picked it up and flung it at Woody like one of those star thingies in a Kung Fu movie. It connected with Woody's shoulder. It was light as a wafer, no harm done, but Woody felt the need to retaliate. He pulled the disc off the other trophy and whizzed it past Keith's ear. Before you knew it, it was an all-out war.

It made me think about the people who get that trophy and treasure it the rest of their lives. Certainly, the Coasters don't use them as coasters. But here you've got the Stones. What could this statue mean to *them*? What kind of validation or promotional boost could it provide? How many of these paperweights can they bring home?

After getting hit by Keith and Woody's flying discs, I realized it was safer to get off the couch and say hello to Mick. I hadn't spoken to him in almost a year and had recently written some stuff he might not have been pleased with. I described his 1988 solo tour as "a calculated risk." He performed twenty Stones songs a night—compared to five solo songs—and played only the Stones-starved countries of Japan and Australia. Mick "can't get too cocky about his critical and commercial success," I wrote.

In another commentary, which I titled "State of the Union," I predicted the Stones would reunite, largely for financial reasons: "The whole will always make more than the sum of its parts. Each member will always have the creative and financial impetus to play with the other four." If Mick didn't like my "emotional blackmail" assessment of Live Aid, he wasn't going to love my Stones "State of the Union" address.

As I approached him in Room 39H of the Waldorf-Astoria, I had no idea how he'd react. To ingratiate myself, I played on his "waxworks of rock" comment. "What next?" I asked. "Madame Tussauds?"

"This is *worse!*" he exclaimed. But at least I got him to laugh. We made small talk for a few minutes, and it was very cordial. I steered clear of any Stones discussion.

During my entire time in Room 39H, I never saw Mick and Keith speak to each other. That is, until they were leaving. As Mick put his coat on, Keith came over and cracked a few jokes about Phil Spector's bodyguards. The two of them embraced and said they were looking forward to hooking up again in Barbados. At least they were on speaking terms. But as I exited the Waldorf, I was no closer in predicting the Stones' future (and, by extension, my own) than when I walked in.

In the weeks to follow, all sorts of rumors began to fly. Some were fact, some were fiction, and a couple found their way to the media.

Rumor Number One: A concert promoter is ready to back up the truck. He's guaranteeing the Stones $65 million—cash up front—to get them back on the road.

Rumor Number Two: The Stones are going to tour, but without Bill Wyman. Bill will retire and, like a baseball team shuffling its lineup, Woody will move to bass and Mick Taylor will step in on guitar.

I wanted to hear what Mick Taylor thought about that, so I arranged an interview with him for *Beggars Banquet*. I'd met him a few times over the years, but never got to know him. Video James had his phone number and put us in touch.

Mick was living on Cornelia Street with his wife, Val, in a modest ground-floor apartment. We conducted the interview in his kitchen, which was connected to the living room. His Hall of Fame trophy was on the mantel, a few feet away.

As pleasant as I found Mick to be, I wouldn't describe him as a bellyful of laughs. I don't know whether it was my line of questioning or his normal disposition, but he seemed very introspective.

He reiterated his feelings about the Hall of Fame ceremony—that it "was a privilege and an honor to participate"—and reflected on how nice it was to see the other Stones. He explained that he was on good terms with Keith—he laid down a track for *Talk Is Cheap,* in fact—and that he'd become friendly with Woody through the years. "The Stones found just the right guy to replace me."

But as for Mick Jagger, he revealed, "I really haven't talked to [him] since I left [in 1974]. At the Hall of Fame ceremony, it was very superficial. I saw him for only five minutes before we went up, and then I saw him onstage. That was the extent of it."

I asked him point-blank whether he would tour with the Stones if they asked him.

Before anything, he made it clear that he had *not* been approached and that he didn't expect to be. "*But,*" he added, "if the Stones ever asked me to participate in a tour, I'd obviously say yes. Because I remember enjoying it so much when I was with them."

Okay, so then why did you leave?

"General frustration. Not being able to play guitar as much, or as expressively, as I would've liked. Not that there was anything wrong with what I did in the Stones. . . . But I can't honestly say I ever saw myself being there the rest of my life."

I asked if he experienced "withdrawal symptoms" after quitting.

"Oh, yes, I did. I won't say it was the smartest thing to do, to leave the world's most successful rock 'n' roll band. But at the time, I had no doubt in my mind that that's what I should do, and pursue other things, even though I had no clear idea of what."

No doubt, in the fifteen years since he'd quit the Stones, there was nothing on his résumé as high-profile—or lucrative—as the Stones. A solo album that went nowhere and a few nightclub gigs that didn't sell out. He toured in the mid-Eighties with Jack Bruce, John Mayall, and Bob Dylan, but only in a backup capacity. He was hoping to release another solo album, but added, "I haven't had much luck getting a record deal."

He said he had no regrets about leaving the Stones, but I still felt bad for him. By 1989, anyone with a few bucks or deutsche marks could rent him out. I know this because my P.O. box was crammed with godawful albums by godawful bands looking for a plug. "Dear Mr. Bill German," they'd write. "Will you please put in your fanzine about Mick Taylor on our new record? It is called 'We Love the Blues' and we are from Frankfurt and our band is the Blues Lovers and the song he is on is called 'The Blues Is the Best.' " I got enough of these things to stock two floors at Tower Records. And despite Mick's brilliance on guitar, even he could not cut through the sheer shittiness of them. He did it for the cash and nothing else.

As I glanced around the apartment, I contrasted his life to Woody's, the man who replaced him. For Woody, the night at the Waldorf was nothing more than an excuse to party. He chucked that trophy around like a toy, and, knowing him, he probably forgot to take it. Some bellboy from the Waldorf probably has it today. And if the rumor was true—the one about the Stones getting $65 mil up front—Woody stood to make seven or eight figures that year. Mick Taylor's loss was Ron Wood's gain. It's scary to think how decisions you make in your youth can impact the rest of your life. Mick was only 26 when he quit the Stones, the same age I was as I sat in his apartment.

After buttoning my coat, I walked to the mantel to see his Hall of Fame trophy up close. It was in pristine condition and looked like it had recently been buffed.

Prompted by Howard Stern's Baba Booey, Mick puts Keith in a
wrestling hold at Grand Central.

20

loyal flush

The Stones told us to meet them at Grand Central Station around noon. It was July 11, 1989, and they'd be announcing their upcoming *Steel Wheels* tour.

Normally, Grand Central's waiting room provides refuge for weary travelers and the homeless. But on this day, it was packed with three hundred journalists, hoping for a good quote or photo op. There was no air-conditioning, and the heat was unbearable. We had to suffer through speeches by the tour's promoter and one of the tour's sponsors. The gal from NBC looked like she was gonna pass out, and the guy from CNN was wiping his brow with his tie. Like everyone else, I used my *Steel Wheels* press kit to fan myself.

The Stones' publicists chose Grand Central because of the "steel wheels" train allusion and because they thought it'd match the excitement of the band's 1975 press conference, when they played "Brown Sugar" from the back of a truck on Fifth Avenue. In the 1989 scenario, the Stones would roll into Grand Central on a caboose and then answer some questions. No music.

It'd have been a great visual if they'd conducted the press conference from the back of that caboose, like a Teddy Roosevelt whistle-stop speech, but they didn't. Instead, we had to watch the Stones on a video screen as they deboarded the train. We didn't see them in person until they walked down a corridor and entered the waiting room. It was fairly anticlimactic and made us wonder why the Stones couldn't just meet us in an air-conditioned room somewhere else.

When the Stones finally joined us in our 100-degree hellhole, Mick stripped down to his undershirt and said, "My mascara's running." Keith asked if anyone needed a towel. The Stones fielded questions from the press, including one from Howard Stern's Baba Booey. He wanted to know whether Mick and

Keith had resolved their feud. Mick ran toward Keith, put him in a headlock, and said, "We don't have fights! We just have disagreements!"

Next came the tired questions the Stones knew to expect: "Is this your last tour?" "How much money are you going to make?" "Is this your last tour?" When one reporter asked if the Stones were in it for the money, Woody quipped, "No, that's the Who!" and Keith proclaimed, "We're in it for the glory, darling, the glory!"

Bill Wyman spent most of the press conference looking at his watch. But when someone asked if the Stones had enough energy to survive the tour, he shot back, "Ask my wife!" Those were the only words he uttered all day, but it was three more words than Charlie.

The entire Stones appearance lasted fifteen minutes. I bumped into Jane on my way out and thanked her for arranging my press pass. I also asked about interviewing Keith for my "tour preview" issue. I assumed it would be as uncomplicated as my previous interview with him—Keith wakes up one afternoon and tells Jane to send Bill German down—but she said, "I'm only Keith's manager. I don't work for the tour. If you want to interview Keith, you need to speak with Rogers & Cowan." She gave me their number and told me I was on my own.

Rogers & Cowan was the Stones' new publicity firm. After building a relationship with the Stones' longtime p.r. man, Paul Wasserman, I now had to start from scratch.

The firing of "Wasso" sent shock waves through the publicity biz. He was a legend in his field—his early clients included Bob Hope and Frank Sinatra—and he'd always had great relationships with the press. For a decade and a half, he'd seen the Stones through every conceivable high and low. When Keith got busted in Toronto, Wasso was there. When the Stones played on the back of that truck, Wasso was there. When the band nearly got arrested in San Antone, Wasso was there.

Wasso messed with journalists' heads sometimes, but for their own good. In 1975, he summoned the media to a restaurant on Fifth Avenue. He set up five microphones, presumably for the Stones to announce their new tour. Reporters and photographers clamored for a good spot and awaited the band's arrival. All of a sudden, the strains of "Brown Sugar" could be heard from outside the restaurant. Everyone turned around and looked out the window. There, on the back of a flatbed truck, were the Rolling Stones, performing live. Everyone grabbed their cameras and dashed outside. When "Brown Sugar" was done, Mick tossed out leaflets of the tour's itinerary, and the band rolled off. Every journalist came back to their office with great pictures and a great story. The Stones didn't field a single question, but got their message across. Very different from this Grand Central thing, which bordered on cruel and unusual punishment and never offered a "wow" factor.

Wasso treated my little fanzine like it was *The New York Times*. He supplied me with extra tickets and backstage passes to Keith's *Talk Is Cheap* tour and to Keith's Chuck Berry thing in St. Louis. And every time I'd speak with him, he'd engage me in something funny and unrelated, like, "Who's got the better corned beef sandwich, Bill? Katz's or Second Avenue?" I just knew that if Wasso were on the *Steel Wheels* tour, it would have been a fun trip for me.

Keith wanted to keep Wasso around, but Mick wanted him out. According to people in the p.r. industry, Mick was upset about how much time Wasso was spending with his other client, U2, and was peeved at Wasso's handling of the *Talk Is Cheap* campaign. Mick felt that Wasso should have prevented Keith's incendiary comments about him from reaching the press. Furthermore, Mick felt Wasso was too expensive and, at fifty-five, too old. Mick wanted younger and cheaper.

Rogers & Cowan, I'm told, got the Stones' contract because they put in the lowest bid. That doesn't imply they weren't qualified, it merely implies they were the least expensive. They'd recently lost some big name rock acts and were desperate to land the Stones.

Of course, if Mick wasn't motivated by the bottom line, the *Steel Wheels* tour might never have happened in the first place. It took just the right amount of money, from just the right man, to get the band to bury their hatchets.

Michael Cohl was a bold, relatively unknown concert promoter from Canada. He made the Stones an offer they couldn't refuse. An offer that changed the rock concert business forever.

Cohl got his start by running a strip joint in Ottawa called Pandora's Box. Then he began promoting concerts in and around Toronto. In 1973, he created a company called CPI, or Concert Productions International, and became Canada's top impresario. But he was still unknown in the States.

In the 1980s, he decided to up the ante. He gained financial muscle by partnering with brew master Labatt's. Under a new umbrella, named BCL, he approached the greatest rock 'n' roll band in the world and guaranteed them $65 million. For the Stones, it wouldn't matter if *three* tickets were sold or three *million* tickets were sold, they'd get their dough, risk-free, plus a huge chunk of the profits.

Cohl's offer was an attention grabber. The Stones' business managers—

and you can include Mick in that contingent—were blown away by it. They told Cohl's competitor, the legendary Bill Graham, to not even bother with an offer.

Graham had promoted the band's previous tour and was hoping to do the same in 1989. He appealed directly to Mick and reminded him of the blood, sweat, and tears he'd shed for the band. Didn't his loyalty count for something?

"I'm only doing this tour for one reason," Mick reportedly told him. "The money. And the numbers will be better [with Cohl]."

In exchange for the $65 mil, the Stones gave Cohl the licensing rights to all facets of the tour. He and BCL would own the name "Steel Wheels," as well as the Stones' likeness and logo, for the duration of the trek. In a corporate sense, the Stones literally sold out.

BCL's first priority was to recoup its investment, and, to do so, Cohl took some brash and innovative steps. For better or worse—most fans would say worse—he revolutionized the concert industry.

For starters, he charged $30 a ticket. I know it sounds ridiculous to say today, but that price was *outrageous* in 1989. No one had ever charged that much, especially for a stadium show. On the previous tour, fans paid $15 for Madison Square Garden. But that was eight years ago. Cohl was counting on the Stones' *new* demographic—the matured rock fan, with a good job and disposable income—to plunk down the cash.

Next, Cohl hooked up eye-popping sponsorship deals and unleashed a crass merchandising campaign. *Steel Wheels* jackets were now available at Macy's and JCPenney for $450.

Lastly, Cohl cut out the mom-and-pop local promoters who'd had relationships with the Stones since the Sixties. By incurring all the local expenses, such as stadium security and insurance, Cohl didn't have to split the income. But unlike most business models, where cutting out the middleman *lowers* prices, Cohl was asking consumers to pay *more*. He held a monopoly interest in the Rolling Stones, making him unstoppable and unchallengeable.

As in the case of Wasso, I knew that if Bill Graham were running the tour, I'd have been in for a smoother ride. I'd met Graham only a handful of times, but he identified with *Beggars Banquet*'s grassroots ethic. Like me, he would go the extra mile for his customers, regardless of the bottom line. He took his business dealings personally and would often hand out donuts to fans waiting in line.

On the Stones' last tour, Graham knew that the ticket itself was part of your concert experience. So, whether you were seeing the Stones at the Tangerine Bowl or at Candlestick Park, your ticket featured graphics from the *Tattoo You* album. And when some fans in Illinois petitioned him, saying the Stones should play their town, he actually responded: "We are overwhelmed by your gracious invitation by petition. We accept." He booked the Stones into the 9,000-seat Metro Center in Rockford, and the audience was entirely comprised of petitioners—a way to reward hardcore Stones fans for their loyalty and passion. On each ticket, instead of some sponsor's name, it read: "The Music Fans of Rockford present the Rolling Stones."

Another Graham story involves Keith's boot. The Stones were about to go onstage when Keith's heel broke off. Graham scrambled backstage until he found someone with a similar heel. He paid the stranger a hundred bucks, yanked off the heel, and sat on his hands and knees, hammering it into Keith's boot.

On the *Steel Wheels* tour, every ticket was an impersonal printout from a Ticketmaster computer, and I could not envision anyone from BCL fixing Keith's shoes, much less indulging a fans' petition. Keith's preference was to stick with Graham, but he knew which battles to pick with Mick and ultimately got outvoted. Graham and Wasso *out,* BCL and Rogers & Cowan *in.*

The day after Grand Central Station, I phoned Rogers & Cowan and requested an interview with Keith. They didn't know me from Adam, so I had to explain myself.

"Now tell me *again,*" said the secretary. "*What* magazine are you from?"

I cringed as I listened to myself. "Well, no, it's a newsletter, the Stones' official newsletter."

She had no idea what I was talking about, but said she'd leave a message for Linn, the head publicist.

Over the next couple of weeks, I tried reaching this Linn woman, with no success. After eleven years of *Beggars Banquet,* I felt I had nothing to show for myself. Keith talked about me on national TV that summer, and it still didn't help my cause. MTV profiled *Beggars Banquet* as part of its *Week in Rock* program and got sound bites from the Stones. "I know Bill German real well," Keith told MTV's Kurt Loder. "Where do you think he gets his information?"

Unfortunately, no one at Rogers & Cowan saw the clip, so they figured I was a delusional psychotic: "That kid with the fanzine called again. He thinks Keith Richards is talking about him on TV."

The great irony is that Rogers & Cowan was the firm that Woody's manager had hired two years earlier to publicize *The Works.* Meaning, Rogers & Cowan had represented *me*. But just my luck, no one who worked on the Woody account in 1987 was still with the firm in '89. The other great irony is that I'd contributed to Rogers & Cowan's very own press kit for the *Steel Wheels* tour. I was hired by CBS Records to write a twenty-page history of the Stones, which was then included in the Rogers & Cowan materials, and it carried my byline. "My name is in *your* press kit," I told the secretary.

Eventually, something clicked over there. A girl named Jill phoned and said I was in luck. "We can't let you have Mick and Keith, but we can let you have Ron Wood."

"I'll *take* him," I replied. "What's the best way to Wykeham?"

By "Wykeham," I was referring to the Stones' temporary rehearsal space, Wykeham Rise, in the sleepy town of Washington, Connecticut.

"No," said Jill. "We'll get back to you about when and where. I just wanted to let you know that we did get your messages and that, yes, you can interview Ron Wood."

Two weeks went by and nothing was arranged. In the meantime, I spoke to Woody on the phone. He invited me to the compound—"We'll do the interview in *my* room"—but I declined. I knew it'd be penny-wise and pound-foolish to circumvent anyone's authority, so I continued to wait.

By mid-August, the Stones switched their operations to Long Island. They were staying at the Garden City Hotel and rehearsing at the Nassau Coliseum. I asked Jill, "Should I go out to the Island?" but she answered, "We still don't know."

A month had passed since my initial request, and I began to doubt it would happen. Thousands of my readers were anticipating my "tour preview" issue, but I had to keep them waiting. I felt stuck.

At the end of August, the Stones switched locations again. This time to Philadelphia, the first stop of the tour. The opening show was two days away when my phone finally rang. "You can interview Ron this afternoon," said Jill.

"I'll hop the next Amtrak," I replied.

"Don't. You'll be doing it over the phone. I'll call you from Ron's room in a few hours, probably around 3."

I told her I preferred doing it in person, but she said I was slotted for a "phoner." When she called at 3 PM, she said, "Okay, I'm passing the phone to Ron now. You'll have ten minutes." Woody grabbed the horn and said, "You should be here. Room service just sent some bananas." And I said, "Yes, I *should* be there."

It was weird interviewing him from ninety miles away instead of twelve inches. His banana remark was a nod to the good ol' days on 78th Street, when we'd sit in his kitchen, sip Jack Daniel's, and open the door for Stevie Ray Vaughan. If I got hungry, he'd tell me to take a banana from the fruit bowl.

I asked him about the *Steel Wheels* rehearsals, and he said "You Can't Always Get What You Want" was giving him trouble. "We're doing [it] just like the record, with all the builds and crescendos. In '81, we would just start the song and kind of wing it. . . . But now we've got to work within limitations. . . . That song has got a lot of tricks in it for me."

I asked if he was nervous.

"Yeah, I *have* been. I fell ill for a few days, but now I'm ready to go."

I asked about the outrageous ticket prices.

"Well," he sighed, "the people are definitely getting their money's worth, not just from us, but from the pyrotechnics, the inflatables. And we've got the largest stage ever."

What about the crass merchandising campaign?

"*Moichandising?* I guess it's all fun. I never thought I'd see the day when merchandising—*moichandising*—would become as big as it is in rock 'n' roll. But maybe some good will come out of it."

I told him that I'd heard about a "clean and sober" rule for this tour. No drugs, no booze.

He skipped the drug part of my question, but did address the booze part. "Well, we *are* being sponsored by Budweiser and Labatt's, so the alcohol bit is not exactly true. But we *have* cut down a lot."

Budweiser, it should be noted, forked over a cool $10 million as the tour's primary sponsor. They got their name on every ticket—"Budweiser presents the Rolling Stones"—and got to use the Stones' name and likeness on posters, neon signs, and promotional displays. By the end of 1989, you couldn't enter a bar without being reminded of the Stones-Bud nuptials.

For 5 million bucks, MTV put their name on the tickets, too, in a deal that scored them the tour's TV rights. That's why they had exclusive live coverage of the Grand Central press conference and why the Stones performed "Mixed Emotions" on the MTV Video Awards. It's also why the Stones participated in the network's *Week in Rock* and *Rockumentary* programs.

Even bus rides were for sale on this tour. A company called Event Transportation Systems bought the "fan transportation rights" for $1 million. They offered fans a ride-plus-ticket to various shows. It was a bus trip that'd normally cost 10 bucks, combined with a ducat legally priced at $30, but, as a package, ETS charged $80 to $90 per passenger. Presumably, they were scalping the rides, not the tickets.

Considering that everything on this tour had a price tag, I felt lucky that my ten-minute phoner with my former co-author didn't cost me a dime. Before I hung up with Woody, he asked if I was coming to Philly for the opening show.

"I wouldn't miss it for the world," I told him.

"Good," he said. "Then stop by my room. I'll save you some bananas."

It was reassuring to know that despite all the obstacles and intermediaries, I still had Woody in my corner. But at the same time, I couldn't help but wonder: If the Stones flushed two guys like Wasso and Graham down the toilet—two guys who'd shown loyalty to this band and were recognized as legends in their fields—then what was in store for a nobody like *me*?

Escorted by cops and bodyguards, Mick (in baseball cap)
exits Toad's Place.

21

the gatekeepers

Navigating the *Steel Wheels* landscape involved more bumps than I expected. Just when I thought I'd figured it out—acquainting myself with the Stones' new publicists and the Stones' new tour promoter—I ran into another wall: the Rolling Stones' bodyguards. The most impenetrable wall of them all.

The difference between the Stones' bodyguards and those other folks was that the bodyguards would let you know where you stood—or where you could *not* stand—immediately. There were no secretaries to leave messages with and no mealy-mouthed I'll-get-back-to-yas. The bodyguards' responses were swift, direct, and could sometimes ouch.

These guys were the gatekeepers. The ultimate arbiters of who shall enter and who shall not. You did not want to get on their bad side or get off on the wrong foot with them.

Me, I got off on the wrong foot.

On August 12, 1989, the marquee at Toad's Place said, "Rock Dance Night, $3." Toad's was a nightclub in New Haven, Connecticut, that would advertise "rock dance nights" from time to time. On this night, however, they failed to mention the Rolling Stones.

The launch of the *Steel Wheels* tour was fast approaching, and the Stones wanted to test themselves before a live audience. Toad's held just five hundred people, so it'd be a tight fit and could only be pulled off in secret.

The night before the show, I was on the phone with Woody and he said he'd get me in. "You've got good timing," he added. "Because JC [the Stones' head of security] is comin' round my room. I'll give him your name and he'll put you on the list. But no plus-ones. They're only letting us have a few names, and Keith's already got forty!"

Minutes later, Video James phoned me. He insisted that I call Woody back and get *him* on the list, too. I told him that wouldn't be polite. "Woody and I left things on a good note, and I don't wanna bother him." But Video James kept laying a guilt trip on me—"Who helped you in the early days?"—so I finally relented.

"Woody, hi. It's me again. Sorry to bother you. I know you said no plus-ones, but I just heard from Video James. Can you put him on the list, too?"

"Video James wants to come? Well, you can ask JC, 'cause he just walked in." Woody passed him the phone. "Who *is* this?" he demanded to know.

"Um [gulp], Bill German."

"And you're a friend of Video James?"

"Um, yes."

"And you'd like to come to the show tomorrow?"

"Uh-huh."

"Well, then you and Video James find me outside the club." Click.

The next night, August 12, Video James and I shared a stretch limo from Manhattan to New Haven with six of Keith's friends. By the time we got to Toad's Place, it was a mob scene. Word had leaked on the Yale University radio station, so hundreds of fans packed York Street. Accompanied by news vans, police cars, and fire trucks. A sergeant on a megaphone told everyone to disperse. "No more tickets are being sold!"

Two hundred early birds indeed gained entrance for the $3 cover, but, beyond that quota, you had to be on the guest list. Video James, Keith's friends, and I fought our way through the crowd and got to the front door. A skinny girl sporting a nose ring was holding a clipboard. She worked for the club, not the Stones, and didn't seem thrilled to be there. Keith's friends gave her their names and went in. I gave my name and heard, "Sorry, you're not on the list."

"Maybe they spelled German with a 'J,'" I suggested. "Can you check that?"

"Nope, you're not on here. Can you move to the side, please?"

"Wait, are you sure that's the *band's* list? *Ron Wood's* list?"

"Look, there's only two lists. The band list and the house list. And you're not on either one."

Video James called out to JC. But JC was stationed near the backstage door, behind a barricade, and it was impossible to get his attention. He had his ear pressed to a walkie-talkie and was occupied with police sergeants and fire captains.

So Video James approached the frazzled Nose Ring Girl, took an upside-down peek at her guest list, and used someone else's name. She wasn't check-ing IDs, so it worked. I watched him disappear into the club. Everyone from our limo ride was in, except for me.

The scene on York Street remained chaotic. Cops, firemen, news crews, fans—I couldn't even get near JC. I resigned myself to spending the show out-side. I sat on the curb, contemplating what went wrong.

It began with the fact that JC had never heard of *Beggars Banquet* and didn't know who I was. He lived in England, and his bodyguard services weren't required when I was hanging at the Stones' houses in New York. On the other hand, he did know Video James, from the deals they'd struck in the past. Remember the Sony Walkmans on the '81 tour? That was JC. Video James would find a bunch of fans who wanted tickets and then act as a go-between. JC would get his Walkmans (or sometimes cash), the fans would get their tickets, and Video James would get a "commission" in the form of a free ticket or backstage pass. Point being, instead of associating me with some-thing legit, such as being Ron Wood's co-author, JC associated me with Video James. He presumed I was a desperate fan he could make a buck off of. He didn't put my name on the guest list and my entry into Toad's rested on a last-minute negotiation between him and Video James.

The whole thing made me miserable. The Stones were playing their first U.S. show in eight years, but the best I could give my readers was a second-hand report. I decided to get up off the curb and make a last-ditch plea to Nose Ring Girl. "I know you hear this all the time," I said, "but I'm *really* sup-posed to be on that list. Ron Wood told me so. I wrote a book with him, and I've been publishing the Stones' official newsletter for eleven years. There's a hundred people inside that'll vouch for me. You can even ask Ron Wood and Keith Richards. Ask them whether Bill German should be inside or outside."

At that point, she sensed I wasn't making it up. She dropped the clipboard to her side and, in exasperation, said, "Go! Just go already! But if I find out you're lying, I'm sending someone in to get you!"

The concert was pretty special. "We've been playing to ourselves," Mick told the crowd, "so it's nice to finally play for some *people*." They ran through eleven songs, including "Little Red Rooster," "Start Me Up," and their new one, "Mixed Emotions." They made a bunch of mistakes, but it added to the charm and intimacy. At the end of the show, Mick blew kisses to the crowd, and Keith shook hands with the fans up front.

As soon as I got back to my apartment, I cranked out a special bulletin about the show, scooping both *Rolling Stone* and *The Week in Rock*. I'd love to

say, "All's well that ends well," but I can't. Because the Toad's scenario re-
peated itself throughout the tour. Just because Keith or Woody invited me
somewhere, it didn't mean I was getting in. I still needed to be placed on a
guest list or let through a door, usually patrolled by JC and his behemoth
henchmen. They were the last word when it came to access, and, in their
world, might made right.

S'TEEL WHEELS' ...

Vol. 2   *The Rolling Stones*   No. 17

BEGGARS BANQUET

Get Rolling!

22

that's the ticket

As soon as I entered Room 227 of the Four Seasons, I knew this wasn't the Stones tours I'd read about in my mid-Seventies *Creem* magazines or seen in movies like *Cocksucker Blues*. The room registered to Mr. Simon Templar, aka Ron Wood, was littered with candy wrappers, confetti, and *Sesame Street* balloons. The groupies and syringes were noticeably absent, replaced by Barbie dolls and toy airplanes.

"We had a party for the kids," explained Woody. "Their last hurrah before going back to school."

It was August 31, 1989. In a few hours, 56,000 fans would cram Philadelphia's Veterans Stadium for the official *Steel Wheels* debut. I got to Philly that morning via Amtrak and went straight to the Four Seasons, where I rang Mr. Templar from the house phone. "Come on up," he said.

Jo made space for me on the sofa, by tossing the kids' stuff on the floor. Since the band's last tour, three of the Stones (Mick, Keith, and Woody) had sired a total of five children. The running joke, said Jo, was that this tour required a day care center.

Woody offered me a banana from the fruit bowl, and I declined. But when Jo said, "Oh, come on, you know you want one!" I grabbed one for old times' sake. As I peeled it, I looked over the set list for that night's concert, which Woody placed on my lap. The opening song was "Start Me Up," and the finale was "Jumpin' Jack Flash."

Woody was feeling some butterflies. "But we'll be fine once we get the first two or three numbers under our belt."

I glanced down at the list and made a mental note: second song, "Bitch"; third song, "Shattered." I was impressed to see twenty-eight songs on the list, including surprises like "2000 Light Years." The Stones would be exploring all tangents of their career, from blues and country to disco and psychedelia. "Twenty-eight songs must be a record for a Stones concert," I surmised. "You're really gonna *do* all these?"

"That's the plan," he said. "Or at least we'll die trying."

From Woody's room, I headed to the Ticket Lady. Believe it or not, the Stones hired someone to sell tickets to friends and family members. Repeat: To *sell* tickets to their friends and family, not *give* tickets to their friends and family. As part of the Stones' deal with Michael Cohl, there were absolutely no freebies on this tour. Even the Stones' wives had to pay.

I first learned of this policy when I phoned Jane's office and requested a ticket to the tour's opening show. As was Jane's new tack, she referred me elsewhere, this time to Shelley Lazar, the Ticket Lady.

Shelley would be traveling with the tour. In each city, she'd set up a box office in her hotel room, where the band's friends and family would purchase their tickets. Everyone would be charged the $30-or-so face, plus a nominal fee for Shelley's salary and travel expenses. The privilege of going through Shelley meant you didn't have to pay a scalper for a good seat. She usually gave you something between the 20th and 30th rows, which wasn't bad for a stadium show. (This tour was stadiums-only, with one exception.)

Over the course of the tour, Shelley sold tens of thousands of tickets to Stones "insiders," sometimes several thousand for a single concert. And the fun part was, you never knew who you'd bump into in her room. I once spotted Patti Hansen buying tickets for her sisters, and Karis Jagger (Mick's daughter by Marsha Hunt) laying out money for her college buddies.

The Stones' wives and kids, it should be noted, *were* able to see the shows for free. They possessed laminated "All Access" passes that allowed them entry into every stadium. But they could not take a seat in the regular audience without paying. They'd watch the show from an upstairs press box or squeeze next to the sound engineer in the mixing booth.

Unfortunately for Shelley, not everyone who came to her room was as gracious as Patti Hansen or Karis Jagger. Shelley had pains-in-the-ass who'd bounce checks on her or who'd literally pay her in nickels and dimes. Some of them were groupies who happened to meet someone in the entourage. Chicks who gave some roadie a handjob, in exchange for the referral. And ultimately, it was that type of person who'd bitch to Shelley about their seat. "I told you I wanted *Keith's* side! Gimme a refund!" Shelley was exposed to the worst side of human nature on this tour, but I never saw her lose her friendly disposition.

She used to be a fourth-grade teacher in New York, so maybe that's where she got her patience.

She handed me a 26th-row ticket and a VIP pass that I hadn't requested. "It comes with the ticket," she said. It was a stick-on patch that contained the date, as well as Keith's initials. "You're with *him*," she said.

From the Four Seasons, I hailed a cab to the Vet. Feeling like a VIP, I strutted to the stadium's backstage entrance. I soon discovered, however, that my pass would not grant me access to the Stones. For that, I needed one of those laminated passes like Patti Hansen. Instead, I was in a room with people who *knew* the Stones, but not *well enough*. For refreshments, we were served stale potato chips and warm Budweiser, king of all Stones sponsors. At 9 o'clock, a stadium security guard told us to clear the backstage area and head to our seats.

Although my Shelley seat was in the 26th row, I wound up sitting front row center. Some subscribers of mine had an extra ticket and invited me to take it. As soon as the house lights went down, all 56,000 people in the stadium jumped to their feet. A tape of the band's new song, "Continental Drift," blared through the PA. The song's haunting sound, replete with Moroccan chants, added to the anticipation. It built to a crescendo when—BOOM!—there was an explosion so hot and so loud, it singed my eyebrows and blew my eardrums. When the smoke settled, I had the Rolling Stones right in front of me, launching into "Start Me Up."

The rest of the show was no less spectacular. There were more explosions, more fireworks, plus raunchy inflatables that could've kicked the Macy's balloons' asses. Not to mention a 300-foot stage that served as the Stones' playground. The band had staircases to climb, ramps to roam, and were constantly in motion.

For purists like myself, the whole thing could've come off too Kiss-like. But I actually got caught up in it. I had just seen the Stones in a small bar, and that will forever be my preference. But for the duration of the *Steel Wheels* trek, I was willing to give this a shot. To see how far the Stones could take it by going HUGE. The show featured all sorts of dramatic moments—Mick emerging from a ball of fire during "Sympathy"—and was unlike any concert I'd ever seen.

After "Start Me Up" and "Bitch," the Stones rolled out their postpunk anthem, "Shattered." They got halfway through it when—*zap!*—everything went dark. No lights, no sound, no nothing. Mick realized what was going on and, as I described in *Beggars Banquet*, "bolted off the stage." The audience thought it was part of the act.

The four remaining Stones were as clueless as the rest of us. Keith and Woody kept strumming, but nothing was coming out. Charlie kept pounding, but only the first two rows could hear it. When it dawned on Keith what was happening—or *not* happening—he began pointing and laughing at Bill Wyman, implying it was *his* fault. After receiving direction from the wings, everyone removed their instruments and left the stage.

For what seemed like an eternity, we were kept in the dark. Nobody knew what was going on, and it began to get scary. Is the show over? Do we leave? There wasn't a single announcement to clue us in.

The grandiosity of the *Steel Wheels* production had made it seem invincible. But now, the Stones' indestructible ship was sinking. Fifty-six thousand fans grew restless and started chanting, "We want the Stones!" Debris was hurled at the stage, and I began to fear a Who-in-Cincinnati. I didn't feel safe in the front row.

After several minutes, the power was restored and the Stones returned, picking up like nothing happened. Mick offered no explanations or any of his usual quips. In fact, for the rest of the night, he hardly spoke to the crowd. I wrote in my next issue that "the band seemed distant."

After the concert, I went to the Four Seasons for a quiet reception with Keith and Woody. Keith had no idea what caused the power failure, but was willing to talk about it for *Beggars Banquet*. He told me why he was pointing at Bill Wyman: "I went up to him [during 'Shattered'] and asked him how things were going. He said, 'So far, so good.' And then, five seconds later, bam, we're dead."

Keith provided me with his latest pseudonym, Mr. LaFaccia, and told me to stay in touch through the tour. The only way to reach him on the road was by staying on top of his names.

After speaking with Keith, I drifted over to Jane. I told her that it had been my dream since childhood to follow the Stones on tour and produce a book about it. "Not a druggy tell-all," I stressed. "More a document or diary, like what I do in *Beggars Banquet*."

"Forget it," Jane said. "The band will never go for it."

I had no idea what she based her opinion on, but I didn't question her. It was only the first night of the tour, so I could put the idea on the back burner. My *other* idea was much more immediate, and that was to host a Stones-only radio show.

I'd always fantasized about being a DJ and had always been told I had the voice and diction for it, if not the face. But I'd been working on *Beggars Banquet* since the age of 16 and never had the chance to pursue it. I was busy with printers and post offices when I should have been interning at WNEW or making tea for Howard Stern. In 1987, however, I tried using my Stones expertise as my ticket into the radio biz. I proposed a "*Beggars Banquet* of the airwaves," a weekly program that would offer news and stories about the Stones. I dreamt about all the rare songs I could play and about all the clever segues. A weekly Beatles show already existed, so it wasn't far-fetched.

I pitched it to D.I.R., the company that produced *King Biscuit Flower Hour,* and was ignored. So I brought it to Westwood One, the largest radio network in America. An executive named Gary Landis liked my demo and said he'd consider it "if the Stones ever tour again."

He was true to his word. In August 1989, he called me up and hired me. He wanted me to host a daily—not weekly—program, where I'd report from every stop of the *Steel Wheels* tour. It'd only be a few minutes a day, but I'd be on a hundred stations across the country. I'd provide concert updates and backstage reports, in addition to sound bites from the Stones. Westwood One would pay me $500 a week and pick up my travel expenses. An absolute dream come true.

Unfortunately, when I mentioned it to Jane at the party, she shot me down. "Forget it," she said. "You can't do it." She told me that the Stones had auctioned off the rights to their speaking voices for $1 million. No one but the winning bidder could interview them on the radio. The tour's radio rights package, licensed through Michael Cohl, included the FM simulcast of the Stones' pay-per-view concert, as well as an exclusive two-hour interview with the band. A bunch of radio networks vied for the deal, but it was snagged by ABC.

"What it means," said Jane, "is that you can't interview the Stones on the radio. Not even for a second. And if you try, we'll throw you off the tour. We can't risk a breach of contract."

According to Jane, Westwood One was hiring me only because they were desperate. "They're using you because they lost the auction," she said. "They're looking for anyone with access to the band. So, you can work for Westwood and do your little show, but you won't be allowed into parties like this one, and you won't have a backstage pass like the one you're wearing, and you won't be allowed to get tickets through Shelley like you did for tonight. The choice is *yours.*"

In the morning, I phoned Westwood One from my hotel room in Philly. Instead of filing my first on-air report, I told them I was out. "It's not worth the risk," I said. "I've invested too much of my life into the Stones to piss them off at this point. I'm sorry, but I'm gonna have to side with *them.*" Better the devil you know.

Earlier in the year, Woody was in D.C. to jam with
(left to right) President George H.W. Bush,
Lee Atwater, and "soul man" Sam Moore.

23

the saint

Big Bob Bender was stationed outside Woody's room. It didn't matter that the Woodman had personally invited me, I still had to get past Bob. It was September 1989, and we were at the Omni Georgetown Hotel near Washington, D.C. The Stones had just come offstage at RFK Stadium.

Woody told me to knock on his door after the gig, but Bob was sitting in a chair right in front of it, reading a book. He looked up when I said, "Hi, I'm here to see Mr. Templar." Woody's secret pseudonym wasn't a required password, but I needed to convey I wasn't a stranger off the street. Although Bob had been bodyguarding the Stones since the Seventies, he'd never met me until this moment.

The first thing you noticed about Bob Bender was his girth. In his hands, that paperback book looked like a postage stamp. He was as wide as he was tall and, with his hillbilly beard and ponytail, reminded me of the old wrestler Haystack Calhoun. After interrogating me, he stood up, laid the book on his chair, and told me to wait in the hallway while he checked inside. A minute or so later, he opened the door and let me in. "Woody'll be down in a second," he said. "He's taking a pee." I took a seat on the couch and looked around.

I didn't know they made hotel rooms this large. It had a kitchen, a living room, and an upstairs. For a minute, I felt jealous. I didn't envy the luxury as much as I envied the ease and convenience. I was arranging everything on my own—planes, hotels, tickets from Shelley—while Woody had people doing it *for* him. He never had to book a hotel and he got a free ride to every gig.

To cover the tour as thoroughly yet economically as possible, I strategically picked which cities to visit. I predicted where the exciting stuff might take place and geographically spread myself out. I often stayed at the Stones' hotels and, to defray my costs, I'd sometimes take a roommate.

For a postconcert atmosphere, the Omni was surprisingly quiet. In fact, moments earlier, I witnessed room service bringing four glasses of milk to Keith's room. (He had his two little girls with him.)

Woody's pee was taking forever, so I leafed through some papers on the coffee table. One said, "Promotour Group Rooming List." It was a telephone directory of the tour's major players. Everyone from Michael Cohl to the band members. Except that the Stones were listed by pseudonyms. Mick went under "G. Fanshawe," his paternal grandmother's maiden name, while Bill went under "B. Stevens" and Charlie was "R. Roberts" (possibly because his middle name is Robert). Keith was still LaFaccia (I never found out the reference) and Woody was still "Simon Templar," the character from the 1960s TV show *The Saint.*

Another interesting item I found was the entourage handbook. It had a travel calendar—hotels, flight times—plus a list of instructions. Things like "Be on time for soundcheck" and "Make sure your luggage is properly tagged." But there was also an edict from the tour's sponsor: "If you are photographed during the tour and there is an alcoholic beverage in your hand, make sure it is Budweiser and not any other brand." I'm paraphrasing, but that was the gist of it.

Woody came downstairs and poured me a Jack & Ginger. He asked what I thought of the gig.

"Better than Philly," I answered. "I think you're in midseason form."

"Yeah, but me and Keith keep fucking up the beginning of 'It's Only Rock 'N Roll.' One night it's *his* fault, next night it's *mine.* We're gonna keep it in the set, but Keith thinks we should do 'Carol' instead."

He reached behind the sofa and grabbed a gorgeous red guitar. He placed it on his lap and plucked the opening notes to "Carol." "It's a 1937 Gibson," he said, knocking on its body. "I bought it when we were in St. Louis last week. And the best part is that Scotty Moore [Elvis's original guitarist] came to the show that night and taught me and Keith how to play 'My Baby Left Me.' And then Johnnie Johnson [Chuck Berry's original pianist] came onstage to play 'Little Red Rooster' with us. You've got to put that in *Beggars Banquet.*"

Jo came downstairs and announced that Lee Atwater had invited them to the White House for lunch. "I told him we can't make it."

Woody first met Atwater, the controversial chairman of the Republican National Committee, at that year's inaugural ball for George H.W. Bush. (Woody was a guest performer.) It didn't matter that Woody disagreed with everything Atwater stood for; they became fast friends. Woody invited him to the RFK gigs and gave him a guitar.

Woody acknowledged what Jo said and continued to caress his '37 Gibson.

I never got attached to a typewriter the way Keith and Woody loved certain guitars. He began strumming "Lady Jane" and told me, "Keith and I wanna do this instead of 'Play with Fire,' but it's hard convincing Mick. We also wanna add a lot of the new stuff, like 'Hold On to Your Hat' and 'Terrifying,' but Mick keeps saying we're not ready."

The mere mention of Mick's name prompted Jo to lodge her own complaint. "Can you believe," she said, "that Mick yelled at me the other night because I'm blond? It's true! I was walking behind the amps during the concert, and I was wearing black, like I'm supposed to. But after the concert, he pulled me aside and said he saw my blond hair sticking out my hat. He said, 'Jo, if I can see your hair during the concert, then everyone in the audience can see it. It's a distraction.' I told him, 'Do you want me to dye my hair black?' I'm sorry, but I am not dying my hair black for Mick Jagger."

"Oh, well," I sighed. "I guess he was just being a perfectionist."

To switch gears, I asked Jo if she had any pictures of the Stones with Scotty Moore or Johnnie Johnson. She said she didn't. Photos like that were hard for me to obtain. Tight restrictions meant that some of the tour's most magical moments—both onstage and off—were never seen by the masses.

The policy, put in place by the Stones' publicists, Rogers & Cowan, went like this: Photographers were not allowed to shoot past the first two songs. Whether you were shooting for *Time* or *Beggars Banquet,* you were escorted out of the photo pit—and out of the stadium—after "Bitch."

The result is that anything that occurred onstage after the first ten minutes went unphotographed by the media. Mick emerging for "Sympathy" in a ball of fire? Not photographed. The band's bow, during which Charlie would grab Keith's guitar? Not photographed. Clapton's guest appearances? Not photographed. The powers that be were very tight about it, and I'm not sure why. Either Mick didn't want close-ups after his makeup smudged, or the Stones and Michael Cohl felt like, "Hey, you wanna see the best moments of this tour? Buy a ticket!"

The policy wasn't a problem for *Time* or *Newsweek* because they could run a generic photo from the concert: "The Rolling Stones, performing last week at XYZ Stadium." But I *specialized* in the Stones, so my readers expected more. To get the situations I described above, I had a friend stuff a telephoto lens down his Fruit of the Looms and shoot from the 30th row.

I also begged and pleaded with Rogers & Cowan. There was one photographer who shot the entire concert each night, but was a mercenary for the tour. He had to surrender his film to the tour's muckamucks, who decided what to do with the pictures. Tons of people would have to approve them—Mick, Tony King, Michael Cohl—before Rogers & Cowan could release them to any magazine. It killed me when they gave some backstage photos to *People* instead of *Beggars Banquet.*

Woody didn't know the difficulties I faced on this tour. As usual, he assumed every door was open to me and that everyone was being helpful. It was not my intention to have him think otherwise, so I didn't talk about it. I never told him about my JC-Toad's fiasco, because I knew he and Keith didn't like snitches or crybabies. But it was Chuch Magee, who stopped by Woody's room at 2 AM, who got me to open up.

Chuch (pronounced "chooch") had been Woody's guitar tech since the Faces. When Woody joined the Stones in the mid-Seventies, he brought Chuch along, and he soon became chief of the road crew. Big Bob let him into Woody's room without screening.

Chuch was one of the most down-to-earth people I ever met around the Stones. When the band wasn't touring or recording, he led a decidedly non–rock 'n' roll life in Marquette, Michigan. He made syrup from maple trees and mentored youth groups at his local church. I got to know him during the *Dirty Work* sessions in New York, and he was a huge supporter of mine. He appreciated *Beggars Banquet*'s grassroots ethic, yet felt it deserved wider exposure. "They should offer it at the concerts," he suggested to me this night.

I told him I had no idea how to go about that, so he gave me the name of BCL's top merchandising guy, Norman Perry. "Keith and I can't stand him," Woody interjected, "but he's the guy who sets up the T-shirts and jackets at the stadiums."

Next, Chuch asked about my airfare, hotels, and concert tickets. "Who's paying for that stuff?" When I said it was coming from my own pocket, Woody seemed surprised. "That's not right!" he exclaimed. "First off, we should have you on the plane with us. I'll talk to Keith about that. Second, after everything you've done for this band, you should not have to pay to see us play."

I explained that my "business arrangement" with the Stones was "I make my own money and I pay my own way. That's how I *like* it."

"Nah," Woody argued, "that's not right. I've got an *idea.*"

I leaned in to hear his idea, but he drifted into one of his ADD moments. "Hang on," he said.

"What, Woody? What's wrong?"

"Hang on."

He stared at the center of my face. Then, he tapped the bridge of my nose with his index finger. "Do you realize, Bill, that your nose is broke?"

"Yeah, Woody, I know. I broke it when I was a kid. I never got it fixed."

"How'd you do that?"

"Football. I was playing football without a helmet. But we can talk about that later, Woody. Tell us your idea!"

"Hmmm," he said. "I never noticed that before. American-style football?"

Great. The guy worked inches from my face for the better part of 1986, but he chooses now to obsess over my nose. And like *he's* one to talk about schnozzes. "Yeah, Woody, yeah. American football. What's your frickin' idea?"

"Oh, *right*. My idea is to get you a laminate straight away. That way, at least you won't have to pay to see us play."

He grabbed the "Promotour Group Rooming List," looked up a number, and dialed: "JC, it's me. I've got Bill German here and I'm gonna send him down to get a laminate." He listened to JC's response, and then said, "Sorry about that. I didn't realize. I'll tell him."

As if I already hadn't made a bad impression on JC, this 3 AM phone call woke him up. He told Woody I should knock on his door "first thing in the morning," around 9 o'clock.

The thing is, I'd already been to JC's room on this trip, but under a different guise. Before the concert at RFK, I'd gone to JC's room to purchase a wad of tickets. They weren't for me, and I had nothing to do with it. I was simply a courier. Video James had arranged for twenty fans to get tickets at JC's "special price." Video James couldn't make it to Washington, so he'd asked me to collect the money from the twenty fans and then bring it to JC. I said, "I don't wanna get involved," but he said it was too late. "JC's already expecting you, and I already told everybody to come to your room and give you the money."

Unlike the '81 tour, JC was not bartering for Sony Walkmans. This time, he enacted a flat fee of $100 per ticket. A considerable markup from the $30 face, but cheaper than what scalpers were getting. In fact, scalpers were coming to JC for *wholesale* deals.

Because there were no freebies this tour, JC had to pay the Ticket Lady the requisite $30 per. But unlike the average bear, he had carte blanche regarding how many tickets he could purchase from her. This particular transaction netted him $70 per ticket, times twenty tickets, so do the math. If he averaged twenty tickets for all sixty shows, it'd be some serious coin.

Before you say, "I bet Keith would be pissed if he knew about JC's wheeling and dealing," let me tell you that Keith *did* know and that he wasn't pissed. What mattered to the Stones and Michael Cohl was that JC was the best security man in the business. He knew every nook and cranny of every hotel and stadium the band was visiting. He moved the Stones swiftly and safely from Point A to Point B every day. If he pocketed a few "gratuities," it was merely a perk.

If asked about it, Keith would tell you his general philosophy in life, which is caveat emptor: "Buyer beware." You don't like the setup, don't buy the tickets. Second, he'd remind you that you're getting a great fucking deal. You're getting a 30th-row seat for a hundred bucks. Try getting a deal like that from some scumbag scalper in the parking lot. To Keith's thinking, JC was performing a service. The harsh reality was: Some of the best tickets in the house weren't put on sale to the public. They were held back by BCL and/or the Stones organization. If JC didn't scalp 'em, *someone* down the food chain would have, and for a lot more.

Before I knew it, a dozen or so Stones freaks were banging on my door and dropping off C-notes. After collecting the money, I headed to JC's room by myself. I was absolutely dreading this. It was going to be my first time speaking with JC face to face, and I wished I could wear a bag over my head. I did not want him to associate me with this crap. First Toad's Place and now *this*.

The transaction went quick. I handed him the cash, he handed me the tickets, and I left. I wanted to let him know I wasn't one of the twenty desperate fans who needed to overpay for a ticket, but I kept my mouth shut.

Anyway, that was *Sunday* morning, September 24. Now let's flash to *Monday* morning. This time, instead of visiting JC's room as a flunky for Video James, I was visiting as a friend of Ron Wood's—which still didn't guarantee my "All Access" laminate. I knocked on JC's door at 9 on the dot.

"Who's *that*?" he barked. He sounded annoyed.

"Um, Bill German. Woody spoke to you last night—"

He cracked the door an inch. "Bloody hell. You here again? What you want?"

"Remember, Woody called you last night—"

"Oh, right," he sighed. "So I'm to give you a laminate, then? Is that why you woke me from a dead sleep last night?"

"Um, well, that was Woody's idea."

He swung the door open and invited me in. His room was small like mine. I sat on a chair in the corner, and he sat on his bed, putting his socks and shoes on.

"So let me get this right," he said. "You're a friend of Video James?"

"Yes, you can say that."

"And how do you know Woody?"

"Well, I wrote a book with him. And I've also been running the Stones' newsletter, *Beggars Banquet,* for the last eleven years. Their official newsletter. They advertised it in one of their albums."

This was my one chance to plead my case and change his opinion of me. He didn't seem impressed by my résumé, nor by my friendship with Woody, but I suppose I passed his test. After several minutes, he reached into his dresser drawer and pulled out the pass. "Woody said to give you a laminate, so, young man, here's your laminate."

Through it all, I think he still viewed me as nothing more than an over-achieving Stones fan. And, as such, he felt he was losing out on a customer. Like, "Woody's gone and ruined it for me." For the remainder of the tour, we had a weird cat-and-mouse relationship. He'd be nice to me one day and put me through hell the next.

Either way, this laminate would make my life easier. It would save me a thousand bucks on tickets and was an upgrade in my backstage mobility, something that'd improve my reportage.

The pass featured a green *Steel Wheels* logo and said "All Access." On the top, there was an ID number. And, of course, there was a string attached—a green lanyard, so you could wear it around your neck.

Whether other strings were attached, I'd soon find out.

After jamming on "Little Red Rooster," Clapton joined me
in the cubbyhole.

24

sympathy for the
devil's advocate

When my favorite baseball team messed up, my favorite rock band took their turf. The Mets missed the '89 playoffs, so it freed Shea Stadium for some early October Stones dates. On October 10, I rode the 7 train like I would to a ballgame. The difference was that a sing-along erupted at Queensboro Plaza. My entire car was belting out "She's a Rainbow." We were packed like sardines, but everyone was singing at the top of their lungs and drinking from paper bags. I was the only one not participating and was feeling anxious. This was the first time I'd be using my All Access laminate and had no idea if it'd work.

I'm sure I was the only person on the 7 train with an All Access pass because anyone else who possessed one was in a limo or in a van with the band. I hid it in my pocket because I didn't want to be hassled by drunken fans. I finally whipped it out at the stadium and was let right through.

I headed to the backstage area and began looking for friendly faces. But the first guy I ran into was Alan Dunn. He pulled me over like a highway patrolman and asked to see my license and registration.

Alan was part of the Mick Camp. He was basically Mick's Jane Rose. He worked in London and was the senior member of the Stones' entourage. He began as Brian Jones's chauffeur in 1967, but had been Mick's right-hand man the last two decades. He asked my name, so I said, "Bill German, from *Beggars Banquet*. I'm looking for the buffet." He didn't laugh at my lame joke—my attempt to break the tension—and acted like he'd never heard of me or my newsletter.

Alan possessed a pasty British complexion, with a husky physique and scraggly beard. I'd seen him from afar a few times, but never approached him because he seemed so serious. Even at parties, he'd never smile or laugh.

Unfortunately for me, it was Mick's people, not Keith's people, who were running the store. They all held official positions on this tour, and worked with the promoter, publicists, and bodyguards. It stemmed from the fact that Mick was considered "upper management," while Keith was merely "talent." While Mick was conducting business meetings and analyzing ticket sales each morning, Keith was facedown in his pillow.

As the general of the Mick Camp, Alan Dunn was as high-ranking as you could get. His tour title was "logistics director," which meant nothing transpired without him knowing. When he spotted me with that laminate, his eyebrow went up two inches and he approached me immediately. After asking my name, he reached to my chest and grabbed the laminate. He examined it closely to make sure it wasn't fake. He noted the ID number. My "270" revealed I was a guest of Woody's, which did not impress him.

Alan Dunn outranked Ron Wood on this tour. Alan was schlepping Brian's luggage when Woody still had zits. Furthermore, the Mick Camp—including Mick—viewed Keith and Woody's friends as parasites. Lowlifes who'd attached themselves to Keith and Woody in New York, and who were now gunking up the "steel wheels." According to Alan Dunn's first impression, that's who I was.

Eventually, he let go of my pass, and it dropped back to my chest. He dryly mumbled, "Up the lift"—the answer to my buffet question—and let me walk away. But he'd eye me with suspicion the rest of the tour.

I rode the elevator to the stadium's Diamond Club level and walked into a mass of chaos. Dozens of people were scurrying around like ants. They were wearing backstage passes and seemed pretty self-important. But their bubbles burst when they discovered their backstage passes didn't really mean backstage.

The Ticket Lady doled out thousands of passes to people who bought tickets from her. I don't know what some of these people envisioned, but a lot of them seemed disappointed, if not frustrated. People began suffering from pass envy and couldn't resist looking at each other's chests. "What pass does *he* have? Why don't *I* have that pass? Does *his* pass get him into the *real* backstage?"

The reality was that your so-called backstage pass determined the food you could eat, not the Rolling Stone you could meet. I spotted at least eight types of passes and learned that each corresponded to a specific buffet, sponsored by a different host: MTV offered pasta shells, CBS Records had meatballs, and Budweiser had pepper steak. The passes were in every kind of shape—round, square, oval, triangular—and read "VIP," "Hospitality," or "Guest." I even saw one that said "Steal Meals." There were so many types, a reference chart was posted on the wall. Like a rock 'n' roll caste system.

As usual, I had no idea where I belonged. I assumed my All Access pass would act as a master key, but it didn't. When I tried to peek in on the Budweiser buffet, I was told I needed room-specific pass. I eventually wound up at CBS. I spotted Dustin Hoffman and Milli Vanilli in there and the meatballs weren't bad.

My All Access pass did allow me into some "privileged" places. At one point, I found myself in the *real* backstage area, on the stadium's ground level. The Stones were shaking hands with some "non-VIPs."

I asked Jill-the-publicist what was going on, and she explained it was a meet-and-greet for some Budweiser folks. Not the suits, but the rank and file. Truck drivers and gals from the bottling plant. I don't know if they were employees of the month, but they were getting to meet the Stones. They posed for a group photo, got a handshake, and were escorted out. The whole thing took a minute, but, for those fans, it'd last a lifetime.

I'd never heard of this "meet-and-greet" stuff and knew it was new for the Stones. If you got backstage on their previous tours, it was more like meet-and-fuck, not meet-and-greet. But things were different now. The event took place for one reason, and that's Budweiser's $10 million sponsorship. Regardless, a bunch of regular fans met the band, and I thought that was cool.

To get to the field from backstage, I walked through the Mets' bullpen, where my beloved Tug McGraw and Jesse Orosco used to reside. It led me to an area behind the stage, where I discovered that the Mets' outfield wall had not been taken down. In fact, the Stones' stage had been built *over* it. So I went under the stage, where no one was looking, and rammed into the wall like Rusty Staub in Game 4 of the '73 playoffs. So far, it was the best part of my All Access pass.

It was a few minutes before showtime and I still had no idea where I'd be watching it. Patti Hansen told me she was going to stand in the mixing booth, so that's where I headed. But I was told I needed a separate "Mixer" pass, in addition to my All Access pass. In most cities, All Access was good for the mixer—the booth in the middle of the field where the sound engineer sits—but in New York, where the band had so many friends, relatives, and business associates, the booth was too crowded.

Dustin Hoffman was watching the show from an upstairs press box, but I heard the view was crappy. I remembered I had friends in the 25th row, so I squeezed in next to them. But during "Tumbling Dice," an usher shined a light in my face and asked to see my ticket. When I pointed to my All Access pass, he told me to move along. No ticket, no seat.

I wandered around for a few more songs, before visiting a subscriber in the wheelchair section. The guy said his chair was wired for sound, recording the show for a bootleg. I asked how he snuck the equipment in, and he said, "They never search the cripples."

During "You Can't Always Get What You Want," I went to the VIP bathroom. From the urinal behind me, I heard a thick Eastern European accent: "Come on, vee have to go votch Clapton."

It was Keith's friend Freddy Sessler, the 66-year-old Holocaust survivor. I could barely zip my fly, let alone wash my hands, before he grabbed my wrist and dragged me out the door. We went through the Mets' bullpen and out behind the stage. I had no clue where he was leading me, but he was huffing and puffing. "Vee can't miss it, vee can't miss it! I know Clapton since he vuz a nuttink! A little pisher! Dat's vy he wrote dat song about me, 'Hello Old Friend.' Dat song is about *me*!"

I could barely understand him, let alone argue with him. I followed him up a ramp that led to the stage. As the Stones were hitting the crescendo of "You Can't Always Get What You Want," a security guard shined a light on my pass and told me I could go no further.

Freddy had an orange All Access laminate, as opposed to my green one. His pass could beat up my pass. Orange allowed the bearer onstage—on the frickin' stage!—whereas mine did not. But Freddy exclaimed, "He's vit me!" and it worked. Before I knew it, I was *onstage* with the Rolling Stones.

Freddy led me to a cubbyhole, right next to the backup singers. It held a dozen or so people and was sort of like a baseball dugout. Jerry Hall was in there, and so was Keith's dad. We were getting a slightly skewed view—one of the reasons Patti Hansen usually didn't sit there—but the intensity was mindboggling. When Mick ventured down the stage-left ramp, you lost sight of him. But when he and Woody strolled down the stage-*right* ramp, you literally could grab their ankles and trip them.

For better or worse, I was seeing what the Stones see. And it helped me understand why rock stars get fucked up. Being in front of 60,000 screaming fans for two hours can be an overwhelming experience. There's no way to healthily match that intensity when the tour is over and you're home in your slippers eating corn flakes.

Eric Clapton took the stage to jam on "Little Red Rooster." And as soon as he finished, he entered the cubbyhole to sit between me and Keith's dad. During "It's Only Rock 'N Roll," he actually danced. I was too bashful to say hello to him or to remind him that we'd met before.

The cubbyhole afforded me the opportunity to peek behind the curtain, so to speak, and see how the tricks were done. The Stones had a whole city back there. Dozens of people with headsets and walkie-talkies. Chuch Magee tuning guitars, and Jo rummaging through Woody's coat rack. Not to mention the "blow-job team"—the dozen or so guys who inflated the 50-foot-high "Honky Tonk Women" balloons. Behind the scenes, you could see them falling over each other, struggling against the elements.

The opening of "Sympathy for the Devil" was the most dramatic part of each concert. That's where the stage would go dark, and nothing but a tribal bongo beat and piercing howls could be heard. Suddenly, out of the darkness, Mick would appear from a ball of flame, high atop the stage.

As dramatic as it was for the audience and for Mick, it was remarkably nondramatic for the four Stones below. While the audience fixated on the Stones' lead singer a hundred feet in the air, the four remaining band members, unseen on the dark and smoky stage, had nothing to do but mill around. To pass the time, they'd come to the cubbyhole and chat with us. Keith would light a cigarette or blow kisses to his kids. Charlie might talk to his wife, Shirley. And Woody would invite the celebrity du jour to his hotel room after the show. On this particular night, October 10, Woody said hi to actor David Keith and asked me how I was doing. I never imagined I'd be conversing with the Rolling Stones *during* a Rolling Stones concert.

High above the stage, Mick struck a daunting pose during "Sympathy." The light behind him would cast his giant shadow across the stadium. But from the cubbyhole, I could see him return from his mighty perch via a tiny elevator. Like catching Houdini in a secret compartment.

The cubbyhole perspective also allowed me to detect the subtle, nonverbal communication between the band members. Stuff not meant for the audience. Keith winking to Charlie, Bill sighing, or even Keith playing with Mick's head. He'd do it by messing up Mick's cues. Mick would be waiting for Keith to hit a certain note, but Keith would make Mick wait for it and throw off his timing. Mick would pretend to ignore it, but Keith would make a face to Woody or Charlie like, "The fucker got *his* right there."

I was surprised to discover that the Stones, primarily Mick, were using a teleprompter. The person operating it was inside the cubbyhole, and I could read what he was posting. It wasn't like the latter-day Sinatra, who needed a teleprompter to remember his lyrics, it was more like stage direction. "Brown

Sugar: Mick left ramp, Ronnie right." "Tumbling Dice: Take off green jacket." And, "Hey, New York, how ya feelin'?"

"Mick left ramp, Ronnie right" was for the lighting guys to avoid surprises. It also prevented Mick and Woody from colliding on the runway or pushing each other down the steps. In other words, the teleprompter served as a traffic cop. And as for "Hey, New York," it wasn't that Mick didn't know what city he was in—the old showbiz cliché—but to ensure he said it at the right moment and without repeating himself.

"Brown Sugar," the third-to-last song, was Alan Dunn's cue to fish the family members out of the cubbyhole and to place them into waiting vans. When he spotted me, he didn't seem pleased, but he was too busy to throw me out. He escorted Jerry Hall and Bert Richards from the cubbyhole and disappeared.

The Stones' family members never got to see the end of a Stones concert. They were already in the idling vans that were set to zoom out of the stadium. The only passengers missing were the Stones themselves. After taking their final bow onstage, the band would be ushered down a ramp (with towels on their heads, like Muhammad Ali) and shoved into the vans. Within seconds, the Stones' caravan would be racing out of the stadium, through the city streets, escorted by a police motorcade. Sirens blaring in the night. So fast, so precise, so imposing, it'd resemble a military operation.

I was lucky to catch several *Steel Wheels* concerts from that cubbyhole, and I shared my observations with my readers. I assumed they craved such behind-the-scenes scoops, but that wasn't always the case. During a chance meeting one night, a fan took me to task. "No way do the Stones use a teleprompter!" he shouted. "Take that *back!*"

He also didn't like when I told him that, contrary to rumors, the Stones would *not* be jamming in any nightclubs. On the '81 tour, they stopped into Chicago's Checkerboard Lounge to jam with Muddy Waters. But this time, their massive insurance policy didn't allow such spontaneity. "If Keith breaks his leg during a Stones concert," I explained, "it's covered by the insurance. But if he breaks his leg in a bar during an off night, it's not."

The fan told me I was full of it. He held to his illusion that the concerts were still spontaneous and that the Stones were still rebellious rock stars, who could do whatever they wanted. I envied his illusions. I began to wish that I didn't see how the magicians did their tricks and that I didn't know so much about the band's day-to-day operations. It was making things less fun for me.

Keith and Freddy (second from left) were never far apart.
(Flanked by Don Covay and Sarah Dash at my 1988 party.)

25

rock 'n' roll
rasputin

If you had to pick a "Rolling Stones insider" out of a line-up, Freddy Sessler would be your last candidate. He was a Holocaust survivor with two decades on Keith and *four* decades on *me*. Yet he's the one who possessed that orange All Access laminate and brought me onstage at Shea.

I met him in the mid-Eighties, during an all-nighter at Woody's house. His first words to me were "So vot are you vorking on vit Voody? You vant maybe some blow?" His accent was so thick, I can't do it justice in print. He pronounced Keith "Keet" and Woody "Voody" and sounded like Peter Lorre from those old horror films. His big schnoz and thick lips made him a cross between Chico Marx and Yasir Arafat.

By his own estimation, Freddy had been on every Stones tour since *England's Newest Hitmakers.* He had supposedly laid more groupies than Mick Jagger and Bill Wyman and snorted more toot than Keith and Woody. His biggest claim to fame, however, was his participation in the "Fordyce Four incident."

It took place in 1975, after a Stones concert in Memphis. The band was boarding its private jet to Dallas, when Keith made an announcement: "Leave *without* me, 'cause I'm *drivin'.*" He wanted to experience America's Deep South firsthand and not from the window of an airplane, so he rented himself a Cadillac. The tour's promoter, Peter Rudge, begged Keith not to do it, but Keith told him to fuck off. He got behind the wheel and brought along three passengers—Freddy, JC, and Woody. A quartet that would come to be known as the "Fordyce Four."

Fordyce, Arkansas, I'm told, was the kind of place where hog-calling contests made front-page headlines. The most heinous crime was the theft of a peach pie from Aunt Bea's windowsill. So when Keith Richards and Ron Wood of the Rolling Stones stumbled into the town's greasy spoon, no one knew what to make of it. The town's police force kept its eye on these suspicious-looking characters.

After a burger and a pee, Keith and his traveling companions hopped back in the Caddy. But when Keith drove off, the car kicked some dust and spun out a bit. Deputy Barney Fife flipped on his siren and pulled them over. A search of the car turned up an illegal knife and a stash of cocaine. "The Fordyce Four" were hauled to jail—passing Floyd's Barber Shop on the way—and it looked like the Stones' concert in Dallas, if not the whole tour, might be canceled.

Two things worked in Keith and Woody's favor. First, Barney Fife found only a smidgen of the coke that was actually in the car. As Keith would reveal to me years later, "There was more *drugs* in that car than *car*." And second, Freddy Sessler played the fall guy. He convinced the judge, who also ran the general store and was the mayor on Tuesdays and Fridays, that he was a hitchhiker and that the drugs were all his. "Vot means Rolling Stones? I don't know dem."

The others shrugged in agreement. "Yeah, we never met this guy before today." After seven hours in jail, they were allowed to leave. Freddy got booked.

No one ever forgot that Freddy took one for the team. He was credited with saving the tour and was rewarded for his loyalty. He was granted carte blanche and was loosely recognized as the Rolling Stones' team mascot—like Paul's grandfather in *A Hard Day's Night,* but nowhere near as cute.

As the years rolled on, however, familiarity bred contempt. There was a time when Freddy was as friendly with Mick as he was with Keith, but not on the *Steel Wheels* tour. It was clear to me that Freddy wasn't welcomed by the Mick Camp as much as he was tolerated.

Freddy epitomized everything Mick despised about Keith Campers. He saw Freddy as a drug-dealing boor. If Keith slept through a rehearsal, he knew it was a Freddy pill that knocked him out.

In her Hollywood memoir, *You'll Never Eat Lunch in This Town Again,* film producer Julia Phillips described her backstage encounter at a 1975 Stones concert: "There is a smelly Israeli named Freddie [*sic*] who seems to be very important to everybody. He carries two medium-sized bottles filled with rock cocaine. He offers some to Goldie [Hawn] and some to me, [but] we turn him down."

She got it wrong. Freddy was Polish, not Israeli. But he *was* important to a lot of people, including Keith. When Freddy entered a room, even if the Stones were there, he was impossible to miss. He was loud, boastful, and opinionated, and you never knew when he was telling you the truth or shoveling you horse crap. I begged him once to tell me his life story, and here's what I got:

He was born in Krakow, Poland, in 1923. When he was 15 years old, Hitler's forces came through his Jewish neighborhood, torching homes and shooting people in the street. Freddy, along with his entire family, was rounded up and sent to a nearby concentration camp.

He attempted an escape one night, and it worked. He left his family behind and made his way to Russia. But when the Communists got hold of him, they shipped him to Siberia. They then sent him to England during World War II, because the Allies needed translators in London. Freddy spoke English, Polish, Russian, German, and Yiddish.

When the war was over, he returned to Poland to search for his family, but learned they were dead. The house he grew up in was no longer standing. Freddy had to start his life over.

Being a jazz fan, he romanticized New York, so that's where he headed. He became a fixture at nightclubs like Birdland and supported himself by taking a job as a busboy. While working at the famed Lindy's, he hobnobbed with some of his idols, like Louis Armstrong, Duke Ellington, and Billie Holiday. He befriended them and began scoring them drugs.

Eventually, Freddy took a job with Volkswagen. In 1961, as the Berlin Wall was going up, he was transferred to the company's headquarters in West Germany. He frequented the strip joints and music clubs of Hamburg, where he caught a show by an unknown band from England. A bunch of kids who called themselves the Beatles. *I became good friends vit John Lennon. Very good friends.*

A year or so later, Freddy moved to London, where he stayed in touch with John. He would see John's band at the Cavern in Liverpool. One night, John introduced Freddy to a kid who said, "I'm gonna be the greatest guitarist in the world someday." *And you know who dat kid vuz? Eric Fucking Clapton! Dat's vy he wrote dat song about me, "Hello Old Friend."*

Lennon also told him to check out an up-and-coming band at London's Crawdaddy Club. *And you know who dat vuz? De fucking Stones! I became good friends vit Brian and vit all of dem.*

That's the journey that led Freddy Sessler to the Rolling Stones. If even a tenth of it is true, it's still pretty amazing.

When Freddy appeared on the scene, he immediately stood out from the pack. He was twenty years older than anyone else in the room. Keith immediately gravitated to him. As I've pointed out before, you need to bring something to the table, like drugs or celebrity, to hang with the Stones. Freddy had the drug part covered, but he offered Keith something more. To Keith, Freddy represented a father figure. Keith's *real* dad had split on him when he was young, so Freddy filled a definite void. Keith and Freddy may have acted like mischievous siblings at times, but there was an undeniable father-son thing underneath.

In real life, Freddy was married four times and sired two girls and three boys. His daughters wanted nothing to do with his Stones exploits, so I never met them. But his two eldest sons signed up for the family business. They became gophers and roadies for the band. One of them married Mackenzie Phillips, making Freddy and Papa John Phillips proud in-laws.

Another thing that bonded Keith and Freddy was World War II. Keith takes the war personally—"Hitler dumped a V-1 on my bed"—and has been obsessed with it most of his life. To Keith's thinking, he and Freddy had each stared down Der Führer and won.

The two became inseparable and were constantly bailing each other out of bad drug deals and near-overdoses. And so, no matter what anyone thought of Freddy on the *Steel Wheels* tour, no one was allowed to fuck with him. He was under Keith's constant protection.

One day in Washington, Freddy invited me to lunch at a fancy restaurant inside the hotel. I met him out front, where the sign said, "Jacket required." I happened to be wearing a blazer, but Freddy showed up in shorts, sandals, and a ratty Stones T-shirt. His hair was a mess. I tapped him on the shoulder and pointed to the sign. "Jacket required, Freddy."

"Fuck dat!" he said emphatically. "Dey *know* me here! I vuz in here vit Keet!"

We received stares from the other patrons (straight-laced suits conducting power lunches), but the maître d' didn't bristle. He brought us in and addressed Freddy as "Mr. Sessler." When the waiter took our order, Freddy asked if they had any coke.

"Yes, sir, we do," came the answer. "Would you like a lemon with that?"

"No!" exclaimed Freddy. "I vant *coke*, not *Coke*! *Blow!*"

"Never mind," I told the waiter, "just bring him a Coke."

At a nearby table was Norman Perry, the tour's merchandising honcho—a major figure in the BCL regime. "Freddy," he said with disdain, "when are you gonna clean up your act already, or at least comb your hair?"

Freddy let him have it. "Who de fuck do you teenk you are? You teenk you're my mudder? Don't tell me how to dress! I been vit de Stones for a hundred years and den *you* and Cohl come along? You're de *new* kids on de block, you little *putz!*"

Freddy was scared of no one and was constantly telling me to stand up for myself on this tour. "You ver around in de Stones' lean years," he'd say. "You kept de fans believing in dem. De fucking Stones *owe* you!"

The Stones were surrounded by so many "yes" people, Keith found it refreshing to have someone give it to him straight. If Freddy thought a Stones show sucked, he'd tell him, "Keet, you sucked!"

Conversely, if Keith had a problem with Freddy, he wouldn't pull punches, either. Or bullets. Woody once told me how Keith got so pissed off at Freddy, he whipped out a .45. It was at Keith's old apartment on 10th Street. Woody couldn't recall what the disagreement was about, but he said Keith aimed for Freddy's feet and made him dance an Irish jig.

Freddy caught almost every show on the *Steel Wheels* tour, and I had no idea how he hacked it financially. He got a discount at some of the hotels and occasionally hitched a ride on the Stones' private jet, but the numbers did not add up. He was not a paid employee of the tour and was not a dependant of Keith's. Yet he was staying at the Ritz-Carlton or Four Seasons in every city, and ringing up impressive room service tabs. Even if he was making money from drugs or ticket scalping, it could not have been enough to support his on-the-road lifestyle. From what I saw, he gave away a lot more than he sold. Free hits for the Stones and free tickets for certain groupies. He also took a bath on his coin scheme.

His "Rolling Stones Commemorative Coin Set" was a brilliant idea, but failed miserably because most fans never knew it existed. The sets were offered at only one concession stand in each stadium. "Norman Perry is screwing me!" he'd say.

Perry and BCL charged Freddy $250,000 for the licensing rights. And that was before the minting costs, silver costs, etc. The coins were like the ones you see for the Olympics, except that these commemorated the *Steel Wheels* tour. There was one coin depicting the tour's official logo, plus five others bearing each Stone's profile. It was truly unique. But Freddy got stuck with a ton of 'em and had to melt them down.

Freddy was full of get-rich-quick schemes. He claimed he made a fortune selling aglets, the things on the tip of your shoelaces, and a fortune selling lightbulbs to the Empire State Building. But he'd always lose his shirt in the long run. "I been a millionaire eight times, and I been broke eight times!"

.   .   .

Freddy had an audience for his stories because no matter what city we were in, his room was packed with people. As soon as we got back from the concert, he'd put on the music and spread out the coke. There were regulars, like Bobby Keys and certain roadies, but also locals. Fans and groupies you'd see for one night and never see the rest of the tour.

Freddy loved being the center of attention. But it was sad how everyone wanted something from him or was there because Keith might walk through the door. (Keith was smart enough to steer clear.)

Freddy knew that I didn't need him for tickets, passes, coke, or access to Keith. I visited him simply for his friendship and developed a genuine fondness for him. I knew how crass and vulgar he could be, but also saw his charming and intelligent side. He could be snorting coke one minute, and devouring *The Wall Street Journal, The Jewish Press,* or *The New York Times* the next. He was a man of many contradictions, but offered his unwavering support to *Beggars Banquet,* for which I was grateful.

If you're wondering how a senior citizen could ingest more drugs than Janis Joplin did at age 27, I don't have the answer. But I do know that Freddy had conquered a laundry list of health problems in the previous few years. He'd been hit with strokes, gout, heart attacks, blood clots, diabetes, and cancer, but it only steeled his resolve. No prognosis could make him miss a Stones tour and, like Rasputin, nothing could kill him off.

I visited him in a New York hospital shortly before the *Steel Wheels* tour. Without warning, he opened his robe to show me his latest scar. He was standing in his red Speedos, with his gray pubes sticking out. "Alright, Freddy! I get the point!"

He said the song "Struggle," from Keith's solo album, was about his health problems. "Keet wrote it about *me!*" I asked Keith if it was true, and he doubled over in laughter. "But that's Freddy," he sighed. "That's why we love him, right?"

The challenge for me—primarily as a journalist—was to discern which of Freddy's statements were true and which weren't. It wasn't always so easy.

During the Stones' *Voodoo Lounge* tour, Freddy insisted that Keith was going to announce his birthday in the middle of a concert. For days, he wouldn't shut up about it. "Keet's gonna announce my boit-day from de stage, Keet's gonna announce my boit-day." He told every roadie, every groupie, and even the bellboys and chambermaids.

"The Stones aren't Willard Scott," I said. "They don't do birthday announcements. They've *never* done a birthday announcement." But sure enough, when Keith stepped to the mic to sing "The Worst," he dedicated it. "There's a special friend of mine here tonight, and it's his birthday. Freddy, this one's for *you.*"

The more I got to know Freddy on the *Steel Wheels* tour, the more I understood why he needed to be there. People labeled him a dope pusher, starfucker, bullshit artist, and dirty old man, but he was a lot more complex than that.

"Hitler killed my family," he reminded me one night. "My mudder, my fadder, viped out. But vot can I do about dat now? Sit in de house and cry? Vait for my blood clots to kill me? I gotta *live,* baby! I gotta prove dey couldn't finish me off."

The groupies, glamour, and fast pace offered Freddy a vibrancy he couldn't find anywhere else. While folks his age were playing shuffleboard, Freddy was hangin' with the Stones. Every line he snorted and every groupie he laid was an affirmation of life and a proclamation of survival. "Look vehr *I* am today, and look vehr *you* are, you Nazi cocksuckers!" Every time he danced at a Stones concert—and man, you should've seen him—it was like he was dancing on Hitler's grave. "I'm gonna dance not just for me, but for all my relatives who *can't.*"

Mick entertains Barbra Streisand, Meryl Streep,
and Michael Douglas at the L.A. Coliseum.

26

mick and keith
on the couch

If people are to be judged by the friends they keep, then Mick and Keith revealed their true colors in Los Angeles.

I caught all four October concerts at the L.A. Coliseum, while staying at a subscriber's house. I couldn't afford a week at the Four Seasons, but kept on top of things anyway. One night, Bill Wyman invited me to cover a book party he was hosting on North Robertson Boulevard. Another night, Woody invited me to his art exhibition on La Cienega. And one afternoon, Keith invited me to lunch at the hotel restaurant.

I went to the Four Seasons with my subscriber to see the Ticket Lady and bumped into Keith and Patti in the lobby. They were headed to the hotel's restaurant and asked us to join them. They were with their two little girls, Theodora and Alexandra, and with Marisa (Patti's niece), Joe Seabrook (Keith's bodyguard), and Bernard Fowler (the Stones' backup singer). Over breadsticks, Keith informed me that he was changing his hotel pseudonym from LaFaccia to R. Soul—as in "Rubber Soul." It was an important piece of information and the kind I could never get from Jane.

Another day, I was at the Four Seasons to breakfast with Norman Perry, the czar of BCL's merchandising division, Brockum. Although the *Steel Wheels* tour was half over, I wanted to talk with him about offering *Beggars Banquet* at the stadiums. I also wanted to discuss my radio show idea, which I was still hot to pursue.

I had tried pitching my "*Beggars Banquet* of the airwaves" to the ABC Radio Network—the company that sewed up the tour's radio rights—but was unsuccessful. I left numerous messages for Tom Cuddy, the vice president of programming, but never heard back. So I thought that if BCL, the company that *sold* them those rights, sponsored my idea, it might help my cause with ABC. Norman agreed to meet with me at the Four Seasons.

Before we even ordered, he snapped at our busboy. The kid asked if he wanted orange juice, and Norman yelled, "If I wanted juice, I would have *asked* for it!" I quickly realized that Norman and I were coming from two different places and speaking different languages. I broached my radio show idea, but he kept changing the topic. He kept telling me to fork over my mailing list to him, free of charge. When I said no, he suggested I buy a ton of merchandise from him to offer my readers.

We danced around, getting nowhere: him trying to sell me *Steel Wheels* leather jackets, and me trying to get him to sponsor my nonexistent radio show. He asked if I had any merchandise ideas, and I jokingly suggested a "Jaggerobics" video. "Like Jane Fonda's, but with Mick." He didn't smile and signaled for the check.

At night, I was off to the Coliseum, where the backstage setup was the most elaborate and star-studded of the tour. I spotted Bowie, Springsteen, and Nicholson, to name a few.

Calling the backstage scene a circus wasn't a metaphor. To accommodate the beautiful people, a series of circus tents was erected. The big top was decorated like a 1950s luncheonette, and the wait staff were dressed like soda jerks. There were video games for the kids and a pool table for grownups, on which Clapton was pitted against Bill Wyman. Woody got winners.

Mick and Keith each had a hospitality tent, and the difference between their respective visitors spoke volumes. When I peeked in on Keith, he was deep in conversation with Phil Spector. He also hosted Tom Petty, Little Steven, and Waddy Wachtel. In Mick's tent, however, you could find Barbra Streisand, Meryl Streep, and Michael Douglas.

Keith had music people, Mick had Hollywood people. It wasn't an absolute—Springsteen did say hi to Mick—but it was clear who was aligned with whom. Mick very much wanted to be part of the Hollywood scene (as an actor, director, producer), so he was courting its powerbrokers. He'd already conquered rock 'n' roll, so he was looking for a new frontier. How many more times could he play to the same schlubby Stones freaks?

For Keith, there was no other place to be. He didn't want to be a movie star and didn't feel the need to impress Barbra Streisand any more than some blue-collar Stones freak in the last row. Keith considered himself the Stones' number one fan. When he wasn't onstage, you could spot him by his *Steel Wheels* leather jacket, the same one sold at the concessions. I think he even slept in it. He was like that guy in the commercial: "I liked the product so much, I bought the company."

The reason you should care about Mick and Keith's differences in philosophies and social circles is that they trickled down to what you saw and heard on the *Steel Wheels* tour. Mick's desire to be hip and well connected might have driven Keith crazy, but it did invigorate the Stones. In the seven years since the band last toured, Mick had investigated a lot of new music and had affiliated with a lot of young and successful bands. He was intent on bringing that to bear on the Stones.

Keith, of course, rejected that notion. He viewed Mick's musical cronies (Duran Duran, Paul Young, the Eurythmics) as "flavors of the month" and viewed Mick's relationships with them as superficial and misguided. But then, if there was one thing that bugged me about Keith, it was that he could be *too* dismissive when it came to new music. If you weren't a hunchbacked blind black dude from the Mississippi Delta, Keith wasn't interested in you.

Keith had a very short list of musicians he respected, and most of them were either dead or close to it. One night, when the tour was on a break, Mick went to the Ritz to see the Red Hot Chili Peppers, while Keith was at Carnegie Hall, watching 86-year-old Carlos Montoya. Mick viewed Keith as stubborn, myopic, and living in a bubble.

But there was an interesting irony to this tour. As much as Mick professed his love for new music and as much as he despised the "retro rocker" label, he was hesitant about adding the band's new songs to the repertoire. Mick was happy with the tour's formula and refused to screw with it. "Spontaneity usually means mistakes," he told *Rolling Stone.*

Mick's formula dictated a rigid approach, which applied not just to the repertoire, but to the arrangements themselves. Mick wanted each song, be it "Brown Sugar," "Tumbling Dice," or "You Can't Always Get What You Want," to sound exactly like the original album version. The Stones had never done it that way before. On previous tours, the Stones would show up and wing it. The result would be a new version of each song—a "road version, a rounded-off version," as Keith described it to me—that differed greatly from the familiar recording.

But not this time. According to Mick, the *Steel Wheels* tour was too grand and too important to leave to chance. There was one way to play each song and *only* one way. He'd already test-marketed the theory. When Mick did his Japanese and Australian solo tours in 1988, I criticized him in *Beggars Banquet* for including twenty Stones songs in his repertoire each night. Why call it a solo show if you're doing twenty frickin' Stones songs? But in assembling his Stones cover band, Mick worked out the arrangements and made them resemble the original records, putting all the subtleties back in.

By seeing a lot of new and commercially successful acts—not the barroom blues guys Keith was dropping in on—Mick got a sense of what was going on in the music industry. He learned that the way to reach the vastest audience, not just hardcore Stones freaks, was to play the hits the way people remembered them. Don't ask people to indulge the Stones' onstage idiosyncrasies, and don't assume the Stones' unpolished sound would be endearing. Most baby boomers want "Gimme Shelter" the way they heard it in their dorm room twenty years ago, so that's how we'll give it to them. It was more a business decision than an artistic decision, but it worked.

Keith, of course, would've preferred the old way. Throw everything in the air and see where it comes down. Take some risks and embrace the vulnerability. Keith didn't want the show to turn into a predictable greatest hits package, so he fought for the new material. The repertoire featured three *Steel Wheels* numbers—including "Mixed Emotions," which Keith privately referred to as "Mick's Demotions"—but Keith wanted more. Mick felt the band and audience weren't ready.

By October, Keith got antsy. "I'm ready to wing anything," he told me. "There's inexorable pressure to keep things the same, because [of the] incredible amount of coordination, the lights, [and] even down to the wardrobe. [But] at the same time, it makes you stale."

Keith let go of a lot of authority on this tour, but the one thing he held tight to was the set list. He lobbied to include new songs like "Terrifying," "Hold On to Your Hat," and "Almost Hear You Sigh," but Mick refused. Two of those songs eventually made it in, but not until late November and not before some heated debates took place.

Keith went along with Mick's ideas because, frankly, he needed the Stones more than Mick did. He loved the Stones and didn't have Hollywood to fall back on. "Being in the Stones is the only thing I know how to do," he told me. "I can't do anything else. What am I gonna do, go to DeVry?"

So Keith learned how to pick his battles. And rather than confront Mick at every turn, he had his own way of getting even. I first noticed it when I watched the concert from the cubbyhole at Shea Stadium. At the beginning of "Honky Tonk Women," Keith would play those famous chords. Well, on some nights, Keith would drag it out longer than he had to. He'd string Mick along for an extra few seconds until the vocal cue. It'd keep Mick guessing and fuck up his timing in front of 60,000 people.

Same thing with "Midnight Rambler." You know the break in the middle? "You heard about the Boston"—CRANK! Mick would jump and/or simulate a whipping motion at the exact moment Keith struck that chord. But if Keith held off for a few seconds, it'd leave Mick hanging and feeling a bit stupid.

It was subtle, but you could spot it if you were watching closely enough. It was textbook passive-aggressive behavior, but it got Keith through the tour without strangling anyone.

I kept trying to reach Tom Cuddy at ABC, but had no luck. The guy had no idea who I was, so I can't blame him for not returning my calls. Besides, my weekly update show became moot when ABC began broadcasting *daily* updates. A stringer from the local ABC affiliate would file a two-minute report. A different person each day. Unfortunately, most had little knowledge of the band's history or a feel for what fans wanted to hear. Many focused on the weather. "It was quite blustery here in Pittsburgh last night, but, despite the cold, the Stones delivered plenty of satisfaction." When one reporter cornered Milli (or was it Vanilli?) to get his professional opinion of the Stones, I reached my boiling point.

I FedExed a letter to Tom Cuddy the next day, saying, "Your Stones updates suck." I told him that ABC could redeem itself if it hired someone who knew the subject matter. Someone like *me*. Of course, I left out the part about my lack of professional radio experience. But I did include a demo of my own update, featuring exclusive info and anecdotes from the tour. "This is how it should sound," I wrote.

To my surprise, he called me while I was in L.A. He said he liked my demo and that KLOS, the local affiliate in Los Angeles, wanted me on as a guest. They were doing a live broadcast from the concert.

When I showed up for my big radio appearance, a stadium security guard said I needed a "Working Personnel" pass to get to the radio booth. I had just been in the band's lounge, but this guy wouldn't let me up to the roof. I flashed him my All Access pass and said, " 'All Access' means everywhere," but he said he didn't like my attitude. I was not about to have my prime-time radio debut destroyed by some rent-a-cop, so, when his back was turned, I pulled a Lucy Ricardo and slipped into the elevator.

The KLOS DJs made a big deal out of me. Steve Downes and Gayle Murphy told listeners I was a Stones insider who'd "seen the tour from every angle." They provided me with a chair, a mic, and even my own set of binoculars. I liked seeing the concert from yet another perspective, but I was freaked out by the booth itself. It was a makeshift wooden thing that was literally on the stadium's roof. San Francisco's deadly earthquake had occurred days earlier, so, if an aftershock hit L.A., our lemonade stand would tumble over and we'd be dead.

The DJs asked about the scene backstage. "Is Clapton here? Is he gonna play?" I answered all their questions and discussed all the things the Stones had done in L.A. that week. I also got into deeper subjects, like the impact of Stu's death and the controversy over Guns N' Roses, the Stones' opening act. (Onstage the night before, Axl assured everyone he wasn't a racist or homophobe, as had been widely reported. "I got nothing against niggers and queers," he stated, "as long as they don't try to touch me or rip me off." A race riot almost broke out between G N' R and the Stones' other openers, Living Colour.)

I remained on the air for a span of three hours, which included portions of the actual concert. What I mean is, there were moments when we'd be talking in the foreground as our listeners could hear the Stones in the background. The station did not have permission to do that, but they flouted the rules, and I love them for it. To me, it captured the true spirit of what FM radio was founded upon: a passion for music and a willingness to be spontaneous and relevant. I was excited to be part of it.

By keeping the mics open, we got to discuss the concert like a sporting event. The two DJs were the play-by-play announcers, and I was the color commentator. Before "Sympathy for the Devil," I said, "Okay, Mick is boarding a secret elevator right now, so he can get to the top of the stage." During "Brown Sugar," I explained how the Stones' families were exiting the cubbyhole for the idling vans. The KLOS brass liked my appearance so much, they had me back a second night.

Unbeknownst to me, the folks at ABC were also listening to the feed. Tom Cuddy phoned me in L.A. with an interesting proposition: "We want you to interview Mick and Keith for our national broadcast next week."

October 29, 1989: My day started in the Mets' laundry room with Keith, Charlie Kendall (left), and Dave-the-engineer . . .

. . . and ended at the Ritz-Carlton with (left to right)
Michael Woods, Marisa, Keith, Carrie Woods (Michael's wife),
James Woods, Woody, and Patti.

27

radio days

I still find it hard to believe that ABC trusted me with their million-dollar baby. A hundred stations across America were set to carry the program—an interview with Mick Jagger and Keith Richards, conducted by Bill German.

The network paid BCL a million bucks for the tour's exclusive radio rights (which also included the simulcast of the Stones' pay-per-view concert), and they were putting their biggest rock broadcast since Live Aid in the hands of a 27-year-old kid with no professional radio experience. I guess the novelty factor—a regular fan interviewing the Stones—had some p.r. appeal.

It also could've made for a train wreck, which is why they teamed me up with radio veteran Charlie Kendall. He and I would be interviewing Mick and Keith as a panel, alternating our questions.

Originally, the format for the program, as spelled out in the million-dollar agreement, was for the Stones to participate in a live call-in show. All five members, with the help of a moderator, would field questions from the public during a two-hour broadcast. But as the airdate approached, the Stones kept chiseling down the concept. They told ABC to scrap the phone-in idea. "Let's just do a regular interview. The five Stones, together in a room, on live radio, interviewed by a DJ." ABC wasn't happy about the change, but didn't put up a fight. The Stones were the biggest music story of 1989, so a regular interview was still a coup.

But then BCL dropped another surprise. It wasn't gonna be all five Stones. Only Mick and Keith. Again, ABC swallowed it. Mick Jagger and Keith Richards in the same room on live radio was still a special event. *Billboard* magazine went to print with it: "ABC Radio Networks has set its two-hour live Rolling Stones interview program with Mick Jagger and Keith Richards. . . . The show will be hosted by veteran air personality Charlie Kendall, and Bill German, editor/publisher of Stones fanzine Beggars Banquet."

Days before the broadcast, however, BCL phoned ABC with another change. "We'll give you Mick and Keith, but you're going to interview them separately, an hour each, pre-taped, not live." At that point, ABC got tired of the bait-and-switch and contemplated a breach-of-contract suit.

It was too late to publicize the change. "Mick Jagger and Keith Richards don't act very chummy on stage these days," reported the New York *Daily News,* "but they'll be buddying up on the airwaves."

Of course, none of it made a difference to *me.* Mick and Keith together, separate, live, or on Memorex. I was so psyched to be part of this thing, I'd have done it upside down on the moon.

Mick's interview was scheduled for Saturday, October 28, at ABC Studio on West End Avenue. Keith's was set for Sunday, prior to the concert at Shea Stadium. (This was the Stones' second stint in New York that month. They did two concerts at Shea, October 10 and 11, before the four in L.A., and four more back at Shea.)

Mick had rules. He wanted no unnecessary people at ABC while he was there. No secretaries, no receptionists, no cleaning ladies, no exceptions. He didn't want anyone asking for his autograph or talking to him. He was going to use the building's back entrance, slip into the radio studio around 10 AM, conduct his one-hour taping, and leave. If anyone inside that building approached him with a camera or pen, he'd exit before doing his interview. I know all this because ABC had to brief me. "I'll keep it in mind," I snickered. "No autographs, no pictures. I'll try *real* hard to restrain myself."

Saturday couldn't come soon enough. I was nervous, but a good kind of nervous. When my phone rang at 9 in the morning, I let my machine get it. I was too busy studying my questions and combing my hair.

"If you're there, Bill, pick up. It's Tom Cuddy."

I grabbed the receiver.

"Glad I caught you. I don't know how to tell you this, but Mick doesn't want you, so stay home."

Mick had not been informed until that morning that I was his interviewer. He instantly said no way. Either he wanted to punish me for something I'd written in *Beggars Banquet,* or he was scared I'd ask the same questions I'd already asked Woody—about the high ticket prices and the crass merchandise campaign. Whatever the case, he told his assistant, Tony King, to call ABC and nix me.

.   .   .

My Keith interview was still on for Sunday at Shea Stadium. I got a lift from a friend who was headed to the concert. But when we hit bumper-to-bumper traffic on Second Avenue, I began to panic. "If I miss this interview, I'll shoot my-self." I jumped out of the car and rolled over some guy's hood, Starsky-and-Hutch style, to get to the sidewalk. From there, I ran to Lexington Avenue to grab the 6 train, which connected me to the 7 train. I made it to Shea just in time.

Charlie Kendall and Dave-the-engineer were waiting for me behind the Mets' scoreboard. The Stones' head publicist, Linn, came to fetch us and handed us each a "Working Personnel" pass. She escorted us through a tunnel and into a small, dimly lit room. "Keith'll be here any minute," she said. When I looked around, I realized we were surrounded by washers and dryers. It was the New York Mets' laundry room, which Keith and Woody had been using as a tune-up space. I found a bunch of their guitar picks on the floor, including one inscribed, "Woody's Pecker."

Dave-the-engineer set up the equipment, as Kendall and I compared notes. We paced the room for twenty-five minutes, like anxious dads in a maternity ward, waiting for Keith. We were next door to the Stones' private lounge, so we could hear him laughing and joking. We then smiled at each other as his inimitable chortle came closer to us from the other side of the door. Keith en-tered the room and greeted me first. "We've been *expecting* you," he joked.

Keith knew what a big opportunity this was for me. He'd had a hand in making it happen, by simply approving it. I didn't know if he was aware of my Mick situation, so I felt compelled to bring it up. "Did you hear?" I said. "Mick called ABC yesterday and said he didn't want me to interview him."

Keith's response, which I'll never forget the rest of my life, was: "Yeah, well, he don't know what's good."

I introduced Keith to my colleagues, before Linn closed the door and left us alone. It was just the four of us, sitting at a rickety poker table. Considering the million bucks exchanged, our setup was rather primitive. "Where did you bring us?" I teased Keith. "This is where Darryl Strawberry washes his jock-strap."

I knew so much about the *Steel Wheels* tour and felt so comfortable with Keith, I wasn't scared to fire some hardballs. One of the first subjects I broached was the Stones' use of pre-recorded music onstage.

"There's some percussion sampling," admitted Keith. "But I will say, what sampling there is has been *closely* supervised by Mr. Watts. *Very closely.* So I'm not really worried about that. To me, the important thing about synthesizers and sampling is how to use it and not just use it indiscriminately. Sometimes, you walk in and think you've entered the typists' pool, 'cause nobody's playing anything, they're just pushing buttons."

Keith said that because the Stones were trying to replicate the arrangements of the original records, they needed to fabricate a few things to get the sound right. He said he'd invoked the spirit of Ian Stewart, the purest of all purists, to make sure it passed muster. "Charlie and I, and Ronnie, too, we look at each other onstage sometimes, and we say, 'He woulda liked that.' The biggest compliment you ever got from Stu was, 'Not bad.' So you kinda look up now and go, 'How was that, ol' sod?' How about a bit of 'Not bad,' so you know it's alright?"

That's all I wanted to do: ask Keith some of the questions that were on people's minds. Why *are* the Stones using recorded music onstage? And what *is* the story with the merchandising? Keith's a big boy, so I knew he could handle it.

"Most of the merchandising," he explained, "I left in Charlie Watts's capable hands. [It] dragged up the quality a bit."

I felt Keith was passing the buck on that one, but he was merely admitting that he controlled very little on this tour. He delegated the rest to the people he trusted. Charlie was a graphic artist by trade—he was so successful, he almost chose his day job over the Stones—so he took great pride in designing the stage sets and merchandise, the stuff Keith couldn't be bothered with. "Charlie knew I had enough on my hands getting the songs together," Keith said. "He's normally, 'Point me to the drums,' but he's taken the reins on a lot of behind-the-scenes stuff this tour. The reason I'm wearing this jacket is because of Charlie Watts."

Ah, yes, the jacket. Glad you brought that up, Keith. "We should tell our listeners that Keith is wearing the highest-ticket item of the 'Rolling Stones Rockware.' The $450 leather jacket. Complete with tongue zippers, tongue patches, and tongue pins." (I made myself sound like the *Price Is Right* announcer.)

Keith seemed slightly embarrassed, if not confused, by my pointing out the price. "Um, well, this one's *mine*," he mumbled to no one in particular. He might not have known the jacket was for sale, let alone the price Brockum/BCL was charging for it.

Keith pleaded ignorance to a lot on this tour, which might be an unsatisfactory excuse, but I believe he was telling the truth. He might've glanced at some memos during his bourbon and corn flakes each day, but if it had nothing to do with keys and chord changes he couldn't get too involved.

I asked him what concessions he'd made to Mick on this tour, and he said he couldn't think of any. I then asked how they were getting along.

"We don't have time not to relate well," he replied. "We don't have time to argue about anything 'cause we're on the job and we gotta roll, go, and not argue about it. Give us some time off, and we'll have a *really* good fight!"

Regarding his on-tour relationship with Woody, he sighed, "[We] don't even hang out all night anymore." He cited the tour's demanding pace: "When I was 20 years old, a rock 'n' roll show was twenty minutes long. I'm 45 years old now, and it's not forty-five minutes long. It's two and a half hours."

The party curtailment also had to do with their expanding broods. I asked Keith what his two daughters, ages 3 and 4, thought of Daddy's life on the road.

"I think they think everybody's dad does this sort of thing. 'Is *your* daddy doing a show today?' They love the ending when they can watch the fireworks and get the police escort. The motorcycles and the wee-wee-wee of the sirens. I have to tell them, 'I can't guarantee you this [all the time], y'know.' "

Keith's dad, Bert, was also a constant presence on this tour. I sat next to him a few times, and he seemed to be having a ball. "Sure he is," confirmed Keith. "Free rum!"

The tour's backstage guests ranged from porn stars to presidential progeny, so I wanted to know who Keith's favorite was. I predicted he'd say Scotty Moore, Elvis's old guitarist.

"You took the words out of my mouth. An incredibly interesting guy. He told us some great stories, which I will not repeat. But he showed me and Woody how to do that lick on 'My Baby Left Me' and 'That's All Right, Mama.' "

I asked what it was like meeting Seka, the porn star, and he exclaimed, "I'm the only one who didn't touch her!" I then asked about the tour's groupie situation. From what I'd seen, it wasn't living up to legend.

"I won't say they're not there," Keith testified. "I just haven't taken up the option!"

Of course, from the looks of 'em, you wouldn't *want* to. Most were way past their prime and had been hanging around since *Exile* or *Aftermath*. I met one who used to service Brian Jones as a teenager, but was now the size of a house. "No one fucks her anymore," a roadie told me. "Now it's just phone sex." This was also the first Stones tour since AIDS, so you had to be careful. In the old days you caught the clap; now you could catch death.

I asked Keith if he missed the intimacy of smaller venues and the chance to interact with fans. I mentioned how, on his solo tour, he gave a fan a ride home.

"Hey," he interjected, "I'm a nice guy, Bill."

"I know! That's a given! But have you had the chance to do something like that on *this* tour, or are things too hectic?"

He leaned in to share a story: "We were on the freeway yesterday, coming here to the gig, and there's this van full of guys. . . . They could tell [it was us], and they start going, 'Tickets, tickets, we need tickets.' . . . So I put my hand out and went, 'Money, money, money.' And they saw the ring, y'know. Eventually, they drove up alongside us, so I had one of our guys give 'em the name of [JC]. We told 'em to come round the back. We pressed the flesh a bit, and we got the guys in. They were originally just hoping to pick up some scalper's tickets."

Not only was that a great story, it was a national advertisement for JC's side business. "So here's the advice to everyone listening," I announced. "If you want tickets, just follow the Stones' van."

"Yeah," Keith concurred, "take a look around. And if you see me, I'm a nice guy, you stand a good chance."

Overall, it was an informative, fun interview. I proved Tom Cuddy right for hiring me. No other journalist knew to ask Keith about his father or Seka or the taxi service he ran for his fans.

At the end of the hour, Keith got up and hugged me. Then he obliged Kendall's and Dave-the-engineer's requests for autographs. For one day, I felt as professional as anyone else on the FM dial. To prove it, ABC paid me 300 bucks. I walked out of that room feeling great.

Usually, when I felt this good on the *Steel Wheels* tour, someone would come along and stick a pin in my balloon. But on this night, the pins must've been hidden. Freddy offered to take me onstage, but I declined. Instead, I sat next to some childhood friends in a regular seat that I paid for. After the show, I brought them to a free buffet in the stadium's Diamond Club. The Stones weren't expected, but my friends were still thrilled.

At one point, as I stood with my empty plate in the linguini line, a guy in the steamed vegetable line nodded like he knew me. It was actor James Woods. I'd never met him, but always loved his work. *Cat's Eye, The Onion Field,* and his Oscar-nominated performance in *Salvador.* I even sat through the long version of *Once Upon a Time in America.*

The guy played sick fucks on the big screen, but was being polite in real life. I didn't know why he was nodding to me, but I nodded back, before walking away. Thirty minutes later, as the room was clearing out, he tapped me on the shoulder. "You gotta do me a favor, Bill. Tell Keith it wasn't *my* idea to do that joke last night."

I had no clue what he was talking about or how he knew my name. He disappeared into the elevator before I could ask him. But when I exited the stadium and walked through the parking lot, I heard two male voices calling from the back of a limo: "Hey, Bill! We love the newsletter!"

The window was rolled down, so I peeked in. "Hey," said James Woods, "we just wanna let you know how much we love the newsletter. My name is James, and this is my brother, Michael. You send the issues to Michael's house, and then he gives them to *me*."

"Yes! Of course! Michael Woods! I've seen that name a million times in my files. You're one of my old-timers."

James explained that he'd hosted *Saturday Night Live* the night before, where he took part in a vampire skit that unflatteringly referenced Keith. I assured him that Keith wouldn't hold it against him. We shook hands, and they told me to keep up the good work. My childhood friends were impressed. "All this," said one, "from a thing you started in your bedroom."

When I got back to Manhattan, I headed to the Ritz-Carlton Hotel, where the Stones were staying. I wanted to have a postconcert drink with some roadies, but I noticed a commotion in the back of the hotel bar. Seated at a banquette were Keith and Woody, alongside Michael and James Woods. Patti Hansen spotted me in the distance and told Keith's bodyguard, Joe Seabrook, to let me through.

I'm not sure why James Woods told me to pass a message to Keith if he knew he was going to see him anyway, but I didn't inquire. Woody cracked himself up by introducing James and Michael to me as his brothers.

They explained to Keith and Woody that they already knew me: "We're card-carrying members." They also informed us that Michael owned a video store in Warwick, Rhode Island. When James would visit, he'd sit behind the counter, logging the rentals and making recommendations. You could rent a James Woods video from James Woods. Michael, it turned out, was more extroverted and gregarious than his famous brother. He kept us in stitches the whole night, and it came as no surprise years later when he ran for mayor of Warwick.

I always loved meeting my readers, no matter who they were, but this was icing on the cake. I felt like I pitched a perfect game at Shea that day.

The Stones couldn't wait to end their Trump-sponsored
press conference and threatened to leave if he came
anywhere near them.

28

trumped up

Atlantic City wasn't where you'd expect to find the Rolling Stones in 1989. It was, for the most part, a mecca for East Coast pensioners who couldn't endure the trip to Vegas. Church groups would show up by the busload, throw nickels in the slots, feast on a free buffet, and reboard the bus before nightfall. Frankie Valli was as rock 'n' roll as it got.

Donald Trump lured the Stones to this den of decadence with a huge offer. It called for three concerts, December 17, 19, and 20, at the Atlantic City Convention Center, next to Trump Plaza Hotel and Casino. It'd be the Stones' last stop of the tour.

The Convention Center, best known for hosting the annual Miss America pageant, was the smallest venue on the *Steel Wheels* itinerary (capacity 16,000) and by far the most expensive. Tickets in the orchestra cost $250, face value.

I'd heard from fans who couldn't afford the $30 tickets on this tour, so $250 was off the charts. It was the highest-priced concert in rock 'n' roll history. As I told my readers, "You might want to save $230 and catch it at home." The December 19 concert was going to be televised on pay-per-view for a mere 20 bucks.

Trump bought these shows outright for $6 million—a ton of money back then—so he was the boss. He, not the Stones, determined the ticket prices. He also got to sell/distribute the tickets however he wanted. For the December 17 show, he comped the best seats to his high rollers. Blue-haired old ladies and guys who reeked of Vitalis. They couldn't name a single Stones song, but when they saw the value of their tickets—$500 a pair—they couldn't resist the perk.

The Stones weren't happy, but it was their own fault for making Trump their boss for the week. At a preconcert press conference, they avoided all photo ops with him and threatened to leave if he came near them. In his book *Surviving at the Top,* Trump claims that the Stones were jealous and that they were scared to share the spotlight with him. "To put it mildly," Trump writes, "the Stones impress me as a bunch of major jerks. A sorry sight. . . . Pale and haggard far beyond their age. Surrounding them on all sides are their body-guards. . . . A mean-spirited bunch of wise guys who shove and rough up people who aren't even in their way."

Photo op or not, Trump got a bang for his buck. He made sure every ticket said, "The Rolling Stones, in association with Trump Plaza," and rigged it so you had to walk through his casino to get to the concert. A little tumbling dice before "Tumbling Dice."

At the December 17 show, I was depressed by what I saw. After the first couple of songs, people got up to leave. By "Midnight Rambler," the front section was half empty. A mass exodus of senior citizens, all holding their hands over their ears. I had subscribers who would've given their left nut for those seats, but they all went to waste.

As if the December 17 audience wasn't bad enough, the concert itself sucked. The sound man never got used to the room, and everything bounced off the walls like a car crash. Then, what was supposed to be a highlight, a guest appearance by John Lee Hooker, turned into a fiasco. The Hook's guitar wasn't plugged into his amp, and it took a few minutes for everyone onstage to realize it. To cap things off, Woody nearly killed himself during "Brown Sugar." He was attempting one of his patented sprints across the stage, when he tripped on a wire and went flying, nearly cracking his skull.

From the opening chords to the final bow, I'd never seen such a snakebit Stones concert. I reported all the details in *Beggars Banquet* and in *Connection,* the 'zine I'd launched for news flashes. I also spoke about it on K-Rock, the big radio station in New York.

A birthday party for Keith was held at the hotel after the show. We were staying at the Marriott Seaview Golf Resort, in the bedroom community of Ab-secon. Keith was checked in as R. Soul, Woody was checked in as J. Ramsey, and I was checked in as Bill German.

Trump had bragged to the media that the Stones were staying at his hotel, so they opted for the golf resort, eight miles away. It remained a well-kept secret. We were basically in the sticks and had the place to ourselves.

Keith's party was downstairs, in the hotel's basement. Midnight had passed, so it was technically his birthday, December 18. The room was remarkably rustic and very much like the basements you knew as a kid. With its tile floors and wood paneling, it seemed more suited for sock hockey and Twister than a Stones bash.

The self-serve buffet offered Keith's favorite, shepherd's pie. The birthday cake resembled a bottle of HP, his favorite steak sauce. (Keith loved that sauce so much, he traveled with it. Try finding HP in Iowa.)

All the Stones were present. Mick was in a corner by himself, but Keith, Woody, and Bill were shooting pool and mingling with guests. I was able to sneak some subscribers in and introduce them. Woody rolled up his sleeve to show them the gash on his elbow. "Once I tripped," he said, "I either had to fall on the floor and skid, or go straight into this pole and slit my head open."

"It's a good thing you chose the former," I sighed. "'Cause it sure would've put a damper on this party."

Keith's actual birthday was quiet. He spent the day privately with his family and never left his room. There was no gig that night, so everything was low-key. I, however, had much to report from the previous night. I'd been hired by K-Rock—"Howard Stern all morning, classic rock all day"—to phone from New Jersey and go on the air live.

To maintain the Stones' privacy, I never revealed my location. "[We're] technically not in Atlantic City," I told DJ Meg Griffin. "I can't tell you exactly where, but . . . we're out in the woods." I provided a play-by-play account of Keith's party and discussed the previous night's concert. I expressed how shaky it all was and how John Lee Hooker forgot to plug in. I mentioned Trump's involvement in the show and how people walked out in the middle of it.

An hour after I got off the air, I received a call in my room from Jane Rose: "Why would you say such negative things about the show? We thought you'd be on *our* side." A bunch of the tour's bigwigs had heard me on the radio and weren't pleased. They called Jane immediately and said, "*You* know that kid. Straighten him out."

She laid into me: "After all we've done for you, this is how you repay us? We're trying to get people to *buy* the pay-per-view, and you go on the radio so you could *badmouth* it? To tell everyone the show is gonna be lousy?"

I tried explaining that I was merely reporting the facts. Did John Lee Hooker forget to plug in? Yes. Did the sound engineers use the show as a run-through for the pay-per-view? Yes. Did blue-haired ladies walk out in the middle? Yes. I never implied the Stones would repeat those mistakes on pay-per-view night. I gave an account of what had already happened, not a prediction of things to come.

"Look," sighed Jane, "all I'm saying is, we were expecting you to be less negative. Everyone's really upset about this. They're asking me, 'What is he up to?'

We're the ones who got you onto that station, and then you use the opportunity to put us down? Be more positive next time. Help us *sell* this thing."

I didn't want to be argumentative, so I didn't bring up an important point: They did *not* get me onto that station. They helped me get on ABC (by approving me for the Keith interview), but the K-Rock gig I got by myself. I'd personally known the K-Rock DJs for years and had guested on their airwaves several times prior to the Stones-ABC pact. K-Rock had dubbed me their Stones Guy (an unpaid position), the way your local news show has the Fruit Guy or Tech Wiz.

But the larger question remained: Did I *owe* anything to the *Steel Wheels* tour? The Stones and BCL let me into their concerts for free, and I was eating their shepherd's pie, so, in that sense, I was their guest. But if becoming a shill was the price I had to pay for my All Access pass, no one had ever told me.

I was an independent journalist, employed by my subscribers, not by the Stones. Negative or not, the December 17 show was a man-bites-dog story that needed to be told.

Unfortunately, the tour's higher-ups had a certain perception of me, and that's what threw them off: "What's this kid up to? With a fan club like *his,* who needs enemies?" It must've driven them crazy that they couldn't fire me. And if they wanted to strip me of my access or of my Ticket Lady privileges, it was too late. The tour was just about over.

On my December 19 radio report, I didn't shill for that night's pay-per-view, but predicted it'd be less chaotic. And it was. John Lee Hooker remembered to plug in, Woody didn't trip, and no one in the audience got up to leave. The Convention Center was packed with Stones fans, not Trump fans. Clapton turned in a searing guest performance on "Little Red Rooster" and stuck around for the Hook's "Boogie Chillen." Even Axl Rose rose to the occasion. He performed a duet with Mick on "Salt of the Earth" and made no mention of "niggers and queers."

A publicist told me that 400,000 households purchased the telecast. BCL and the Stones' business managers were very pleased. But there was a glitch. During "Satisfaction," the feed went on the fritz. From what I was told, the U.S. military had knocked the Stones' satellite off the air because they were invading Panama at that moment and needed the frequency. As a result, the pay-per-view company offered everyone a free repeat.

The final night of the tour, December 20, was bittersweet. It elicited, dare I say, mixed emotions. I'd had a great time on this tour—watching the concerts, meeting subscribers, doing my radio broadcasts—but the constant uncertainty of my "insider-outsider" status exhausted me. The higher-ups on this tour made me feel like I was always begging them for favors and like my motives were always in question. That part, I wasn't going to miss.

Prior to the concert, I visited the band lounge. I assumed it would be my last chance to say goodbye to some people and wish them a Merry Christmas. In light of my K-Rock controversy, I feared I'd be barred from backstage, but Big Bob Bender, who was manning the door, reluctantly let me in.

It was a pretty emotional scene back there. People were exchanging gifts and hugs. The roadies were asking the Stones to autograph their tour programs, not as collector's items, but as personal mementos. Like getting your teachers to sign your yearbook.

I, too, asked for some autographs. Not for me, but for the contest I was running in *Beggars Banquet*. I'd promised the winner that "at least one member" of the Stones would sign a tour program, but was hoping to get the whole band. I dreaded asking for autographs, so I started with Woody, always the easiest. Then I moved to Bill Wyman, who was also easy.

Woody said that the key to getting Mick was to get the rest of the band first. I was too intimidated to approach Charlie, so I zoned in on Keith. He said, "Of course." He laid my program on the snooker table, pulled the cap off my Sharpie, and hunched over, ready to sign. But just then, his mother, who'd flown in from England for his birthday, called to him from the other side of the room. Keith excused himself—"One second, Bill"—and ran to her.

Unfortunately, Big Bob then entered the room with his nightly announcement: "The band's going on, so everyone has to leave the backstage area. Everyone, go to your seats." My winner would have to be content with two signatures, not five.

The Stones put in a dynamite performance that night. One of my favorite shows of the tour. When it was over, the band stuck around. Unlike their previous high-speed escapes from the venue, they remained backstage to bid farewell to the crew.

This time, the scene was sadder than before. People were openly weeping, and it made me feel like a trespasser. I was friendly with some of these people, but could not delude myself into thinking I was one of them. The roadies, the sound engineers, the makeup girl, the seamstress—they were integral parts of the *Steel Wheels* production, while I was not. And so, feeling like an outsider, I headed for the exit, when someone grabbed my shoulder. It was Keith. "You still need me to sign that book?"

I was floored. With all the stuff he had on his mind and with all the emotions of the night, *he* was approaching *me* about my request. He knew it was for a Stones fan and didn't want to let them down. In the three hours since I'd last spoken to him, he'd had to concern himself with chord changes, not tripping over wires, making sure his mother was alright, making sure John Lee Hooker was plugged in, and with saying goodbye to two hundred people. Yet he never forgot that autograph.

Everyone went their separate ways from Atlantic City. Mr. Soul went to Connecticut; Mr. Ramsey caught the next Concorde. I planned to take a bus to Manhattan, but Freddy insisted I ride in his rent-a-car. I assumed his girlfriend would be driving, but I was wrong. I didn't think Freddy had a driver's license, and I'm still not sure he actually did. All I know is, he grabbed the keys from her and got behind the wheel. We argued with him, but it was too late. Freddy started the motor and off we went.

For the next two hours, we zigged and zagged along the Garden State Parkway and Jersey Turnpike. He straddled the yellow line for much of the trip, and we narrowly missed a head-on collision. It got to the point where I *hoped* we'd get stopped by the cops, because it would've been better than flying through the windshield or rolling down an embankment. His girlfriend begged him to let her drive, but he kept yelling, "Shut de fuck up! Leave me alone!" He rambled on about Donald Trump, the invasion of Panama, and the Stones' upcoming tour of Japan, as I turned pale in the backseat.

Freddy's girlfriend was less than half his age. She was blond, slim, busty, and gorgeous. She had traveled with him for much of the tour, and I assumed she was using him for drugs and Stones access. But she revealed to me during our harrowing car ride that she'd never done drugs and wasn't a Stones fan. She was a "working girl."

I finally connected the dots on how Freddy could afford to follow the tour. He'd sought out wealthy fans to be his "sponsors." In return for backstage passes, they'd pick up his airfare and hotel bills. They'd even pay for his "girlfriends." There was no shortage of fans willing to do the deal, no matter how expensive.

As Freddy dropped me off at my apartment, he said, "See you in Tokyo!"

Woody has me do a guest spot during his press conference in Tokyo.

29

lost in
translation

If the Stones hadn't made a habit of getting busted, they could've played Japan a lot sooner than they did. When they petitioned Hirohito's government for visas in 1973, they were flatly denied. The government took one look at Mick and Keith's rap sheet and branded them "undesirables" and "corrupters of youth."

But now it was February 1990. Hirohito was dead, and the people in power either liked the Stones or knew they were good for business. The yen was stronger than Godzilla, and the nation was in a spending mood. A concert promoter offered the Stones $30 million to come over.

Similar to the Trump deal, the Stones took the money up front. Ten concerts, all at the Tokyo Dome, for fifty thousand people a night. The promoter set prices at a steep 10,000 yen—70 U.S. dollars—but the half million tickets sold instantly. Fans had been waiting their whole lives for this. History in the making.

American media outlets were interested in the story, but didn't send anyone. I was the only Western journalist to make the trip and was hired by *Rolling Stone* to write an article and by three radio outlets to do phone-in reports. The money I made went toward my travel.

When the Stones landed at Narita Airport, thousands of fans threw flowers at them and shrieked like little girls. The Stones were slightly embarrassed. I flew in separately and didn't get the same reception, but there was a welcoming committee. Somehow, the members of the Japanese Rolling Stones fan club found out my flight information and were waiting for me at the gate. Two guys were waving at me, and a girl was jumping up and down, trying to get my attention. I had no idea who these people were, so I thought they were gesturing to someone else. But the girl ran up to me and said, "Mr. German-san, we drive you to Okura Hotel."

"Arigato," I said. "But sorry, so sorry. I have car ride *already.*" The girl turned around and translated to the two guys. They seemed truly deflated, as though it would've been an honor to chauffeur me around. One of them had a loose-leaf binder full of *Beggars Banquet*s and asked me to autograph it.

It was common knowledge that the Stones were at the Okura Hotel. After checking in, I paid a visit to Freddy's room. It was uncharacteristically quiet. His only company was a local girl who called herself Mary. Freddy made it clear she wasn't his girlfriend. "She's a Stones fan," he explained, "but I'm not fucking her. She's my translator."

Freddy was in a foul mood. "I can't get no pussy and I can't get no blow!" he whined. "De whores don't fuck Americans because our cocks are too big! Dey still remember Kenny Norton!" He added that the Stones were being watched like hawks, so they couldn't bring coke into the country. They also didn't know the local dealers, so they were out of luck. The entourage had been there a week and were getting edgy.

Freddy was seated in front of a rolling cart and was nibbling a tuna sandwich from room service. He'd also ordered a bowl of miso soup and a plate of flan. He complained between bites of his sandwich and only shut up when there was a knock at the door. He told me to open it, and in walked Keith, trailed by his assistant, Tony Russell, and his bodyguard, Joe Seabrook.

Keith pulled up a chair next to Freddy and stole a spoonful of Freddy's flan. The room was small, so Mary and I sat on the bed and Joe and Tony sat on the dresser. For Mary, this was the payoff for putting up with Freddy. The chance to meet Keith is why she took the job.

Freddy went to his nightstand and pulled out a plastic baggie. He poured its contents onto the cart. It looked like M&Ms, but was a bunch of pills. Keith scooped a handful and popped them in his mouth, as did Freddy. Keith chased it with some flan.

I hadn't seen Keith since Atlantic City, so we had a lot to talk about. From the Stones and Mike Tyson to Nelson Mandela and the fall of Communism.

A day earlier, Keith, Mick, Woody, and Charlie were at the Tokyo Dome to see Tyson lose the heavyweight crown to Buster Douglas. "Mike ain't been the same since Rooney split," observed Keith. As for Mandela, Keith said it was "about time" he got out of prison, an event that had also occurred the day before. As for the fall of Communism, Keith said he was looking forward to seeing it for himself that summer, if the Stones toured Europe. He maintained it was rock 'n' roll diplomacy, not bullets, that brought down the Iron Curtain.

It was a great conversation, and it could've gone deep into the night, if Keith didn't lose his motor skills. The pills suddenly kicked in, and he began slurring his words. His speech was a 45 RPM record at 33. His body slowed down like a wind-up toy.

Freddy slumped forward and his face careened into the bowl of soup. He momentarily righted himself. Keith tried to keep the conversation going, but wasn't succeeding. The only things coming from his mouth were gibberish and flan. At that point, Mary began spoon-feeding Keith like a Gerber's baby food commercial. Most of the flan was dribbling on Keith's chin, so she'd scoop it up and put it back in his mouth.

Joe and Tony knew it was time to get Keith out. They grabbed him under each arm and lifted him from the chair. They dragged him from the room, with his feet dragging behind him, scraping the carpet. Freddy, meanwhile, slumped forward again. I picked him up, for fear he'd drown in his soup. Mary and I managed to pull him from the chair and dump him on his bed, with his shoes still on. He was mumbling, "No pussy, no blow," as we turned out the lights and left.

The next day, I found myself at the Tokyo Dome for a dress rehearsal. When it was over, Mick scurried down the backstage ramp before everybody else. He walked right past me and intentionally avoided eye contact. There's no way he didn't see me, but he didn't say hello. I took it personally.

Keith followed a minute later, with a cup of whiskey in his hand and a cigarette dangling from his mouth. He apologized for his "early exit" the night before. Together, we walked through the stadium's tunnel and toward the dressing room area. He then came to a sudden stop and opened one of the doors. I could see Mick standing in the room, all by himself. Mick glared out at me and seemed a bit agitated.

"Alright," Keith sighed. "I gotta hash this out with the old lady."

I nervously chuckled at Keith's remark. I don't know what he and his "old lady" needed to discuss—no one dared follow them into that room—but I was relieved to learn that Mick was pissed at Keith, not just me.

I shook Keith's hand and pointed out that the ash from his cigarette had fallen into his cup. "You might not wanna drink that," I said. But he muttered, "Hmmph, *protein,*" and, in one swift move, downed his Jack-and-ash, stepped into the dressing room, and closed the door.

The first show was Wednesday, February 14. My All Access pass was no longer valid, but the Ticket Lady gave me a stick-on pass that got me in free. It didn't allow me into the band's lounge, but into a VIP room with non-English-speaking B-listers. There was dried squid to eat, and mucus and sweat to drink. No kidding, the tour's Japanese sponsor was a soft drink called Pocari Sweat, and another drink was called Mucous.

The concerts were identical to those in America. The Stones performed the same repertoire and brought the same stage, pyrotechnics, and inflatables. Mick, however, attempted some Japanese from a teleprompter. "Hello, Japanese people," he said. "We've waited so long to come here." The audience squealed with delight.

Keith didn't bother to speak the language, but still got a rise from the crowd. When he stepped to the mic for "Can't Be Seen" and "Happy," he said, "I feel better than Mike Tyson." And unlike the shows in America, everyone stayed for his set, not using it as a pee break.

For me, observing the audience was as entertaining as the band. The fans were excited, but never allowed themselves to fully cut loose. Most of them never undid their ties. They were coming straight from the office, so the guys were in business suits and the girls were in skirts. They stood throughout the whole concert, but, unlike their American counterparts, never stood on their seats. I'd call it a restrained wildness. They clapped, cheered, and shrieked, but the American accoutrements were missing. The scent of pot never wafted through the air, and nary a bra was flung to the stage.

The starkest contrast came *after* the show. Everyone sat in their seats and waited to be dismissed, like a grade school assembly. A voice came over the PA system with instructions: "Section 1, it is permissible for you to leave now. Section 2, now it is *your* turn." It was in Japanese, so I didn't understand a word, but it was scary to watch. One section at a time would robotically stand up and walk single file, like a science fiction movie.

Of course, Freddy didn't wait for instructions. "Fuck dat!" he yelled. "*Vee* von de fuckin' var, not *dem*! Dey can't tell us vot to do!" I followed him out to the street, and, when we had trouble hailing a cab, he let loose again: "*Vee* von de fuckin' var, not *you*!" The lack of blow was getting to him.

Tim Kellogg came just in time. He flew in from the U.S. and got past customs with a bag of coke up his ass. Kellogg (not his real name) was the official "provider" for the *Steel Wheels* tour. The Mick Camp couldn't stand him, but, here in Tokyo, the Keith and Woody Camps hailed him as a hero. He was rewarded with money, tickets, passes, and access. Roadies let him sleep in their rooms, so he got to stay at the five-star Okura for free. His stash lasted just a day or so, but everyone's mood seemed cheerier.

The concerts were great, but I found the man-bites-dog stories elsewhere.

During one of the off nights, Woody hosted an exhibition of his artwork at the Isetan department store, the one-stop shop for yuppies on the go. In a single visit, you could purchase a refrigerator, life insurance, and a Ron Wood litho.

I hitched a ride with Woody's cute sister-in-law. When we arrived, we found Woody behind a desk, looking like a deer caught in the headlights. He'd shown up thinking it was a regular art exhibition, but got roped into a formal press conference. TV lights were shining in his face, and he seemed pretty uncomfortable. Every question and every answer was translated from Japanese to English and from English to Japanese.

Woody spotted me from across the room and tried to deflect attention from himself. "I think I see Bill German over there," he announced over the mic. "He *better* be here." The camera crews turned around to see who he was talking about. Masayoshi Koshitani, the emcee, urged me to join Woody for a photo op.

I approached the desk as Woody held up a copy of *The Works*. "He's the co-writer, the ghostwriter," Woody told the press corps. "Also the publisher of *Beggars Banquet* Rolling Stone magazine." I mugged it up with Woody for several moments—the flashbulbs went off like fireworks—and I think he was relieved to unload his burden.

After the Saturday night concert on February 17, a party was held in the banquet room of the Okura Hotel. I didn't receive a formal invitation, but didn't think one was necessary. Big Bob Bender was blocking the door. "They told me not to let you in," he said, "but let me see what I can do."

At first, I thought he was joking. But when he checked inside to make sure the coast was clear, I realized he was telling the truth. "Alright," he said. "Make your move." I thanked him and slinked inside. It had taken me months to realize that Bob was a decent guy who hated the tour's hierarchical bullshit. Nonetheless, *someone* in the Stones' entourage didn't want me around.

I knew I was being watched at this party. As I chatted with Keith and Woody—the latter wearing a kimono—I spotted Jane, JC, and Alan Dunn huddled in a corner, staring at me. Nobody asked me to leave—no one *would,* as long as I was standing next to Keith—but I got the distinct and creepy impression I wasn't welcome.

Woody said he was headed to a bar called Red Shoes, in Tokyo's Roppongi district, and that I should meet him there after the party. I tried hailing a taxi, but none of the drivers knew what "Red Shoes" meant. Someone suggested I try the Japanese pronunciation—"Red Shoozda"—and, to my amazement, it worked.

By the time I got there, Woody was three sheets to the wind. He and Jo were at a table with Bernard Fowler and Lisa Fischer, the Stones' backup singers.

"Bill Fucking German!" Woody shouted. "You made it!"

"Ron Fucking Wood! I most certainly did!"

"Well, have a seat, Bill Fucking German! Bill Germ-Fucking-Man!"

He made a place for me at his table and offered me some lizard juice. It's a Korean drink that's similar to—well, *nothing*. You know how a bottle of tequila has the worm in it? This bottle had the six-inch carcass of an iguana.

Woody was downing it like water. I tried a sip and opted for bourbon. I stepped to the bar to place my order, where I came across JC. He was sitting on a stool by himself and told me to buy him a drink.

"Who wouldn't want you here?" he asked.

"Huh?"

"Who do you think doesn't want you here?"

"You mean, in this *bar*?"

"*No*! On this *tour*! Who do you think wouldn't want you around?"

"Ah, so what you're saying is, there *is* someone who doesn't want me here."

"I'm not saying that. I'm saying, if that were the case, who do you think it would be?"

"Well," I said, "I guess there are people in the Mick Camp who might not be in love with me. Maybe Alan Dunn, maybe Tony King, maybe Mick himself. I mean, I've written a lot of sarcastic stuff about Mick through the years, and maybe he's sensitive to it. I don't know. Are you going to tell me what this is about?"

"I'm just posing a hypothetical," he said. "I never said someone didn't want you around. I simply asked who you *think* wouldn't want you around."

Woody got up from the table to see what we were discussing, but we shooed him away. JC and I wanted to feel each other out.

He informed me that his first bodyguarding gig was the Monkees in 1967. He'd gotten out of the army and needed a job. His brother was already a body-guard and fixed him up. In 1969, his brother was hired for the Stones' Hyde Park concert. JC tagged along and approached Mick: "I'm gonna work for you someday." The Stones indeed hired JC for their 1973 tour of Europe, and he never left. He developed other clients—Bowie, Dylan, the Who—"but I drop everything for a Stones tour."

When I told him how I came to the Stones, I think he felt a kinship. We had both approached them as brash-yet-naïve young turks. He said he had respect for journalists and mentioned a columnist he used to read in *The Guardian*. "The guy was an absolute arsehole," he said, "but I loved his writing. That's a wonderful talent to have, to be a writer. I wish *I* could write. But look at me, look at Seabrook. We were destined to work with our hands, not our minds."

I never expected him to open up like this. "Did it ever occur to you," he added, "that some of the people on this tour are jealous of you?"

"*Jealous*? Of *me*? I never thought about it."

"Well, you *should*. Because here you are, a journalist in his twenties, while people on this tour, twice your age, have no prospects. They'll be working for Mick and Keith the rest of their bloody lives because they can't do anything else."

This was too much for me to digest. For most of the *Steel Wheels* tour, I worried that everyone viewed me as an incapable dork. But if I understood JC correctly, I was perceived as quite the opposite. As someone capable of doing "damage."

JC's job was to protect the Stones by weeding out the physical threats and nuisances. He knew that I presented no such problems. So if someone told him to keep me at bay, it had nothing to do with my physical actions and everything to do with my writing.

JC knew I knew stuff. "Look," he said, "you're obviously aware of some of the dealings I've had. But let me tell you something, Bill. What you *don't* know is the things I *don't* do for money. The fans that I've let in, completely free of charge. The fans I've taken backstage, without a single dollar changing hands. Do you know what progeria is?"

"Pro what?"

"Progeria. It's a kids' disease. Makes children look like senior citizens. By the time they're 9, they look 90. Shriveled, toothless, and bald. I read about this kid who had it. He was 15, pushing his life expectancy. The article said he loved the Stones, so I contacted the newspaper and they gave me his number. I invited him and his mother to one of the shows and sorted them with back-stage passes, tickets, the whole lot. His mum said it was the happiest day of his life."

"Wow," I said, "that was pretty nice of you."

"Well, here's the point, Bill. If some rich arsehole is willing to give me a mil-lion dollars to let him backstage to impress his girlfriend, I'm not gonna be foolish enough not to take it. So long as I know he's not a nuisance or a trou-blemaker. But if I see a kid who's got progeria, who's not got much time on this earth, and only wants to see a Stones concert, then I'm gonna do my best to make him happy. I've had some illness in my family, so I know it's not an easy road. If I see someone sick, or someone in a wheelchair, I'll go out of my way to help them—free of charge."

I sensed he was telling the truth. And I realized he was much more complex than I initially gave him credit for. By gouging the rich and helping the poor, he was a rock 'n' roll Robin Hood. "So what you're saying is, if I bring you a busload of Stones fans in wheelchairs, you'll take care of them?"

"That's right," he answered. "But for every busload of cripples you send me, bring me *two* busloads of rich arseholes!"

JC never revealed who in the Stones entourage had it in for me. He ended our conversation by saying, "I like you. And I've enjoyed sharing a few drinks with you tonight. And that's why, at the end of the day, if I fuck with you on this tour, I'm merely doing my job. You've got to realize it's nothing personal, it's just business."

At the next concert, Freddy sought me out backstage. "Did you speak vit Kellogg?"

"Um, no. Why should I speak with Kellogg?"

"Go find Kellogg."

Freddy wouldn't tell me what this was about, but I sensed the urgency in his voice. I located Kellogg in a backstage tunnel and asked what was up.

"Well," he said sheepishly, "you know that video I sent to your room? It's gonna get here tomorrow, and it's got some 'stuff' in it."

"*Stuff*? You're joking, right? Please tell me you're joking."

He wasn't joking. When Kellogg's initial supply of coke ran out, everyone begged him for more. He phoned his wife back home and told her to send some. He instructed her how to use a videotape to hide the blow, by screwing open the cassette and inserting the baggie inside. If you do it right, it won't fuck up the tape's playability. Meaning, if a customs officer gets curious, he'll pop it in a VCR and it'll play perfectly.

How did *I* get involved? Well, Kellogg never had a room at the Okura. The roadies were so happy to have him, they let him sleep on their floors. A different room each night. "Bill," he said to me one day, "would it be okay if my wife FedExed a video to your room? It's for Woody. He wants to see the L.A. '75 concert. Just pick it up from the front desk when it shows up, and I'll come get it from you. 'Cause I don't know which room I'll be staying in that day."

I was so clueless and naïve, I said, "Sure, no problem." I didn't think twice. I never imagined that a videotape could have cocaine in it. And I never thought he'd be stupid enough to send a package of drugs to himself. Which, of course, he *wasn't*. He was sending the package to *me*.

He said it was JC's idea to use *my* room instead of anyone else's. Nothing personal, just business. *Let's send the coke to the one guy who doesn't want it.* I guess it had to do with the fact I wasn't on the tour's manifest. If Keith or Woody got busted, the tour would be canceled. If some roadie or sound engineer got busted, it'd affect the show. But if Bill German got busted, no big deal.

Whoever wanted to get rid of me found the perfect way to do it. A decade earlier, Paul McCartney spent ten days in a Tokyo jail for a handful of pot. The hard-liners wanted to give him seven years. Imagine what they'd do to me for some coke.

When Freddy got wind of the situation, he blew up at JC. Freddy wanted coke, but knew this wasn't the right way to get it. I collapsed into a chair backstage and put my hands over my face. Freddy elbowed JC in the ribs and got him to offer me a booby prize. For tonight only, even though I didn't possess the right pass, JC would allow me onstage to watch the show. Like the last meal of a condemned man. I didn't have the strength to yell, so I followed Freddy up the backstage ramp and took my seat in the cubbyhole. "Dat's boolshit vot dey did to you," he said. "Keet vud be very upset if he knew about dis."

I paid no attention to the concert that night. My eyes were open, but I didn't see a thing. I assume Mick was prancing just inches from my face and, for all I know, Keith and Woody spoke to me during "Sympathy for the Devil." But I can't recall a minute of it. I sat there catatonic, with scenes of *Midnight Express* flickering through my head.

I went back to the hotel that night, but couldn't sleep. I was truly convinced I'd be going to prison. How could the cops *not* search a package intended for the Stones' hotel?

In the morning, I got a phone call from Narita Airport. An English-speaking customs officer said she had a FedEx package with my name on it. She needed to ask me some questions before she could release it.

"What is the contents of this package?"

"A videotape, a VHS videotape."

"And what is the contents of this tape?"

"Music, rock 'n' roll music."

"Can you tell me the name of the artist on this tape?"

"The Rolling Stones."

I'd heard that Japan was cracking down on porn, so I prayed that's all they were looking for. If they popped it in the VCR, they'd see the Stones doing "Wild Horses" at the L.A. Forum. But if they waved it in the snout of a drug squad bloodhound, I'd be going to prison.

A few hours later, I got a call from the Okura front desk. The girl said a package had arrived for me and they were sending it up. "No!" I stressed. "Don't send it up! I'll have someone come and get it. The package really isn't for me, so the person who it belongs to will come downstairs."

Kellogg and Freddy went to the front desk. Kellogg signed for it and wasn't asked for ID. No one jumped out to bust him. To be on the safe side, however, he and Freddy zigzagged through the hotel's back stairwell to throw off the trail. For some reason, they brought the tape to *my* room.

As soon as they walked in, Kellogg cracked the cassette open with his bare hands. They laid some lines on my table and devoured it like starving puppies. I doubt there was anything left for Keith, Woody, or a single roadie.

I remained nervous for the rest of my trip, expecting to get cuffed at any moment. I couldn't breathe until I was safely on board Northwest Airlines, en route to JFK. Sitting on a plane for fourteen hours wasn't easy, but it sure beat ten years in the big house.

A boy and his dog.

30

welcome
to the jungle

When the Stones hit Europe in the summer of 1990, they changed the name of their tour to "Urban Jungle." They'd already licensed *Steel Wheels* to Michael Cohl, so the new moniker meant a new contract with him and new merchandise opportunities.

Europe had changed quite a bit since the band last visited in '82. The Iron Curtain was gone, and the Stones were hoping to play Moscow, Prague, and the shipyards of Gdansk.

Prior to the tour's debut in Holland, I visited Jane Rose in her New York office. She greeted me not with "Hello," but with "Everyone's pissed at you." My stomach did flips. "You printed the wrong dates for the tour!" she said. "You weren't authorized to print *any* dates, but you printed them anyway, and they were wrong. So everyone's pissed at you."

I asked who she meant by "everyone"—there's no way Keith could give a shit—but all she'd offer was "*Everyone.*" She seemed to enjoy saying it. The fact is, I did print some wrong dates, and no one felt worse than I did. In March 1990, two months before the launch of the Urban Jungle tour, it was widely rumored that the Stones would visit Europe that year, but Tony King and Jane were mum.

Letters poured in from my American subscribers, begging me for details. They wanted to see the Stones overseas, but needed to book flights and request vacation time as soon as possible.

I had a draft of the itinerary—which I obtained from a reliable source—so I went to print with it. In the March 11 issue of *Connection,* the smaller and speedier sister of *Beggars Banquet,* I ran the entire list. But in the two months between publication and the launch of the tour, several dates got switched. I printed that the Stones would be in Rotterdam on May 19, 21, and 23, but it turned out to be May 18, 19, and 21. I placed them in Helsinki on August 9, when it turned out to be Copenhagen. I had them in Knebworth on June 30 and Moscow on August 12, but both fell through.

I'm fully aware that a scoop isn't a scoop if the information isn't accurate. It would've done me no good to have my subscribers show up in Rotterdam a day late or go to Helsinki in a handbasket. So I intended to print, in small letters, "Subject to change"—but I forgot.

In the next issue of *Connection,* April 14, I humbly printed a correction. But the damage had already been done. Jane said that a bunch of European newspapers picked up on my March 11 list and began calling Mick's office in London. Supposedly, the Mick Campers were besieged by reporters, trying to confirm my scoop.

Anytime I made a mistake in *Beggars Banquet,* I'd want to stick my head in the oven. I still kick myself for spelling it "the Grammies" and for reporting that Keith saw a Sam Shepard play when it was really a Tom Stoppard play. So Jane's "Everyone's pissed at you" added to my stress. I knew that "everyone" didn't include Keith or Woody, but it did mean the tour's bigwigs.

I flew to Rotterdam for the debut. To cut my expenses, I traveled with two female Stones fans. We shared a rent-a-car and a room at the Hilton.

After check-in, I met with some of my Dutch subscribers in the hotel bar. My two traveling companions—who I'll refer to as the Pigeon Sisters—met with Alan Dunn. They'd known him for years, and he was the one who vouched for them with the Ticket Lady. When he saw me from across the room, he told them, "See Bill German over there? He's persona non grata on this tour."

It freaked out the Pigeon Sisters. They feared that their Ticket Lady privileges would be revoked if Alan Dunn knew we were rooming together. So we had to come and go separately and keep a low profile. Unbeknownst to me, the girls even struck my name from the hotel register. And after the first concert, they stranded me at Feyenoord Stadium. We drove there together, in the rent-a-car I chipped in for, but they went home without me. I roamed the parking lot like an Alzheimer's patient, until there were no cars left to look for. I sprinted to the railway station and caught the last train.

This "persona non grata" stuff left me so demoralized and homesick, I phoned a friend back in the States. It cost me a hundred bucks. I also knocked on Jane's door, to ask her advice. She explained that the problem wasn't the wrong dates per se, but what it represented. The itinerary was an internal memo, not meant for publication. When I printed it, it prompted someone to say: We've got a mole among us, and we need to get rid of him.

She never revealed who in the organization specifically blackballed me, but said, "Why can't you be more like the *Japanese* fan club? Those guys are just happy to be here. Everyone thinks you're not a fan and that you've got ulterior motives. Like you're here to profit off the band."

Me? Here to profit off the band? A funny notion, that. I'm the one who eked out twenty-something grand that year, while Michael Cohl raked in millions and the Janes, JCs, and Alan Dunns made six figures apiece. To one degree or another, we *all* profited off the band—from Prince Rupert and Michael Cohl to the guy selling bootleg shirts in the parking lot. An entire economy existed because five kids in 1962 played some Chuck Berry songs.

Freddy, I can reveal today, was my Deep Throat for the tour dates. He possessed a copy of the proposed itinerary and lent it to me back in February, when we were in Japan.

I'd gone to his room to say sayonara. He was in bed, with the covers up to his neck. He asked me if I had a list of the European dates, and I told him no. He rolled out of bed, walked to his desk, and handed me a copy—while in the buff.

I printed the list. It was on official stationery from Mick's British office, so I trusted it. But it was merely a draft, subject to final ratification. Most of the dates were solid, but some were changed. The price I paid for obtaining that list was seeing Freddy naked, and the price I paid for *printing* it was my "persona non grata" status.

I remember thinking how cool it was when Chet Flippo, writing for *Rolling Stone,* got tossed from the Stones' '78 tour. The magazine had written something critical, and Mick took offense. "Flippo's off the tour," he decreed.

When I read about it as a 15-year-old, I dreamed that one day I'd be like Flippo. Well, here I was, twelve years later, and it didn't feel so good. The difference, of course, is that Flippo had a major magazine behind him like *Rolling Stone.* I was in this all by myself and in a foreign country.

From Holland, the Pigeon Sisters and I headed to West Germany. During the drive to Hannover, they said they were reneging on our roommate deal. They couldn't risk being associated with me. When we got to the InterContinental—same hotel as the Stones—they checked into the room we'd reserved, while I asked for a separate one.

The front desk said, "We're booked," so I found a bed-and-breakfast around the corner. Close enough to the action, yet less than one-third the price of the InterContinental.

There was no concert that night, and I was feeling lonely, so I walked the grounds of the Rathaus. It's a centuries-old building that's like a city hall and museum. By coincidence, a limo pulled up to the curb, and a voice cried out: "Look! It's a Bill German in Germany!"

It was Woody, of course, returning from dinner. He invited me up to his room, where we watched the Uruguay vs. England soccer match. Either he didn't get the memo about my "persona non grata" status or he chose to ignore it. We hung out 'til dawn, and he invited me back the next night. He was there for me when I really needed a pal.

Another person who ignored the "memo" was the Ticket Lady. I visited her at the InterContinental, and she invited me to sit for a while. She must've sensed how low I was feeling. We talked about how she used to live in Brooklyn and how she'd eat at the deli where my parents worked. It made me feel less homesick. Regardless of my status, she continued to let me purchase tickets from her. And although I wasn't permitted into the band's backstage lounge, she gave me passes for the B-list VIP room.

The concerts in Europe were similar to those in the States, except for the stage set. To save money, they used drapery instead of the *Steel Wheels* metalwork. At first, the drapes were adorned with a jungle scene (Mick's idea), but it looked pretty tacky, so they scrapped it.

As for the repertoire, they added "Street Fighting Man." And to spice it up, they'd inflate huge dog balloons that Mick would wrestle. He'd smack their snouts and balls with a huge stick. Then, at the end of the song, he'd disappear into one of the dogs' mouths and be devoured.

After the concert in Hannover, a local subscriber tracked me down. He said he was insulted by the spectacle. He believed the Stones were making a mockery of his country's situation. "My country has been through a lot," he said, "and that song is very important to us. It tells the story of how we feel. But Mick makes a stupid joke from it."

He was truly upset, and I could see his point. A line like "My name is called disturbance" resonated with kids who had chiseled down the Berlin Wall six months earlier. And, "Everywhere I hear the sound of marching charging feet, boy" was a rallying cry for thousands of protestors. "Street Fighting Man" had stood the test of time and had become an anthem on both sides of the Wall—as well as in Tiananmen Square, Johannesburg, Prague, Moscow, and Gdansk. But Mick chose to go with the gimmicky dog balloons.

"Sympathy for the Devil," at least, still packed a punch. The Stones did the same thing as in America, with Mick singing the first verse high above the stage. Except that at Hannover's Niedersachsen Stadium, Mick's mic didn't work. He was up there by himself, singing, "Please allow me to introduce myself," and no one heard it. He promptly came down the elevator, peeved. The audience could sense his irritation.

Postconcert, I found myself at the InterContinental bar, sitting next to JC. He told me Mick was so angry about the glitch, heads were going to roll. At that very moment, Mick himself entered the room. JC jumped off his barstool like the Führer had just walked in, and pretended not to know me. Mick shot me a look like the glitch was *my* fault.

Mick's presence made me so tense, I darted to the elevator to visit Woody. He was eating a hamburger from room service. I never burdened him with my aggravation, but I did tell him about Mick's evil eye. He told me not to worry and that he'd get Keith to straighten it out. Bobby Keys stopped by, and, when the subject of Mick's moodiness came up, he said, "Aw, hell, that's *nothing*. Mick Jagger hasn't said two words to me this whole year."

It was consoling to know that Mick wasn't singling me out. Bobby was someone who'd been recording with the Stones for over two decades. He played the signature sax solos on "Live with Me" and "Brown Sugar" and had been touring with the band since 1972. But I guess none of that mattered in 1990.

I returned to Europe for the July shows at London's Wembley Stadium. I roomed at the Y, like I did for Stu's memorial in '86. It was ten times cheaper than where the Stones were staying. Keith, Woody, and the entourage were at the Mayfair, while Mick was at the Halcyon.

I spent a lot of time at the Mayfair. One day, I brought Keith to meet a bunch of my subscribers in the lobby. Another day, I brought a belated birthday gift to Woody's room. One of those Mexican Day of the Dead dioramas, depicting a skeleton shooting pool. Woody said he loved it and told me what everyone else got him: "A pair of pajamas from Bobby Keys, a chain from Jo, Mick gave me a rug, Bill gave me a Chagall lithograph, and Keith gave me a silver bracelet. But he didn't have a box or wrapping paper, so he stuck it in a grapefruit peel." Good gossip for the newsletter and for my K-Rock radio reports.

The Wembley concerts were fun and provided a study in British culture. At the July 4 show, the fans largely ignored the Stones because they were consumed by the World Cup semifinal: England vs. West Germany. Mick didn't want to take the stage because he was watching it in the band lounge. The concert started while the match was still on, so fans listened on earplugs or watched it at the stadium's bar. Cheers and jeers erupted throughout the concert, but it had nothing to do with the Stones. England lost, so everyone was in a pissy mood, including the Mick Campers.

I didn't know whether my "persona non grata" thing was still in effect, but I walked on eggshells anyway. I avoided the Mick people and the tour's bigwigs as much as possible. The one guy who sought me out was Norman Perry. He didn't care what I wrote in my newsletter, so long as I was willing to buy merchandise from him. A lot of my American subscribers were dying for Urban Jungle stuff, so I arranged to visit his London office on Marylebone Road.

Norman made me buy a minimum of three hundred pieces of each item, payment up front, no return policy, and I went for it. It was a financial risk, but I didn't mind. If anything, I appreciated his straightforwardness. I'd grown so frustrated by everyone's evasiveness on this tour, I was happy to know where I stood. Norman was always honest with me and never tried to stab me in the back, only the front.

When I left his office and walked the Marylebone district, I got a sinking feeling. I remembered that this was where, on a Langham Street rooftop, Edward R. Murrow did his famous radio reports during the blitz. One of journalism's holiest shrines, yet I was there to haggle *moichandise*. It made me realize that, as a journalist, I was way off my charted course.

At the next concert, a line in "Ruby Tuesday" hit me like a V-1 bomb. When Mick sang, "Cash your dreams before they slip away," I felt he was singing to *me*. For years, my biggest dream was to write a book about the Stones on tour. With the yearlong *Steel Wheels*/Urban Jungle junket winding down, the time to pursue that dream was now.

This was hanging in Keith's poolroom.

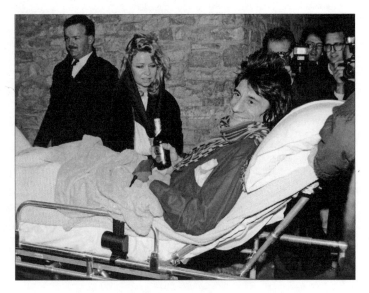

Beer in hand, Woody gets wheeled out of the Princess
Margaret Hospital.

31

a degree
of separation

By the end of the *Steel Wheels*/Urban Jungle campaign, I'd witnessed more of its shows and logged more of its miles than any other journalist. I crossed the U.S., as well as the Atlantic and Pacific Oceans, to catch thirty-four concerts from every conceivable angle—onstage, on the roof, and all points in between. I reported for a dozen *Beggars Banquet/Connection* issues, two dozen radio broadcasts, and one *Rolling Stone* article. My plan was to compile my observations into one cohesive book.

When I mentioned my idea on the first day of the tour, Jane Rose told me to forget it. She said the Stones would have no desire to participate in such a project. And now that the tour was over, she was telling me to forget it *again*. The Stones *had* agreed to do such a book, but Mick wanted someone else to write it.

I'd sacrificed an entire year of my life to cover this tour. With few exceptions, I did not leave my apartment for anything but the Stones. I didn't go on a single date and didn't get laid. I saw Keith's parents more than I saw my own. So I was extremely bummed not to get this assignment. No one was preventing me from doing my *own* book about the tour, but remember two things: The Stones organization was sitting on the tour's best photos. It was *their* hired photographer who had the best access. Moreover, if I competed with the Stones organization in the marketplace, I could kiss their cooperation goodbye forever, effectively ending *Beggars Banquet*.

Mick and his aide-de-camp, Tony King, commissioned a glossy fluff piece instead of a document for posterity. The book was well written and had some nice pictures, but there were unforgivable gaps.

I still can't fathom how a book about the Urban Jungle tour could ignore the Stones' visit to Prague. They played to a hundred thousand people and broke bread with Václav Havel, the playwright-turned-prisoner-turned-president. When Czechoslovakia was under Communist rule a year earlier, a visit from the Stones was unimaginable. But on August 18, 1990, Prague was welcoming the Stones like conquering heroes. Posters were plastered all over the city that read: "The tanks are rolling out, the Stones are rolling in." Giant billboards, which previously featured portraits of Stalin, now displayed the Stones' tongue logo. The country was going through a "Velvet Revolution," and the Stones' arrival was its most visible symbol.

At Strahov Stadium, 107,000 Czechs, Poles, and Ukrainians watched the Stones through a driving rain. Havel declared your Stones ticket a temporary visa, so, if you were crossing the border to see the concert, you merely flashed it to the officer and were waved right through.

Before the gig, Havel invited the Stones to Hradčany Castle, the presidential palace. Thousands cheered as their democratically elected president stood on the castle's balcony with their favorite rock 'n' roll band. At the concert that night, Havel wore an Urban Jungle T-shirt, while fans who'd been repressed their whole lives got to finally enjoy the Stones openly.

None of this was mentioned in the Stones' self-produced book. Not a single photo of the Stones with Havel—I ran three in *Beggars Banquet/Connection*—and not a single reference to Prague. Also neglected were the Stones' trips to Berlin. They played *East* Berlin before "East" was dropped from the geopolitical nomenclature, and they played *West* Berlin in the same stadium that hosted the 1936 Olympics. Where Hitler watched Jesse Owens, fans were now cheering the Stones. But that fact wasn't significant enough for Mick's book. Two pages were instead dedicated to the tour's moving trucks.

As frustrated as I was, I had little time to sulk. I had a newsletter to run and plenty of news to report. Within months of the tour's conclusion, Woody broke both his legs, Mick married Jerry, and Bill Wyman threatened to quit.

On November 12, 1990, Woody was returning from the funeral of his father-in-law in Devon, England. He and Jo were on the M4 motorway when they skidded on a rain slick. "[We were] butt-first in the *fast* lane," explained Woody. Their car got smacked and, when Woody got out to check the damage, a third car skidded and sandwiched him in between. His legs were crushed, and he was rushed to the Princess Margaret Hospital. "It wasn't my time to go," he told me on the phone. "And the best part is, the doctors prescribed me a pint of Guinness."

On November 21, Mick and Jerry were traveling through Bali and got the urge to merge. They found a Hindu priest to perform their wedding ceremony. From what I was told, it involved Mick sprinkling chicken blood on Jerry and hitting her over the head with a banana. Alan Dunn was the best man, and the only guests were Mick and Jerry's toddlers and nanny. The whole thing didn't seem kosher. I knew it'd never stand up in civil court and, duh, that's why Mick did it in the first place. Years later, when Jerry demanded half of Mick's income—after his gazillionth affair—he denied they were married and the British legal system agreed.

Early in 1991, the Stones released a live album called *Flashpoint*. It featured a bonus studio track, "Highwire," inspired by the Gulf War. They shot a video for it at the Brooklyn Navy Yard, minus Bill Wyman. His absence sparked rumors that he was leaving the band.

Toward the end of '91, the Stones followed *Flashpoint* with the release of *At the Max,* a concert film from the Urban Jungle tour. It utilized a new format known as IMAX. It was supposed to premiere at the Museum of Natural History, the only place in New York with a legitimate IMAX screen, but, due to a conflict, was shown at the Beacon Theatre. Keith conducted a formal press conference in the lobby and, when asked if he liked the way he looked in the film, quipped, "Hey, man, I *never* like the way I look!"

Beggars Banquet was rolling along nicely, but I'd hit a glass ceiling. After covering the Stones for thirteen years, I was making shit money and couldn't even write a book about them. I moved to a studio apartment on Manhattan's Upper West Side, in a building for low-income New Yorkers. I pursued other job possibilities—auditioning for VH1 and writing copy for a friend's mail-order catalog—but life without the Stones seemed daunting. The epilogue of Stones quitters and castoffs was not encouraging: Brian Jones was fished out of a swimming pool and Mick Taylor was looking peaked.

And how about Bill Graham? When the Stones rejected him for the *Steel Wheels*/Urban Jungle tour, he sank into a deep depression and developed an addiction to Halcion. "Losing the Stones," he said in his autobiography, "was like watching my favorite lover become a whore." He'd worked with dozens of legendary bands, but considered the Stones "the filet." From Halcion, he graduated to Prozac and lithium, and, by October 1991, he was dead. It may have been a helicopter crash that killed his body, but it was losing the Stones that killed his spirit.

Let's also not forget Paul Wasserman, the publicist who was dumped for a younger and cheaper p.r. firm. Wasso had orchestrated the Stones' flatbed truck stunt in '75 and had seen them through years of turbulence. When they got rid of him before the *Steel Wheels* tour, he felt lost. So he hatched a scheme worthy of Max Bialystock. He convinced people that his famous clients—U2 and Jack Nicholson—needed investors for their nonexistent production companies. When nothing materialized, his victims confronted him and he attempted suicide. He was convicted of fraud and, at age 66, spent six months in the L.A. County Men's Central Jail.

Life after the Stones ain't pretty. Nothing you do will ever be as exciting as what you've done with *them*. And you can't put them behind you like any job you've ever quit or been fired from. They'll haunt you when you're trying to watch football ("Start Me Up" before every kickoff) or Letterman (Paul Shaffer striking up "Bitch" before a commercial) or Scorsese (De Niro icing some guy to "Monkey Man" or "Gimme Shelter"). The Stones will be everywhere *you* are—movies, commercials, the Super Bowl—and you'll constantly be reminded of what you no longer have. If your life isn't in order or you've got nothing good lined up, you're gonna feel stupid and alone.

Perhaps that's why Keith said, "Nobody leaves the Stones except in a coffin." I wasn't sure if he meant it as an observation or as a decree—he *was* threatening to break Wyman's legs if he quit—but the point was clear: Almost no one leaves willingly. And that extends to the Bill Germans, Freddy Sesslers, and Jane Roses.

The pull of the Stones is like a vacuum suction. And when you're in that vacuum, nothing in the real world matters. On a tour, you blow into town and walk past dozens of envious Stones freaks at the hotel. You then go to the venue and rub elbows with celebrities and walk through the same tunnel as the band. You already know the set list, and Woody told you to come back to his room after the show. You look around at the 50,000 people in the stands, and you know that every one of them wishes they were you.

You're in a world where everyone you meet is judging your worth by your proximity to the band, not for anything you've done in your *own* life. Do you have a backstage pass? Did you go to Keith's party? That's all that matters. You buy into it and derive your self-esteem and identity from it. It becomes an addiction and you'll do anything to keep it.

But after thirteen years of *Beggars Banquet,* I wanted more. The band's machinery had beaten the enthusiasm out of me, and I realized that my high school history teacher was right: "The problem with mixing hobby and profession is that it'll make your work feel like fun, but it'll eventually make your fun feel like work."

As much as my readers envied me for hanging with the Stones, I was the one envying *them*. They'd send me pictures of themselves at the concerts—

hoisting beers, wearing Stones shirts, and completely letting loose. For me, the Stones had become a day at the office, and the visceral joy of cheering "yeah-yeah-woo!" at the end of "Brown Sugar" was something I missed.

With all this conflict swirling through my head, I found myself at Keith and Patti's house in Weston, Connecticut. They'd invited me to their holy trinity of late-December celebrations: Keith's birthday, Christ's birthday, and their wedding anniversary.

I wanted to bring something special to thank them for their kindness and support, but I was stumped. (To quote Letterman, "Keith Richards is a hard guy to shop for. What do you get the man who's taken *everything*?") I'd always heard about the gifts they got from their famous friends—gold watches and Warhols—but I couldn't compete with that. I knew they loved board games, so I stopped by a store that sold chess sets. Deluxe pieces, like Robert E. Lee vs. Ulysses S. Grant, and Luke Skywalker vs. Darth Vader. It made me long for a Mick Camp vs. Keith Camp: Keith as the king, Jane as his queen, and Freddy as a rook vs. Mick as the king, Tony King as the queen, and Alan Dunn as a bishop. Plenty of pawns on both sides.

The chess sets were too expensive, so I went with a Day of the Dead diorama like I had for Woody. This one depicted several skeletons as mariachi musicians. Fitting, because Keith and Patti had a mariachi band at their wedding.

It was my first time at their relatively new home, so Patti gave me the tour. When we got to Keith's private study, I was flattered to see a copy of *The Works* prominently displayed. The party itself was in the basement, so Patti and I hopped over the sleeping Labrador to get down the steps.

The basement had a fully stocked bar and a jumbo video screen. At the basement's far end was an actual classroom, complete with a blackboard, erasers, and kiddie chairs. Patti would read to the girls in there. Alexandra and Theodora were 5 and 6 and were the primary reasons the Richardses moved from Manhattan to Weston. On the bulletin board were their drawings of "Daddy." A stick figure with a stick guitar.

The basement also had a game room, where the main attraction was the *Steel Wheels* pool table. The walls had paintings of the Stones by Sebastian Krüger. My favorite, near the pool-cue rack, depicted Mick as Keith's hand puppet.

Keith and I made eye contact, and he approached me from the other side of the room. I was so confused by the conflicts in my life that it reflected in my body language. I wasn't sure if I should shake Keith's hand like a business associate or hug him like a friend, so I awkwardly settled for something in the middle.

I didn't want to discuss the Stones with him, so I made an attempt at small talk. I'd noticed a poster in the bathroom, autographed by the Broadway cast of *Six Degrees of Separation,* so I asked, "How'd you like *Six Degrees*?"

He flipped through his mental Rolodex, but had no idea what I was talking about.

"The *play,*" I said. "The poster was staring at me while I was peeing."

"Oh, *that,*" he replied. "Patti went without me. You'd have to ask *her.*" So much for small talk.

A few minutes later, Steve Jordan and Charley Drayton arrived. Keith's X-Pensive Winos mates greeted him with soul-brother hugs and high-fives. I envied how nonconflicted they were when it came to the Stones. They knew exactly where they stood in relation to Keith, while I wondered, "Am I a fan? A friend? A journalist? Or what?"

When I looked around the room, I realized that no one from the Stones tour was there—no bodyguards, no promoters, and no publicists. Backstage passes weren't required in Keith and Patti's basement, and this party, contrary to JC's mantra, was *personal,* not *business.* The twenty invited guests were strictly friends and family.

As I stood there, I realized I could remain friends with Keith and Patti, while giving up *Beggars Banquet.* I could still attend Stones shows, without having to chronicle them. And I could still be a journalist, reporting on everything else in the world, while enjoying parties in Weston. No conflicts or entanglements.

My daydream in Keith's basement was interrupted by Jane Rose. "Make sure," she said, "that whatever you write about this party, you run by me first. And don't forget, you *cannot* write 'Connecticut.' Just say this party was *outside New York City.*"

It was Christmas, so I wasn't about to argue. She was concerned for Keith's privacy and I understood that, but she was taking it too far. Connecticut's a big place, and a stalker would have to ring lots of doorbells to zero in on Keith's house.

In my next issue, I mentioned the party just briefly. It was such a small item, I didn't run it past Jane. To me, it was nothing more than a private celebration with some nice people. I was invited to my friend's house, and he happens to be a Rolling Stone.

Ultimately, I stuck with *Beggars Banquet,* the way Jack Paar stuck with *The Tonight Show.* He's the guy who preceded Johnny Carson as host. In 1960, he felt the network was dicking him around (telling him what he could and couldn't say), so he abruptly announced his resignation on the air. His parting words were: "There must be a better way to make a living than this." But he crawled back to the show a few weeks later, saying: "I've *looked*. And there *isn't*."

Chuckles visits New York.

Woody introduced me to Izzy, but Izzy wasn't too friendly.

32

bird not
in the hand

With the Stones embarking on five separate solo projects, I had to deal with a slew of new middle people. Charlie was the first Stone out of the gate, with his brilliant jazz album, *From One Charlie*. On it, he paid homage to the late Charlie "Bird" Parker.

To promote the 1991 release, he brought his jazz quintet to New York for a one-night stand at the Blue Note. He was also doing interviews, so I asked Sherry Daly to slot me in. Sherry was based in London and, for lack of a better description, was Charlie's Jane Rose. She told me I could have fifteen minutes with Charlie before his June 3 Blue Note gig. "Come down for soundcheck round noon," she said, "and when he's done, he'll have some time for you."

I was thrilled. Charlie was the one Stone I'd never interviewed, much less had a conversation with. I'd been in some intimate situations with him, but could never get more than a nod from him. He could be very introverted around strangers, and I got the distinct impression he never remembered who I was. I hoped my interview would change all that.

I sat quietly during the soundcheck at a table near the stage. Sherry said, "Charlie will join you shortly," but I waited for two hours. Charlie was the consummate perfectionist, involved in every aspect of the show. After rehearsing each song with his band, he jumped inside the sound booth to test the monitors and lighting. He shuffled past me on several occasions, but was too focused to notice me.

At a certain point, he finished his tinkering and scampered upstairs to his dressing room. I don't think he ever knew I was there. Sherry apologized and told me to call her at the hotel. "Ring me at the Mark," she said, "and we'll set something up before he leaves. I promise."

I left several messages, but didn't hear back. Charlie did interviews with *Good Morning America* and several print outlets, but not *Beggars Banquet*. By the time Sherry returned my call, she and Charlie were back in London.

I think she perceived an interview in *Beggars Banquet* as preaching to the choir. If the *Steel Wheels* business model taught anything to the Stones, it was to focus on the bottom line. And so, the people who needed to be pitched weren't Stones freaks, they were the people combing their hair and packing their kids' lunches during *Good Morning America.*

A year later, I got a second chance. In July 1992, Charlie and his quintet returned to the Blue Note for a six-night stint. Sherry promised to fit me in. She told me to come to the Hard Rock Cafe, where Charlie was scheduled to donate a drum skin. "After the presentation," she said, "he'll have five or ten minutes for your interview." I hustled down there, tape recorder in hand.

Unfortunately, Bill Clinton came between us. Charlie's limo got stuck in bumper-to-bumper traffic outside the Democratic National Convention. Thousands of people were demonstrating near Madison Square Garden, bringing midtown to a standstill. By the time Charlie arrived at the Hard Rock, there was no time. He posed for photos and split. Sherry apologized to me as she and Charlie rushed out the door: "Ring me at the hotel!"

I attended two of Charlie's shows at the Blue Note, including one I wasn't supposed to. What I mean is, Sherry put me on the guest list for the Friday show, but I turned up a day early. Keith said he'd be there on Thursday, so I asked Sherry if she could switch me. She said no. My thinking was, if I attended *one* show, with everything else being equal, I should witness the one Keith's at. That way, I'd be killing two Stones with one Bird. If anything interesting took place as a result of Keith's presence, I'd get the story firsthand.

I went to the Blue Note on Thursday, since tickets were still available. But when I got to the door, Sherry, who was standing there with the guest list, said, "This is *not* your night."

"I know," I replied. "But I *also* wanna come *tonight.* I'll *pay.*"

"But this is not your night," she reiterated. "I told you on the phone, you're on the list for *tomorrow.*"

"I know. But I *also* wanna come *tonight.*"

She wasn't grasping what I was saying and acted like I was putting one over on her. "Bill German," she declared, "you're a naughty boy! A very naughty boy!"

I had no idea what that meant, but I pulled out my wallet to show I didn't want a freebie. "Well," she said, "I'll let you in tonight, you naughty boy, but I cannot seat you next to Keith."

"That's fine," I said. "I wasn't *expecting* to sit with Keith. And look—*money!* I'm willing to *pay!*"

She ushered me to a table in the paid-customers section and said, "This is where I can put you." I wound up next to three guys, all stinking of booze. They were wearing Stones shirts and called out Stones requests throughout the show.

This was a jazz club, with tablecloths and candles. Charlie was playing with brushes, not sticks. Low-key. But these schnooks were yelling, " 'Brown Sugar'!" and, "Charlie's good tonight, ain't he?" When one of them hollered, "Hey, Chuck! Yo, Chuckles!" I wanted to die. I tried sliding under the table, so Keith wouldn't see me.

After the show, I did chat with Keith. Luckily, he didn't associate me with the three idiots. But as I left the club, Sherry's "naughty boy" comment reverberated in my head. I was about to turn 30 and had a schoolmarm scolding me like a child. By week's end, Sherry didn't grant my interview, saying, "I'm sorry we couldn't fit you in."

I felt slightly consoled when Charlie skipped Letterman, too. He bailed out last-minute after learning the show's policy: Paul Shaffer and Co. had to accompany each musical guest. Charlie admired Shaffer, but had painstakingly arranged his song for a jazz quintet, not a rock band.

Ten minutes before showtime, neither side was backing down. Charlie said he was leaving, and he wasn't bluffing. He exited the green room and headed for the elevator. I heard from an eyewitness that it played out like a vaudeville skit. The show's producer followed Charlie to the elevator, begging him to stay. Charlie got on and pressed the Lobby button, so the producer got on and pressed Cancel. It went like that for two minutes. Lobby. Cancel. Lobby. Cancel.

Charlie darted to another elevator. Again, it was lobby-cancel-lobby-cancel, until lobby won and Charlie was gone. It happened so close to show-time that Letterman had no idea. He announced during his monologue that Charlie was on the show, but Shaffer corrected him. Letterman said something like "Are you *serious*?" and Paul replied yes. It then became the running joke of the night: "What's that, Paul? Charlie took a powder?" Gary Busey was the show's other guest, so no one expected *Charlie* to be the problem.

With two strikes against me, I tried again in October 1993. *Warm and Tender,* a collection of Tin Pan Alley songs, was Charlie's new album. To promote it, he flew to New York for a private concert at the Algonquin Hotel.

I asked the record company if I could interview him, but they said, "He's booked." It's possible they were still pissed at me. Months earlier, when I printed an advance listing of the album's song titles, I received a phone call from the label's publicist: "How did you get the track listing? Who gave it to you? You weren't authorized to print that!"

I didn't reveal my source—Bernard Fowler, the Charlie Watts Quintet's lead singer—and I held the phone from my ear as she ranted and raved. The record company was two years old and was located in the swamps of Jersey, so you'd think they'd be grateful for publicity. *Warm and Tender* was a great disc, but they had an uphill climb with Charlie's third jazz album in as many years. Stones fans considered it too much a diversion, and jazz purists never gave it a chance.

Charlie's people put him on *Regis and Kathie Lee* instead. He sat speechless on live TV, as Reege teased him about the Stones, and as Kathie Lee, in her perkiest airhead tone, compared Charlie's repertoire to her own insipid cruise-ship act: " 'Time after Time' is my new closing song!" Charlie was like, "Who *is* this person?" But for Charlie's handlers, it was more important to reach the housewives in curlers than the fans who read *Beggars Banquet.*

Woody, meanwhile, had his *own* album to do. He kept me abreast of his progress at every stage. He began recording at his new house in Ireland, and he'd play it for me over the phone. He then mixed the album in Los Angeles, where I hooked up with him for a proper listen.

The album was called *Slide on This* and featured guests like U2's the Edge and Def Leppard's Joe Elliott. Woody's manager hired a publicist to help promote it. She'd never heard of *Beggars Banquet* and, frankly, I'd never heard of her, either. But to schedule an interview with Ron Wood, I needed to go through her. I sent her a package of *Beggars Banquet* issues, so she could familiarize herself. She was based in New York, so I strolled to her office, to pick up some promo photos and remind her about the interview. I asked if she'd had the chance to look through my issues and she replied, "Ugh, it's such an overload of information." I chuckled and said, "Yeah, I try to cover *everything,* and I've been doing it since 1978."

"Wow!" she exclaimed in a patronizing tone. "That makes you a fan's fan!"

I rolled my eyes, suggesting I wasn't comfortable with that assessment, but she misinterpreted me. Instead of backing off, she upped the ante: "Let me correct that—you're a *fan's fan's fan!*"

I felt like saying, "Listen, lady, I may be a fan, but I run a legitimate news publication. I might cover *just* the Stones, but tell that to Sam Donaldson. He covered *just* the White House for twelve years. I'm sorry I'm so knowledgeable and passionate about my subject."

Of course, that's what I *should* have said to her. But I was too polite and hated pulling rank. She'd been working with Woody for five minutes, while I'd written a book with the guy. Yet she considered *herself* the professional and me an obsessive nerd.

So here's some irony: When Woody appeared on Bob Costas's *Later* program, she and I were both in the wings. And when Costas, during a commercial break, asked for the dates of Woody's upcoming solo gigs—so he could plug them on the air—she didn't have a clue. I'm the one who had to say, "St. Petersburg on Friday and Miami on Saturday." And after the show, *I'm* the one who got Costas and Woody to pose for a photo, something that should have been the publicist's job.

She never did fit me in for that interview.

The other *Slide on This* head-scratcher was how Woody couldn't get a record deal for it. A member of the Rolling Stones—not to mention the guy who co-wrote "Stay with Me"—was being ignored by the major labels. So on March 28, 1992, a listening party was held in Hollywood. Woody and his manager invited friends and record executives to A&M Studio.

I attended as both a supporter and reporter. Woody was happy to see me and introduced me around. First was Izzy Stradlin from Guns N' Roses. I tried being cordial, but he didn't say a word and didn't shake my hand. If anyone was dopier than Axl, it was *this* guy.

Next, Woody brought me to Richard Lewis, the comedian. Richard had his back to everyone the whole night. He was dancing in a corner by himself, grooving to Woody's album and playing air guitar. Occasionally, he'd turn around and give Woody a thumbs-up, before returning to his trance. He must've forgotten to cut his pills in half that day. Woody startled him by tapping his shoulder. "Richard, I'd like you to meet Bill German. He co-authored my book with me."

Richard shook my hand. I knew he collected Woody's artwork, so I asked him what he had. But all he answered was, "I'll call ya! I'll call ya!"

"No, I just wanna know, which pieces of Woody's artwork do you have?"

"I'll call ya! I'll call ya!"

I didn't bother telling him that he didn't have my number. He was very hyper, but at least he was more sociable than Izzy and less scary than Phil Spector.

Phil was seated at a banquette most of the night and never mingled. He had two bodyguards with him and kept his back to the wall. Woody plopped down next to him and was flattered to hear him say, "*I* should have produced this album!" Although I'm not sure Phil meant it as a compliment.

A couple of *Beggars Banquet* photographers were in the room, so I asked Woody if it was okay to snap a photo of him with Phil. Woody said yes, and I waved my friends over. But as soon as their cameras clicked, Phil lost his cool, directing his anger at *me*.

"Stop!" he yelled. "Gimme that film! I want that film! If you don't gimme that film, I'll have you killed! Then I'll have you arrested!"

Being a fan's fan's fan was dangerous work.

Woody and Rod up to no good.

33

spare the rod,
spoil the child

Keith's *Main Offender* album came out in October 1992. To promote it, he appeared on the syndicated radio show *Rockline*. I knew the show's producers, so I helped them prepare for the interview. The broadcast took place on October 19, and I went to the ABC building on West End Avenue to witness it in person.

When Keith, Jane, and Tony Russell (Keith's assistant) showed up, they were surprised to see me. Keith retreated to a sound booth by himself and donned a set of headphones. The rest of us, including two engineers, watched Keith through a window. The show's moderator, Bob Coburn, was in L.A., speaking to Keith via satellite.

The show began at 10 PM, and Keith fielded questions from Coburn and from listeners who phoned in. "Is it true you collect knives?" "Yeah, I like blades." Off air, Coburn asked Keith if he'd seen that night's presidential debate between Bill Clinton and George Bush Sr. Keith said he hadn't, but referred to the Clinton-Gore ticket as "the pussy-whipped double act."

Rick Nielsen, the guitarist from Cheap Trick, called in to the show like a regular fan. "[You're] one of the main guys in my life," he told Keith. "I'm as nervous as that girl that called before. . . . Keith Richards, [I'm] a fan for life." He was phoning from his car, so Keith joked, "Rick, you take it easy, stay on the road."

Rick interpreted "stay on the road" to mean that Cheap Trick should keep touring—"I can't afford to get *off*," he responded—but Keith was referring to Rick's dialing-while-driving. "Keep your eyes on the road," Keith clarified.

During the next commercial, Keith admitted he had no idea who he was talking to. I tried clueing him in—"Y'know, the guy with the baseball cap"—

but it didn't register. The engineer even sang, "Your momma's alright, your daddy's alright," but Keith drew a blank.

When the show was over, Keith stuck around a bit, to sign stuff for the engineers. "I'm headed to Woody," he told me. "You wanna hitch a ride?"

Woody was in town, rehearsing for his solo tour at SIR Studio. He'd finally scored a record deal—from that same company in Jersey that put out Charlie—and was ready to bring *Slide on This* to the masses.

Keith and I took the building's freight elevator to the garage, where a car was waiting. Jane said, "Alright, Bill, *good night*"—implying that I couldn't join them—so I informed her that Keith had *invited* me. Limousine protocol dictates that the celebrity rides face-forward, so Keith got the choice seat, while I got the backward seat. Jane and Tony sat on Keith's side.

When the car pulled out of the garage, there was a group of fans waiting at the curb. Our driver sped off without stopping. In fact, for the next twenty minutes, we played cat-and-mouse with a car that was following us. We had only forty or so blocks to go, but we added an extra twenty to shake them off. We zigged and zagged from east to west and west to east. Tony spent most of the trip peering out the back window, barking instructions to our driver. "They're still following us! Make a right on 42nd!" "A left on 34th!"

"Make a U-turn!" yelled Jane. "Go through the light!"

Keith was oblivious and calmly faced forward. It gave us a chance to chat. I told him I'd recently been to the Magritte exhibition at the Met and that one of Magritte's paintings, *The Rape,* must have inspired the Stones' 1973 tour advertisement. (Both depicted a woman's torso as a face. Her nipples were the eyes, her pubic region the mouth.)

"That sounds about right," said Keith. "Rape is what the Stones do, right? Rape and plunder."

I laughed and asked him if he ever met Magritte in the Sixties.

"Probably," he said. "But I can't recall."

Jane and Tony weren't interested in Magritte. They were still consumed by our car chase. "Take Seventh Avenue! Get in the left lane!" We pulled up to SIR around 1 AM. Again, there were two dozen people surrounding our limo. Keith's a patient guy, but this was a mob scene. Without waiting for the driver to open the door, he dashed out, *A Hard Day's Night* style. Several people grabbed Keith's arm, but he yanked his way through.

When we got inside, Woody's first words—before greeting Keith—were "Bill German! We just heard your name on the radio!" (I was thanked in the credits.) Woody said he tried phoning the show, but "I kept getting a busy signal!"

Woody unhooked his guitar and sat next to Keith on the drum riser. Whether he planned to end his rehearsal at 1 AM didn't matter. As soon as Keith showed up, the point was moot. Even at his own rehearsal, Woody took a backseat. For the next couple of hours, we listened to *Main Offender* through the studio's speakers. Woody hardly said a word about his own solo album. It was reminiscent of the nights I spent at Woody's when we were working on our book. The minute Mick or Keith came over, everything stopped and it was all about *them,* not Woody. Keith didn't intend to hijack Woody's rehearsal, but that's the way it played out. I left at 4 AM and told Woody I'd catch him later in the week.

When I next visited the studio, the employees immediately buzzed me in. "You're Keith's friend from the other night, right?" Woody had a lot of stuff going on that he never mentioned when Keith was there. For starters, his dog had just died in Ireland. Second, he had a touch of the flu. Third, he'd cracked a rib. Fourth, he had a zit on his face so big, he'd given it a name. He was calling it Brian for some reason, and it was hard not to stare.

Overall, Woody was in good spirits and looking forward to his tour. I watched a full rehearsal and convinced him it was great. His repertoire included Stones and Faces tunes, like "It's Only Rock 'N Roll" and "Stay with Me," as well as solo nuggets, like "Breathe on Me" and "I Can Feel the Fire."

I attended his warm-up show at Toad's Place and his official debut at the Ritz, Halloween night. He then played Electric Lady Studio for a special radio broadcast. "I'd just like everyone out there in radio land to know that we *are* playing naked."

In the lounge at Electric Lady, he urged me to come along for the five-week tour: "We've got a spot for you on the bus!" He said he'd get the driver to stop at my apartment so I could pick up my toothbrush and underwear.

I was flattered by the invitation, but had an issue to get out and postage stamps to lick. I couldn't run off and join the circus.

Woody and I next saw each other in May 1993. He was in New York with Rod Stewart and was in his more comfortable role as second banana.

The two of them had recently taped an *Unplugged* episode for MTV. Woody played on thirteen songs, including "Maggie May," but it was billed as a Rod thing. In fact, the ensuing CD was called *Rod Stewart: Unplugged . . . and Seated,* with Woody's involvement a mere footnote.

Woody was happy to promote the project, so he tagged along with Rod to *Rockline.* Again, the show was conducted at ABC, in a studio normally used for news reports. When Woody walked in, he greeted me with a big hug and a "Heyyyyy!" Rod asked, "Who-*zee*?"

"Bill's me co-author," Woody informed him. "You remember *The Works,* right? Bill co-wrote it with me here in New York. He's also editor of *Beggars Banquet* Stones magazine. Been doin' it since the year dot."

"You don't *look* that old," said Rod. (Woody had introduced us once before, but I didn't expect them to remember. It was at the Hard Rock Cafe, following the first MTV Awards in 1984. Rod stole French fries off my plate and never explained why he and Woody brought an ironing board onstage.)

"Hey," Woody suggested, "Bill should do *your* fan magazine!"

Rod and his manager nodded, as though it was something they'd consider, but I told them the Stones were enough for me.

Woody and Rod retreated to the booth behind the glass. Their managers, as well as Jo Wood and Chuch Magee, watched with me from the other side. Again, the show's moderator was in Los Angeles and, again, some of the best material came off air. Rod and Woody sang a couple of Faces numbers during the commercials. And when the show was over, Woody taped a public service announcement, going slightly off script: "In recent years, there's been a lot of progress in the fight against AIDS. And when we catch the bastard that started it, we'll strangle him." Rod laughed so hard, he literally fell off his chair.

With Rod as his partner in crime, Woody possessed a giddiness he could rarely express around the Stones. He and Rod were like mischievous teenagers.

They invited me back to their hotel. When our limo pulled up to the Peninsula on 56th Street, a bunch of autograph seekers were waiting outside. Woody was done signing before Rod, so he grabbed me and said, "Let's head for the bar!" When we got there, we found the place closed. "It's only one-thirty!" cried Woody. The bar didn't have doors, it was an open area off the lobby, so Woody ventured inside. "Make Rod think we're having a party!" He began hooting and howling, but I was too self-conscious to join him. A minute later, Rod and the others arrived on the scene.

"What have we here?" asked Rod rhetorically. "*Closed? That's ridiculous!*"

Of course, nothing could deter these recovering hotel wreckers. Rod promptly got behind the bar and began taking drink requests. He wasn't joking. He pulled glasses off the rack and foraged around in the fridge. Then he wielded the soda spigot. "Watcha want, mate?" I requested a Jack & Ginger and he provided. I left a dollar tip, but he didn't take it.

"I've been working here since the early days," he quipped. "I remember when Gerry and the Pacemakers came through."

We drank for twenty minutes, and at no point did security check in on us. And through it all, I was shocked at how nice Rod was. But he eventually put the spigot down and left with these parting words: "It's time to shag the wife." The rest of us piled into Woody's tenth-floor suite.

Jo showed me souvenirs she got at the previous weekend's Kentucky Derby. "We bet on Sea Hero and won." Woody, meanwhile, popped in a video of *Unplugged*. He told me to concentrate on his "Cut Across Shorty" slide work.

At a certain point in the program, Woody was shown wearing glasses—for the first time onstage—prompting Rod to lament, "We're getting *ooooold*." As we watched it, Jo said to me, "That reminds me, Bill. Please avoid calling him 'Woody' from now on. He's more mature now, so we prefer Ron or Ronnie, but not Woody. That's part of his *old* life."

I told her I'd try, but that the adjustment wouldn't be easy. For years, I'd addressed her husband as Woody. Plus, I sensed this was *her* idea, not his. To her, "Woody" was the guy who overdid everything—drank too much, snorted too much, and, in the Faces days, groupied too much and wrecked hotels too much. "Ron," I suppose, was the responsible father, faithful husband, and inspired painter-musician. His 46th birthday was approaching, so it was time he grew up. But man, I'd sure miss the old Woody if he grew up *too* much.

Most people, after pulling an all-nighter with Rod Stewart and Ron Wood, would be sleeping it off the next morning. Not me. I had mountains of snail mail to answer, stacks of small checks to deposit, and a *Beggars Banquet* to write. I was drowning in paper clips and index cards when my phone rang at 11 AM. It was my friend in L.A., the producer of *Rockline*.

"Did you see what they did last night?" he asked. "ABC is throwing a shit fit." He explained that ABC's news guy had a cow that morning when he walked into the studio and looked at the console. In fact, the damage was so disturbing, ABC was threatening to never rent space to *Rockline* again.

"What," I asked, "what did they *do*?"

"They took a knife and carved into the console."

"Like what, their *initials*?"

"No! A humongous cock!"

Same ol' Woody.

Backstage at Webster Hall. After the show, I tried to thank
Mick for the forty tickets, but he was hard to approach.

34

tombstone blues

"I could end up as the next Guy Lombardo," joshed Keith. Better than watching Dick Clark's ball drop.

We were at the Academy nightclub on New Year's Eve, steps from Times Square. A thousand fans packed the club, but millions were watching on TV. CBS was airing Keith's concert live.

Of course, if Keith Richards had to work New Year's Eve, so did I. At midnight, as he and the Winos rang in 1993 with "Time Is on My Side," I was busy taking notes for *Beggars Banquet*.

The new year launched a busy period for the individual Stones, so I had to stay on my toes. Keith's Academy show was merely a warm-up for his five-week *Main Offender* tour. Woody, meanwhile, brought his *Slide on This* tour to Japan. Charlie was working on his latest jazz album. And Bill Wyman was officially resigning from the Stones. "I really don't want to do it anymore," he announced on January 6. "It's been wonderful . . . but I thought the last two tours with them were the best we have ever done, so [I'm] quite happy to stop."

Mick appeared on the February 6 edition of *Saturday Night Live*. He had no plans to tour behind his new solo album, *Wandering Spirit,* but there were rumors of a one-off club gig in New York. I phoned Mick's people—Tony King, Alan Dunn, and a new employee with the unfortunate name of Janice Crotch—but they all knew nothing.

Out of nowhere, I received a call from Michael Cohl: "I'm promoting Mick's show tomorrow at Webster Hall. One show only, twelve hundred fans, and we're not selling tickets. We're giving them to radio stations. But Mick thought it'd be a good idea to get you involved."

I was stunned. The last time I'd spoken to Mick, in 1992, I thought I'd made a bad impression and that he'd want nothing to do with me. It was at the Hammersmith Odeon in London, after an all-star benefit concert. Mick and Woody were on the bill, playing blues covers, and I attended as Woody's guest. When I greeted Mick backstage, I had a drink in each hand, so I only extended my pinky finger. Mick smiled, shook my pinky—the old Jagger charm—and said, "Aha, two-fisted drinker!" I figured, "Great, now he thinks I'm a lush." But I guess I worried for nothing.

Cohl explained that hundreds of radio stations were getting two tickets apiece, but that I was getting forty. The show was Tuesday night, February 9, and I had two days to decide which of my readers would go. He asked how I planned to pull it off.

"Well," I said, "I'm running a contest in my latest issue for an autographed copy of Mick's album. I'll pick from those entries, and I don't think anyone'll be upset when I tell 'em, 'Hey, you didn't win Mick's autograph, but you're seeing him at Webster Hall tomorrow.' "

As soon as I got off the phone, I stuck my hand into the bag of contest entries. None of the postcards had phone numbers, so I had to call 411. When I reached some of the winners, they freaked: "Is this really Bill German? I'm seeing *Mick* tomorrow?"

One guy told me he'd been cruising Long Island, in search of WBAB's ticket van. "You caught me and my wife on a dinner break," he said. "The station says they have one pair and they're giving it to the first listener who spots the van. We've been driving around like maniacs!" I told him to relax and that I'd FedEx him his tickets.

Another winner asked me whether Webster Hall was wheelchair-accessible. I checked with the club and informed her it wasn't. "Y'know what?" she said. "It doesn't matter. There's no way I'm missing Mick in a nightclub! If I have to, I'll climb the stairs on my hands and knees!"

One of the postcards I picked was from Berlin. On it, the guy wrote, "If Mick plays a nightclub in New York"—as I'd suggested in my January issue— "my mother and I will come from Germany." I called his bluff, as well as his house. He and his mom booked a last-minute flight.

I loved helping my readers, but problems arose when word leaked out. "Bill German has forty tickets" became the worst-kept secret in New York, and my phone rang off the hook. Even the gossip columnist at *Vanity Fair* called. "[Ahmet] Ertegun got two tickets to the invitation-only show," wrote Deb Mitchell in the magazine's next issue. "[But] Bill German, the editor of the fanzine *Beggars Banquet,* got 40. Jagger wanted to play to fans, not socialites."

All of a sudden, everyone was my best friend. People crawled out of the woodwork, demanding I help them. Some were pretty aggressive—"You better get me in!"—and it felt like a feeding frenzy. A few played the guilt card. "It's my birthday!" sobbed a girl I hadn't heard from in years. Another beggar happened to be a ticket scalper. When I asked, "Why can't you get your *own* ticket?" he said, "This show is so tight, even scalpers can't get in!"

Ultimately, I got all the pains-in-the-ass into the show for free. What they lacked in good manners, they made up for in fandom, so I wanted to help them. But when I gave them their tickets, almost none of them said thanks.

Up until Tuesday night, I was dropping off tickets at people's hotel rooms and workplaces. By showtime, I was exhausted. Mick and his band, featuring guitarist Jimmy Rip and keyboardist Chuck Leavell, put on a tremendous set. They ran through eleven *Wandering Spirit* tracks and returned for a wild encore of "Rip This Joint," "Live with Me," and "Have You Seen Your Mother"—songs the Stones hadn't played in decades. Mick got the crowd going in a way that Charlie's jazz band at the Blue Note could not. Even Keith and Woody's shows never matched the intensity of Mick's three-song Stones set. Things got so frenetic, a woman collapsed in front of the stage. The bouncers scooped her up and carried her limp body off the dance floor.

I later discovered she was one of my contest winners. "It was the greatest night of my life!" she raved. "During the encore, I got close enough to see the hairs on Mick's arm! That's why I fainted!"

After the show, I attended Mick's private party at a club called Tatou. I wanted to thank him for the tickets, but he was difficult to approach. He was chatting up Robert De Niro and never made eye contact with me.

When I got home, I was physically and emotionally drained. As I reflected on the last two days, I grew very depressed. I felt like a lot of people had used me for my Stones connections. Some of them would've knocked down their own grandmothers to score a ticket. They put their love of the Stones over common decency, and it made me question who I'd been busting my hump for all these years.

Whenever I caught shit from the Stones organization, I always reminded myself, "I don't work for *them,* I work for my *readers.*" No matter how bad or lonely it got, I had the perceived loyalty of my subscribers to fall back on. But now I wasn't so sure.

I'd given my blood, sweat, and tears to my readers and never had a problem with that. But this time, they made me feel like an automated ticket dispenser instead of a human being. I was charging $1.67 an issue (20 bucks for twelve) and giving them news and opportunities they couldn't find anywhere else, so why couldn't they be more gracious?

I also realized that, while tending to the needs and dreams of my readers, I was neglecting my own. I was too consumed with *Beggars Banquet* to pursue my outside goals as a writer or to take care of my health. My choppers made Austin Powers look like Donny Osmond, but I had no time for a dentist. I was squinting like Mr. Magoo, but had no time for an optometrist. I was suffering excruciating backaches, but hadn't seen a doctor since the Carter administration. From the day I turned 16, I'd been under the crush of *Beggars Banquet,* and the nonstop pace was finally catching up with me.

Don't get me wrong. Hanging with the Stones was great. But it had come at the expense of every other thing in my life since high school. I had no time for senior proms, no time for spring breaks in Daytona, and no time for marriage or kids.

I'd created a monster that was slowly killing me, and I didn't know how to stop it. I'd never held a job except *Beggars Banquet,* and I was compulsively obsessed with documenting the Stones. At the same time, they never broke up and, unlike their idols, Otis and Buddy, never had their plane hit a lake or a cornfield. They kept busy even when they weren't touring, and the public's fascination with them never faded. As a Stones reporter, I had no chance to catch my breath or to jump off the moving locomotive.

If I were running a Who or Zeppelin 'zine, I'd have wrapped things up the minute their drummer choked on his vomit. If I were running a Police 'zine, I'd have had just three members to follow, each one boring as hell, and a group that folded after a handful of albums. I mean, how could I have known in 1978 that the Stones were in the *early* stage of their career?

As I sat down to do my taxes in February '93, I realized I'd made just 14K the previous year. That would've been fine if I wasn't putting in ninety-hour workweeks or if I didn't encounter so many hassles. But as I continued dealing with the Stones' middle people and the folks in the music industry, nothing came easy for me. In fact, one such person made fun of me on national TV.

VH1 approached me to profile *Beggars Banquet.* They wanted to film me interacting with Mick, but Mick's people said no. So I suggested a walking tour of New York Stones landmarks. A camera crew tailed me to the Palladium, the Ed Sullivan Theater, St. Mark's Place, the 79th Street Boat Basin, and the exteriors of Mick and Woody's old houses on the Upper West Side. I provided anecdotes at each location. (St. Mark's is where they shot the "Waiting on a Friend" video. The Boat Basin is where, in 1966, they lived afloat for three days.) It was an informative segment. But when the VJ introed it on prime-time TV, he said, "Now here's a guy who's dedicated his *whole life* to the Rolling Stones." He then, after pausing for sarcastic and rhetorical effect, added, *"Whyyyyyyy?"* He made me sound like a *Star Trek* nerd who needed to get a life.

Ironically, as I was being ridiculed for my dedication and knowledge, I had people stealing that knowledge for financial gain. In the early 1990s, a bunch of Stones books were produced by know-nothing biographers. They'd order a set of *Beggars Banquet* back issues, read through them—as well as through *The Works*—and reword my anecdotes for their own book.

Imitation may be the sincerest form of flattery, but, trust me, when someone takes your work and makes more money and gets more recognition from it than you do, it's the sincerest form of ripping your guts out. I was living off itsy-bitsy checks from my readers, while these people were getting six-figure advances from major publishers, using *my* firsthand accounts. Some of the anecdotes involved me as a major player, but they'd cut me out of my own stories. Instead of writing, "Keith said to Bill German," they'd write, "Keith said to a friend. . . ." The Ian Stewart eulogy that Keith gave me in Woody's kitchen has appeared in so many places, biographers now steal it from *each other.*

All I know is, these writers didn't go through the crap that *I* did to get my stories firsthand. None of them spent thousands of dollars on airfare or international phone calls, and none of them got stranded at a stadium in Holland or saw Freddy Sessler naked in Japan.

As each one of these Stones books hit the marketplace, my stomach did flips. Combined with the hassles from the Stones organization and the rudeness of my readers, I felt pretty miserable by early '93. To make things worse, my girlfriend was threatening to leave me.

We'd met in December 1991 and, for our third date, I invited her to Keith's house in Connecticut. When she turned me down—because she didn't want to break a dinner date with her sister—I knew she was girlfriend material. Her co-workers told her she was nuts for skipping Keith's party, but she stuck to her guns. I asked her out again because she represented a respite from my Stones stuff. She'd *heard* of the Stones, but didn't care about them and thought Keith was the drummer.

By 1993 she was the longest-running girlfriend I'd ever had, but she was getting frustrated. I was constantly telling her, "I can't see you tonight because I've got Woody's show in New Haven" or "I'm interviewing Charlie at the Hard Rock." She hated the mess in my apartment and how faxes and calls would come in at 4 AM. She hated the pittance of money I was making and how the Stones organization pushed me around. She hated the fact I was a 30-year-old man whose course in life had been charted by a 16-year-old Stones fan. She kept asking, "When are you going to get to where you're going?" and I didn't have an answer for her.

I grew extremely depressed and felt very alienated. I realized that the guy on VH1 was right. I *had* dedicated my life to the Rolling Stones. Every decision I ever made was dictated by them and their activities: where I went to school, where I lived, where I traveled, who I dated, and how much money I earned. It also explained why I quit NYU, why I never learned to drive, and why my health was deteriorating. The Stones affected every minute of my existence, and I couldn't take it any longer.

I felt overwhelmed and had thoughts of suicide. It seemed like the only way out for me. I wasn't living my own life anyway, so what would the difference be? I'd spent my entire adult life indulging *other* people's whims, celebrating *other* people's accomplishments, instead of my own. *Their* albums, *their* tours, *their* ideas, that's what my life was based on.

As glib as it sounds, I considered killing myself at Keith's upcoming solo concert. I figured I'd climb to the balcony of the Beacon Theatre and take a dive. Maybe I'd borrow that line from *The Omen.* "This is for *you,* Keith!" My tombstone would read, "Dedicated his life to the Rolling Stones," but I'd be dead, so it wouldn't bother me.

Keith booked five gigs at the Beacon, and I had a ticket for each one. I could pick my night.

Mr. Venice makes his getaway from the Beacon,
February 1993.

35

keith's
absolution

Killing myself at a Keith concert had a distinct administrative advantage. My readers, many of whom would be there, wouldn't have to guess why their issues stopped coming. It'd save a lot of explaining and clerical work.

As for Keith, I didn't think he'd be fazed. As much as he liked me, he'd had so many people croak on him, he would've taken my midconcert splattering in stride. He probably would have used it to intro his next song: "Hey, Bill, ya shouldn't take it so hard."

Keith's stint at the Beacon—the final stop of his tour—ran February 19–24. When I got to the theater on opening night and saw the mezzanine, I instantly had my doubts. I'm not a doctor or physicist, but it seemed too low for a fatal leap.

"It's nice to be back with the people I know," Keith told the hometown crowd. He opened each night with Eddie Cochran's "Somethin' Else," before pounding out material from his two solo albums. During the first night's encore, "Take It So Hard," the audience showered him with red roses and a black bra, which he gathered up when leaving the stage.

Keith was checked in as Mr. Venice at the Mayflower Hotel on Central Park West. I headed there after each concert, to share a drink with a Wino or two. One night, when seated at a table in the hotel bar, I smelled a powerful aroma wafting through the room. I turned around to discover Mr. Venice, sneaking up behind me. He must've splashed a whole bottle of cologne on himself. He sat down at my table.

It was rare to see Keith in the hotel bar after a show—I can't recall a single time during *Steel Wheels*/Urban Jungle—but a solo tour afforded him the intimacy he craved. "I ain't gonna stay long," he told Freddy Sessler and me. "Just pressin' the flesh a bit."

This was the first time I'd spoken to Keith since Mick did an impression of him on *Saturday Night Live* two weeks earlier. It was a great skit, with Mike Myers impersonating Mick and Mick impersonating Keith. (In *Beggars Banquet,* I dubbed it "the most intentionally hilarious role in Mick's acting career.")

"Didn't see it," Keith told me. "Even if I wanted to, I was workin' that night."

I asked Keith if *he* had plans to perform on *SNL,* but he quipped, "Mick's done it *for* me."

Keith informed me that Marianne Faithfull had come backstage that night at the Beacon. "Her tits look great," he confided. Marianne's escort for the night was the notorious Allen Klein.

Keith didn't comment on Klein, nor on his tits, but he volunteered some unrelated Stones news: "Charlie was just in Phoenix, buyin' horses with Shirley."

"Thanks," I said. "I'll put that in the newsletter."

"That's why I'm *tellin'* ya. You hear from Woody lately?"

"Yeah, he played with Rod at the Brit Awards last week. A full Faces reunion, but with Bill Wyman on bass."

Keith wasn't pleased that Bill played with Rod Stewart, just weeks after quitting the Stones. He offered his take on Bill's resignation: "You can't force a guy to do somethin' he don't wanna do. I did everythin' except hold a gun to his head. At the end of the day, if he don't wanna be in the Stones, ya gotta let him go."

I asked about a replacement.

"Well, Mick wants to hold auditions, but I like Joey Spampinato, the cat I used on *Hail! Hail!* But do me a favor. Sit on that, don't put it in *Beggars Banquet,* for at least a week. I want it to come from *me.* I don't want Mick sayin' no before I bring it up."

I told Keith I'd respect his wishes. He then suggested we continue our conversation upstairs. "Come to my room in twenty minutes." He rose from the table and proceeded to shake hands with every fan in the bar. When he approached a tiny Japanese girl, who'd flown in just for the Beacon shows, she began hyperventilating.

After twenty minutes, Freddy and I headed upstairs. Keith's bodyguard, Joe Seabrook, was stationed outside Keith's room and opened the door for us. By now, Keith was shirtless and barefoot, wearing blue jeans and a white captain's hat. A tape of Jimmy Reed was blasting from his boom box on the floor. It was a moderately sized suite, with a living room, bedroom, and kitchen.

Keith explained he was flying solo that night. Patti and the kids had gone back to Connecticut after the concert, but they'd left behind some mementos. Above the desk, taped to the wall, were the girls' crayon drawings, as well as the current cover of *Mirabella,* featuring Patti. On the desk itself, I spotted a bottle of Fahrenheit—the cologne in question—and a beer stein, functioning as a pen and pencil holder.

"See that mug?" Keith asked me. "I got it from one of your readers. We flew into Canada, second show of the tour, and this chick, one of the customs officers, comes up to me. 'Mr. Richards, I'm gonna need you to step in the other room.' I'm goin', 'Fuck, I don't need *this* again.' So I'm gettin' ready for the rubber glove, y'know? But she tells me, 'I'm a subscriber to *Beggars Banquet,* and I want ya to sign the latest issue.' I sign it, and she gives me this mug. She knew I was comin', so she made sure to be on duty. Her name's Marilyn. I still got the mug, which I been packin' and unpackin' the whole tour."

That was one of the nicest stories I'd heard in a long time. I knew exactly which subscriber he was talking about. Marilyn was one of my old-timers, and she'd once sent me a picture of herself in uniform. She was a sweet girl, so I was thrilled she met Keith—even if it made him clench his butt cheeks.

"For a minute, I was expectin' another Toronto," mused Keith, referring to his 1977 arrest. "I remember dat," said Freddy, pulling a coke vial from his pocket.

Freddy was closing in on 70, but went line for line with Keith this night. Keith knew I didn't want any, so he said, "Make yourself a drink." I went to his fridge, and it was filled with Orange Crush. "You *drink* this stuff?" I asked. "It looks like you won a year's supply on a game show."

"I'm off the Jack," he explained. "Now all I drink is vodka, mixed with *that* stuff. It's better on the vocal cords." I didn't ask which vodka he preferred, but his fridge offered Absolut, Stoli, and Smirnoff.

Keith began reminiscing about his '77 bust. "First, they had to wake me up. No warrant for me and no probable cause. Then they tell me I'm tryin' to *sell* the stuff. But ah, one of those officers conveniently met his demise in a car wreck shortly thereafter." (As comfortable as I felt around Keith, he'd sometimes let out cryptic comments that'd scare the shit out of me.)

"The judge ordered me to see a shrink," he added. "Part of my probation. But the shrink was more fucked up than *me*. I'd listen to *her* bitch about *her* life. Then they'd make me pee in a cup, but I'd slip 'em Marlon's instead."

It was great hanging out with Keith. But I was still depressed and was still being hounded by overzealous Stones fans. Each night in the Beacon lobby, it was "Bill German, you gotta get me backstage!" "Bill German, get me a bass audition!"

I had bass players sending me demo tapes in the mail. One droned on for forty-five minutes, with only a solo. At one point, you hear his mother calling him for dinner and him yelling, "Leave me alone, Ma! I'm trying to record!"

I also had people begging for jobs. *I want to be the Stones' roadie, publicist, secretary.* They'd send résumés, and I'd try to be diplomatic. One guy wanted to be their bodyguard and included a list of his firearms—a Glock and an AK-47—so I was *real* diplomatic.

One girl insisted I hire her for *Beggars Banquet.* She sent pictures of herself and wanted to come to my apartment to discuss it. A few days later, I saw her on the Howard Stern E! show. She was telling Howard that the guy who runs the Stones' fan club might hire her. He just laughed. The reason he had her on, you see, is that she was Charles Manson's pen pal. She probably would've hacked me to pieces and scrawled "Let It Bleed" on my refrigerator door.

At the final Beacon show, Keith told the crowd, "I'll never forget this week, I owe ya," and it was obvious he meant it. There were points during the concert where his humility bled through his pores. Like he couldn't believe his luck, playing for the two greatest bands in the world. "They're a band in a million," he said of the Winos. "As good as bad gets."

There was no official end-of-tour party, but Keith invited fifteen or so people to his room. He wanted us to help him stay awake until his early morning flight to St. Bart's. The coke was flowing, courtesy of Kellogg.

Tim Kellogg was the tour's official drug dealer and had quite a racket going. He was granted carte blanche—no Mick Camp to hamper his mobility—and possessed an All Access laminate. He bartered his blow for additional tickets and passes from the tour's entourage. He then turned around to Keith's fans and bartered those tickets and passes for airfare, hotel rooms, blowjobs, and cash. If he wasn't so shady, I'd have envied his entrepreneurial spirit. Next to Keith, he was the most popular guy in the room.

At 3 AM, the hotel got complaints about the noise. "Why now?" asked Keith. "It's been this fuckin' loud all week!" By the time I left at 7 AM, things were still going strong. I was the first of Keith's guests to head for the door. Keith's personal assistant, Tony Russell, had arrived to pack Keith's suitcase, and I knew that was my cue. I never forgot Svi's advice about knowing when to leave. I may have stayed *years* too late, but not *hours.*

I was still feeling miserable, but, in the days following the Beacon, two letters lifted my spirits. One was from that girl in the wheelchair—the one who was determined to see Mick at Webster Hall, whatever it took. She told me that two of the club's bouncers had chivalrously carried her, plus her wheelchair, up the two flights of steps. It restored my faith in humanity.

The second letter was from another Webster Hall winner. In a heartfelt note, she told me how she'd been going through a low point in her life. She'd recently been diagnosed with cancer. But when she won the contest, it changed her outlook and gave her hope. Suddenly, she felt *lucky*. And the concert itself brought her so much joy, it helped her endure her painful treatments.

The letters reminded me of why I started *Beggars Banquet* in the first place. And it reminded me that there were plenty of great people in Beggars Banquet Land. The problem was, I rarely heard from the silent majority of contented people, I only heard from the vocal minority of malcontents. The ones who harassed me for tickets, accosted me in the Beacon lobby, and demanded I get them a job with the Stones. They were a small percentage of who was out there, but the largest percentage of who I heard from. I needed to remember that.

And maybe it worked like that with Stones employees. Maybe it was a vocal minority that drove me nuts, and if I could figure out a way to handle them, my life would get easier. I quickly came up with a Pavlovian experiment for Jane. What if I wore the same cologne as Keith? Maybe there's an olfactory impulse that'd prevent her from yelling at me, the way she'd never yell at *him*. I bought a $40 bottle of Fahrenheit and splashed some on before visiting her.

It didn't work. In fact, my next issue had her wailing like a banshee. "You weren't supposed to write about the writing! Or about the auditions! You had no right to write that!" She was steaming over a simple paragraph in Volume 3, Number 14: "Mick and Keith have just returned from a month in Barbados, where they began throwing around ideas and writing a bunch of new songs. . . . It looks like the next move on the agenda is for all four Stones to regroup in two weeks right here in New York, where they'll continue writing songs and probably even audition a few bass players."

According to her, I wasn't supposed to say anything about writing songs or auditioning bassists in New York, due to tax laws. I already knew the Stones couldn't *record* in America, but I'll swear on a stack of pancakes and Bibles that Jane said I could mention jamming or songwriting. Both are vague activities that are not considered work, she once explained. So either the IRS had changed the rules or *she* had.

I had no idea she'd get so upset. The entire world knew the Stones needed to replace Bill Wyman. It would have been impossible—and insulting to my readers—to ignore that fact. And if it was something that Keith, who was my source for that info, didn't want mentioned, he'd have told me so.

There were *other* problems with Volume 3, Number 14. Janice Crotch called me from Mick's office in London. She said Mick didn't like the photos I ran of him and Keith at JFK Airport, en route to their Barbados songwriting sessions. Mick felt it was an invasion of privacy.

I apologized, even though I didn't mean it. I printed the photos because they were *newsworthy*. They were the first signs of renewed Stones activity and the first time in two years that Mick and Keith were in public together. It was a *Beggars Banquet* scoop, so I wanted the photos as proof. Photos that were taken in a very public place by an unobtrusive fan who happened to be there.

According to Ms. Crotch, Mick also felt that I'd given too much coverage to Woody's activities with Rod Stewart. Every day, someone was telling me what to do and what not to do. It wasn't bad enough that I had people stealing my work or that I'd sacrificed my health and love life to cover the Stones. On top of that, I had to worry about stepping on land mines each day. I felt extremely overwhelmed and returned to my thoughts of suicide as the only way out.

I searched my bathroom and realized I was completely unprepared to kill myself. Can you overdose on Bufferin? What about Drano? The one thing I didn't want was to wake up in Bellevue with a tummy ache, having to stare at Rorschach tests. I thought about wrapping my lips around a revolver, but had no idea how to get one. I considered slitting my wrists, jumping in front of a train, and putting a bag over my head like Jerzy Kosinksi.

Needless to say, I didn't go through with it. I thought about it for months, but never attempted it. My biggest apprehension was my folks. Even on my worst days, I knew that parents shouldn't bury children. It goes against nature. So I plodded through 1993, hoping for an answer.

In December, I received a cheery call from Jane. She informed me of the party that Patti was planning for Keith's 50th birthday. "It's Saturday night at Metropolis, near Union Square."

"And you're telling me this because . . . I'm *invited*?"

"Yes," she said. "Patti and I have you on the list. But you have to keep it hush-hush because it's a surprise."

On Saturday night, December 18, a hundred and fifty people gathered at Metropolis. Keith was lured, believing it was a quiet dinner. But when he walked in, he realized he knew everyone. Guests included Eric Clapton, Jann Wenner, Phil Spector, a bunch of Winos, and Adam Clayton from U2. Also, the Stones' new bassist, Darryl Jones, and a gaggle of Patti's model friends, like Kate Moss and Naomi Campbell. Johnnie Johnson provided the entertainment, during a buffet-style dinner. Keith joined him on piano for a bit.

I brought my non-Stones-fan girlfriend. When I introduced her to Keith, she treated him as nothing more than a friend of mine. If anything, she was more impressed by Kate Moss.

There was a five-piece birthday cake, which spelled "K-E-I-T-H," and a "10" cake to commemorate Keith and Patti's wedding anniversary. Jane was in a good mood, but explained that the surprise was almost blown. The gossip page of the *New York Post* had leaked the event. Jane phoned Patti and cautioned her not to bring the paper into the house. But Patti said, "That's alright, Keith never reads those things anyway." Jane suspected the leak came from Naomi Campbell. She didn't say how she came to that conclusion, but I was glad she wasn't blaming *me*.

I made sure to say hello to Keith's dad, Bert. He was sitting in between Keith and Clapton, smoking his ever-present pipe, and sporting a huge grin. I asked him rhetorically, "Where were *you* fifty years ago today?" and he came back with a sobering response: "I was on the battlefield fighting for my country." I wasn't expecting that.

After singing "Happy Birthday" and downing some cake and champagne, everyone retreated to the restaurant's basement. There, on a small stage, an a cappella group ran through "Papa Was a Rollin' Stone" and "Speedo," the old Cadillacs song. Keith loved it and was gyrating in front of the stage.

When that was done, a DJ played some Seventies disco music. Do the Hustle! A bunch of girls kicked off their heels and really got into it, including Patti and her blond sisters and nieces. Jane danced with Peter Wolf of the J. Geils Band.

My girlfriend wanted me to dance with her, but I refused. I'm not the disco-dancing type. She grew agitated, and we exchanged a few words. She stormed off to the ladies' room and said she was finally breaking up with me.

I followed her to the restroom area, where I ran into Keith. He was standing outside the men's room, holding court and directing traffic. He told me that the Stones' recent recording sessions went well and that after New Year's they'd begin mixing the album and planning a tour. "We're gonna give you a lot to write about," he said.

For some reason, maybe because of the tension with my girlfriend, I snapped at him. "Oh, yeah?" I said sarcastically. "Like I haven't given you *enough* of my life? I been writing about you for fifteen years!"

I smiled as I said it, but he must've sensed the edge in my tone. He looked me straight in the eye and went, "Hey, man, I didn't *ask* ya to. No one's *makin'* ya."

His remark saved my life. On the surface, it sounded like he was snapping back at me and, to a certain extent, he *was*. A lot of people have blamed the Stones for a lot of things, so he didn't need to hear it anymore. But in reality, he was absolving me and telling me I was free to go. When he made his comments, he half-smiled and supportively put his hand on my shoulder.

Keith liked me and liked *Beggars Banquet*. But he was reminding me that he'd never held a gun to my head. True, the *Stones* approached *me* about making my 'zine official, but that was a decade ago, before my 21st birthday. I was now 31 and responsible for my own life. If I felt trapped inside the Stones' vacuum, it was no one's fault but my own. As obvious as that seems today, I needed to hear it from Keith back then.

I also think I needed his permission to leave. Not only was it Keith who decreed, "No one leaves the Stones except in a coffin," it was Keith to whom I felt the strongest sense of loyalty. He'd stuck by me through so many situations, I felt I'd be betraying him if I left. But here he was, saying it's okay. "No one's makin' ya." Perhaps the recent departure of the *other* Bill got him to soften his stance and to realize that if you care about someone, you have to let them go.

Keith once spoke to me in an interview about surviving one's demons. He acknowledged that a lot has to do with "your personality and your ego and your physical makeup," but that, ultimately, it comes down to personal responsibility. "Anything you thrown yourself into," he advised, "you better get yourself out of."

The next move was mine.

To announce their *Voodoo Lounge* tour on May 3, the Stones
arrived at their New York press conference by boat.
Days later, Mick gave Ben Stiller my number.

36

something
about ben

True to Keith's word, the band gave me lots to write about in 1994. In January, the four Stones gathered in L.A. to finish their *Voodoo Lounge* album. In May, they officially announced their tour. I resolved to stick around and cover it, while finding a new direction in life. But days after the announcement, a new direction found *me*.

Ben Stiller wanted to do lunch. His personal assistant phoned from L.A., saying Mick had given Ben my number. Mick wanted Ben to write, direct, and star in a film about two Stones freaks who'll do anything to meet the band. They'll smuggle themselves in trucks, crawl on precarious catwalks, and pose as bellboys. I envisioned *Wayne's World* meets *Bill & Ted's Excellent Adventure*. "The band will appear in the film," explained Ben's assistant, Mia, "but probably no speaking roles."

The Stones were financing the project, and Universal Pictures had already shown interest in theatrical distribution. Other possibilities included HBO, VH1, and Fox. The whole thing was Mick's idea, so he asked Lorne Michaels to suggest a writer/director. Lorne suggested Ben.

Ben had appeared on *SNL*, but was far from a household name. (He did only five episodes.) He hadn't yet caught his frank-and-beans in his zipper or milked De Niro's cat. His breakthrough roles in *There's Something About Mary* and *Meet the Parents* were years off. But he'd just won an Emmy for his sketch comedy program, *The Ben Stiller Show* (despite its cancellation by Fox), and had just directed/starred in the critically acclaimed film *Reality Bites,* making him the darling of the X Generation.

In the mid-1990s, there was no demographic more desirable to advertisers and the media than Gen X, the segment of population aged 20 to 29. Mick wanted to connect with those kids, so he jumped at the chance to work with Ben. He then instructed Ben to call Bill German. "He deals with our nuttiest fans."

In early June, Ben and I met at an Italian restaurant in my neighborhood. It took several calls for Mia to hook it up. Ben was a busy guy and was only in New York a few days. Plus, he had dietary issues. When I told Mia I'd picked Italian, she said she'd have to ask Ben if that was okay. She then phoned to say he couldn't eat anything oily. She asked me to stop by the restaurant, check out the menu, and get back to her. "Yup, they have some non-oily items," I informed her. "There's a ricotta ravioli with fava beans and green peas he might like, and a grilled breast of chicken, served on a bed of wild mushroom risotto, with a generous helping of sultana raisins and pine nuts he might go for."

Ben was late to the restaurant, so I began thinking he flaked. I wasn't sure what he looked like, so, at one point, I approached the wrong person. "Are you Ben?" *"Nope."* I hadn't seen *Reality Bites,* and whenever I'd seen his skit show he was dressed as Eddie Munster.

Eventually, he pulled up in a taxi. My negative impressions were instantly dispelled. He apologized for his tardiness and was extremely polite. At first, he wasn't sure where to sit. We went from outdoors to indoors to outdoors, schlepping our water glasses and menus, until he found just the right table. He'd obviously retained his New York neuroticism, so I felt I'd known him for years.

He told me he grew up a few blocks away, at 84th and Riverside, and that he'd attended the Hebrew school on 83rd. I told him I grew up in Brooklyn. He told me he was 28, and I said 31. Almost like a first date. Eventually, we got around to the film. "I'm still putting it together in my head," he said. "I'm thinking of getting Brad Pitt to be the other Stones fan. Do you know who he is?"

I told him the name rang a bell, but that I couldn't place the face. Brad's ass might've made an impression in *Thelma & Louise,* but, in June of '94, the average filmgoer didn't know him. *Interview with the Vampire* and *Legends of the Fall* weren't out, and his biggest roles had been in *Cool World* and *A River Runs Through It.* So maybe this Stones thing could put him on the map.

Ben suggested I let loose with my wacky fan stories. I began with a girl who'd called me that very morning, demanding to know the meaning behind "Brown Sugar." "I don't know how she got my number," I told Ben, "but she wouldn't let me off until I answered her."

"So what'd you say?"

"I said, 'Look, it means whatever you want it to mean. People write songs, artists paint pictures, and they don't have to tell you what it means. It's for you to interpret.' But she got mad and told me I better ask Mick and Keith 'cause she's calling back *tomorrow.* She said she won't stop calling until I give her an answer. I said, 'It's about sex and drugs and rock 'n' roll, alright? It's about slavery and cunnilingus, whatever you want.' "

Ben was jotting notes on his memo pad. "That's *nothing,*" I said. "I got *much* better stories than *that.*" For the next three hours, I regaled him with dozens of anecdotes. (Like about the girl who handcuffed herself to Mick, etc.) He seemed to enjoy them, not just as a writer, but as a lunch companion. I was giving good Stones. I yakked so much, I had no chance to eat. It wasn't until he took a pee break that I scarfed down my tortellini.

I admit I was "auditioning" for Ben. Hoping he'd say, "Hey, Bill, come to *our* side, where we spend our days doing *creative* stuff, not licking postage stamps."

When he returned from the restroom, he told me he had an idea. "I think I'll put you in the film," he said. "Maybe a scene where Brad and I approach you at a Stones concert and drive you crazy. You'll play yourself."

"I can do that," I joked. "I've been playing myself for years." I fully expected to steal the scene from this Brad Pitt fellow. Ben also said I'd be a script consultant, which I interpreted as my "in." I couldn't wait to launch my career as a screenwriter.

The only person more excited than me was Ben. He hoped that affiliating with the Stones would give him his big break. He said he was nervous dealing with Mick—he was in such awe, he'd surreptitiously tape their phone conversations—and I told him not to be. "You're in the driver's seat," I stressed. "You gotta realize how horny Mick is for you."

He laughed, but didn't get what I was saying. "Look," I explained, "Mick's got this hard-on for anything Gen X. He desperately wants to seem hip and to reach out to younger fans. Part of it's an ego thing, and part of it's business. He wants to see if he can break through to a new generation. That's what this film represents to him. If he honestly wanted to depict his fans, he'd get 40-year-old stockbrokers and soccer moms, not you and Brad Pitt."

Ben confessed he was a little sick of the Generation X tag because it had become nothing more than a marketing tool. Advertisers were targeting twentysomethings for profit and were trying to exploit him as the demographic's poster child. "At least you're a *somebody,*" I teased. "I'm 31. Too young to be a baby boomer, too old to be a Gen Xer. I don't know *what* the fuck I am."

At the end of our lunch, Ben picked up the tab and gave me his home number. I felt so optimistic, I skipped along Columbus Avenue, back to my apartment. A few days later, a gift basket showed up. Fruits, nuts, and chocolate-covered pretzels, accompanied by a note from Ben: "Thank you for your help. I look forward to working with you."

· · ·

In the course of my dealings with Ben and Mia, I was instructed to keep the project under wraps. "That's Mick's rule," they said, "not ours." I wasn't about to fuck this up, so I was happy to oblige. But in that Sunday's New York *Daily News,* an article titled "Rolling Stiller to Gather Stones" appeared, spilling the beans: "Stiller will intersperse [Stones] concert footage with a fictional story-line, involving a character played by him, and another by 'A River Runs Through It' star Brad Pitt. They'll play two Stones disciples who follow the band around . . . in a never-ending quest to get backstage to meet their idols. While the deal's still being finalized, sources said the film will be distributed by Universal."

I didn't know where the leak came from, but I prayed it wouldn't jeopardize the project. Mick's people were pissed, but told Ben it was still on. Mia asked if I had any clues as to how it got out—unlike the usual Stones inquisition, she was being curious, not accusatory—and I told her I didn't. "The waitress had no idea who Ben was, and our table wasn't close enough for anyone to eavesdrop."

The Stones began tour rehearsals in Toronto, and Ben went up there with his writing partner, Judd Apatow, to meet with Mick. (Apatow would go on to write *The 40-Year-Old Virgin* and *Knocked Up.*) Ben called me as soon as he returned to L.A., but the reception on his cell phone was breaking up.

"I JUST GOT BACK FROM TORONTO!" he yelled into the phone.

"WHAT'S THAT? YOU'RE IN A TORNADO?" (My attempt at humor.)

"I'M BACK FROM TORONTO! I MET WITH MICK ABOUT THE SCRIPT!"

He said he was driving through the Hollywood Hills. It was hard to hear him, but his enthusiasm was crystal clear. He told me he sat in on a Stones rehearsal and that Mick treated him and Judd royally. "HE OFFERED TO MAKE US TEA!"

Ben said he'd call me the following week to keep me posted. We wound up playing phone tag for a while, until word came over the summer that the film wasn't happening. From what I could piece together, the other Stones—or their business managers—lost interest in the project. It was going to cost them $10 million, and they didn't think it was worth it. I'd have to look elsewhere for my new direction.

The next time I saw Ben was in Washington, D.C., outside the Ritz-Carlton Hotel. It was opening night of the *Voodoo Lounge* tour, August 1, and he was on his way to the Ticket Lady's room. We spoke about the film, and he seemed really bummed that it didn't work out. I felt bad for him and tried my best to console him. "Hang in there," I said. "You'll get other projects."

. . .

As for Mick, he was undeterred. He landed the Stones a spot on *Beverly Hills 90210,* the most popular TV show among teens and Gen Xers, and it didn't cost him or his fellow Stones a cent. Mick convinced the show's producer, schlockmeister Aaron Spelling, to script the most unlikely storyline in the series' history.

In an episode titled "Rock of Ages," the kids in the famous zip code get downright Stones-loopy. Forget that last week the gang was listening to nothing but Brian McKnight and Lisa Stansfield. This week they're obsessed with the Stones. They're tripping over themselves to attend the band's concert at the Rose Bowl and can't wait to don the latest Stones apparel.

Brandon (portrayed by Jason Priestley) races to the concert in his *Voodoo Lounge* varsity jacket. Donna (Tori Spelling) sells *Voodoo Lounge* tour programs as a vendor. Kelly (Jennie Garth) scores a ticket from her modeling agent. Steve (Ian Ziering) contacts a Jane Rose–type person in the Stones organization and, after experiencing difficulties with her (just like the *real* Jane), finally gets into the show.

Bad boy Dylan McKay (played by Luke Perry) is the only one who can't make the concert. That's because he's in rehab. In a product placement coup, however, he sports a *Voodoo Lounge* baseball cap the entire episode. In fact, it becomes the central theme of his storyline. A fellow rehabber, y'see, hates the cap—hates what the Stones *represent*—and literally tries to knock it off Dylan's head. In the end, the two of them work it out in group therapy. The guy admits to Dylan that he actually *loves* the Stones and was merely jealous of the cap. He begs to borrow the cap so he can wear it awhile.

If you saw the episode, you know I'm not making it up. It aired on network television in prime time. A Rolling Stones infomercial disguised as a TV show. The Stones didn't speak, but were shown onstage in exclusive *90210* footage. And if all that product placement wasn't enough, you got a full-blown ad during the episode's closing credits. (You won't see it in the syndicated reruns.) A still photo of Mick and Keith, accompanied by a booming voice-over: "Watch the Rolling Stones this Friday night on pay-per-view! Call your local cable company!"

Perhaps Aaron Spelling was itching to attract baby boomers to *Beverly Hills 90210* the way Mick was itching to lure Gen Xers to the Stones. All I know is, the Stones used to work with groundbreaking filmmakers like Godard, Robert Frank, and the Maysles brothers, and used to hop into bed with Anita Pallenberg and Marianne Faithfull—not the guy who gave us *The Love Boat.*

But such was the new and biting reality. ·

In a reciprocal arrangement, Vice President Gore's kids
watched the band rehearse.

37

road worriers

The Stones opened their *Voodoo Lounge* tour on August 1, 1994, in Washington, D.C. They stayed at the Ritz-Carlton. I was at the Holiday Inn.

I needed to save money this tour because I'd made the conscious decision to pay for my tickets. In an effort to remain as independent as possible, I eschewed the all-important All Access laminate. I didn't ask for one, and nobody offered. I remembered how compromised that pass made me feel on the *Steel Wheels* tour, so I was glad to pay 55 bucks per concert and not feel beholden.

The day before the first show, I went to the Ritz-Carlton to visit the Ticket Lady. Woody, Jo, and Big Bob Bender were in the lobby. They didn't see me because they were surrounded by overzealous fans. I stood back and observed the scene as an outsider. One fan had a *Black and Blue* LP, and Woody said, "I'll sign it, but you've got to hold my drink." The kid gladly exchanged his LP and Sharpie for Woody's plastic cup. After autographing a dozen items for various fans, Woody was hustled into a van.

The Woods were on their way to see Jim Carrey's *The Mask*. The van inched down the hotel driveway and suddenly stopped. The door swung open and out popped Jo. She rushed back to the lobby, found the kid with the *Black and Blue* album, and said, "Excuse me, may I have my husband's drink back?" The fan sheepishly handed her the cup, which she carried back to the van. She hopped inside, and the van rolled off.

Seconds later, Freddy Sessler came bounding off the elevator. "Vot? Dey left vit-*out* me? I can't believe dey left vit-*out* me!" I told him he missed Woody by the blink of an eye. "No!" he cried. "I don't care about fucking Voody! I mean de Holocaust group. I can't believe dey left vit-*out* me!"

By "Holocaust group," he was referring to the dozen or so Stones employees who'd scheduled a trip to D.C.'s new Holocaust Museum. In every city, the red carpet was rolled out for the entourage, and they'd get free perks. Freddy signed up for the museum, but overslept. "I can't believe dey left vit-out me!"

He said he'd get there by taxi. He urged me to come with him, but I said no. I felt uncomfortable glomming off the entourage's perks and, frankly, if I was going to bawl my eyes out in public, I'd prefer not doing it in front of Pierre-the-roadie or Benji-the-sound-man. Freddy got into a cab and told the driver, "Take me to de Holocaust!"

The tour hadn't begun, but I'd already witnessed its absurdities. My goal was to follow the *Voodoo Lounge* tour and cover its man-bites-dog stories, but I vowed to keep a healthy distance and not let the chaos get to me. It was a huge adjustment, made possible by my willingness to end *Beggars Banquet*. In essence, I was using this tour as a test. If things went smoothly for me, I'd keep the 'zine going somehow. But if people made things difficult, I'd walk away with a clear conscience.

The debut concert at RFK Stadium was a virtual marathon. The Stones performed twenty-seven songs, culled from thirty years of recorded history—*England's Newest Hitmakers* to *Voodoo Lounge*. The show began with a tribal drumbeat and the sight of a giant cobra spitting fire. Mick made a dramatic entrance by rising from a trap door, as the band played "Not Fade Away."

Although I possessed the VIP pass for B-listers, I spotted some A-list guests, like Jack Nicholson and Graham Nash. Senators Bill Bradley, Al D'Amato, and Chris Dodd were there, too. "Bill Clinton wanted to come tonight," announced Mick onstage, "but he's still trying to make up his mind." Mick told some good jokes, but that's because he had writers, provided to him by Lorne Michaels.

The stage design was just as spectacular as the one from *Steel Wheels*. Three hundred feet wide, adorned with giant balloons of Elvis and the Virgin Mary. During "Monkey Man," two stilt walkers joined the spectacle. One, I presume, was Satan. He sported horns, a tail, and an erect penis that almost poked Mick's eye out. The other was a she-devil. I didn't think a Stones concert could get tackier than Mick wrestling those dogs in Europe, but when he wrestled Satan for the she-devil's affections, I believe they topped themselves. Thankfully, Mick realized it, too. As I reported in the next *Beggars Banquet*, "The two stilt walkers, good actors and nice people I'm sure, were on a plane home after the D.C. shows."

A party was held in the Ritz-Carlton's main ballroom on opening night. No guest list, just show your laminate and you're in. Which meant I wasn't in. The door was guarded by hotel security, who were given strict instructions. I hoped that Keith or Woody could walk me in, but they entered through a back door.

I retreated to the hotel bar, where I spoke with Jane Rose's assistant, Robyn. I informed her I was staying at the Holiday Inn. "Next to St. Matthew's," I said, "where JFK's funeral was." She replied, "Hey, if you're into president stuff, you should come with me to the White House. I'm getting a private tour and I have no one to go with."

I jumped at the chance. I'd been to D.C. only once before, in 1989, and spent the entire trip in Woody's room and at Stones concerts.

For weeks, there was speculation about the Stones at the White House. Supposedly, the Clintons had personally invited them. A visit was scheduled for Thursday, August 4. Robyn was instrumental in hooking it up, but Jane wouldn't let her attend. "So many people are going, you need to stay at the hotel and hold down the fort."

Robyn was in her early twenties and had been working for Jane a short time. She performed all sorts of tasks for her, like picking up her dry cleaning and watching her dog, Delilah. Robyn was a sweet kid and put up with Jane's crap—and with Delilah's crap—because the job was a temporary stop for her. She wasn't a Stones fan and had bigger aspirations. Jane brought Delilah on tour—the dog possessed its own All Access laminate—so Robyn had lots of dogsitting to do.

Robyn's contact at the White House offered her a tour of her own. He told her she could invite whomever she wanted. All I had to do was provide my Social Security number for a background check.

On Wednesday afternoon, August 3, Robyn and I secretly left Delilah with a Ritz-Carlton employee. We slid out the back door and into a taxi. "Sixteen hundred Pennsylvania Avenue, please." Within moments, we were greeted at the East Gate by Assistant Deputy Director of the White House Wayne Skinner. He possessed a Southern drawl thicker than Gomer Pyle's and explained that he'd worked for Governor Clinton in Arkansas. He handed us each a laminated pass.

What made this a "private tour" is that we visited areas not included on the regular jaunt. Thousands of citizens traipse through that building every day and it *is* accurately dubbed "the People's House," but they need to limit access so it isn't overrun. Keep in mind, however, if they considered *me* worthy of a private tour, it isn't all that exclusive.

Wayne took us through the Rose Garden, site of Tricia Nixon's wedding, as well as through the kitchen, where we met the White House pastry chef. We went out to the South Lawn, which is where the presidential helicopter takes off and where President Clinton would jog.

Throughout our walk, I fantasized I was on a journalistic assignment. I asked Wayne all sorts of odd questions: "Are there food tasters?" "How do they watch for assassins when Clinton is jogging?" If I'd gone with the forty-person Stones delegation the next day, there's no way I could've spoken up or made myself conspicuous. But because it was just Robyn and I, we had Wayne's full attention. Every inch of that place, including the portraits, light fixtures, and floral arrangements, has an amazing story. Under the East Room chandelier, for instance, seven presidents have lain in state.

I was impressed by how many regular folks worked there. You realize it's an office building, with menial tasks to be done. (Which isn't to say there weren't guys talking into their cufflinks.) Wayne knew all the workers and was constantly introducing us. "Ted, I'd like you to meet Robyn and Bill. They're with the Stones camp."

Each one said how excited they were to have the Stones in town. "I hope they do 'Beast of Burden' tonight," said one. In a reciprocal arrangement, the Ticket Lady sent a stack of tickets for that night's concert, and Vice President Gore's kids had already witnessed a rehearsal.

Problem was, most of these folks thought the Stones were dropping in on them the following day. "That's gonna be so cool to have them here. They've never been here, right?" It presented an awkward situation for me and Robyn because, by Wednesday, we knew the Stones were *not* visiting the White House on Thursday. The Stones' families and roadies were coming, but the Stones themselves would be sleeping in. Nothing partisan or political, it's just that a photo op with Bill and Hillary would benefit Bill and Hillary more than it would the Stones. (Later in the tour, they snubbed the Republican governor of New York, George Pataki, who wanted to shake their hands at Syracuse Airport.)

Robyn and I possessed intelligence that had eluded the Secret Service, FBI, and CIA. We weren't sure how to handle it, but, after whispering to each other, concluded it wasn't our place to speak for the Stones or to burst anyone's bubble. So if anyone said, "We can't wait to meet them tomorrow," our response was, "Yeah, that'll be great!" And when a Gore staffer asked if the Stones are nice people, we said, "Ha, ha! You'll find out tomorrow!"

The highlight of our private tour was the Oval Office. Wayne explained that we would not be meeting the president—he was next door in the Cabinet Room—but that we could sniff around his office a bit. On the way in, we were introduced to the president's secretary, Bettie, who shook our hands and told us she wasn't going to the concert. "It's not my thing," she said, "but it's all anyone can talk about around here."

The first thing you notice when you enter the Oval Office is the presidential seal on the carpet. Then you notice the desk. Wayne instructed us not to touch it—I guess they don't want you pressing The Button—but he let us glance at it awhile. Behind the desk were busts of Lincoln and FDR.

The Oval Office is a relatively recent addition to the White House, but it's seen its share of awe-inspiring moments. It's where JFK mulled the Cuban missile crisis and where Truman announced Japan's surrender. It's where Martin Luther King retreated after his "I Have a Dream" speech and where Reagan addressed the nation about *Challenger*. It's where Nixon's eighteen-minute gap has seeped into the walls. As I stood there, my knees began to weaken. To cap it off, the door swung open and Graham Nash walked in, also on a private tour.

I still consider August 3, 1994, one of the greatest days of my life and it was made possible because I published a Rolling Stones fanzine. Credentials good enough for the Oval Office, if not a Stones party at the Ritz-Carlton.

I still had a strong desire to host, write, and produce a weekly radio program about the Stones. Sort of a *This Week in the Voodoo Lounge,* with news and interviews. But the Stones' publicists limited access to the band. With few exceptions (like MTV, who paid for the privilege), interviews were not granted to anyone not named *60 Minutes* or *Rolling Stone.* I spoke with a tour bigwig about my idea, but he said, "Even if we were interested, we wouldn't have you host it."

"Who would you rather have," I asked indignantly, "a corporate shill like Casey Kasem?"

And his answer was, "Well, come to think of it, *yes.*"

I wound up doing intermittent reports for WNEW. Their DJ Tony Pigg would invite me to the studio and put me on live. I hoped that if I ended *Beggars Banquet* after the tour, I could find a job there as a DJ. But when he told me he couldn't play "Midnight Rambler"—it was no longer on the station's playlist—I had second thoughts. The end was near for rock 'n' roll radio as we knew it.

WNEW is where I listened to the Stones' 1975 press conference and where I first heard the *Some Girls* album. It's where I turned the night John Lennon died. But the bean counters were now in charge of rock 'n' roll and were more interested in the bottom line than in respecting their audience.

Nowhere was that more evident than at VH1, the station that ridiculed my Stones knowledge. They telecast a *Voodoo Lounge* concert and put the titles of each song on the bottom of the screen. Except that they listed one song as "I'm Gonna Walk" and another as "I Used to Love Her." Apparently, no one at

VH1 had ever heard "Before They Make Me Run" or "It's All Over Now." It sure would've been nice if a network founded on rock music actually hired someone who knew a tiny bit about it.

The over-corporatization of rock 'n' roll also affected how fans got tickets. Ticketmaster had a monopoly. You had to put up with exorbitant fees and with concerts that mysteriously sold out in minutes. For the average fan, it was expensive and frustrating.

I saw a way I could help. I asked the Ticket Lady if I could buy blocks of tickets to sell my readers at face value. She said, "Yes, but let me check with Michael Cohl."

Cohl agreed—he was, after all, in the business of selling tickets—and I was allowed to purchase fifty "VIP" seats per show. I posted a notice in *Beggars Banquet,* offering three locations: New York, Los Angeles, and Chicago. I chose those cities because they were the toughest of the tour and because they were geographically and chronologically diverse.

Within days, my P.O. box was flooded. I was drowning in envelopes, but didn't mind. I wasn't expecting any thank-yous and didn't stand to make a dime. I simply felt that sharing my Ticket Lady privileges was the right thing to do. I knew there'd be bad apples, but I focused on the "silent majority" who honestly needed the help.

Demand far outweighed supply, and I didn't want to disappoint anyone, so I offered alternatives. I had to phone people as far away as Tokyo to ask them if they'd rather go to Oakland, San Diego, or Philadelphia. In the end, I doled out almost eight hundred tickets for fifteen different concerts in six different cities. It was an indescribable amount of work, and I lost money on the phone calls, but it was gratifying. "If this is *Beggars Banquet*'s last stand," I told myself, "it's a nice way to go out."

For me, the most pleasant surprise of the tour was the support I got from Alan Dunn, the loyal Mick Camper. The guy who had viewed me suspiciously throughout *Steel Wheels* came around for *Voodoo Lounge.* Back in '89, he barely knew me and had probably never seen *Beggars Banquet.* But I put him on the comp list, and he began appreciating my work. It took a while, but Alan realized I wasn't one of the ill-mannered, drug-addicted hangers-on he encountered every day of a Stones tour.

Alan provided me with a lift for much of *Voodoo Lounge.* And I mean that literally, as well as figuratively. Alan's title was "logistics director," so he was responsible for moving the entourage from city to city and street to street. He arranged the vans that brought everyone from the hotel to the stadium, and he'd voluntarily put me in one. I'd sit next to Mick's accountant or the backup singer's cousin, en route to the concert. It saved me tons in carfare and provided an emotional boost. It was good having someone so high in the food chain looking out for me.

It came just as I was getting less cooperation from Jane. She still donated the occasional snapshot to *Beggars Banquet,* which was very nice of her, but she dried up as a source of information. When I asked her in early '94 if the Stones would be playing the Rose Bowl, she said, "Um, well, yes, but don't print that. The Stones don't like being told where they're going." And when I asked her about the band's upcoming video, "Love Is Strong," she said, "It's too hard to describe."

I obeyed her instructions and didn't print the Rose Bowl item. But I hated it when I got scooped by the *L.A. Times.* As for the "Love Is Strong" video, I told my readers it's "too difficult to describe," when it could've been summed up in a sentence: The Stones are made to look like giants, roaming through Manhattan like Godzilla. When the video debuted on MTV, my readers probably thought I was an idiot. But Jane didn't want headaches from the tour's muckamucks, and I honestly can't say I blame her.

When the Stones played a secret pre-tour gig in Toronto, she said she couldn't help. She told me to call Alan. I reached him at the Four Seasons, and he said, "I'll get you in, but it'll cost you."

At first, I thought he was trying to shake me down, like JC at Toad's Place. But it was his dry sense of humor. "The club's charging $5," he explained, "and everyone has to pay, as it's going to charity."

I told him I could afford it and caught the next flight to Toronto. It was July 19 at the RPM nightclub. The club's capacity was a thousand people—a hundred of whom were on the guest list, and nine hundred who were driving past the club when a sign went up: "Rolling Stones Live Tonight 8:30 PM Reg Cover $5." There were people on their way to work who swerved off the road, called in sick, and immediately got in line. Dan Aykroyd rolled up on his Harley.

I couldn't believe how easy Alan made it for me. He fixed me up with a guest pass, so I strolled there leisurely and hung with Keith and Woody. Keith gave me some gossip—"We been rehearsin' 'Moonlight Mile' "—and signed an RPM matchbook for my next contest.

The concert was just a warm-up, so the sound was rough. They opened with "Live with Me" and surprised everyone with "No Expectations." The place was a sweatbox, so girls flung their brassieres onstage and bartenders sprayed the audience with soda water. For the encore, they performed the Temptations' "I Can't Get Next to You" with local blues whiz Jeff Healey.

Healey was blind, so Keith clasped his arm and served as his Seeing Eye dog to bring him onstage.

I knew that obtaining pictures of this event wouldn't be easy. The Stones permitted only one photographer, so I smuggled my own camera. After clicking one photo, however, I was accosted by the club's 300-pound bouncer: "Gimme the fuckin' film!" I pointed to my pass and pathetically stated, "I'm with the band," but he hollered, "I don't give a fuck!" and ripped the camera out of my hands.

The next day, I called Tony King. His tour title was "Mick Jagger press liaison." I asked if he could supply me with exclusive photos from the show, and he said no. Mick approved only three of the photographer's images, and they were being serviced to the Associated Press. I'd have to use the same photos as every publication in the world.

Tony King was mild-mannered and quintessentially British. As Mick's mouthpiece, he often delivered bad news to me, but in a too-polite way. Following a September show in Philadelphia, he approached me at the hotel. "Mick has a request to ask of you," he said. "He would really prefer it if you no longer printed the restaurants he visits."

"Alright," I retorted, "but at least I don't print what he *tips!*"

When I got home, I checked the latest issue of *Beggars Banquet* to see what this was about. I noticed an item about the Stones' trip to D.C.: "Mick celebrated his birthday, July 26, dining quietly with Jerry and Charlie at a place called Rakui, following a rain-drenched rehearsal at RFK."

The Stones were on track to gross $300 million this tour, but that's what got Mick's nads in a knot. I could fully understand if it was a security issue, but it wasn't. It'd probably be years before Mick returned to that restaurant.

There had to be more to it, I thought. And that's when I recalled how Janice Crotch, Mick's secretary in London, phoned me right before the tour, saying, "Mick thinks you're too personal in the newsletter."

She didn't give examples, but was probably referring to Mick's partying in L.A. Mick had been renting a house near Beverly Hills since 1991 and was cozying up to lots of stars and starlets. He attended a party one night at the Hollywood Hills home of producer Rick Rubin that was catered by Heidi Fleiss and got broken up by the cops.

My theory is that Mick was nervous about Jerry Hall. While he was cavorting on tour, she was primarily in London, using *Beggars Banquet* to keep tabs on him. Instead of being told to take Jerry Hall off my mailing list, I was being told to get "less personal."

"Fine," I thought. "If Mick doesn't want me reporting on his social life, it's not worth fighting over." Frankly, I no longer gave a shit where—or, for that matter, who—Mick Jagger was eating out. Even when I obsessed and reported on that stuff as a teenager, it usually had a humorous slant to it or something to do with the Stones' music career. I might've told you that Woody ate chicken vindaloo at an Indian restaurant, but that's because, after the chicken vindaloo, he sat in with the sitar player.

With the Stones' increased corporatization and tight control of access, the man-bites-dog stories became harder to find. But I knew the Stones were still the Stones and that if I looked hard enough I'd dig up some nuggets. After sixteen years, I still felt the adrenaline rush of sniffing out a story and putting it in the newsletter.

One of my favorite *Voodoo Lounge* stories took place on August 17, during a driving rain at Giants Stadium. My B-list pass allowed me into an enclosed booth with some A-listers. Willie Nelson was there, smoking some funny-looking cigarettes.

The Stones rewarded the rain-soaked crowd with a truly great performance. Before the encore, the booth cleared out and everyone headed downstairs. Willie and I positioned ourselves by the backstage tunnel, right by the Stones' motorcade. Everyone was waiting for the band to come off stage and zoom into the night. The engines were running, and the motorcycle cops were ready to tear out. A very intense scene.

Mick came through first and got right in, making eye contact with no one. Next came Keith, sporting a towel over his head. He spotted Willie from the corner of his eye and broke away from his minders. People were yelling, "Keith, we gotta get outta here," but he didn't care. He gave Willie a huge hug and started chatting. When Woody and Charlie realized who Keith was talking to, they ran right over. It turned into a love-fest, as the cops and drivers watched impatiently. (Mick never got out.) I recognized a great moment when I saw it and wrote about it in *Beggars Banquet*. It was pure, not staged.

My other favorite story came in Chicago. Keith and Woody were dining at the Ritz-Carlton on September 10 when a kid approached them with a request. He said he was proposing to his girlfriend the next night at the concert and could use Keith's help. Keith said okay and took the kid's name. Probably just humoring him, right?

The next night, after singing "Happy" in front of 50,000 people, Keith said something into the mic like "Hey, Debbie in the 7th row. Jason's got somethin' real important to ask ya." The kid got on his knee and popped the question. Keith went, "What'd she say?" before informing the crowd, "I don't even *know* these people!" "Debbie" and "Jason" got a story to tell their grandkids, and I got a story for *Beggars Banquet.*

Unfortunately, I soon discovered that my human-interest stories were violating the tour's mission statement. In an October 5 memo to the entourage, Michael Cohl said, "We are generating far too many sidebar stories . . . about shepherds pie, other individual projects, likes and dislikes, [which] bury the main message we need to disseminate. . . . Objectives for the balance of the tour are as follows: 1) sell the remaining tickets, 2) publicize the pay per view, 3) generate merchandise awareness. . . . All the press stories should be steered to these main points."

Cohl was essentially the tour's owner, so I understood his position. He was always friendly to me in person, but was a businessman who had every right to earn as much money as possible. To that end, he was letting everyone know—the publicists, the Tony Kings, and even the roadies and backup musicians—that *Beggars Banquet* was irrelevant and not worth cooperating with. I mean, what was *Beggars Banquet* but one "sidebar story" after another? Anecdotes about Keith hugging Willie or playing matchmaker in Chicago do not generate "merchandise awareness."

In a weird way, it was a relief to finally see in writing how much the game was rigged against me. At least I knew I wasn't imagining it.

Springsteen attends the so-called nightclub gig
at the MGM Grand.

38

viva las vegas

Freddy Sessler wanted to die on tour. "If I *have* to die, it should be doing vot I love. Votching de Stones and being on de road." I envisioned him collapsing during a concert or discovered lifeless by a hotel chambermaid. Probably with a shit-eating grin on his face and a vial of coke in his hands. "I'd be de talk of de whole fuckin' tour!" he gushed.

He was telling me this at the MGM Grand Hotel in Las Vegas. Today, seeing a major rock act on the Vegas strip is standard fare. But in 1994, when the Stones first visited, it was practically unheard of. Places like the Hard Rock and House of Blues didn't exist—Hard Rock came in '95, House of Blues, '99—and recent visits from McCartney and U2 were out at the university and not part of the gambling and tourist trade. The Vegas strip, for the most part, was still for the AARP set. Men in Bermuda shorts and black sox, bringing their blue-haired wives to see Wayne Newton and Robert Goulet.

But the old guard was slowly dying off. Liberace and Sammy Davis weren't around, and Robert Goulet's fans were in motorized wheelchairs. To survive as a tourist destination, Vegas needed to cultivate a new customer base and a new image.

Enter the Rolling Stones.

The Stones were wooed by Steve Wynn's Mirage, but opted for the MGM, October 14 and 15. MGM had been closed for thirteen years—a 1980 fire killed eighty-five people—but reopened with five thousand new rooms and a virtual city on its ground floor: a shopping mall, theme park, comedy club, concert arena, and casino.

MGM needed the Stones to put it back on the map. And for the Stones, no stop on the *Voodoo Lounge* tour was as lucrative. Tickets in the orchestra were priced at $300, face value. Higher than Atlantic City in 1989.

Back in '89, the Stones laid the blame on Donald Trump. *He's the one doing the gouging; we knew nothing about it.* But in 1994, they knew. And while no one winces at a $300 Stones ticket *today,* the point is, *this* is where it started. Here is where they tested the model: "Can we make $300 our standard? Will the market bear it?" The answers to those questions would have far-reaching effects for both the Stones and Las Vegas.

The two concerts sold out immediately. Stones fans were so conditioned to stadiums, they considered a fourteen-thousand-seat venue a "nightclub gig" and the 300 bucks a bargain. (On the band's next tour, 300 bucks was indeed the standard for any indoor venue. And when they returned to Vegas to play the Hard Rock, they charged a staggering $1,000 a head, face value.)

The Stones got free room and board, so they saved on the motorcade. To get to the gigs, they just rolled out of bed and onto the elevator. I couldn't afford the MGM, so I stayed at the Tropicana. Only $35 a night, thanks to a subscriber who worked there. My room faced the MGM, where a neon sign advertised its upcoming events. Next to the Stones, you had Sheena Easton, Manhattan Transfer, the Professional Bull Riders Championship, and the UWF Wrestling Black Jack Brawl.

The new Vegas understood three things about rock 'n' roll–loving baby boomers: They had disposable income, young children, and guilt. Unlike our parents' generation, boomers didn't want to leave their kids at home with Grandmom. They preferred to take them along for the ride.

Back in the Sixties and Seventies, it would've been unthinkable, if not criminal, to bring little kids to Vegas. But by the mid-Nineties, it was clear that catering to families was the way to go. The hotels spent millions of dollars on kid-friendly attractions. At the Mirage, you had the buccaneer battle and erupting volcano. At Excalibur, you had the jousting knights. At MGM, you had the Emerald City and Wizard of Oz. Vegas made a conscious decision to adapt to the new demographic and to become the "Disneyland of the Desert." Mom and Dad got the Stones, the kids got Hulk Hogan, and Grandma got Manhattan Transfer. Mick, as I reported in my "Casino Boogie" article, took in Siegfried & Roy.

The Stones concerts were great. I couldn't justify the $300, so I sat toward the back. I possessed only the B-list pass, so I couldn't schmooze with Cruise, dish with De Niro, or eat spring rolls with Springsteen. They, along with Sean Penn and Kelsey Grammer, were in the band's private lair, conveniently dubbed the Voodoo Lounge. The Stones' "nightclub gig" was the place to be seen.

Freddy capitalized on the "small gig" perception by scalping tickets. He bought a bunch from the Ticket Lady and turned them over for twice the face. On Friday the 14th, right before the concert, he was selling outside the MGM when cops approached. They said scalping was prohibited within five hundred feet of the venue. He flashed them his laminate and said he was "with the band." They let him go with a warning: "We're watching you. And if we catch you again, we'll arrest you."

Back in his room that night, 71-year-old Freddy grew defiant and yearned for the Vegas of yore—the bodies-buried-in-the-desert, Bugsy Siegel Vegas. That's probably the one Keith had in mind when he signed off on this thing. But then he showed up and they put umbrellas in his vodka.

Freddy was determined to put the "sin" back in Sin City. He refused to mind his p's and q's and refused to play nice. "You vanna bring in de Stones? You gotta deal vit *me*. Fuck Dorotee and her dog, Toto, too!"

On Saturday afternoon, I bumped into him in the MGM lobby. He looked like shit. Very sweaty and bleary-eyed. His hair was flipped in an unintentional comb-over. It was 3 PM, but he hadn't slept yet. I suggested he nap before the concert.

"I vill," he responded. "I'll tell dem to gimme a vake-up call."

I escorted him to the elevator, and he went to his room—or so I thought.

When I returned to the MGM at 6 PM, I saw Alan Dunn. "I assume you've heard about Freddy," he said.

"No, what *about* him?"

"Well, he spent the day in jail. Apparently, you're the last to know."

I couldn't tell if he was joking. "How can that be?" I asked. "I just saw him three hours ago."

"Well, he's back in his room, so I suggest you ask him *yourself.*"

I dashed to Freddy's room and found him in bed, looking shittier than before. His girlfriend du jour opened the door. "Dat's right!" he gloated. "I got busted! Right dehr in de lobby! But doze cocksuckers didn't know who dey ver dealing vit!"

According to eyewitnesses, the scene went like this:

Right after I left Freddy in the lobby—and right before he was to board the elevator to his room—he made a U-turn. He had extra tickets, so he scoured the casino for potential customers. He then proceeded to the lobby, where, not far from the front desk, he bumped into JC.

In the course of their conversation, Freddy produced a vial of coke from his pocket. Freddy opened it, sprinkled some on his wrist, and began snorting in public. Within seconds, a dozen officers, most in plain clothes, sprang from behind slot machines, desks, and potted plants. "Hold it right there! You're under arrest!"

In a slick move, Freddy tried handing the vial to JC, who shoved it right back to him. Two grown men playing hot potato. "*You* take it." "No, it's yours, *you* take it." Didn't matter to the cops. They slapped cuffs on both of them and hauled them into a hidden room behind the front desk. Apparently, Vegas hotels have holding cells, like a mini–police station.

For JC, this was particularly embarrassing. Here was the head of Rolling Stones security, who'd been coordinating all week with the hotel's detectives and Vegas PD, and they've got him in cuffs.

They determined that JC did nothing wrong and let him go. But they hustled Freddy to a squad car and took him to a *real* police station for booking. From there, I can rely only on what Freddy told me:

"So I'm sittin' in de police station, and you know who I call?"

"I don't know. Who?"

"Oscar Goodman."

"Who?"

"Oscar Fucking Goodman!" He slammed his fist on the night table, annoyed that I didn't know the name.

Goodman was the most notorious defense attorney in the history of Las Vegas. Since the 1960s, he'd represented every dirty rotten scoundrel who ever set foot there, including Meyer Lansky. He was nicknamed the "Barrister of Butchers" because his clients were so brutal. He's such a staple of Vegas lore, he portrayed himself in Scorsese's *Casino* and was controversially elected the city's mayor in 1999. (Re-elected twice.)

Freddy made it sound like he and Oscar were old pals. Like he could reach him on a Saturday afternoon and have Oscar drop everything to take his case. "I said, 'Oscar, I don't vanna miss de Stones tonight,' and he said, 'Freddy, I'll get you out vit plenty of time.' De sergeant den gets a call and dey let me go."

I couldn't tell if Freddy was bullshitting, but this much I knew: In the span of three hours, he'd been arrested, brought to a police station, and sprung without charges.

My theory is that someone high up, perhaps the DA, understood what was at stake. The city's future was riding on this weekend. Rock bands of the Stones' caliber had to feel comfortable there. If it got around that narcs had busted the Stones' friends or employees in Vegas, a lot of acts would shy away. Aerosmith and the Who don't need the hassles or legal fees.

"And you know vot else?" said Freddy. "De cops gave me a lift back to de hotel and gave me back my blow!"

He strutted into that night's concert like a returning war hero. He was the talk of the entire Stones camp. He wore a shit-eating grin and didn't have to drop dead to earn the attention.

Viva Las Vegas, viva Freddy Sessler.

Mick, Woody, and Jo arrive at the American Legion Hall.
Woody came with a smile, but left without one.

39

surreality bites:
the slums of beverly hills

When *Rolling Stone* asked Woody to list the most "surreal moments" of the *Voodoo Lounge* tour (for its 1994 year-end issue), he cited two nights in Los Angeles: "A. C. Cowlings was in our room. That was kinda surreal. [And another] night, my friend Harry Dean Stanton was playing guitar and singing in my room [while] Sean Penn was reciting poetry."

Following the trip to Vegas and a brief stop in San Diego, the Stones and I checked into the Four Seasons in Beverly Hills. I couldn't afford it, but a subscriber wanted to thank me for some tickets. I wouldn't accept gifts from him, but I was willing to crash in his suite. A bellboy wheeled in a rickety cot and set it up in the living room.

The Stones were slated for two concerts at the Rose Bowl in Pasadena—Wednesday, October 19, and Friday, October 21. Celebrities were tripping over each other for tickets and passes. And yet, for all the star power in the house—Jack Nicholson, Whoopi Goldberg, Goldie Hawn—it was A. C. Cowlings and Robert Shapiro who turned the most heads.

Cowlings, of course, was behind the wheel of O. J. Simpson's Ford Bronco during the nationally televised slow-speed chase. And Shapiro was O.J.'s lead defense attorney. This was eighteen weeks after the murders and chase (pre-Cochran and pre–"Dream Team"). Everyone craned their necks to look at these guys. While poor O.J. was in his orange jumpsuit, rotting in a jail cell, his best friend and lead attorney were livin' large at the Stones. During "Start Me Up," Shapiro's mug appeared on the JumboTron. Each night, the camera would pan the audience and show some potbellied bald guy singing the song's chorus, but on this Friday night in L.A., the potbellied bald guy was

America's most famous defense attorney. Fifty thousand fans cheered the sight of him.

After the show, I grabbed a drink at the hotel bar. I had Nicholson and James Caan to my right, Gary Busey to my left. I was told that Cowlings was already upstairs, hanging out in Keith's room. According to Woody in that *Rolling Stone* article, "[Cowlings] couldn't say much . . . he didn't give anything away." But Freddy gave me his own version of events.

"Dat cocksucker Cowlings! He sold out his best friend! Just to hang out vit Keet, to impress Keet!" According to Freddy, A.C. dished all the grizzly details. "He showed Keet how O.J. slit dehr heads off! Den he told Keet vehr O.J. hid de knife!"

When I pointed out to Freddy that he himself wasn't present during Cowlings's visit, he grew agitated.

"Vot, you don't believe me? Keet told me de whole fuckin' ting! Vord for vord!"

Not only wasn't Freddy in Keith's room with Cowlings, he wasn't even in L.A. He was phoning my cot from his son's house in Arizona. Freddy was urged to take a leave of absence after the Vegas incident. A lot of people were amused by Freddy's Sin City bust, but not Mick and Michael Cohl. In fact, Cohl made it clear in writing—via the minutes of a production meeting—that "Fred Sessler" was not an official member of the tour, and that "all entourage" were discouraged from mingling with this undesirable hanger-on. It was Cohl's way of indemnifying himself: *We got nothing to do with this Sessler guy.*

Earlier that month, Cohl had to bail out a roadie—caught snorting in the stairwell of a New Orleans hotel—so he didn't need crap from a non-employee like Freddy. He told Freddy to leave the tour and, this time, Keith didn't stick up for him.

Freddy sounded depressed, like he was suffering from Stones withdrawal. Missing a week of Beverly Hills starfucking had to be killing him. But he insisted that Keith was constantly updating him and that's how he could call me from 300 miles away to tell me what was happening 300 *feet* from me. "Cowlings told Keet everyting! Vehr de knife is, *everyting!*"

I never asked Keith or Woody to confirm Freddy's claim because, frankly, I didn't want to know. But from what I saw at the Rose Bowl and Four Seasons that night, I can tell you Woody was right. It was certainly surreal.

Now to Woody's *other* surreal night—Wednesday, October 19. It started innocently enough at the American Legion Hall in Hollywood. The Stones were guests of honor at a party hosted by their label, Virgin Records.

Despite the fact that Virgin had hired me to compile their *Voodoo Lounge* press kit, and despite the fact they still owed me $300 for said work, no one at the label thought to invite me. I called Jane and asked if she could intervene. She kindly said yes and called me back at my cot: "They say they'll pay you next week and that your drinks are on the house tonight. You're on the guest list."

When Alan Dunn saw me hailing a cab outside the hotel, he offered me a ride. He was organizing shuttle vans to and from the party. He sat me next to Suzi-the-wardrobe-girl and Lisa Fischer, the backup vocalist. When we pulled up to the club on North Highland Avenue, our blacked-out van was swarmed by paparazzi. They huffed when no one more marketable than a backup singer, seamstress, and fanzine editor spilled out.

I milled around the club and spotted some famous faces: Nicolas Cage, Shannen Doherty, two guys from R.E.M., and Richard Branson, the head of Virgin Records. Branson was seated on a giant pillow, playing sitar, as Egyptian-looking servants fed him grapes and fanned him with large feathers.

At 1:30 AM, I was standing in a vestibule when I was approached by Alan Dunn's brother, Arnold. Like Alan, Arnold worked in the London office during the "off season" and was a 100 percent Mick Camper. He started with the Stones as a glorified bellboy—his title on the '81 tour was "baggage supervisor"—but now held a prominent role in the Jagger regime.

Normally, Arnold wouldn't give me the time of day. I'd see him backstage or in the hotel lobby and never get more than a nod from him. But he was shaking my hand and telling me to follow him. In fact, he continued to clasp my hand and pull me along like a tugboat. I had no idea what this was about or where it was leading.

He walked me to another part of the club, before stopping, letting go of my hand, and saying, "Don't move, stay right here." Then he disappeared. He returned thirty seconds later, accompanied by Mick Jagger of the Rolling Stones. They shuffled through the same vestibule I'd just been standing in and headed up a staircase.

Suddenly it clicked. What Arnold had done—what that walkie-talkied toady had done—was deposit me out of Mick Jagger's sight line. As Mick was waiting in his car, Arnold's task was to sweep a path for him before bringing him inside. For whatever reason, Arnold deemed me unworthy of breathing the same air as his boss.

Mick left the party at 2 AM. Keith and Charlie were no-shows. At 2:30, Woody and Jo stumbled in and headed straight to the bar. I waited to say hello until they got their drinks. But the bartender said he couldn't serve them. Something about California's liquor curfew.

"You're not serious!" cried Woody.

"I'm sorry," came the answer, "but that's the law."

Woody got exasperated. "Hang on a minute. *You* invited me here, and now you're telling me I can't *drink*?"

"I'm sorry," the bartender restated. "But we have a 2 o'clock curfew."

"But it's *our* party," interjected Jo. "We're the guests of honor."

"I realize that," the bartender said, "but I can't. I already made last call."

Harry Dean Stanton, the actor, was standing nearby and tried to intervene. "This is a private party. You're not *selling* us drinks. You're *pouring* them, like the host at a party. Which means the curfew doesn't apply."

"I'm sorry," the bartender stressed, "but I've got to close out."

"Alright then," said Woody, "if *you* won't do it, I'll make my *own* fuckin' drink." He slid behind the bar, poured a glass of JD, and handed it to Harry. Then, he shoveled ice into another glass before hearing, "Sir, that's *enough*. You can't *do* that!"

Woody blew a gasket, and things almost got physical. "I'll get my *own* fuckin' drinks!" he ranted. "Why the fuck did you get me here in the first place?" In all the years I'd been around Woody, including the year I virtually lived with him, I'd never seen him this angry. He stormed out of the room, repeating, "I'll get my *own* fuckin' drinks!" and I made no attempt to go near him.

With no more booze or Stones in the house, I decided to call it a night. When I got to the Four Seasons, I ran for a closing elevator. I pressed the button and, when the door reopened, I was face to face with Woody and Jo. Their limo must've arrived a minute before my van, but I didn't see them walk in.

I boarded the elevator and said hello. Woody was in a much better mood. I pressed the button for my floor and asked him what he was up to.

"Not much," he said. "Hangin' round."

"Can you use some company?"

"Of course, we can always use one *more*."

The elevator stopped on my floor, but I didn't get out. We continued to the Stones' private floors. There were other people in the elevator, but I couldn't see who they were. We were pretty cramped, and the girth of Bob Bender was blocking my view. When we exited, the passengers' identities were finally revealed: Harry Dean Stanton and Sean Penn.

We piled into the Woods' living room and plopped on the sofas. Woody, as an inside joke, offered me a banana. Sean, clad in a black leather jacket and sporting short hair, reached across the coffee table to shake my hand. "I'm Sean. How do you know Ronnie?"

I told him about *The Works* and *Beggars Banquet*.

"Cool," he said. "So you're a journalist."

Woody hopped up to retrieve the latest *Beggars Banquet* from the kitchen counter. "This is it," he told Sean. "Bill's been doin' it since puberty."

Sean perused its pages and seemed mildly interested. He informed me he still used a typewriter, as opposed to a computer. I told him I was partial to typewriters, too, and that I still designed my issues with scissors and glue, not a computer program.

"That reminds me," said Jo. "I saw in your latest issue that you've still not made the change to 'Ronnie.' Promise me you'll do that. To only call him Ronnie, not Woody."

"I promise," I said. "Next issue." (*Beggars Banquet* aficionados will note that in my October issue—Volume 3, Number 22—I was still referring to him as Woody. In my November issue—Volume 3, Number 23—I began calling him Ronnie. After sixteen years of "Woody," my readers must've wondered, "Who the hell is *Ronnie*?")

Sean was very polite. I'd been a fan of his a long time, so it was a bonus to find him so friendly. As for Harry, I didn't chat with him much. As soon as he spotted Woody's acoustic guitar on the couch, he grabbed it and never let go. The first song he played was "Danny Boy." Then he played some flamenco tunes. Next thing we knew, he was yodeling in Spanish. He said he had a regular gig in some L.A. nightclub, but that he usually played to an empty house.

Woody—I mean, Ronnie—was mesmerized by Harry's talent. "How *old* are you?" he asked.

"Sixty-eight," came the reply.

"That's almost Freddy's age! But look at *Freddy* and look at *this* guy. Fantastic, man! Brilliant!"

Ronnie grabbed an electric guitar, plugged into a tiny practice amp, and tried to keep up with Harry. Sean, meanwhile, was pacing the room, talking to himself. He was completely oblivious to the music and to our conversation. He was moving his lips as he paced. Ronnie would occasionally look at Sean and roll his eyes. We had no idea what Sean was up to.

At 5 o'clock in the morning, Bobby Keys and Bernard Fowler stopped by. By then, the jam session had moved to the dining room. Sean was still pacing the living room, and no one wanted to break his trance. We were a little scared of him.

To change the focus, I asked Jo about a Post-it note that was stuck to the lampshade in the living room. "Tell Shelley we're NOT paying for A-smith tix," it read.

She explained that Ronnie had invited the guys from Aerosmith to the

Stones' concert in Boston. Ronnie, of course, didn't realize those tickets had to be *paid* for. He assumed that, because he was a Rolling Stone, he could invite whomever he wanted. Well, *someone* had to pay for those tickets and, when Aerosmith's management claimed Ronnie told them not to worry about it, the Ticket Lady (Shelley) stuck Ronnie with the bill.

"Can you *believe* that?" cried Jo.

I shrugged my shoulders and told her my own tale of woe. About Arnold Dunn removing me from Mick's airspace.

"That's Mick for ya," chimed Bobby Keys. "I'm surprised he announces my name each night. Probably wouldn't, if the teleprompter wasn't tellin' him to."

Jo said she would speak to Mick about Arnold's treatment of me. "We'll also tell him you deserve a laminate for this tour. It's absurd to make you pay. Isn't that right, Ronnie?"

Ronnie nodded, but I don't think he heard a word she said. He was preoccupied with Harry's yodeling and with Sean's mumbling and pacing. I begged Jo *not* to talk to Mick about me because I didn't want to stir things up. "Besides," I said, "I prefer being my own person. I might even quit after this tour. I haven't decided yet."

She again called out to the dining room—"Ronnie, did you hear that?"—but got no response.

It must have been around 6 AM when Bob Bender brought a note from outside. It was the entourage newsletter. If you were a member of the tour, a note would get slipped under your door every morning, containing little bits of information. Things like "We leave for soundcheck at 3 PM today" or "If you want to see Siegfried & Roy, don't forget to sign up by Tuesday."

Today's said: "Contrary to popular belief, to the best of our knowledge, the Rolling Stones will not be playing tonight at the House of Blues."

It referred to the rumors that had spread like wildfire. Every fan in California thought the Stones would show up at the club on Sunset Boulevard for a surprise gig. Buddy Guy was the announced headliner, so everyone made the leap: *Keith and Ronnie love Buddy Guy. He opened for the Stones last week in Vegas. They jammed with him in a nightclub in 1981. It all adds up!*

The club sold out weeks in advance. Scalpers were getting 200 bucks a throw, based on speculation and hysteria. Ronnie read the note and said, "Hey, we never committed anything to *anybody.*" He told me he'd be spending the night at Le Dome, dining with Slash from Guns N' Roses.

With a break in the jam session, Ronnie began focusing on Sean. He was still talking to himself, still gesticulating, and still in his own world. Ronnie got concerned: "Uh, hey there, Sean, what exactly are you doing?"

"Poetry," he answered. "I've got some poetry in my head."

"Well, then let's *hear* it, boy!"

Sean recited a couple of verses, and it wasn't bad. Dylanesque musings about screwing a chick in the back of a Cadillac. I'm not sure if it had a deeper metaphorical meaning or if it was just about, well, screwing a chick in the back of a Cadillac. Whatever the case, Ronnie seized the moment. He grabbed his guitar and dragged his amp into the living room area. "We'll turn it into a song!"

Ronnie and Harry strummed to Sean's monologue, as Bernard sang backup and Bobby used the coffee table as a bongo. I enjoyed the creativity of it all, but wished I had more to offer. I did nothing but sit on my hands. After so many years as an observer, I began feeling uneasy in these situations. The more I was surrounded by greatness—in this case, two Oscar-caliber actors and a Rolling Stone—the farther I felt from it. And let's face it, if *I'd* been talking to myself in that room, I would not have been indulged the way Sean was. I'd have been physically removed by Bob Bender.

By 8 AM, everyone was still jamming in the living room, except for Sean. He and Jo were in the bedroom, deep in conversation. On my way out of the bathroom, Sean called out to me.

"Bill," he said, "you're a journalist, so maybe you can answer this."

I was flattered that he remembered not just my name, but my occupation. I entered the bedroom, but, before he had the chance to ask his question, Jo yelled, "Sean! Stop it! Don't! You've got to stop it!" She tried to muzzle his mouth, but he pushed her hand away. "Let me talk, Jo! Let me talk!"

"Bill," he said, "why is it that America always has to Hitlerize someone? I mean, like Saddam Hussein or Noriega or Castro. Why does the media and the White House constantly Hitlerize these people and never show both sides?"

I had no idea where he was going with this. His political views are well known *now,* but, back then, he kept them to himself.

"Stop worrying!" yelled Jo. "It's got nothing to do with you, Sean! Relax!"

"It's true those guys aren't Hitler," I said to Sean, "but let's face it, they're not champions in the human rights department, either."

"No, you're right, Bill. You're definitely right about that. I'm just saying that, no matter who it is, we always pick someone to pick on. Know what I mean?"

"I guess it keeps us focused," I suggested. "Maybe we always need an enemy. We don't have the Russians anymore."

Sean seemed serious about this stuff, and I could tell it really weighed on him. He could've easily buried his head in the sand and enjoyed the trappings of celebrity, but I sensed he was honestly distressed by the world outside L.A.

"Who cares?" yelled Jo. "I'm sure you feel bad for these people, Sean, but what does it matter? You can't do anything about it, so relax."

She began massaging Sean's shoulders, but he ignored her. He pointed out that America's imprisonment of Noriega wasn't for human rights violations, but for drug trafficking.

"We are *not* talking about this!" declared Jo. "Bill, don't encourage him! Besides, who's Noriega?"

"From Panama," grumbled Sean.

"That's *thousands* of miles from here," Jo argued. "You're in Beverly Hills, Sean. That's what you should focus on. Care about Paneema if you're *in* Paneema. If the Stones go to Paneema, then it would concern me." She called out to the other room: "Ronnie? Are we going to Paneema?"

"Wazzat?"

"I said, are the Stones playing Paneema?"

"Uh, nah, don't *think* so."

"So who *cares*, Sean? It doesn't mat-*ter*! Re-*lax*!"

Jo and Sean's argument continued in circles, as the boys played in the living room. I said good night, and Ronnie asked why I was leaving so early. "Well," I answered, "it *is* 8 AM and I'm due back at my cot."

Enough surreality for one visit.

BEGGARS BANQUET
The Rolling Stones

Volume 3, Number 26

June 14, 1995

The Stones' Dutch Treat!

Some people referred to it as "The Stones Unplugged." The band's entourage loosely referred to it as "The Foot Tappers and Wheel Shunters Club Gig." But whatever you called it, the Stones' two-night stint at the Paradiso Club in Amsterdam, Holland, was an event that most Rolling Stones fans could only dream of.

On Friday and Saturday, May 26 and 27, seven hundred people a night were treated to a Stones performance like none other in the group's three-decade long career. Not only did the Stones rearrange some of their classic live tracks, like "Gimme Shelter" and "Street Fighting Man," they also dusted off some numbers they hadn't played in a while, like "Respectable," "Rip This Joint," and "Spider And The Fly." And then there were a few they had never played in concert at all, like "Shine A Light," their new one "Jump On Top Of Me," and even a cover of "Like A Rolling Stone."

More than the usual pre-tour warm-up gig, these two shows will make up the Stones' upcoming CD and video release--the next best thing to being there.

Although the Stones tried to keep the exact date and location of these shows a secret, it seemed like everyone in Amsterdam knew about it for weeks. It was mentioned on the radio, in the newspapers, and on TV. The Stones didn't even bother using a pseudonym. The sign outside the club boldly proclaimed "Tonight: Rolling Stones-- Uitverkocht." (That's "sold out," for you English speaking readers.)

Tickets--or actually, wristbands--were sold the morning of the show (Friday) for the mere price of 25 guilders (approximately 18 U.S. dollars). The catch, however, [cont. next page]

Above: Mick goes acoustic.
Below: Stones in Stockholm, June 1.

Paradiso, May 26
Amsterdam, Holland

Not Fade Away
It's All Over Now
Live With Me
Let It Bleed
Spider And The Fly
Beast Of Burden
Angie
Wild Horses
Sweet Virginia
Dead Flowers
Shine A Light
Like A Rolling Stone
Connection
Slipping Away
The Worst
Gimme Shelter
All Down The Line
Respectable
Rip This Joint
encore:
Street Fighting Man

40

frank discussion

When my flight touched down at Schiphol Airport in Holland, I lied to passport control, like I'd been instructed. The Stones were in Amsterdam to play two shows at the Paradiso nightclub, but I wasn't to let anyone know.

It was May 1995, and the band was about to extend its *Voodoo Lounge* tour to Europe. I had a feeling they'd pull a secret nightclub show, but Jane and Tony King said no. I finally got through to Alan Dunn, who confirmed it. "May 26 and 27," he said. "I can put you on the list, but we don't want this in the press. So don't tell *anyone,* not even the customs agent at the airport."

When the guy stamping my passport asked, "The reason for your visit?" I told him, "I wanna see the Heineken brewery. Also, the Van Gogh Museum."

When I got to my hotel, I realized the secret was out. Before I put down my suitcase, I had messages from local Stones fans. They correctly assumed I was flying in and that I'd be staying at the American Hotel near Leidseplein Square. The Stones were at the five-star Amstel, but their roadies were at the American.

Per capita, I'd say Holland possesses the most rabid Stones freaks in the world. You can't put anything past them. They knew the Stones were in town and knew they'd be playing the Paradiso. It was the one nightclub in Amsterdam that didn't have an advertised band for Friday, the 26th, and Saturday, the 27th. The only question was how to get tickets.

The local rock station, Arrow 107, instructed listeners to tune in Friday morning for an announcement. It was easy to predict the gist of it—"Tickets for tonight's Stones concert are on sale *now!*"—but not the specifics. The concerts were happening at the Paradiso, but that didn't mean tickets would be sold there. For *that* detail, you had to listen at 10 AM. I told the fans who called me that I had no advance knowledge. All I knew was that *my* tickets were at the Amstel with the Ticket Lady.

That's where I headed first thing Friday morning. I left my hotel around 9:30 and noticed a mob scene across the street. Hundreds of people were lined up in front of the Melkveg nightclub, listening to radios. I walked around the corner and found the same scene at the Paradiso. Tickets were going on sale at the moment of the announcement, so you had to be standing in the right place at the right time to have a chance. For thousands of anxious fans, it was like betting on the ponies. Everyone played a hunch. At a dozen locations throughout the city, mostly record stores and nightclubs, thousands of fans queued up, praying *their* horse was the one. At one location, it got so rowdy, a fan fell in the canal.

The winner was the Melkveg. All the tickets—seven hundred for Friday, seven hundred for Saturday—were snapped up in minutes. People who'd staked out the Paradiso frantically ran to the Melkveg upon the radio announcement, but I doubt they made it in time.

It was nice not dealing with the madness. The Ticket Lady's office was quiet, and she was courteous as always. I paid 25 guilders per concert, which was around 18 U.S. dollars. To prevent scalping, nontransferable wristbands accompanied each ticket. Friday's was orange, with the words "Rolling Stones, Paradiso, 26 Mei 1995," and Saturday's was blue. I stuck out my right arm and Shelley snapped Friday's into place. I stuck out my left arm for Saturday's. "This blue one has to survive a day and a half," she advised, "so when you bathe, you might want to stick your arm outside the shower stall."

She then handed me a yellow card with instructions. It read: *"Let Op! Alleen toegang met polsbandje."*

"Translation on the other side," she said.

"Attention! Only access with wristband." The card listed several prohibited items: cameras, audio equipment, video equipment, and pocketknives. "You will be body searched," the card stressed. "If we find any of the objects, you lose your right to enter Paradiso."

The strict policy was in place because these nightclub shows weren't like the ones in the past. Sir Morgan's Cove in '81 and Toad's Place in '89 were about warming up for a tour. These shows, however, were commercially motivated. The Stones were filming their own version of MTV's *Unplugged.* As you'll recall, bands would play a small venue, tone down the sound (thus the term "unplugged," which was technically a misnomer), and telecast it exclusively on MTV, before releasing it on CD and video. Clapton, Rod, and Nirvana had all taken part. The Stones wanted to do it, too, but outside the aegis of

MTV. That way, they could keep all the loot. They filmed it themselves and titled it *Stripped* instead of *Unplugged.*

The band performed acoustic versions of "Street Fighting Man" and "Not Fade Away." They dusted off "Connection," "The Spider and the Fly," and "Shine a Light." They even covered "Like a Rolling Stone."

Before the show, I was approached by a hysterical subscriber outside the club. "Mr. German! Wait! You must help me! I must see this show! I have been a Stones fan my whole life!" He had tears streaming down his face, but I explained there was nothing I could do. There were only so many rafts on the *Titanic.*

I was then approached by another subscriber. "They won't let me in! I got a wristband this morning, but they cut it off with a scissor!"

"Why'd they do that?"

"Because they found my tape recorder. I had it hidden in my sock."

I reminded him that the card clearly said "no audio equipment" and that "you will be body searched." The Stones were so vigilant about bootleggers, I saw one guy get his wheelchair inspected.

Eventually, I made it to the front door, where a bouncer poked and prodded my wristband. He rubbed it and tugged it to make sure it wasn't counterfeit. He then patted every inch of my body.

Inside the lobby, there were "traffic cops" telling you where to go. They were Mick employees, not Paradiso employees, so they addressed me by name. "Bill, you're upstairs." The show was no-seats general admission, but these guys determined who went where—up to the balcony or down near the stage.

When I got upstairs and looked around, the whole thing became clear. They wanted the beautiful people on camera and the ugly folks out of sight. I'm not saying this was an absolute, but it was definitely the rule.

I learned that some of the hotties near the stage weren't even Stones fans—they were hired models. I was also informed, by eyewitnesses, that Stones employees ran to the Museumplein—the popular town square—to recruit additional babes, last-minute. The girls were instantly given wristbands and escorted right to the front of the stage.

I realize that planting an audience with gorgeous chicks is a common showbiz practice. Alan Freed did it, and so did Jay Leno. But Leno put in two hundred shows a year, visible to millions, while the Stones had done *five* of these secret shows in the past fifteen years. For every paid model on that dance floor, a Stones fan was robbed of that once-in-a-lifetime experience.

.   .   .

One of the first things I did when I got to Amsterdam was visit the Anne Frank House. It's the actual place where the famous girl hid from the Nazis. Located at 263 Prinsengracht, it's now a museum. Parts have been preserved from when she lived there. On her bedroom wall, for instance, you see pictures she pasted of her favorite Hollywood movie stars. It reminded me of *my* walls as a teen, full of Stones posters.

I'd read Anne Frank's diary when I was a kid, but couldn't remember the details. I did recall that her father, Otto, built a bookcase that served as the family's secret door. That way, if the Nazis stormed the building, they'd never suspect that anyone lived there. When I saw the bookcase in person, it gave me chills.

It also gave me the sign I was waiting for. I'd flown into Amsterdam with this big "secret" to keep. But now I had to rethink the word. The Stones and I have a *secret*? That's a relative term when you're in front of Otto Frank's bookcase.

I suddenly felt embarrassed for thinking *my* secret was so important. I enjoyed the concerts tremendously and I understand why a secret show is the Holy Grail for Stones fans. But I could never get swept up in its mania again. And upon that conclusion, I realized I no longer qualified for my job.

To Bill German ~

Dear Bill,
   We shall miss
the great instructional
~ monthly very much
   How will we know
from now on ~
where we all are
and what each
of us has been
  up to? . . . .
Don't dissappear
too long
we want you near
for the next thing . . . .

♡ Ronnie
     '96

epilogue

the departed

Keith's first words to me in my post–*Beggars Banquet* life were: "You look like a great weight has been lifted off you." As usual, he was right.

After covering the European leg of the *Voodoo Lounge* tour, I finally threw in the towel. "This is the day some of you thought would never come," I wrote in my January 1996 issue. "After seventeen years and a total of 102 issues, you now hold in your hands the final edition of *Beggars Banquet.*"

Seventeen years at the same job is quite a commitment. I was 33, and *Beggars Banquet* had consumed more than half my life. The banner headline of my final issue was "BB: The Last Time." Some people told me they cried when they read it. Hundreds of subscribers—many of whom had previously lurked in that "silent majority"—poured their hearts out to me. "*Beggars Banquet* was a part of my life," they'd say. "I loved coming home and finding it in my mailbox. I'd read it on my front steps." A girl in Austria said, "It is from *Beggars Banquet* that I learned to speak English." I had no idea my little 'zine impacted so many people.

Usually, when fanzines fold, they take the money and run. But I was determined to settle everyone's account. I went through every subscriber's file—thousands of handwritten index cards—and cut individual refund checks.

Two weeks after my final issue, I was tempted to return. It was February 1996, and I was at the Bottom Line for a show by Chris Jagger.

Chris's older brother, Mick, entered the club while the opening band was on. Fans approached him during the intermission, so he darted into the club's office. Jerry Hall and Jann Wenner, the publisher of *Rolling Stone,* remained at the table, so I walked over. Jerry shook my hand and said, "I'm so sad you're stopping. I'm really going to miss it." (Of course. How *else* to keep such accurate tabs on Mick?)

Jann, who I'd met a year earlier at a Stones show, put his arm around me and told me he had big news. "This is off the record," he prefaced. "And I'm telling you because there's no *Beggars Banquet* to print it in. But the Stones are going back on the road next year. Mick just told me in the car."

For a moment, my heart sank. I mean, if I'd known this information two weeks earlier, would I still have pulled the plug on *Beggars Banquet*? The answer, ultimately, is yes. I knew that dealing with the Stones' machinery was only getting harder, not easier. But I have to be honest. When the *Voodoo Lounge* tour ended, I didn't expect them to hit the road for a long time, if ever. I knew they were *capable* of sticking around and remaining relevant, I just didn't think they'd *want* to.

In the months following the *Voodoo Lounge* tour, the Stones were dealt a series of blows. Charlie's mother died. Two of Keith's close friends died. Alan and Arnold Dunn's parents died. And one of the Stones' roadies killed himself. All between September '95 and January '96.

But death, I should have realized, had never stopped the Stones in the past. They've had plenty of people depart on them, and they've always just stepped over the bodies. That's what makes the Stones the Stones. But in January '96, I sensed a certain finality I can't put into words. It was like, after all the prosperity of the *Steel Wheels* and *Voodoo Lounge* tours, the Stones were being slapped to reality. Like the devil was here to collect.

The Canadian government was also here to collect. Michael Cohl, the businessman behind the Stones' wildly successful tours, was facing a criminal investigation. He allegedly charged a phony tax on every ticket he sold at Toronto's CNE Stadium. Fans paid an extra $3 apiece for Springsteen, U2, and Stones tickets, all pocketed by Cohl. According to government auditors, he made $5 million from the scheme, including a half million from Stones shows. He avoided jail time, but had to sell his BCL stock back to Labatt's. It looked like his career was over.

When I mentioned it to Jann Wenner, he said the Stones didn't care. Cohl had a new company and a new project: the 1997 Stones tour.

Mick, by the way, did catch his brother's act that night at the Bottom Line. He waited until the house lights went down before returning to his seat. But Chris thrust him back in the limelight by inviting him onstage. Mick declined, so Chris jumped into the audience. For a minute, the two of them regressed to their childhood, playing a bizarre game of cat-and-mouse. Mick ducked to the left, then to the right, and hid behind a pole. Chris eventually gave up. When the show was over, Mick raced out of the club like Secretariat. No autographs, no handshakes, no nothing. I never had the chance to say hello to him or to thank him for the note he'd contributed to my farewell issue.

"I've always enjoyed reading *Beggars Banquet* when it dropped through my letterbox," he wrote. "So I'm very sad that this is the last issue. Thanks Bill for all your time and effort. We've had fun!"

In putting together my final issue, I'd phoned Mick's office to see if he'd write a note. It arrived within forty-eight hours, via fax. Very efficient. I asked Jane if Keith could do one, but his took over a month.

I didn't think I had space in the issue for more than two notes, so I didn't approach the others. But Ronnie volunteered to draw something and insisted I ask Charlie. So I called Sherry Daly. "Charlie will be devastated," she said of *Beggars Banquet*'s demise. I told her I didn't think he knew it existed. "Quite the contrary," she claimed. "And I'm sure he'd love to do something for your finale. But he's busy recording a jazz album and visiting his mum in hospital each day, so hopefully he can get to it." He never did.

Ronnie's drawing arrived about two weeks after New Year's. He depicted me from the back, walking away from it all. With my long hair, raincoat, and ever-present briefcase. And per our inside joke, he put a banana in my hand. I was really moved by it. His note read: "Dear Bill, we shall miss the great instructional monthly very much. How will we know from now on where we all are and what each of us has been up to? Don't dissappear too long. We want you near for the next thing!!!"

Keith's contribution arrived last. I waited so long, I laid out the entire issue, minus a space for him. It showed up the final week of January, but was worth the wait: "Bill, I'm going to miss the old rag—a big hole in the month. Thanks for so much pleasure and information. You always knew something we didn't. One love. Forward, brother." By "Forward, brother," he was encouraging me to get on with my life—outside the Stones' vacuum.

When I saw him a few months later, at a Charlie Watts jazz concert in New York, he apologized for taking so long. He said he didn't want to rush something so important. We were at a place on 47th Street called the Supper Club, and the contrast between Keith and Mick's public personas could not have been starker.

Unlike Mick, Keith let everyone know he was in the house. He cracked up the audience several times by playfully heckling Charlie. After the show, he stuck around to shake hands and sign autographs. I introduced him to some fans, and when one said her name was Donna, he serenaded her with the Ritchie Valens song. I never got the chance to speak with Charlie.

In August 1997, the Stones announced their *Bridges to Babylon* tour at a press conference in Brooklyn. As a photo op, they rode a Cadillac convertible across the Brooklyn Bridge—Mick at the wheel, Keith shotgun—and parked near the East River. With the World Trade Center as a backdrop, they took questions from the press. It was odd for me not to attend, but, if I wanted to get on with my post-*Banquet* life, I needed to stay away. I was still a Rolling Stones fan, but not a "Rolling Stones reporter."

I limited myself to a handful of shows. In October, they played the Capitol Theatre in the New York suburb of Port Chester, as part of MTV's *Live from the Ten Spot* series. The place held just 1,200 people, and most of the attendees were contest winners and VIPs, like Governor Pataki. The Ticket Lady got me in. MTV paid the Stones a gazillion dollars, but the band had to break for commercials, right in the middle of the concert. I expected Mick to hold up a can of Alpo like Ed McMahon.

Later in the tour, the band accepted $5 million from Pepsi to play a private show for its executives. "We used to do coke," announced Mick from the stage, "but now we do Pepsi."

One of the tour's sponsors was Sprint. In a highly publicized campaign, the Stones set aside the best seats at each concert for the company's customers. Meaning, hardcore Sprint fans, not hardcore Stones fans, got priority. To Keith's credit, he did anything but shill. "[Their] phones were shit," he told *Rolling Stone*. "I don't use cellular phones, so it makes no difference to me. It's like sticking your head in the oven. They're very bad for you." It warmed the cockles of my heart that Keith had some piss and vinegar left.

In November '97, I was hired to lecture about Ronnie's artwork at the San Francisco Art Exchange. It coincided with the Stones' concerts in the Bay Area. For a cut of the night's profits, I discussed his paintings, etchings, and monoprints. I stood at a lectern and blathered endlessly, as everyone looked around for Ronnie. He never turned up, but Alan Dunn did. I'm not sure Ronnie even knew about it.

I told Alan I missed Keith and Ronnie and that I wanted to surprise them backstage. "Come to the tour office tomorrow," he said, "and there'll be passes for you."

I knew that Ronnie's pseudonym at the hotel was Mr. Harrington, but I didn't want to disturb him there. He was with his kids. I preferred to surprise him backstage. To do that, I needed not the B-list "VIP" pass, but the almighty "Bar Babylon" pass. That's what they were calling the band's lounge this time.

The "tour office" was the room at each hotel where the Stones organization would conduct their day-to-day business. Sort of a "war room," with maps and pushpins, fax machines and trunk lines. I entered to find Arnold Dunn, not Alan, seated behind the desk. When I told him why I was there, he said, "Bar Babylon passes can only be given upon a band member's approval. If a primary band member phones this office to approve you, then I can release a Bar Babylon pass to you."

I knew he was full of it, so I left the office and called the Ticket Lady. Without hesitating, she said, "No problem, how many do you need?"

On the night of the show, I got caught in traffic and arrived late to the Bar Babylon. The Stones had already retreated to their dressing rooms. But Freddy grabbed me and said, "Do Keet and Voody know you're here? Come vit me!" He pulled me down a corridor, where I passed Mick. We nodded politely, but didn't say anything.

When we got to Keith's dressing room, he wasn't facing us. He was standing at a clothing rack that only held scarves. "Ah," he was asking himself, "what to wear?"

"Keet!" yelled Freddy. "Look who's here!"

Keith turned around and grinned. "Mr. Gerrrrman! What brings *you* here?"

I told him I happened to be in town. He gave me a big hug and said, "Well, I'm glad you made it. Ronnie's havin' his face done, so that could be a while."

Keith sat on a sofa and began strumming a gorgeous red Gibson. He said it was from 1947. Eventually, Ronnie walked in. He was wearing a makeup bib and seemed confused to see me out west. "I'm here to sell your artwork," I explained. "I gave a lecture at the Art Exchange for a cut of the sales."

"That's great," he replied. "You have my *permission* to keep the *commission!*"

For the twenty minutes I was in that room, it felt like old times. But as for the concert itself, I don't remember much. I know I loved "Little Queenie," but I spent most of the show having flashbacks. Whenever I've seen the Stones since ending *Beggars Banquet,* my mind has wandered—to Woody's basement, Mick's den, or Keith's terrace. The private moments I shared with those guys.

Freddy, by the way, did not die on a Stones tour. But in 2000, at the age of 77, he pulled the next best thing. He died on Keith's birthday. Almost like, "Keet, you'll never forget de day I croaked!" He was buried with his backstage passes.

That same year, Keith lost his bodyguard, Joe Seabrook, to a brain hemorrhage, and his father, Bert, to natural causes. Keith would later make headlines by saying he snorted Bert's cremains.

And so, what about Bill German? How did *I* end up? Well, I sat down to write the great American novel—nothing to do with rock 'n' roll—but had trouble getting it going. Rolling Stones flashbacks kept cluttering my brain. It didn't help that I was living on Manhattan's Upper West Side, where many of my experiences took place. In the course of my daily life, I'd pass Mick and Woody's old houses or the Beacon Theatre.

To unclutter my brain, I began scribbling my Stones flashbacks whenever they hit me. On phone bills, grocery receipts, and airplane vomit bags. I tossed them in a shoebox and went on my way. I caught up on movies, museums, and my social life. I didn't have to work for "the man" because I'd sold off some back issues and lived frugally in a low-income housing unit.

Upon the twentieth anniversary of my high school graduation, I reconnected with an old English teacher. She reminded me of the axiom "Write what you know." At the same time, a former subscriber of mine, Cameron Crowe, released his semi-autobiographical film, *Almost Famous,* about a teenage rock journalist. Everywhere I went, people said, "That's just like *your* story!" So I began organizing the notes in the shoebox.

The Stones hit the road again in 2002. Ticket prices on the *Licks* tour were so outrageous, I couldn't afford to go. At Madison Square Garden, they were charging $350 for anything but nosebleeds, not counting the $30 surcharge from Ticketmaster. The prices at Giants Stadium—a friggin' stadium!—were similar.

My only hope was to reach Keith or Ronnie. I knew they were staying at the Palace Hotel during their New York stint, but I didn't know their pseudonyms. The night before Madison Square Garden—and two nights before my 40th birthday—Ronnie had an art exhibition downtown.

Jo spotted me among the crowd and yelled, "Look, Ronnie, it's Bill German!" He asked if I was coming to the Garden, and I said I couldn't afford it. He instructed me to call his twentysomething stepson, Jamie—who was now his manager—to get a "Shebeen" pass for free admission. ("The Shebeen" was what they were calling the band's lounge this time. A Gaelic word, meaning "illegal pub.") I phoned Jamie, but he claimed he couldn't help me. So I missed the entire tour.

Death and scandal on the *Licks* tour again tempered the Stones' financial conquests. Chuch Magee, one of my favorite people in the entourage, died of a heart attack at a rehearsal. He felt queasy and took a nap, feet from where the Stones were jamming. He never woke up. He'd been with the band twenty-seven years, but was so humble, his neighbors back home knew little of his employers. The Stones descended upon Marquette, Michigan, to sing "Amazing Grace" at his funeral, for a congregation that barely recognized them.

When it moved to Europe in 2003, the *Licks* tour also marked the departure of JC. From what I was told, a scalper got busted in Germany and revealed how he got his tickets. The authorities weren't concerned about the scalping per se, they were concerned about the Stones' potential for undeclared income. The Stones didn't need that kind of scrutiny, so they tossed JC overboard, despite his thirty years of service. Not even Keith could overrule it.

Fans always ask about my current relationship with the Stones. I tell 'em that Keith and Ronnie feel like long-lost uncles to me. They no longer live in New York, and they've added too many layers. Not to mention ever-changing phone numbers and pseudonyms. In the past decade, I've spoken with them only sporadically.

I did get quite concerned for Ronnie's health in the late '90s and early 2000s. He was in and out of rehab. When I saw him at that gallery in New York, the first thing he said to me was "Look, Bill, I'm seven months clean!" He was holding something that looked like cranberry juice. But when I saw him in 2004, at another exhibition, he made no such proclamations. He seemed in good spirits, however, and reported that Charlie was conquering throat cancer. The Stones, he predicted, "will be back next year."

They announced their *A Bigger Bang* tour on May 10, 2005, with a press conference and mini-concert at Lincoln Center. Walking distance from my apartment.

I was not about to pass up a free Stones show, so I called their publicists to be put on the press list. But the girl I spoke with at Rogers & Cowan had never heard of me and said I couldn't come. After providing my life story in an e-mail, she finally deemed me worthy. I strolled to Lincoln Center and was assigned a third-row seat. The Stones played three songs, including their new one, "Oh No, Not You Again." At one point, Ronnie spotted me and waved.

After the mini-concert, a suit from Ameriquest, the mortgage company sponsoring the tour, gave a spiel about "making the American dream come true." Ameriquest ran national TV ads that showed the Stones performing onstage, with a guy saying something like "I'm Bob, your Ameriquest agent. Whether you're looking to refinance or see the Rolling Stones in concert, I'm here to help you." It was no longer a joke to say you had to mortgage your house for Stones tickets.

At the time, the attorneys general of twenty-six states were investigating Ameriquest for predatory and fraudulent lending practices. I received e-mails from several distraught fans. "Last year, in the middle of hurricane season, we were scammed by Ameriquest," wrote one. "They ruined our credit . . . we lost everything . . . they were ruthless. I can't believe the Stones are letting them sponsor."

The tour's prices made 2002 look like a bargain. A decent seat—even at a stadium—was $480 through Ticketmaster. I was content with my free Lincoln Center show and had no intention of going. But an old subscriber insisted on treating me to Madison Square Garden. My $180 ticket was so high up, I could've touched Willis Reed's retired jersey. I never thought about visiting the band's lounge—dubbed the "Rattlesnake Inn"—because, frankly, the folks I liked seeing back there were dead.

I caught one other show on the *Bigger Bang* tour for free. Remember how one of the fans I got into Mick's Webster Hall show in '93 happened to be a scalper? Well, he promised to return the favor, but it took thirteen years. On October 29, 2006, he got me into the band's gig at the Beacon Theatre, the toughest ticket of the tour. Bill and Hillary Clinton were coming, so everyone got searched by Secret Service. Martin Scorsese was filming it for his *Shine a Light* documentary. It was wall-to-wall celebrities. My seat was way upstairs and the Stones had no idea I was in the house, but I was happy just to be there. The Stones felt like fun for me again, not work.

Of course, the only reason the band was playing a small theater is that Scorsese was paying them to. (Or more accurately, producer Steve Bing.) The film company bought out the Beacon and determined who got in. They pulled out hundreds of seats to make room for the cameras, leaving a little over 2,000. Then they gave a thousand seats to the Bill Clinton Foundation. Lastly, they hired good-looking models to sit up front and be captured on film. A few hundred tickets were offered to the public, gone in half a minute.

The Stones put on a great show. Mick was recovering from laryngitis, but you'd never know it. He was in top form, gyrating his 63-year-old body through "Sympathy," "Shine a Light," and "She Was Hot." Keith pulled up a stool for "As Tears Go By" and struck a Bogart-like pose (long frock, no guitar) for "You Got the Silver."

Backstage before the show, Ahmet Ertegun fell and sustained major head trauma. Paramedics rushed to his aid, but he lapsed into a coma and eventually died from his injuries. The Stones, of course, went on with the show, thriving on the evening's chaos.

So you know what? I'm *glad* the Stones step over the dead bodies. We *need* them to. I don't see why they can't go on forever and play 'til they drop, like Muddy Waters or Howlin' Wolf. There may be a ton of bullshit that surrounds

them, but if we can focus on what got us here—their music, their charisma—
I think we'll be alright.

As for me, I'm not sure anything I do will ever be as exciting as what I did
those seventeen years. But I know I'm headed in one direction—and that's
forward, brother.

acknowledgments

Writing a book can be tough. And getting one published can be tougher. So I'm grateful to Jim Fitzgerald, my agent, and to Claire Tisne, at Random House, for making the process so painless. Jim showed enthusiasm for this project the minute he learned of it, and Claire championed it through thick and thin. (And I do mean thick. Like *War and Peace* thick.) Their faith in me is something I'll always treasure.

I thank my editor, Ryan Doherty, for helping me trim the fat from my manuscript and for keeping this book on track. And I thank all the good people at Villard/Random House who gave a thumbs-up to *Under Their Thumb*—Libby McGuire, Kim Hovey, Brian McLendon, Steve Messina, and the original mensch on the scene, Adam Korn.

I couldn't have finished this book without the unflagging support and love of Dessie Marinis, Nora Lieberman, the Germans, and Jerry Schulman. Words can't convey my gratitude and indebtedness to them.

I must acknowledge the friends whose names were obscured in the pages of this book and/or who listened to me kvetch while writing this thing: Harriet and Pat Argentiere, Celeste Balducci, Bruce Barch, Christine Baronak, Kevin Barry, Angie and Bill Bechtold, Lisa and Barbara Bechtold, Shirley and Jerry Birenz, the Blue Paradisos, Claudia Boutote, Patty Butler, Sarah Butler, Phyllis Canning, Deb Charych, Sally Cook, David Dalton, Robert DiSalvatore, Stephen Dunkle, David Dunton, Pam and Chris Eborn, Bibi Farber, Mark Felsot, Ed Finnell, Donna Gaines, Anne Garrett, Charlene and Mo Goldner, Arnie Goodman, Meg Griffin, Bob Gruen, Lynnsey Guerrero, Tamara Guo, Iris and Michael Haas, Raquel and Jason Hagen, Jim Hartley, Eva Harvey, Estelle Heifetz, Gregg Heifetz, Ed Hemwall, Rick Hind, Ilana and Howard Horowitz, Andrea and Dale Horstmann, Yuji Ikeda, Charlie Jennemann, Brit Johnson, Scott Jones, Theron Kabrich, James Karnbach, George Kazepis, Jack Kelleher, Linda Kelly, Theresa Kereakes, Jane Kessler, Mayumi and Steve Klapper, Rochelle and Ron Klempner, Koos Kokhuis, Rich Kolnsberg, Mike Koshitani, Susan Krakenberg,

Mike Krowiak, Diane and Arnie Landau, Teri Landi, Shelley Lazar, Chuck Leavell, Matt Lee, Jeff Leviton, Joel Levy, Nat Levy, Allen Lieberman, Gerardo Liedo, Leah Lublin, Jo Maeder, Clare Magee, Rhonda Markowitz, David McGough, Ian McLagan, Ian McPherson, Diane McWhorter, Rhonda Mills, Mayumi Motouchi, Marilyn Murray, Lynn O'Brien, Debbie Palan, Donna Petrozzello, Tony Pigg, Ken Podsada, Doug Potash, Janet and Jeff Prushankin, Chuck Pulin, Marilou Regan, Brett Regenbogen, Carla Rhodes, Ebet Roberts, Denise Root, Norman Ross, Lynne Rossi, Beverly and Bob Rossman, Dagmar Schaefer, Alain Schinassi, Bernd Schonebaum, Carrie Schulman, Jesse Schulman, Lisa Seifert, Andrew Slayton, David Van Sise, Bjornulf Vik, Mark Voglesong, Sue Weiner, Josh Weingust, Miriam Weiss, Eliot Wien, Alan Wilensky, Carrie Woods, and Ed Wright.

I'd like to thank the Stones employees and hangers-on who helped me during my 'zine days. Especially Jane Rose, Alan Dunn, JC, Tony King, Video James, and the late Freddy Sessler. I'd also like to thank the Stones employees and hangers-on who gave me a ton of headaches during that time. Especially Jane Rose, Alan Dunn, JC, Tony King, Video James, and the late Freddy Sessler. Their headaches provided lots of material for this book.

Of course, I can never repay Patti and Keith Richards, nor Jo and Ronnie Wood, for their immeasurable kindness and hospitality. Mick Jagger, Bill Wyman, Charlie Watts, and Ian Stewart were no slouches, either. It was an honor to be in their presence, and I still can't believe they let me hang around for so long.

Lastly, it pains me to no end that Alan Heifetz, Art Collins, Bruce Bechtold, Chuch Magee, Karen Rose, Kathy Voglesong, Michael Woods, Quenby Schulman, Ruth Rosenberg, Vinnie Zuffante, and Virginia Lohle are not here to read this book. I think they would have been proud of me for getting it done.

illustration credits

Page 240: Charlie Jennemann

Page 252: David John Hogan

Page 260 (top): Sebastian Krüger

Page 260 (bottom): Paul Welford/Rex USA Ltd.

Page 268 (both): Bob Gruen

Page 276: Richard Young/Rex USA Ltd.

Page 282: Chuck Pulin

Page 290: Chrystyna Van Sise

Page 300: Bob Gruen

Page 306: Albert Ferreira/DMI/Time & Life/Getty Images

Page 318: Albert Ferreira/DMI/Time & Life/Getty Images

Page 324 (both): Vinnie Zuffante/*Beggars Banquet* Archive

Page 340: courtesy of Ronnie Wood

about the author

BILL GERMAN was born in Brooklyn, New York, in 1962. His life turned upside down when, at age 10, he first heard the Rolling Stones' *Get Yer Ya-Ya's Out* album. By age 16, he was chronicling the Stones' activities in *Beggars Banquet,* the fanzine he launched from his bedroom. The band took note and eventually declared *Beggars Banquet* their official newsletter. German traveled the world with the Stones and was welcomed into their homes. He co-authored *The Works* with guitarist Ron Wood, and wrote about the group for *Rolling Stone* and *Spin.* He's been profiled on MTV and VH1, and has reported on the Stones for various radio stations across the United States, such as WZLX in Boston, KLOS in Los Angeles, WCSX in Detroit, and both WNEW and K-Rock in New York. German majored in journalism at New York University until he dropped out to follow the Stones. He resides in New York City, where he refers to his Manhattan studio apartment as "the House the Stones Built."

www.billgerman.com

about the type

This book was set in Cheltenham, a typeface created by a distinguished American architect, Bertram Grosvenor Goodhue, in 1896 and produced by Ingalls Kimball of the Cheltenham Press in New York in 1902, who suggested that the face be called Cheltenham. It was designed with long ascenders and short descenders as a result of legibility studies indicating that the eye identifies letters by scanning their tops. The Mergenthaler Linotype Company put the typeface on machine in 1906, and Cheltenham has maintained its popularity for more than a century.